The New Deal
and the Triumph
of Liberalism

A Volume in the Series

Political Development of the American Nation:
Studies in Politics and History

Edited by   Sidney M. Milkis and
Jerome M. Mileur

The New Deal and the Triumph of Liberalism

Edited by
Sidney M. Milkis
and
Jerome M. Mileur

University of Massachusetts Press
Amherst and Boston

Copyright © 2002 by University of Massachusetts Press
Printed in the United States of America
LC 2001055501
ISBN 1-55849-320-4 (cloth); 321-2 (paper)
Designed by Dennis Anderson
Set in Galliard by Graphic Composition, Inc.
Printed and bound by Thomson-Shore, Inc.

Library of Congress Cataloging-in-Publication Data

The New Deal and the triumph of liberalism / edited by Sidney M. Milkis and Jerome M.
    Mileur.
        p. cm. — (Political development of the American nation)
    Includes bibliographical references and index.
        ISBN 1-55849-320-4 (cloth : alk. paper) — ISBN 1-55849-321-2 (pbk. : alk.
paper)
        1. Liberalism—United States. 2. United States—Politics and government—
1933–1945. I. Milkis, Sidney M. II. Mileur, Jerome M. III. Series.

JC574.2.U6 N48 2002
973.917—dc21

                                                            2001055501

British Library Cataloguing in Publication data are available.

Contents

Introduction

The New Deal, Then and Now

Sidney M. Milkis and Jerome M. Mileur

The New Deal and the Triumph of Liberalism identifies the New Deal not just as a historical episode that brought about change but also as a critical episode that left a lasting legacy for American politics and government.[1] Indeed, for political scientists, historians, sociologists, and others in the academy, as well as for two generations of journalists, the New Deal was the defining moment in the twentieth century.

To be sure, the New Deal was not cut from whole cloth. This volume treats it as one of three great moments in American politics in the twentieth century, successor of the Progressive Era, precursor to the Great Society, exploring connections between these as well as examining the time itself.[2] Its debt to the earlier era of reform has been and continues to be a matter of some controversy. In many ways, the nationalism and executive-oriented politics of the New Deal are an extension of Theodore Roosevelt's enthusiasms, but enthusiasm is one thing, programs quite another, and the New Deal went beyond the New Nationalism in its use of government as an instrument of reform. A high-ranking official in the Wilson administration, Franklin Delano Roosevelt embraced much of the New Freedom program in his New Deal, as well as Wilson's foreign policy, but went much further in areas of social policy and in institutionalizing the office of the president. The New Deal built as well on many initiatives by Herbert Hoover as both secretary of commerce and president, especially in the use of "brains" in government, but its activism and expansion of the national government's authority exceeded anything contemplated by Hoover. The New Deal also attracted some, though by no means all, old Progressives into its ranks, but was far more diverse socially than was Progressivism, drawing Catholics, Jews, unionists, women, and African Americans into the nation's governance as never before. The New Deal may not exactly have been a wholly "new departure," as Richard Hofstadter has suggested, but in American politics it was a new benchmark which reconstructed what it had inherited and which set the nation on a markedly different course.[3]

Unlike the Progressive Era, the New Deal gave rise to a full-scale partisan transformation. With the realignment of the 1930s, the New Deal took the shape of a "regime" that marked a critical departure in the governing principles, institutional arrangements, and policies that shaped American political life.[4] The Great Society would expand and modify the national state forged on the anvil of the New Deal realignment. But the legislation of the 1960s, along with other important reforms carried out during the late 1960s and 1970s, fulfilled much that was implicit in the New Deal, marking an extension rather than a departure from the New Deal regime.

The view of the New Deal as the defining chapter of modern political life in the United States is the central theme of the essays written by William Leuchtenburg and Morton Keller. Leuchtenburg calls the New Deal "the most creative political event of the twentieth century." Keller goes further, arguing in his conclusion to this volume that the 1930s marked a refounding. The New Deal "should be remembered not as an episode in the long march of American reform," he contends, "but as a defining time, like the Revolution and the establishment of the new nation, that set the stage for and defined the terms of American politics and government for generations to come." Some of the authors of this volume take issue with such celebratory views of the New Deal; many express disappointment over decisions made and directions not taken. But no one dissents from the judgment that the New Deal is the defining moment in twentieth-century American politics. Indeed, in their exploration of important dimensions of change in those years—in the Democratic Party, the labor movement, and the role of government in society and as an agent of public policy—the authors of this volume shed new light on how the New Deal, as Harry Hopkins claimed, "made America over."[5]

Redefining the Social Contract

The foundation of the New Deal realignment was a new governing philosophy, a redefinition of the social contract. Contrary to received wisdom, the New Deal was not merely a series of ad hoc responses to the political and economic emergencies of the 1930s created by the Great Depression. Inheriting broad principles from American history, Roosevelt and his political allies adapted them to new conditions and reshaped them into an enduring public philosophy: New Deal Liberalism. Liberalism in American politics hitherto had been associated with Jeffersonian principles, which followed the natural rights tradition of limited government. Roosevelt was the first statesman to "appropriate" the term "liberalism" and make it part of the common political vocabulary. In doing so, he reworked—or, as Donald Brand claims, perverted—the elements of the old faith into a modern form.[6]

In his Commonwealth Club Address, delivered during the 1932 campaign, and during each key rhetorical opportunity thereafter, Roosevelt announced that the task of modern government was "to assist in the development of an economic declaration of rights, an economic constitutional order." The traditional emphasis in American politics on individual self-reliance should give way to a new understanding of the social contract in which the government guaranteed individual men and women protection from the uncertainties of the marketplace. Security was to be the new self-evident truth of political life in the United States.[7]

Scholars, even ardent New Dealers, have tended to downplay the importance of ideas in shaping the New Deal. "Then and later," the historian David Kennedy writes, "critics have charged that so many inconsistent impulses contended under the tent of Roosevelt's New Deal that to seek for system and coherence was to pursue a fool's errand." "That accusation," he continues, "has echoed repeatedly in assessments that stress the New Deal's mongrel intellectual pedigree, its improbably plural constituent base, its political pragmatism, its abundant inconsistencies, contradictions, inconstancies, and failures."[8] Such a view may be found in this volume. Both Jytte Klausen and Seyom Brown cast skeptical eyes on New Deal Liberalism, arguing that it frequently falls prey to opportunistic political calculations and economic considerations. And Nelson Lichtenstein, while acknowledging the importance of a New

Deal vision of a good society in directing labor policy, laments that powerful business interests overcame it during the 1940s.

Still, the possibility that ideas and ideology played a powerful role in shaping the New Deal receives extensive critical attention in this volume, especially in the chapters by Sidney Milkis, Keller, and Brand. There are important differences in the way these authors characterize New Deal Liberalism. Keller portrays it boldly as revolutionary in the full sense of the term, a transformation from a polity of Protestant hegemony and decentralized power into a regime resting on two new essential features: inclusive popular nationalism and a readiness to use the federal government when necessary to secure prosperity and meet large domestic and international needs.

Milkis too views the New Deal as momentous but claims that FDR heralded and played the principal part in carrying out a *conservative* revolution. Recognizing that the creation of a national state with expansive supervisory powers could arouse the antipathy of Americans to centralized power, Roosevelt considered it imperative that the New Deal be informed by a public philosophy in which the new concept of state power would be carefully interwoven with earlier conceptions of American government. To be sure, Theodore Roosevelt and Woodrow Wilson had anticipated many elements of this argument, but FDR was the first advocate of an ongoing supervisory role for the government to link this new public philosophy to constitutional principles. Wilson's New Freedom, emphasizing initiatives such as antitrust policy and reform activity in the states, remained, in its essentials, committed to the decentralization of power, to a natural rights understanding of the Constitution. In contrast, Theodore Roosevelt, like Herbert Croly, championed an alternative, more radical progressive understanding—a New Nationalism— which all too visibly placed reformers in opposition to constitutional government and the "pursuit of happiness," traditionally understood. Roosevelt termed his philosophy "Liberalism" rather than "Progressivism," thus signifying that the New Deal should be understood as the expansion, rather than the transcendence, of natural rights.

Keller and Milkis view the transformation of American political culture as a critical development in the advent of a positive understanding of government responsibility in the United States. Brand also gives primacy to ideas but argues that "the deepest failure of the New Deal was conceptual and ideological." For Brand, there are considerable strands of continuity between the Progressive Era and the New Deal; more to the point, he argues that New Deal Liberalism was a wolf in sheep's clothing: "Adopting the term 'liberalism' allowed progressives to present themselves as the faithful of the American political tradition and defused the charge of radicalism." But this modernized version of the old faith was "misleading, for these repackaged progressives still took their bearings from" the statist ambitions of their forebears, from a view of progress that denigrated rights, properly understood. Examining the National Recovery Administration, transportation policy, and banking regulation, Brand contends that the New Deal state was built on an anticompetitive ideology.

Brand grants important New Deal successes. Yet animated by an ideology that scorned natural rights, liberal reformers demurred in the face of practical successes such as the National Securities Act, which protected investors from dishonestly advertised stocks and from insider training. Such reforms were "pro-competitive and market-strengthening," thus defying the ultimate goal of liberal reformers: to form a more perfect union in which "government, rather than private profit, should determine the allocation of capital." Once the New Deal order was institutionalized, Brand argues, "it developed its own internal logic and regulatory momentum," yielding a centralized form of administration that was economically inefficient and ideologically abhorrent.

Brand's conservative critique of New Deal Liberalism may have history on its side. As Leuchtenburg concedes, "Over the past generation, not only in America and in Thatcher's Britain but also in the European continent and even in the Third World, the state has come to be regarded as suspect, and there has been a transfer of trust to the market." Still, many other authors in this volume argue that the New Deal principles have had a lasting impact, that the New Deal's relationship to past and present patterns of American politics provides the key to a better understanding of the most pressing problems currently faced by the American people.

The Grand Politics of the New Deal

The discussion of New Deal Liberalism makes clear that the economic constitutional order was not merely a rhetorical flourish. Roosevelt's reappraisal of values is important to understanding not only the New

Deal but also his influence on the institutions that have shaped politics and government since the 1930s. The essays by Marc Landy, Jerome Mileur, and Milkis detail the leading features of Roosevelt's ambitious politics. They are informed, in part, by the cyclical view of American political development, owing much to work of Walter Dean Burnham and Stephen Skowronek.[9] These essays thus begin from the premise that Roosevelt's presidency is akin to those of Thomas Jefferson, Andrew Jackson, and Abraham Lincoln. Each recast the political battle by redefining its terms, and in each case that redefinition had to do with the constitution of American politics and governance. It was within these new frames—our "surrogate for revolution," as Burnham characterizes them—that each used the politics of his times to move the nation along new paths.[10] Each understood that the American constitutional system worked through politics and that, to change its effects on the governance of the nation, one must change the politics so integral to its functioning. Each produced a "new" party system by realigning the forces competing for control of the national government and, in turn, reconstituted the government on bases different from that which went before.

Still, as we see in the essays of Mileur, Landy, and Milkis, there was something distinctive about the New Deal realignment; most important, it was the first in which the executive was at the heart of the voters' approach to politics and government. All previous realignments occurred within the parameters set by a consensus in the United States dedicated to private property, limited government, and administrative decentralization. Even the Civil War, a regime crisis of the first order, failed to signal a departure from the political conditions that sustained this consensus. It is only in the twentieth century, with the emergence of the Progressive movement, that a fundamental challenge to the nineteenth-century liberal consensus is offered. Just as New Deal Liberalism drew on the Progressive tradition, so FDR's leadership was inspired in important ways by the presidencies of Theodore Roosevelt and Woodrow Wilson. But the success of TR and Wilson fell short in advancing progressive democracy, as neither of them had presided over a realignment. It fell to FDR to consolidate or institutionalize the changes in the executive that were initiated during the Progressive Era.

Indeed, with the Progressive movement in disarray after World War I, the nation was left with two major parties in which conservatives were dominant. The 1924 Progressive Party candidacy of Robert La Follette,

who ran third behind the major party candidates with just over 16 percent of the national vote, expressed both the frustration of reformers
with the state of national politics and the limits of their popular appeal.
In the Republican Party, the business-oriented Old Guard had returned
to power, but not as the nationalist party of the prewar years.[11] In the
Democratic Party, the southern Bourbons were similarly hostile to the
expanded federal role that might jeopardize their region's "way of life,"
while the urban bosses of the North had never shared in power at the national level and remained for the most part localist in their political orientation. Within the Democratic Party of the North, however, a new urban progressivism was emerging, nowhere more so than in New York
where Robert Wagner and Al Smith led the way. Franklin Roosevelt, who
began his political career as a Progressive, came increasingly to admire
these champions of working-class America, to understand better the rationale behind their program, and to believe that a political liberalism
that combined elements of the old Progressivism with the new was the
path the national party should follow. The Democratic Party, he believed, should become a liberal alternative to the conservatism of the
Grand Old Party (GOP). Throughout the 1920s, good economic times
sustained the Republican majority, but the coming of the depression led
to a repudiation of the GOP, giving the Democrats and Roosevelt the
opportunity to escape from the political wilderness. In seizing the moment, FDR did more than realign the political forces of the nation; he
reconstructed the terms of the party battle by establishing New Deal
Liberalism as the nation's public philosophy, which governed its politics
well beyond his years in office.

As noted, the New Deal differs in many ways from the Progressive
Era: it produced a partisan majority in the nation built on a new governing philosophy and also transformed the social and professional character of the government itself.[12] The New Deal also differed markedly
from Progressivism in its reformist enthusiasms. The rallying cry of the
latter was to restore popular rule. It marched to the drumbeat of democracy, seeking a more truly popular government through reform of political parties, lobbyists, and political money, as well as nonpartisan forms
of local government and a more direct role of citizens in their government through the initiative and referendum, the recall, and the direct
election of U.S. senators.[13] There was no analogous impulse in the New
Deal. Indeed, as Milkis argues, New Deal Liberalism transmuted the

Progressive cry for "pure democracy" into an economic constitutional order that dedicated reform to new rights.

Landy, Mileur, and Milkis agree that FDR remade national government and politics in the United States. They differ, however, in their interpretations of how the New Deal affected the party system. Milkis highlights New Deal rhetoric and practices that transcended parties and established a rights-based welfare state that diminished their importance. Landy, on the other hand, emphasizes how FDR strengthened partisanship, building, in his view, the most successful political party in the nation's history. Mileur in a sense argues that they are both correct. Picturing Roosevelt as a master politician, he contends that FDR entered the White House as a strong party man and, in his first term, governed as a party leader. It was only after the frustrations early in his second term, owing to opposition in his own party and the failures of the "purge" campaign, that FDR turned away from the party as the political vehicle through which to secure New Deal Liberalism and looked instead to rights-based reform as the more certain strategy. In this, the winners politically were the new groups FDR had attracted to the party; the losers were the traditional bases of the party: the south primarily but also the big-city machines.

Each of these essays reminds us that statesmanship and politician need not be distinct qualities; each shows that Roosevelt was an extraordinary politician who engaged the nation in a struggle for its constitutional soul. The 1936 election, Landy reveals, was an especially critical episode in this surrogate constitutional convention. Rather than take the conventional road of rehearsing his administration's accomplishments and taking credit for recovery, Roosevelt chose instead to castigate the opponents of the New Deal in terms that were harsh and provocative. His depiction of the opposition as "economic royalists," Landy argues, "provided a clear focal point for the anger that ordinary people felt toward those they held responsible for the economic devastation they had experienced. They rejoiced against the forces of darkness: speculators, bankers, and bosses."

Although it sharpened political conflict along class lines, the message of the 1936 campaign was not really class based. Landy contends that, in reconstructing the Democratic Party, FDR took pains to marginalize militantly populist voices, such as Huey Long and John L. Lewis. Rather, Roosevelt's campaign for Liberalism was a promise to overthrow a "monarchy" in the name of the commoners. In a nation where nearly everyone fancies himself or herself a commoner, the breadth of the appeal was enormous. More important, FDR provided a means for partisan identification with the New Deal based on a powerful and enduring understanding of rights. In the final analysis, FDR enlisted New Deal supporters in a war against privilege that reaffirmed the social contract, as he understood it. As the peroration of Roosevelt's militant nomination speech conveyed, this was not a cause simply for labor and the dispossessed but a challenge for a generation. Among these final passages, emphasizing "faith, hope, and charity," are the words for which this address would be remembered: "There is a mysterious cycle in human events. To some generations much is given. Of other generations much is expected. This generation of Americans has a rendezvous with destiny."[14]

Landy and Mileur both stress how Roosevelt made use of this campaign and his immense victory to strengthen the Democratic Party, to secure its status as a majority party for a generation. Roosevelt's rhetoric, Landy writes, "crystallized the terms of the debate between the two parties in a manner that riveted the attachment of those who had been leaning toward the Democrats"; no less important, he carried out structural change, such as the abolition of the two-thirds rule, which weakened the influence of southern Democrats ("the ball and chain of the party's forward march"),[15] and facilitated the adoption of a national reform program. By the end of his second term, FDR had gone far to transform the party from a state and local organization, dedicated to local self-government and patronage, into a national programmatic party. The new liberal coalition, as Mileur shows, included constituencies that embraced the New Deal—most notably, labor, African Americans, Jews, and women—and thus generated the electoral support required to carry its programs into practice.

Paradoxically, the grand politics of the New Deal may have made partisanship less important. As Milkis argues, once the New Deal was in place, such militant partisanship would no longer be necessary or even possible. The distinctive quality about the New Deal realignment—its dedication to executive dominion—transformed the Democratic Party into a way station on the road to administrative government. The reconstituted executive office, which transformed the presidency into an institution, deprived party leaders of the very tasks that gave them status and influence: linking the president to interest groups, staffing the executive department, developing policy, and, most important, providing campaign support. Moreover, Milkis argues, New Deal institutional reform, which FDR established as a party program, was directed not just to creating presidential government but also to embedding progressive principles (considered tantamount to political rights) in a bureaucratic structure that would insulate reform and reformers from electoral change. Thus, the New Deal realignment may have been the last of its kind, for it transformed a decentralized republic into a more centralized and bureaucratic form of democracy that focused political life in the United States on the presidency and administrative agencies.

Building the New Deal State

The "economic constitutional order" may be seen as giving rise to a more active and better-equipped national state, but one without adequate means of public debate and judgment. As the chapters by Lichtenstein, Klausen, and Suzanne Mettler show, however, there were limits to the New Deal state. In truth, Roosevelt was ambivalent about "state building." He never intended to establish the centralized bureaucratic apparatus characteristic of modern states elsewhere; indeed, the New Deal order created new obstacles to statist ambitions. Once viewed as entitlements, New Deal programs became autonomous islands of power, beholden to the rights-based claims of favored constituencies, that would constrain presidents no less than had localized parties.

Lichtenstein poses hard challenges to this interpretation of the American rights-based welfare state. He views the "labor question" as the heart of New Deal politics and argues that the enactment and administration of the Wagner Act could have resulted in the creation of an American version of social democracy. Denying that "Dr. Win the War" displaced "Dr. New Deal," Lichtenstein contends that "a process of politicized bargaining" endured from 1935 until 1946, one that seemed to advance the United States "toward a labor-backed corporatism that would later characterize social policy in northern Europe and Scandinavia." The new self-evident truths in this corporate state would entitle the working class not only to the wages of security but also to redistributive social policy that might disproportionately benefit African American laborers as well as workers in low-wage industries such as cotton textiles.

The potential to create a European-style welfare state in America, Lichtenstein claims, was short-circuited by the enactment of the Taft-Hartley Act and its aftermath. Although this is not a novel argument, Lichtenstein sheds new light on how the effects of Taft-Hartley, passed over Harry Truman's veto, went well beyond the elimination of the closed shop. More important, he argues, Taft-Hartley strengthened the hand of management in the workplace. By making industry-wide collective bargaining impractical, exposing unions to rabid anticommunism, and preventing foremen and first-line supervisors from becoming unionized, it empowered management to carry out a devastating strategy of *divide et impera* on the shop floor. At the end of the day, Lichtenstein believes, the exceptional hostility of American business to collective bargaining and the distinctive structural features of the American political economy that advantaged this antiunion animus destroyed the real possibility of achieving social democracy in the United States.

Like Lichtenstein, Klausen challenges the received wisdom of American exceptionalism. She also shows that the New Deal did not come to an end during the war. But in her essay, an examination of the National Resources Planning Board, she expresses far more skepticism than Lichtenstein about the potential to achieve European-style corporatism in the United States. Indeed, Klausen raises serious questions about the very importance of "state capacities." She does not find that the liberal tradition and the division and separation of powers posed a fundamental obstacle to planning in the United States, and she denies that Great Britain and Western Europe, shaped by political cultures more open to centralized power, embraced planning. The shared experience of World War II, rather than ideological or institutional factors, was critical to the rise of state planning and social welfare policies in industrial democracies. By the same token, the return of peace and prosperity posed serious challenges to the continuation of state controls. In the final analysis, economic exigencies determined whether planning was sustained in postwar industrial democracies. "The dollar's hegemonic position in the postwar world economy"—American prosperity and European scarcity—explains why the "United States achieved less planning and the Europeans achieved more."

Klausen thus argues, contrary to Lichtenstein, that it is misleading to evaluate the New Deal as a failure because it did not bring forth a European-style welfare state. The more limited form of planning that did take hold in the United States not only comported with what the American people would accept once the war was over but also abetted the extraordinary prosperity the country enjoyed during the late 1940s and 1950s. In their affinity for a certain form of Keynesianism, one that emphasized demand management rather than physical controls and had a focus on planning as a matter of forecasting rather than social control of the economy, New Dealers were ahead of their reform counterparts, such as William Beveridge, in Great Britain.

Klausen's essay complements Milkis's contention that Liberals championed a Second Bill of Rights, as FDR framed the New Deal view of justice, that emphasized security rather than redistribution of wealth. To be sure, the concept of an economic constitutional order—the view that responsive state action was an extension of individual rights—was not a theory that supported the formation of a highly centralized and autonomous administrative power. Nevertheless, linking national power to individual rights might have been the only way to transform the governing philosophy of the United States, given the intense commitment the American people have to limited government. As Keller shows, moreover, this rights-based welfare is not a laggard but an expansive supervisory power that has advanced not only economic rights but also social rights, promising a full share of citizenship to all Americans.

Mettler's essay issues the most direct challenge to this view that the New Deal represents the triumph of liberalism, "the moment," as she puts it, "at which the national government began to extend rights beyond the basic fundamentals of naturalization to Americans." A careful examination of New Deal policies shows instead, Mettler argues, "the perpetuation, long afterward, of a nonliberal realm of governance." More to the point, New Deal Liberalism's promise was denigrated by the institutionalization of "neofeudal" policies through the system of American federalism, within the states, "where most women, as well as men of color, continued to be governed long afterward." Such programs as Social Security and the National Labor Relations Act, which codified national standards and were administered in Washington, "endowed Americans with new social and economic dimensions of citizenship." But welfare policy, in the form of Aid to Dependent Children (ADC), and unemployment compensation left considerable discretion to the states, which dealt out social justice unevenly. As as consequence, New Deal citizenship became divided into two distinct forms of governance: men, particularly white men, were endowed with national citizenship, whereas women and minority men were left under the auspices of the states and thus subject to highly variable and often discriminatory treatment.

Mettler thus casts doubt on both Milkis's argument that Roosevelt's pronouncement of an economic constitutional order shaped the New Deal state and Klausen's contention that state capacity was not especially important in curtailing the American welfare state. Mettler does not condemn the New Deal as inherently unjust to African Americans and women. "Unlike programs and rules established in earlier eras," she grants, "which clearly distinguished between citizens on the basis of sex and race, such as protective labor laws, the New Deal social policies were free of such language." Nor does Mettler indict reformers for intentionally structuring programs in a way that would harm women and minorities. She shows, for example, that many architects of the more decentralized programs like ADC (later AFDC) were women and that reformers were convinced they were fashioning a program that would build successfully and fairly on such earlier programs as mothers' pensions.[16] Just as Mileur illustrates that women played an important part in the reconstructed Democratic Party, so Mettler confirms their significance in designing the institutions of New Deal governance.

In its best light, New Deal concessions to federalism may be seen as an attempt to preserve certain virtues of administrative decentralization. Leaving certain important policy decisions to states and localities, as Tocqueville notes, cultivated a sense of citizenship by giving the people a stake in government affairs: "What I most admire in America is not the *administrative* but the *political* effects of decentralization. In the United States the motherland's presence is felt everywhere. It is a subject of concern to the village and to the whole Union. The inhabitants care about each of their country's interest as if it were their own. Each man takes pride in the nation; the successes it gains seem his own work, and he becomes elated; he rejoices in the general prosperity from which he profits. He has much the same feeling for his country as one has for one's family, and a sort of selfishness makes him care for the state."[17]

Yet, Mettler insists that the communitarian potential of local self-government all too easily dissolves into paternalistic arrangements and racial discrimination that denigrates the promise of Liberalism. With respect to the New Deal, the legacy of Jim Crow and discriminatory practices against women, codified under the province of the states' police power, severely constrained the reach of the economic constitutional order. Indeed, she suggests that federalism is inherently unjust. "Although decentralized governance may do much to preserve democratic practices in policymaking," she concludes, "it means that citizenship will be defined according to the political and cultural geography of federalism and that it will be different—in a word, unequal—from one state or region to another."

But Mettler does not go so far as to declare that separate is always unequal, that federalism has no value in sustaining the dignity of the democratic individual. She acknowledges that decentralized administration became less egregious as the civil rights and women's movements arose and the rights revolution was expanded. The laws enacted during the 1930s abetted the expansion of national administrative power in the service of reform; these laws proved to be true "organic statutes," Mettler discovers, "which could be built on and liberalized over time." Through such changes, "even AFDC began to approximate an 'entitlement,' a benefit assured to those who fit nationally uniform, standardized eligibility criteria."

Yet no sooner had this occurred than welfare came under attack. Mettler warns that the culmination of this assault, the welfare reform of the 1990s, which eliminated the entitlement status of AFDC and delegated more administrative discretion to the states than they had known in six decades, risks restoring a fractious and inherently unjust welfare state. The enactment of the Personal Responsibility and Work Opportunity Act did not return us to pre–New Deal arrangements. Unlike Lichtenstein, who fears a restoration of the "slave labor" that characterized working conditions and wages prior to the enactment of the Wagner Act, Mettler fears a return to an earlier, more limited New Deal state. Mettler acknowledges, therefore, that the dawn of a new century is not very likely to mark the demise of the welfare state. Instead, the current debate turns on what kind of welfare state we shall have, a political question that tends to enshrine the New Deal, as well as the national state it spawned, as a permanent part of American political life.

New Deal Policies: Security at Home and Abroad

Just as the New Deal order gave rise to a new understanding of government responsibility and an administrative state, so too it resulted in the expansion of programs that made the welfare state an integral part of politics and government in the United States. We have noted how many essays in this volume point to social welfare policy and collective bargaining as enduring policy contributions. But, as Keller and Leuchtenburg show, Social Security and big labor only begin to reveal the policy dimensions of the New Deal. In one sense, as Mettler argues, the most obvious objective of the New Deal during the Great Depression— providing security for vulnerable individuals—was severely constrained. Indeed, as David Kennedy points out, "the New Deal's premier objective, at least until 1938, and in Roosevelt's mind probably for a long time thereafter, was not economic recovery but structural change." This change prepared the New Deal state not to destroy capitalism, Kennedy adds, but to "devolatize it, and at the same time to distribute its benefits more evenly." Thus, the task was to provide an institutional framework that would achieve security not just for the dispossessed but also "for capitalists and consumers, for workers and employers, for corporations and farms and homeowners and bankers and builders as well."[18]

Much of this task was achieved without draconian state controls or burdensome taxes. As Brand's essay indicates, the political economy's reconstruction was carried out, for the most part, by regulatory commissions, charged with providing rules of competition that would reduce the risk, the terrifying uncertainty, of market forces. Whether these new forums denigrated competition, as Brand argues, or erected the "latticework on which the postwar economy grew," as Kennedy claims, it is impossible to deny that the New Deal transformed America, that it touched nearly every aspect of daily life. As Leuchtenburg puts it, "If an American in the twenty-first century cashes a Social Security check, flies into La Guardia Airport, votes in a union election, deposits money in a government-insured bank account, switches on the lights in a remote farmhouse, drives on the Blue Ridge Parkway, collects unemployment compensation, or watches a football game in the stadium at Ole Miss, he or she will be drawing on the legacy of the New Deal."

Ronald Story's essay on higher education suggests just how far the liberal policy state reached. Challenging the received wisdom that Roosevelt's contribution to higher education was "inconsequential," Story makes a persuasive case that the New Deal "laid the groundwork for the entire modern academic edifice that we take for granted today." Students of this era have missed FDR's impact on higher education in part because the administration did not have a *policy* on it. But, through programs like the GI Bill, Story shows, the Roosevelt administration had a *practice* of using colleges and universities for other purposes: to reduce unemployment, reward veterans, and produce weapons.

The production of weapons, which incorporated universities into a national security state, raises the question of the New Deal's effect on international affairs. This is the topic of Brown's essay. Klausen and Lichtenstein defy the scholarly consensus that the New Deal came to an end with World War II. Brown's essay, which focuses on FDR's foreign policy, shows just how difficult it is to disentangle Roosevelt's domestic and foreign policy objectives. More penetratingly, Brown indicates that New Deal principles did not stop at the water's edge, that Roosevelt, like Wilson, had a concept of progress which extended to a new world order. Nor were these just words, Brown claims, for with the issuance of the Atlantic Charter in 1941, the "progressive liberalism which FDR made a part of his political rhetoric on the way to his presidency and which was now being projected onto the world stage had apparently become very much part of his own Weltanschauung." The Atlantic Charter committed the Allies to "respect the right of all peoples to choose the form of government under which they will live" and "to see sovereign rights and self-government restored to those who have been forcibly deprived of them," principles that presupposed an anti-imperialist front. Believing that this anti-imperialist thrust was crucial to the struggle against the Axis powers, FDR persuaded a nervous Winston Churchill to endorse the charter, Brown shows, even though the language might be and, in fact, eventually was turned against the British Empire.

To be sure, as Brown and other authors in this volume indicate, FDR's idealism frequently gave way to realpolitik and domestic considerations. Roosevelt has been sharply criticized for his cautious approach to war in Europe and Asia, his internment of Japanese Americans in concentration camps, and his concessions to Stalin at Yalta. Taking account of FDR's sincere idealism, as well as his opportunistic departures from it, Brown ends his portrait of Roosevelt with an expression of profound ambivalence: "Internationalism/nationalism, realpolitik/idealism, elitism/populism—no one of the Rooseveltian Janus faces, no particular angle of vision on them, adequately captures the often elusive character of his international . . . statecraft." Yet, Brown concedes, such a complex elusiveness may have been appropriate for the last pre–cold war president:

a less skillful and attentive politician may not have been able to fend off the powerful appeal of isolationism in the country, and a less committed internationalist may not have tried. The current generation of policy-makers, confronting a post–cold war era, could do worse, Brown concludes, "in selecting as their role model the last pre–cold war president."

Whither the New Deal?

The ambivalent, yet celebratory, note sounded by Brown's essay expresses well the spirit with which this volume was produced. The authors contained herein recognize the New Deal as one of the few episodes in American history that brought about profound and enduring change. At the same time, we have chosen to honor it with a collection of essays that capture its richness, complexity, and controversies. We believe the essays that follow reaffirm that, as the historian Barry Karl has written, "the New Deal raises all the most fundamental questions about the character of American government and its relationship to governments elsewhere in the world."[19]

Above all, these essays confirm anew that the political battles of the 1930s marked the most important test of the character of American constitutional government and the liberal tradition that sustained it. The New Deal gave rise to an understanding of rights and constitutional arrangements that enabled the national government to give to many Americans a greater sense of security and thus to renew their attachment to the fundamental law. As Roosevelt put it in his Four Freedoms speech, the precursor to the Atlantic Charter, the traditional liberal freedoms of speech and religion were to be supplemented by two new freedoms: "freedom from want," the commitment to "economic understandings which will secure to every nation a healthy peace time life for its inhabitants," and "freedom from fear," dedicated to "a world-wide reduction of armaments to such a point and in such a fashion that no nation will be in a position to commit an act of physical aggression against any neighbor."[20] That a greater sense of entitlement was accomplished at a time, as Kennedy notes, "when despair and alienation were prostrating many peoples under the heel of dictatorship was no small accomplishment."[21]

Nonetheless, this redefinition of the social contract did not so much resolve tensions between the American constitutional tradition and the New Deal demand for new rights as it did to bring them into bold relief.

Hostility to taxes and centralized administration continued to feed American political conservatism; the extension of the New Deal "rights revolution" in the 1960s and 1970s aroused a new, more confident form of opposition to the Liberal state, culminating in Ronald Reagan's election to the White House in 1980.

Reagan's message as a candidate and as president was but a variation on the theme he had been enunciating ever since he gave a nationwide television address on behalf of Barry Goldwater in October 1964. By acting "outside its legitimate function," a central state perverted, rather than modernized, the concept of rights, he insisted: "Natural unalienable rights" were presumed to be a "dispensation of government" that stripped people of their self-reliance and their capacity for self-government. "The real destroyer of liberties of the people," he warned, "is he who spreads among them bounties, donations, and benefits." Seventeen years later, in his inaugural address—the first by a president in more than fifty years to appeal for limited government—Reagan sounded the same theme. "In the present crisis," he announced, "government is not the solution to our problem; government is the problem."[22]

As many essays in this volume reveal, the Reagan presidency appeared to signal the twilight, if not the end, of the New Deal era. Bill Clinton, the first Democratic president elected in sixteen years, seemed only to ratify the forlorn state of Liberalism. His willingness to sign a bill jettisoning the welfare system first established in the 1930s, to construct a bipartisan coalition in support of a balanced budget, and to trumpet the end of "the era of big government" gave the impression of bestowing bipartisan legitimacy on the Reagan "revolution."

In the face of this development, as Keller and Leuchtenburg point out, the Left has found little to celebrate in the New Deal tradition. In its failure to sustain a vital labor movement, as illustrated by Lichtenstein; in its compromise with virulent provincialism, as detailed by Mettler; in its halfhearted effort to establish a planned economy, as told by Klausen; and in its inability to create a solid national political foundation required to sustain the new and much enlarged national state, as lamented by Mileur, the New Deal has been condemned for what it left undone. For six decades, Leuchtenburg observes, the main criticism of FDR's policies has been that the government did not go far enough, that it was a conservative response to conditions that had revolutionary possibilities.

These assaults from the Left and the Right notwithstanding, the up-shot of this volume is that Liberalism has triumphed, that we live today, as Keller concludes, "in a polity best defined as a lengthened shadow of the New Deal." For all the antigovernment rhetoric of the 1980s, the Reagan presidency failed to curtail the entitlement state, defended Liberal internationalism, and championed an activist presidency that made the prospect of getting government off our backs a chimera. For all Clinton's remonstrations about the need for a "new Democracy," he resurrected his presidency, even as it was condemned as irrelevant by the shock troops of the 104th Republican-controlled Congress, in a defense of New Deal and Great Society programs. Clinton's reelection, the first Democrat to be reelected by the American voters since FDR, revealed just how deeply such programs as Social Security, Medicare, environmental protection, and support for education had become ingrained in our political life. Indeed, the "new" Democratic solution to welfare reform has not been to eliminate poverty programs but to reinvent them as work programs, fulfilling the most sacred New Deal entitlement: the right to a decent job.

But with the triumph of Liberalism has come a recognition, or rediscovery, of its failings. As Story's chapter on education suggests, the New Deal did not create a new kind of American, one who was any less obsessed with rights or more enamored of "collective action for equitable benefits." Instead, it transmuted a Jeffersonian democracy, rooted in individual responsibility, locality, and natural rights, into a suburban republic, dedicated to individual achievement, global awareness, and programmatic rights. One might see, as Story does, a contradiction between the contributions of Social Security and big labor, on the one hand, and education, on the other: the former cultivate "collective action for equitable benefits," he claims, whereas the latter propose "to expand individual consciousness and enable individual achievement." Yet there is a real sense in which New Deal entitlements, as detailed in FDR's 1944 State of the Union message, including the right to a useful and remunerative job, the right of every family to a decent home, the right to adequate medical care, the right to adequate protection from the fears of old age, and the right to good education, were committed to employing collective action to strengthen and enrich, rather than temper, individual consciousness and achievement.[23] Such a commitment brought with it the risk of confounding rights and interests and exposing the New

Deal state to the relentless, selfish claims of interest groups; more telling, the expansion of rights deepens the inherent tension in a liberal polity between rights and obligations, makes more fragile the sense of citizenship in American political life.

In the final analysis, the strengths and weaknesses of the New Deal follow from its attempt to expand the possibilities of individual rights, from an attempt to graft a national administrative apparatus and activist public philosophy onto a rights-based constitutional system and political culture. "In his shrewd, negative rephrasing of positive freedoms," Orlando Patterson has written, "Roosevelt preemptively undermined his liberal critics and, at the same time, foresaw the basic flaw in what would soon become the most celebrated postwar restatement of classical liberalism: Isaiah Berlin's view that there are two concepts of liberty, one positive and inevitably evil, the other negative and uniquely worth pursuing."[24] In formulating a new understanding of Liberalism—one that was less diffident in the face of economic security at home and despotism abroad—Roosevelt and his New Deal allies made a vital contribution to the triumph of Liberalism. But it remains to be seen whether the expansion of rights that characterized the New Deal enables it to sustain a vital civic culture, whether the more centralized, bureaucratic form of democracy to which it gave rise can support a nation of individuals capable of pursuing happiness with dignity and responsibility. In this sense, the essays that follow invite us to consider a dilemma as old as the republic: How can a state that is expansive and powerful enough to protect our rights provide for an active and competent citizenry?

Notes

1. This volume is drawn from a conference held at Brandeis University in June 1998.

2. This volume is the second of three that will examine twentieth-century political reform. On the Progressive Era, see a previous volume in this series: Sidney M. Milkis and Jerome M. Mileur, eds., *Progressivism and the New Democracy* (Amherst: University of Massachusetts Press, 1999). The final volume, *The Great Society and the Rights Revolution,* will be published in 2002.

3. For all their diversity, there was a generational, educational, and cultural coherence to Progressives and Progressivism that was not true of New Dealers and the New Deal. The generation of Progressive activists was, for the most part, born in the years of the decade after the Civil War. They were disproportionately the sons and daughters of mainstream Protestant ministers, whose ancestries

traced primarily to New England, and they were members of an emerging, socially conscious, college-educated elite, for whom reform was at once the product of social scientific research and humanitarian idealism. On the homogeneity
of Progressives, see Eldon J. Eisenach, *The Lost Promise of Progressivism*
(Lawrence: University Press of Kansas, 1994), and Robert Crunden, *Ministers of
Reform* (New York: Basic Books, 1992).

   3. Richard Hofstadter, *The Age of Reform: From Bryan to FDR* (New York:
Alfred A. Knopf, 1959), 300–314.

   4. In calling the New Deal a new "regime," we do not mean to suggest that
it resulted in a new constitutional order. Of the authors in this volume, only
Keller views the New Deal as a "refounding." In our understanding, the New
Deal, like the realignments of 1800, 1828, and 1860, brought about significant
changes within the essential framework of American constitutional government.
On the use of "regime" in this more limited sense, see Richard A. Harris and Sid-
ney M. Milkis, *The Politics of Regulatory Change: A Tale of Two Agencies*, 2d ed.
(New York: Oxford University Press, 1996).

   5. Joseph Alsop and Robert Kintner, "We Shall Make America Over," *Saturday Evening Post*, November 1938, 91.

   6. Louis Hartz, *The Liberal Tradition in America: An Interpretation of
American Political Thought since the Revolution* (New York: Harcourt, Brace,
1955); Ronald Rotunda, "The Liberal Label: Roosevelt's Capture of a Symbol,"
in *Public Policy*, ed. John D. Montgomery and Albert O. Hirschman (Cambridge: Harvard University Press, 1968), 17:377–408.

   7. Franklin D. Roosevelt, *The Public Papers and Addresses of Franklin D. Roosevelt*, ed. Samuel I. Rosenman, 13 vols. (New York: Random House, 1938–50),
1:752.

   8. David M. Kennedy, *Freedom from Fear: The American People in Depression
and War, 1929–1945* (New York: Oxford University Press, 1999), 364. Kennedy
takes issue with this received wisdom. Amid the chaos of New Deal innovation,
he spies a "coherent pattern," one that can be "summarized in a single word:
security" (365).

   9. Walter Dean Burnham, *Critical Elections and the Mainsprings of American Politics* (New York: Norton, 1970); Stephen Skowronek, *The Politics Presidents Make: Leadership from John Adams to Bill Clinton* (Cambridge: Harvard
University Press, 1997).

   10. Walter Dean Burnham, "Party Systems and the Political Process," in *The
American Party Systems: Stages of Political Development*, ed. William Nisbet
Chambers and Walter Dean Burnham (New York: Oxford University Press,
1975), 289.

   11. On the change of Republican Party ideology in the 1920s, see John Gerring, *Party Ideologies in America, 1828–1996* (New York: Cambridge University
Press, 1998), esp. chap. 4.

   12. While Franklin Roosevelt and his New Deal drew lessons in political leadership and public policy from the earlier reformist period, they did not draw great
numbers of old Progressives into their ranks, save for those associated with

Woodrow Wilson's New Freedom administration. Some younger, second-generation Republican Progressives, such as Harold Ickes, Henry Wallace, and Charles Merriam, were prominent in the New Deal, and some older Republican Progressive warhorses in Congress, George Norris and Burton Wheeler among them, backed many of Roosevelt's initiatives, but they were the exception and not the rule. See Otis L. Graham Jr., *An Encore for Reform: The Old Progressives and the New Deal* (New York: Oxford University Press, 1967).

13. For a view of the Progressive Era that emphasizes its commitment to and advance toward a "new democracy," see Milkis and Mileur, *Progressivism and the New Democracy,* especially the introduction to the volume. See also Milkis, *Political Parties and Constitutional Government: Remaking American Democracy* (Baltimore: Johns Hopkins University Press, 1999), esp. chap. 3.

14. Roosevelt, *Public Papers and Addresses,* 5:234.

15. Thomas Stokes so characterized southern Democrats; see *Chip Off My Shoulder* (Princeton: Princeton University Press, 1940), 503.

16. On mothers' pensions, see Theda Skocpol, *Protecting Soldiers and Mothers: The Political Origins of Social Policy in the United States* (Cambridge: Harvard University Press, 1992).

17. Alexis de Tocqueville, *Democracy in America,* ed. J. P. Mayer (New York: Harper and Row, 1969), 95 (emphasis in original).

18. Kennedy, *Freedom from Fear,* 365, 372.

19. Barry Karl, *The Uneasy State: The United States from 1915 to 1945* (Chicago: University of Chicago Press, 1983), 231.

20. Roosevelt, *Public Papers and Addresses,* 9:671–72.

21. Kennedy, *Freedom from Fear,* 378.

22. Ronald Reagan, "A Time for Choosing," October 27, 1964, in *Ronald Reagan Talks to America,* ed. Richard M. Scaife (Old Greenwich, Conn.: Devan Adair, 1983), 4–5, and "Ronald Reagan's First Inaugural Address," in *The Evolving Presidency: Addresses, Cases, Essays, Letters, Reports, Resolutions, Transcripts, and Other Landmark Documents, 1787–1998,* ed. Michael Nelson (Washington, D.C.: CQ Press, 1999), 220.

23. Roosevelt, *Public Papers and Addresses,* 13:40–41.

24. Orlando Patterson, "The Liberal Millennium," *New Republic,* November 8, 1999, 61.

The New Deal at the End of the Twentieth Century

William E. Leuchtenburg

The organizers of the conference at Brandeis University from which the essays in this volume derive could hardly have scheduled it at a more propitious moment—on the sixtieth anniversary of the final enactment of New Deal social legislation (the Fair Labor Standards Act of 1938) and at a time when, on the brink of the millennium, we were at the cusp of seismic generational change.

I have had occasion again and again in recent years to be dismayed by the quickened pace at which the once precociously young generation of the age of Roosevelt has been departing. In the waning months of Jimmy Carter's presidency, I was invited by Secretary of State Ed Muskie to a luncheon of about a dozen people (including the television commentators Walter Cronkite and Eric Sevareid) to discuss what to do about the forthcoming centennial of FDR's birth; of the veterans of the New Deal present that afternoon—Tommy Corcoran, Jim Rowe, Ben Cohen, and Frank Roosevelt—all are now gone. In 1983, on the fiftieth anniversary of the New Deal, I had supper in a big tent adjoining the LBJ Library with Claude Pepper, who entered the U.S. Senate in 1936, and Senator Jennings Randolph, the last survivor of the Congress of the First Hundred Days. The indefatigable Pepper died a few years ago; big Jennings Randolph, with his booming voice and infectious smile, just a few days before the conference at Brandeis convened. At a meeting on the presidency at Princeton in 1986, each scholar appeared in tandem with a practitioner. My mate was Wilbur Cohen, of whom it was said that an authority on Social Security was someone who had Wilbur's telephone number. He first entered the New Deal at the age of twenty-one. Now sweet Wilbur Cohen, too, is gone. When in 1983 I served as consultant to NBC for its documentary on the New Deal, I was able to suggest a number of people from the FDR years for on-camera interviews. When I got a call from a filmmaker a short time ago, I could come up with virtually no one.

We are fast approaching the time when the history of the New Deal will be read by people with no personal memory of it. Writers will no longer be able to assume a commonality of familiarity so that the mere mention of a name has a resonance. Not many years ago, as mail was being sorted by two very well informed women on the staff of the National Humanities Center, they asked me who the woman was whose face was on a postage stamp and what she had done to merit that honor. She was Frances Perkins. Each year in the course I taught for nearly a decade with John Hope Franklin and Walter Dellinger at Duke Law School, I would ask students what is meant by the term "Brandeisian," and each year I would draw a blank.

The problem runs far deeper than absence of name recognition, as an experience at the FDR Memorial in Washington made clear to me. The dedication of the memorial in May 1997 was a special moment for me because I had been asked some twenty years earlier by its creator, Larry Halprin, to select quotations from FDR to be inscribed in granite for generations to come, and on that brilliantly sunny morning I was seeing for the first time what had been wrought. I did not think that all the sculptures were successful—Arthur Schlesinger said to me that the one of Eleanor Roosevelt looked like a suburban housewife on her way to a Wednesday matinee—but the one I found particularly moving was George Segal's *Breadline,* with its queue of despondent, desperate jobless men. Yet I noted on that inaugural day a feature that neither Segal nor anyone else could have anticipated: one tourist after another joining the breadline and mugging, grinning, giggling for a family snapshot. A feature writer on the *Washington Post* phoned Segal and me about this some time later, for she had witnessed the same phenomenon and, baffled by the incongruity, sought to puzzle out what it meant. Afterward, she reported on "a woman who has placed her hand, conga-line style," on the shoulder of the figure of one of the derelicts yelling, "Didja get it?"; noted "one fellow shouting merrily, watching as a man in powder blue jogging gear joins the breadline and squints toward the camera"; and observed four men "guffawing and winking" as they fall in with Segal's "five men in hats and overcoats and crumbling shoes, lined up hunched and stoic." It was, she wrote, "a mesmerizing sight, odd and disturbing. One wonders what sort of homage is being paid to Depression suffering."[1]

What is this coming generation—the generation with no direct experience of the 1930s—likely to make of the New Deal? I can imagine three very different scenarios. One is that, as the country looks back from the perspective of the twenty-first century on the hundred years from William McKinley to Bill Clinton, the Roosevelt era will no longer seem especially remarkable, will no longer appear to be a "watershed." That would not be an altogether new conclusion. I recall that when, on the fiftieth anniversary of the New Deal, I spoke at a forum at the Wilson Center in Washington, Herbert Stein, the former chairman of the Council of Economic Advisers, rose during the question period to say, "What's so special about the New Deal? Wherever you look in the world in the 1930s, you find an expansion of the state. The New Deal was just one aspect of an inevitable worldwide trend." Some years ago, I took part in a conference at the Graduate Center of the City University of New York titled "The Relevance of the New Deal to the Present Situation." Early in the new century, it may be concluded that the answer to the question, "What relevance does the New Deal have today?" is "None."

A second possibility is that the new generation will acknowledge that the New Deal was consequential but decide that it was malign. For six decades, the main criticism of FDR's policies has been that the government did not go far enough—that it missed the opportunity to nationalize the banks, that it failed to establish a planned economy, that it was, as Richard Kirkendall summed up the New Left's censure, an "antirevolutionary response to a situation that had revolutionary potentialities."[2] More recently, though, libertarians and conservatives have been asserting that the trouble with the New Deal was that it did all too much, bequeathing a legacy of cumbersome statist intrusions that have burdened a free society. Commenting on the claim that the Holding Company Act of 1935 "eliminated abusive concentrations of big capital," Richard Posner, chief judge of the U.S. Court of Appeals for the Seventh Circuit, wrote in the spring of 1998: "Who believes that anymore? Who has a good word these days for the Glass-Steagall Act or the Robinson-Patman Act? Who mourns the repeal of the Civil Aeronautics Act? Who regrets the rollback of the Wagner Act, in calmer times, by the Taft-Hartley Act? Or the curbing of the New Deal agencies by the Administrative Procedure Act?"[3]

The New Dealers took pride in the building of mammoth structures—the great dams in the Tennessee Valley, Grand Coulee and Bonneville in the Pacific Northwest, Fort Peck in Montana—but recently Secretary of the Interior Bruce Babbitt raised a sledgehammer and knocked a big chunk of concrete out of a dam on the Rogue River in Oregon to symbolize a resolve to terminate the obsession with dam building. Liberals in the 1930s also rejoiced in vast public housing complexes that replaced noisome slums, only to witness in recent years dynamite charges blow the projects to smithereens because they had come to be regarded as crime-ridden, drug-plagued dead ends.

Over the past generation, not only in Reagan's America and in Thatcher's Britain but also on the European continent and even in the third world, the state has come to be regarded as suspect and there has been a transfer of trust to the market. "From India to Israel, from Mexico to Moscow, it has become a truism that economic activities should be dominated by market forces," observed a writer in *Newsweek* in the spring of 1998. "Around the world, nominally left-of-center governments advance what used to be thought right-wing economic policies. The intellectual climate of the era has been transformed."[4] In the former Soviet sphere, the achievement of a "civil society" has been measured by the degree to which a country has established a market economy. In the United States, former president Clinton jettisoned the Aid to Families with Dependent Children program first established in the 1930s and announced that the era of big government is over. The two major parties wrangle over which deserves the credit not for FDR-style innovations but for balancing the budget. In such a milieu, it is conceivable that the New Deal will come to be regarded as a mercantilist aberration.

There is, though, a third possibility—that as people contemplate the events of the twentieth century they will come to have a greater appreciation of the achievements of the New Deal than numbers of scholars have shown. If they have any sensitivity at all to historic antecedents, they cannot help but be aware of the impact of the age of Roosevelt on their lives. If an American in the twenty-first century cashes a Social Security check, flies into La Guardia Airport, votes in a union election, deposits money in a government-insured bank account, switches on the lights in a remote farmhouse, drives on the Blue Ridge Parkway, collects unemployment compensation, or watches a football game in the stadium at Ole Miss, he or she will be drawing on the legacy of the New Deal.

At least some individuals born well after the end of the New Deal have shown an abiding awareness of its continuing presence. Before Bill Clinton had even met for the first time with his Cabinet, his secretary of labor, Robert Reich, entered in his diary:

> I discover Frances Perkins in a closet and promptly hang her behind my desk. God knows how long the Republicans had locked her away in there—maybe a dozen years. She looks lovely nonetheless: hair pulled back in a neat bun, modest black dress, pearl necklace, her hands folded primly before her. She now has a perfect view of the Capitol and can also gaze over my shoulder to check on what I'm up to. Saint Frances of the Labor Department, Our Lady of Working Americans. . . .
>
> Now that I've liberated her from the Republican closet, she will have a bird's-eye view of what we try to do. I hope she's not too disappointed.[5]

Not surprisingly, Franklin Roosevelt casts a much larger shadow than Secretary Perkins. In April 1995 a journalist, noting that at the time of FDR's death a radio announcer had said that for twelve years "Franklin Roosevelt was the Capital," commented, "Fifty years later, he almost still is." That same month Kevin Phillips, scoffing at Newt Gingrich's "burbling about taking a leaf from the Duke of Wellington's peninsular campaign or following the late 18th-Century fiscal prescriptions of Pitt the Younger," wrote that the Speaker, who "really wants to become . . . what Reagan never tried to be: the genuine anti-Roosevelt," had "about as much chance of wiping away Roosevelt's legacy as a prairie dog does of resculpting Mt. Rushmore." In like manner, another commentator, remarking on Gingrich's ambition to undo the New Deal, observed: "It is some task, dismantling the Roosevelt legacy. . . . The inscription to Sir Christopher Wren in St. Paul's Cathedral comes mightily to mind: 'If you seek his monument look about you.' Mr. Roosevelt's monument is everywhere."[6]

In his lifetime, many, especially those who viewed him as "a traitor to his class," detested FDR, but today his place in the pantheon of American presidents is secure. It has become commonplace to rank him as the greatest president of this century. In the last two polls in which I participated (the *New York Times* and *Time Magazine*), Roosevelt was number one—in a category by himself. Moreover, to everyone's astonishment, the FDR Memorial has become the most popular tourist attraction in Washington. Though it is not easy to find and parking is difficult, it drew as many visitors in its first year as the White House, the Washington Monument, and the Jefferson Memorial combined. So many of the 3 million visitors touched Fala's nose, Eleanor Roosevelt's knuckles, and FDR's fingers that they have changed color to gold.[7]

On the fiftieth anniversary of FDR's death, a Wisconsin editor wrote:

There is an ancient campaign badge that I wear on the cuff of my winter coat.

It's red, white and blue, and it reads, "I want Roosevelt again."

The badge summed up sentiments of the majority of Americans when it was first used during President Franklin Delano Roosevelt's 1940 re-election campaign. And it still expresses my feelings.

Apparently, I am not alone. Chuck Jones, the University of Wisconsin's Hawkins professor of political science, says that—in many senses—"Roosevelt" is the name we give to our oft-denied political longings. "We sort of yearn—constantly—for another Roosevelt, for that sort of leader."[8]

Those who seek the second coming of FDR are doing more than paying tribute to the four-time president. To be sure, they admire his capacity for leadership. A columnist, recalling the grief in his boyhood town of Charlotte when Roosevelt's funeral train went through, wrote, "You want to believe, despite a computer-TV-microwave society, that . . . crisis produces great men. That in a world-class jam—not petty, juggle-the-budget 1990s tantrums—a new FDR would show up."[9] Yet what people miss still more is the compassion and innovativeness of the New Deal. Both Roosevelt and the New Dealers were flawed, but much of the time they carried on in a spirit sadly lacking in recent decades, encapsulated in FDR's words in his Second Inaugural Address: "The test of our progress is not whether we add more to the abundance of those who have much; it is whether we provide enough for those who have little."[10] That conviction may be expected to gain in salience as economic conditions change. When all is going well, paeans to the free market are voiced hourly. But when there is a downturn and millions here and abroad need cushioning from the ravages of the market, New Deal approaches are no longer likely to be thought obsolete.

Even Bill Clinton came to understand this, though he was a slow learner. True, he had repeatedly expressed admiration for Roosevelt and his achievements, but these statements had been largely ritualistic. At Warm Springs in 1995, he even transmuted FDR into a New Democrat who, if he were alive today, would want to diminish the role of the national government. Yet in October 1998, confronted by the prospect of a worldwide economic meltdown, he told the financial leaders of 182 nations at the annual conference of the International Monetary Fund and the World Bank that if global capitalism was not tempered by New Deal–type safety nets and government regulations, democracy and free markets would "shrivel together." Repeatedly, he cited FDR. "Fair and honest regulation, sound social policy are not enemies of the market," Clinton maintained. "We must put a human face on the global economy."[11] Despite the many naysayers, the New Deal, six decades later, continues to exert a compelling influence.

The lively controversy over how to take the measure of FDR and the New Deal shows no sign of relenting. By diverging widely in their conclusions, the two most recent Roosevelt biographers provided fresh evidence of the vitality of earlier debates. Patrick J. Maney ended his 1992 book with the chilling sentence, "Among presidents, alas, Franklin Roosevelt was not a man for all seasons,"[12] while in 2000 George McJimsey reckoned that "no president in our history has faced such critical problems with the courage, vision, and stamina that Roosevelt displayed."[13] No more in the twenty-first century than in the twentieth will historians be able to escape deciding whether, on balance, they regard the New Deal as a Good Thing, but one hopes—and expects—that they will not continue to worry the very same questions that have preoccupied writers in past generations. "To lament the New Deal's deficiencies or to celebrate its achievements has only limited utility," Tony Badger of Cambridge University, one of the most astute scholars of the 1930s, has written. "Instead, what is needed is an examination of the relationship between reforms instituted by the New Deal and the longer-term developments of American society."[14] Historians in the future will build on the work of those of us who first entered the research room at Hyde Park some fifty years ago, but they will ask new questions, come up with new answers.

Notes

1. Liza Mundy, "Bread Lines and Circuses," *Washington Post Magazine,* June 1, 1997, 4.

2. Richard S. Kirkendall, "The New Deal as Watershed: The Recent Literature," *Journal of American History* 54 (March 1968): 849.

3. Richard A. Posner, "This Magic Moment," *New Republic,* April 6, 1998, 34.

4. Michael Elliott, "The Romance of the Marketplace," *Newsweek,* May 4, 1998, 37.

5. Robert B. Reich, *Locked in the Cabinet* (New York: Knopf, 1997), 76–77.

6. Craig Crawford in the *Orlando Sentinel,* April 9, 1995; *Los Angeles Times,* April 2, 1995; William Murchison in the *Dallas Morning News,* April 12, 1995.

7. *USA Today,* May 22, 1998; *View from Hyde Park* 12 (Summer 1998).

8. John Nichols in *Madison (Wis.) Capital Times,* April 12, 1995.

9. Sandy Grady in the *Buffalo News,* April 14, 1995.

10. For the drafting of that address, see Halford R. Ryan, *Franklin D. Roosevelt's Rhetorical Presidency* (New York: Greenwood, 1988), 89.

11. *Raleigh News and Observer,* October 7, 1998; *Washington Post,* October 7, 1998.

12. Patrick J. Maney, *The Roosevelt Presence: A Biography of Franklin Delano Roosevelt* (New York: Twayne, 1992), 203.

13. George McJimsey, *The Presidency of Franklin Delano Roosevelt* (Lawrence: University Press of Kansas, 2000), 295.

14. Anthony J. Badger, *The New Deal: The Depression Years, 1933–1940* (New York: Hill and Wang, 1989), 301.

Franklin D. Roosevelt, the Economic Constitutional Order, and the New Politics of Presidential Leadership

Sidney M. Milkis

Like his progeny the New Deal, Franklin Roosevelt's legacy as a democratic leader is disputed. To be sure, scholars of the presidency and commonsense opinion consider him to be one of our greatest presidents. With Washington and Lincoln, Franklin D. Roosevelt is considered, as Arthur Schlesinger puts it, one of the "immortals" of the American presidency.[1] Yet, most historians and presidential scholars view his principal legacy, the New Deal, as a series of ad hoc responses to the political and economic emergencies created by the Great Depression. The perception of the New Deal as "all brawn and no brain" is more often than not attributed to the nature of Roosevelt's leadership.[2] In James MacGregor Burns's well-known characterization, Roosevelt was a "broker" leader whose "shiftiness" and "improvising" detracted from "hard, long-range purposeful building of a strong popular movement behind a coherent political program."[3]

In contrast, I have argued that FDR had a rather coherent understanding and program of reform and that he made a distinct contribution to both the development of modern presidential leadership and the progressive tradition.[4] Roosevelt's contribution to leadership of public opinion, to the so-called rhetorical presidency, was limited, but it was deliberately so.[5] As he put it to Ray Stannard Baker, Woodrow Wilson's biographer, who in 1935 urged FDR to give the same emphasis to "vision" that his Democratic predecessor had, "You are absolutely right about the response this country gives to vision and profound moral purpose that I can only assure you of my hearty concurrence and my constant desire to make that appeal. . . . I know at the same time that you will be sympathetic to the point of view that the public psychology and, for that matter, individual psychology, cannot, because of human weakness, be attuned to a constant repetition of the highest note on the scale." Reform leadership, FDR insisted, had to combine principled rhetoric and solid accomplishments of administration. In this respect, FDR believed, his cousin Theodore offered valuable lessons on leadership. "Theodore Roosevelt lacked Woodrow Wilson's appeal to the fundamental and failed to stir, as Wilson did, the truly profound moral and social convictions," he acknowledged. But, FDR continued, Wilson "failed where Theodore Roosevelt succeeded in stirring people to enthusiasm about individual events, even though these specific events may have been superficial in comparison with the fundamentals."[6]

Whereas Wilson believed that the burdens of executive administration should be reduced, thus enabling presidents to become strong leaders of their parties and provide rhetorical leadership that would enable the country to form its judgments of party principles and policies, Roosevelt's concept of the modern presidency emphasized executive administration with limits on partisanship and rhetoric. Like his cousin, FDR hoped to emancipate the president from the constraining influence of American political parties, which made national administrative power chimerical. As one of Roosevelt's aides, Ernest Cuneo, put it, "FDR ran against only one opponent his whole life—Teddy Roosevelt, his relative." FDR admired his cousin's New Nationalism, his attack on party, his aggressive use of executive power, and his commitment to building a strong national government, which Wilson's New Freedom made impractical.[7]

FDR's contribution to the progressive tradition was to combine elements of Wilson's New Freedom and Roosevelt's New Nationalism, thus formulating a new American political philosophy: New Deal Liberalism. An important part of this accomplishment was "rhetorical," but in the more classical understanding of this term.[8] His task was to challenge the core belief in the Anglo-American tradition that freedom was inherently *natural* and that the protection of natural rights required that a "wall of separation," as Thomas Jefferson put it, stand between society and the national government. Roosevelt sought not to reject but to revive and renew the American constitutional heritage: to persuade the American people that the expansion of the industrial economy had rendered their understanding of inalienable rights inadequate to assure equality in the pursuit of happiness, and to teach them that a strong national government and executive were not alien to their values.

As Felix Frankfurter put it, FDR had a rare gift for taking "the country to school," for giving the American people "a full dress exposition and analysis" of principles and policies he supported.[9] In "taking the American people to school," FDR explained that the economic system would destroy itself if it were not subject to constitutional reform and that this transformed economic constitution would be based on a new right—the right to economic security. This redefinition of the social contract, obligating the national government to provide an adequate standard of living for all its people, presupposed not only a new understanding of individual rights but also a change in constitutional arrangements; it meant that the executive, as the leading national institution in American politics, would have to be strengthened. The president, rather than the Congress or party organizations, would have to become the leading instrument of popular rule. Like that of Jefferson, Jackson, and Lincoln, Roosevelt's leadership was the principal ingredient in a full-scale partisan realignment, but the New Deal realignment was the first one dedicated to expanding national administrative power and to placing presidential power at the heart of its approach to politics and government. The consolidation of modern executive leadership required not only increasing presidential opportunities to persuade but also enhancing the executive's capacity for solid programmatic achievement.[10]

Franklin D. Roosevelt's program to reconstruct American political life left an ambiguous legacy. In the wake of the Roosevelt "revolution," the presidency was freed from the strictures of party, only to be constrained by an unwieldy bureaucracy and a fractious political environment. These constraints did not result from the absence of serious and original thought but followed from a principled understanding of American political life that allied national administration to a new understanding of rights, to an "economic constitutional order" that gave rise to a more active and better-equipped national state, but one without adequate means of public debate and judgment.

Redefining the Social Contract

Because FDR was a gifted politician who knew when to trim as well as when to set full sail, scholars have tended to underestimate how steadfast and resolute was his course, viewing him as a president of extraordinary political gifts, although one lacking a coherent political philosophy. "At the heart of the New Deal there was not a philosophy but a temperament," Hofstadter wrote. "The essence of this temperament was Roosevelt's confidence that even when he was operating in unfamiliar territory he could do no wrong, commit no serious mistakes." FDR's confidence was born of an "intuitive wisdom" that the people "wanted experiment, activity, trial and error, anything that would expose a sense of movement and novelty."[11]

Yet there was a method to FDR's bold leadership. This was apparent to James Farley, who served as postmaster general and head of the Democratic National Committee during Roosevelt's first two terms. As Farley noted in his memoirs, "Some of the things he has done during his administration, while appearing to the ordinary man on the street as a wonderful accomplishment, quickly performed, are things I have heard him discuss not only before he was elected, but before he was nominated." Roosevelt's discussions with Farley and other close associates revealed that when FDR was "elected President he had a full knowledge of the [office], and had in mind more or less definitely, the program he proposed to put into effect as soon as he could bring about the necessary legislation and other actions necessary in order to carry out his ideas."[12]

Roosevelt's 1936 tribute to Abraham Lincoln hinted at the depth and purpose of the ideas that governed his actions. He praised Lincoln "for transfusing with new meaning the concepts of our constitutional fathers and to assure a Government having for its broad purpose the promotion of life, liberty, and the pursuit of happiness."[13] So FDR defined his own task. It was not to rouse public opinion but to teach the American people a new public philosophy, albeit one that promised to reinvigorate the Framers' understanding of the social contract. New Deal Liberalism did not presume to transform America's public philosophy in the fundamental sense given it by Walter Lippman.[14] Nor, however, was Liberalism merely a set of governing principles that justified the New Deal realignment.

Rather, like the political realignment of the Civil War period, the political transformation of the 1930s gave new meaning to the understanding of rights. Roosevelt first spoke of the need to modernize the elements of the old faith in his famous Commonwealth Club Address, delivered during the 1932 campaign and appropriately understood as the New Deal manifesto. This speech's theme was that the time had come—indeed, it had come three decades earlier—to recognize the "new terms of the old social contract." It was necessary to rewrite the social contract to take account of a national economy remade by industrial capitalism and the concentration of economic power, a new contract to establish countervailing power—a stronger national state—lest the United States steer "a steady course toward economic oligarchy." Protection of national welfare must shift from the private citizen to the government. As FDR put it, in a famous turn of phrase, "The day of enlightened administration has come."[15]

Significantly, a draft of the Commonwealth Club Address, prepared by Adolf Berle, had read, "The day of the *manager* has come." The final version of the address, fashioned by Roosevelt and Raymond Moley, pronounced the day of "enlightened administration" instead, thus pushing home more clearly than the draft language the extent to which the reform of American democracy seemed to bring with it administrative aggrandizement. The objective was not merely to accentuate the role of expertise within public councils but also to elevate administrative officials and agencies to a central position in the realization of a progressive democratic policy.[16]

Yet FDR acknowledged that the creation of a national state with expansive supervisory powers would be a "long, slow task." He was sensitive to the uneasy fit between energetic central government and the Constitution. It was imperative, therefore, that the New Deal be informed by a public philosophy in which the new concept of state power would be carefully interwoven with earlier conceptions of American government. The task of modern government, FDR announced, was "to assist the development of an economic declaration of rights, an economic constitutional order."[17] The traditional emphasis in American politics on individual self-reliance should therefore give way to a new understanding of the social contract, in which the government guaranteed individual men and women protection from the uncertainties of the marketplace. Security was to be the new self-evident truth of political life in the United States.

The defense of progressive reform in terms of an economic constitutional order was a critical development in the advent of a positive understanding of government responsibility in the United States. Although Theodore Roosevelt and Woodrow Wilson anticipated many elements of this argument, FDR was the first advocate of an ongoing supervisory role for the government to link this new public responsibility to constitutional principles. Wilson's New Freedom remained in its essentials committed to the decentralization of power, to a natural rights understanding of the Constitution. Herbert Croly and Theodore Roosevelt expressed an alternative progressive understanding, one that envisioned a "new nationalism" and a dominant president who would serve as "the steward of the public welfare."[18] TR's bolt from the Republican Party in 1912, his rejection of partisan control of presidential politics and government, was part of a broader effort to advance a "neo-Hamiltonian" program that would free national administration from the forces of decentralization.[19]

Theodore Roosevelt's 1912 Progressive Party campaign anticipated many of the social welfare measures that would become central to the New Deal reform program, but the political division between progressives and conservatives, drawn so boldly by TR and Croly, placed reformers in opposition to popular conceptions of the "pursuit of happiness" and constitutional government. The New Nationalism's reform aspirations were wedded to measures of "pure democracy," including the universal use of the direct primary, an easier method to amend the Constitution, the initiative, recall of elected officials (including the president), and referenda on laws that the state courts declared unconstitutional. The Progressive Party's program of "pure democracy" was sanctified as a "covenant with the people," as a deep and abiding pledge to make the people the "masters of their constitution."[20] This vision of democracy rejected traditional party politics as they had worked in the United States. To be sure, localized parties were not part of the original Constitution, but they had become a bulwark of limited constitutional government and federalism during the nineteenth century. Progressives disdained such intermediary organizations that might interfere with "pure democracy" and instead championed a form of popular rule that would reach fulfillment in an independent executive, directly tied to public opinion and freed from the provincial and corrupt influence of party and commercial interests. "It was not in the specific schemes of economic or social change embodied in the Progressive party's platform that the essential point of departure of that party was to be found," the *Nation* observed in its postmortem of the 1912 election. Rather, the editorial continued, "impatience . . . of any restraints as are imposed by a written Constitution is of the very essence of the movement; and even this does not by any means measure the extent of its departure from the American tradition."[21]

Indeed, the Progressives' dream of national community appeared to prescribe an unvarnished majoritarianism that threatened the Constitution's promise to protect individual freedom against the vagaries of public opinion. Croly, in fact, had begun to rethink his celebration of New Nationalism during World War I. Toward the end of 1917, his essays in the *New Republic* began to warn that America's "liberal democracy" risked becoming a "jacobin democracy" unless it tolerated, indeed fostered, "competition" from intermediary economic and social groups.[22]

Croly's anxiety about progressive democracy degenerating into plebiscitary politics was given a more complete elaboration in John Dewey's struggles during the 1920s to reconcile individualism with progressive ideals. For Dewey, progressivism could have an enduring and salubrious effect on the American polity only insofar as it could be transformed into a new liberal tradition, one that did not celebrate a rugged individualism and abhor state interference with private property but instead viewed the state as the guarantor of social and economic welfare. Dewey's concept of "new individualism" was an important precursor to New Deal Liberalism. Indeed, FDR's economic constitutional order pronounced in the Commonwealth Club Address bore striking similarities to the views Dewey had expressed in his six-part series "Individualism: Old and New," published by the *New Republic* during late 1929 and early 1930. Whereas Croly hoped for the "substitution of frank social policy for the individualism of the past," Dewey advocated a reform program suited to a new understanding of individualism, one that was appropriate for the modern social and economic stresses of the twentieth century.[23]

Dewey did not create new individualism out of whole cloth, of course. He greatly admired English liberal thinkers such as T. H. Green. Dewey credited the teachings of this new liberal school for breaking "down the idea that freedom is something that individuals have as a ready-made possession," for fostering "the idea that the state has the responsibility for creating institutions under which individuals can effectively realize the potentialities that are theirs."[24] But Green lectured on the duties and responsibilities of the *individual* as well. He proposed strong temperance measures, for instance, arguing that there "was no right to freedom in the purchase and sale of a particular commodity, if the general result of allowing such freedom is to detract from freedom in the higher sense, from the general power of men to make the best of themselves."[25] This kind of social control, which drew considerable support from American progressives during the enactment and ratification of the Eighteenth Amendment, had been discredited by the early 1930s. In adapting English liberalism for American soil, Dewey spoke less of duties than he did of education as a means to strengthen the character of individual men and women. He emphasized the responsibility of the state, rather than that of the citizen, to create the conditions for individuals to realize their full potential, to advance social welfare policy and foster community participation in the "cause of the liberty of the human spirit."[26]

From Dewey, New Dealers discovered how to circumvent American hostility to administrative centralization and persuade Americans that expansive national power was consistent with revered traditions. "The great tradition of America is liberal," the philosopher H. M. Kallen wrote in 1935, which Dewey "restates in language under the conditions of his time what Jefferson's Declaration of Independence affirmed in the language and under the conditions of his."[27] Borrowing from Dewey, FDR termed his philosophy "Liberalism" rather than "Progressivism" and thereby meant to convey the idea that the dignity of the democratic individual now required a strengthening of national resolve. The New Deal understanding of reform, however, appealed more directly to the American constitutional tradition. For Dewey, liberalism's fate lay not in a new understanding of rights but, instead, with a greater sense of community, more particularly with reform of local communities as forums of educated public inquiry.[28] In contrast, the New Deal asserted a connection between nationalism and rights, albeit rights that looked beyond the original social contract.

New Deal Liberalism was the foundation on which a full-scale partisan realignment arose. Roosevelt's triumph was greatly aided, of course, by the economic exigencies created by the Great Depression. But FDR's deft reinterpretation of the American constitutional tradition was no less important.[29] The economic constitutional order gave allegiance to constitutional principles and forms, even as it required the national government to assume responsibility for protecting individual men and women from unfair business practices and the vagaries of the marketplace. FDR gave legitimacy to progressive principles by embedding them in the language of constitutionalism and interpreting them as an expansion rather than a subversion of the natural rights tradition. As Roosevelt made clear in the Commonwealth Club Address, this new understanding of rights required both a return to and a redefinition of the Declaration: "Under the [Declaration] rulers were accorded power, and the people consented to that power on consideration that they be accorded certain rights. The task of statesmanship has always been the redefinition of these rights in terms of a changing and growing social order. New conditions impose new requirements upon government and those who conduct government."[30]

Roosevelt reaffirmed the principles of the Commonwealth Club Address throughout his presidency. Indeed, each key rhetorical moment represented an opportunity to elaborate on the meaning of an economic constitutional order. Significantly, the new understanding of the Constitution was the principal message of Roosevelt's first reelection bid in 1936, the decisive triumph that established the Democrats as the majority party in American politics for a generation.

Lincoln had "transfused with new meaning the concepts of our constitutional fathers" by defending the Declaration of Independence as America's founding document, by teaching how the centrality of the Declaration to the American constitutional heritage justified a "new birth of freedom." This constitutional teaching was sanctified by the Republican Party's 1860 campaign platform, which included and celebrated the importance of the Declaration.[31] Just as the 1860 Republican platform included the Declaration of Independence, so too the 1936 Democratic platform, drafted by FDR, was written as a pastiche of the Declaration, emphasizing the need for a fundamental reconsideration of rights. As the platform claimed with respect to the 1935 Social Security Act: "We hold this truth to be self-evident—that government in a modern civilization has certain inescapable obligations to its citizens," among which is the responsibility "to erect a structure of economic security for [its] people, making sure that this benefit shall keep step with the ever increasing capacity of America to provide a high standard of living for all its citizens."[32]

The 1936 election appeared to sanction FDR's redefinition of the social contract. Roosevelt, of course, won every state but Maine and Vermont. More significant, FDR won the day on the issue of whether New Deal policies meant greater liberty or tyranny. The *New York Times* reported in February 1936: "Liberalism and all it stands for is coming forward as an issue in the national campaign. Both New Deal and anti-administration spokesmen declare their devotion to the liberal ideal of freedom and democracy; both assail each other as opponents of true liberalism."[33] The 1936 Republican platform declared that "America was in peril" and dedicated the party to "the preservation of . . . political liberty," which "for the first time" was "threatened by Government itself." The Republican Party, with its historical commitment to preserving a large sphere of unrestricted private action, "must become the true liberal party," argued former president Herbert Hoover. The New Deal, he said, was a "false liberalism" that regimented people and extended bureaucracy.[34] But Roosevelt successfully defended the New Deal in terms of liberalism. Excoriating the unreconstructed segment of the business community that opposed his program as "economic royalists," FDR's 1936 convention address was dedicated to the proposition that "freedom is no half-and-half affair":

> The royalists of the new economic order have conceded that political freedom was the business of government, but they have maintained that economic slavery was nobody's business. They granted that the Government could protect the citizen in his own right to vote, but they denied that Government could do anything to protect the citizen in his right to work and his right to live. . . . If the average citizen is guaranteed equal opportunity in the polling place, he must have equal opportunity in the marketplace.[35]

The campaign for a new understanding of rights must have been successful, Ronald Rotunda has written, "for although Hoover continually insisted that he was a liberal, the 1936 election presented the first instances of some Hoover-like liberals who began to admit they were really conservatives."[36]

The Third New Deal and the Consolidation of the Modern Presidency

Roosevelt's reappraisal of values is important to understanding the New Deal, but it is also important in understanding his influence on laws and institutional change. Historians have generally divided Roosevelt's first term into two periods, each identified by a flurry of legislative activity lasting approximately one hundred days. The first (1933–34) responded to FDR's call for "bold, persistent experimentation" to meet the great emergency at hand. Among those measures were the Emergency Banking Relief Bill and other legislation establishing the Public Works Administration, the Agricultural Adjustment Administration, and the National Recovery Administration.[37] The second period (1935–36) brought laws such as the Social Security Act and the National Labor Relations Act that converted emergency programs into ongoing obligations of the national government. The "economic constitutional order" conceived of such programs as Social Security and collective bargaining as rights. In principle, these programs were to be permanent entitlements, like speech and assembly, beyond the vagaries of public opinion and the reach of elections and party politics. Once established, as one New Dealer observed hopefully, "we may assume the nature of the problems of American life are such as not to permit any political party for any length of time to abandon most of the collectivist functions which are now being exercised. This is true, even though the details of policy programs may differ and even though the old slogans of opposition to government activity will survive long after their meaning has been sucked out."[38]

Just as the Roosevelt administration's first term was dedicated to the formulation of a new social contract and to the enactment of legislation called for by the economic constitutional order, so FDR pursued a program during his second term that would thoroughly reconstruct the institutions and practices of constitutional government in the United States. This program—the Third New Deal—was pursued with the understanding that programmatic rights, such as Social Security and collective bargaining, would not amount to anything unless new institutional arrangements were established that would reorganize the institutions and redistribute the powers of government.[39] It included three extremely controversial initiatives: the Executive Reorganization Act, the centerpiece of the program, announced in January 1937; the "court-packing" plan, proposed just a few weeks after the administrative reform program; and the so-called purge campaign, attempted during the 1938 primary elections. These measures had the common objective of strengthening national administrative power. They marked an effort to transform a decentralized polity, dominated by localized parties and court rulings that supported property and states rights, a "state of courts and parties," as Stephen Skowronek has called it, into a more centralized, even bureaucratic, form of democracy that could deliver the goods championed by New Dealers.[40]

Transforming the Institution of the Presidency

The centerpiece of the Third New Deal was the Executive Reorganization Bill, which strengthened the administrative power and capacity of the president. Significantly, the bill proposed to create a number of new administrative tools and support staff, not just for Roosevelt but for the office as an institution. "No measure was closer to Roosevelt's heart," the *New York Times* reported, and none aroused "more determination to force it through Congress than the reorganization bill."[41]

The executive reorganization proposal was based on a report prepared by the President's Committee on Administrative Management (PCAM), which was directed by three of the country's foremost scholars on public administration: Louis Brownlow, the chairman; Charles E. Merriam; and Luther Gulick. Roosevelt formally convened the Brownlow Committee in March 1936 and consulted often with Brownlow, Gulick, and Merriam during the remainder of the year.

Soon after the 1936 election, during a planning session with Gulick and Brownlow, Roosevelt revealed that he considered the Brownlow Committee a surrogate constitutional convention. As Gulick's notes of the meeting read: "[Roosevelt] said that since the election he had received a great many suggestions that he move for a constitutional convention for the United States and observed that there was no way of keeping such an affair from getting out of hand what with [Father] Coughlin and other crackpots about. 'But,' he said, 'there is more than one way of killing a cat, just as in the job I assigned you.'"[42]

The objective of the Brownlow Committee's constitutional deliberations was executive dominion. Its report proposed measures that would significantly expand the staff support of the executive office and greatly extend presidential authority over the executive branch, including the independent regulatory commissions. As Gulick anticipated, the strengthened executive emerging from this reform would be delegated authority to govern. Laws would be little more than "a declaration of war, so that the essence of the program is in the gradual unfolding of the plan in actual administration."[43]

Localized democracy shaped by party politics would thereby be replaced by the activities of a dominant and dominating presidency. Whereas Wilson had proposed and slouched toward a reconstituted party system in the hope of establishing stronger linkages between the executive and the legislature, the administrative program of the New Deal would combine executive action and public policy, so that the president and administrative agencies would be delegated authority to govern, thus making unnecessary the constant cooperation of party members in Congress and the states.[44] The traditional party system had provided presidents with a stable basis of popular support and, episodically, during critical partisan alignments, with the opportunity to achieve national reform. What was once episodic, New Deal reformers insisted, must now become routine. As the Brownlow Committee report put it, "Our national will must be expressed not merely in a brief, exultant moment of electoral decision, but in persistent, determined, competent day-by-day administration of what the nation has decided to do."[45]

To be sure, party politics were not irrelevant to the task of strengthening national administration. In fact, the administrative reform program became, at FDR's urging, a party program. Ironically, a policy aimed at making party politics less important became a major focus of party responsibility. So strongly did Roosevelt favor this legislation that House Majority Leader Sam Rayburn appealed for party unity before the critical vote on the Executive Reorganization Bill, arguing that the defeat of this legislation would amount to a "vote of no confidence" in the president.[46]

Administrative Reform and Party Responsibility

Roosevelt lost this vote of confidence on administrative reform in April 1938, as the House of Representatives, with massive Democratic defections, voted down the legislation. It was a devastating defeat for FDR and had an important influence on his decision to undertake the purge campaign, in which he intervened directly in one gubernatorial and several congressional primary campaigns in a bold effort to replace conservative Democrats with candidates who were "100 percent New Dealers." In June, Democratic senator Josh Lee of Oklahoma urged FDR to "bear down on those who voted against your program, who are now patting you on the back in their campaigns, feeling for a soft place to stick a knife after [the] elections." The vote on the reorganization legislation, Lee suggested, "might be a good one to use as an example or test of loyalty."[47] Two days later, interestingly, FDR announced in a fireside speech his intention to purge the Democratic Party of conservatives. The defeat of the administrative reform proposal, coming on the heels of the defeat of the "court-packing" plan, also closely linked to strengthening administrative power, left Roosevelt little recourse but to go to the country.[48]

Roosevelt's attempt to influence his party's nomination contests was not unprecedented. William Howard Taft and Wilson had made limited efforts to remove recalcitrants from their parties. But Roosevelt's campaign took place on a larger scale than those of Taft and Wilson and, unlike previous efforts, made no attempt to work through regular partisan channels. In all but one case, Roosevelt chose to make a direct appeal to public opinion, rather than attempt to cooperate with or reform the regular party apparatus. Indeed, during the general election, Roosevelt announced that he would prefer liberal Republicans to conservatives of his own party and that he would continue to campaign for the election of liberals in national and state politics, regardless of their party affiliation.[49]

Roosevelt's purge campaign, charged James Farley, Democratic chairman, violated "a cardinal political creed" of American politics "that the President keep out of local matters."[50] The degree to which FDR's actions were viewed as a shocking violation of the norm is indicated by the press's labeling of it as the "purge," a term associated with Adolf Hitler's attempt to weed out dissension in Germany's National Socialist Party and Joseph Stalin's elimination of "disloyal" party members from the Soviet Communist Party. FDR's "purge" was hardly despotic, and yet the "campaign for saving liberalism," as he called it, was a jarring departure from the traditions of party politics in the United States.

Roosevelt and his political allies believed, however, as one aide put it, that "the President, and not either party, was now the instrument of the people as a whole."[51] In truth, the conditions seemed right for such a presidential challenge to partisan responsibility in 1938. Columnist Raymond Clapper, in fact, suggested that developments since Wilson's occupation of the White House had made the sort of campaign FDR waged against conservative Democrats inevitable. "It awaited only the appearance of a strong president in a highly controversial setting."[52]

First, there had been the spread of the direct primary during the first three decades of the twentieth century. This reform had begun to weaken greatly the grip of local party organizations on the electorate. William H. Meier, Democratic county chairman from Nebraska, for example, wrote Farley in 1938 that his state's direct primary law had "created a situation which made candidates too independent of the party."[53]

The spread of the direct primary gave the president the opportunity to make a direct appeal to the people over the heads of congressional candidates and local party leaders. Thereby, it provided an attractive vehicle for an attack on traditional party politics, which Roosevelt saw as an obstacle to his policy objectives. Furthermore, radio broadcasting made the opportunity to speak to large audiences even more enticing. Of course, the use of the mass media was bound to be especially tempting to an extremely popular president with as fine a radio presence as Roosevelt. Indeed, Frankfurter encouraged FDR to go to the country in the midst of the president's monumental struggles with the Seventy-fifth Congress, assuring him that "the contagiousness of your personality over the radio, the warmth of your voice and your being," would "renew [the public's] dependence on you." Frankfurter was "absolutely right," FDR responded a few days later. In anticipation of the purge campaign, he wrote, "I feel like saying to the country—'You will hear from me soon and often. This is not a threat but a promise.'"[54]

Roosevelt's purge campaign thus marked an important event in the development of the "rhetorical presidency." But this advance in popular leadership was hitched to a program dedicated to administrative aggrandizement. In the final analysis, the objective of the Third New Deal, including the purge, was not to persuade Congress to give up its control over the party councils, which were becoming less significant in the scheme of things. Rather, the purpose of the New Deal institutional program was to force Congress to relinquish its control over national administration, which was becoming the center of political life in industrial societies.

The Executive Reorganization Act of 1939

The purge failed at the polls, but it frightened recalcitrant Democrats, who after the 1938 elections became more conciliatory toward their president on a few matters. Administrative reform was one of these, and in 1939 a compromise but nonetheless significant reorganization bill passed Congress.[55] Although considerably weaker than the original proposal, the 1939 Executive Reorganization Act provided authority for the creation of the Executive Office of the President, which included the newly formed White House Office and a strengthened and refurbished

Bureau of the Budget, and it enhanced the chief executive's control over administrative agencies. As such, this legislation was, in effect, the organic statute of the "modern" presidency. Roosevelt's extraordinary leadership was, so to speak, institutionalized by the administrative reform bill, for this statute ratified a process in which public expectations and institutional arrangements established the president as the principal agent of popular rule. It set off a new dynamic whereby executive administration, coupled with the greater personal responsibility of the president enhanced by FDR's political leadership and the emergence of the mass media, displaced collective responsibility in important ways.[56]

With the strengthening of executive administration, the presidency became disassociated from party politics, undermining the latter's importance. As the presidency evolved into a ubiquitous institution, it preempted party leaders in many of their limited but significant tasks: linking the president to interest groups, staffing the executive department, policy development, and, most important, campaign support. Presidents no longer were elected and governed as head of a party but were elected and governed as the head of a personal organization they created in their own image.

But the purpose of New Deal reform was not to strengthen presidential government per se. Rather, the presidency was strengthened on the assumption that, as the one national office, it would be an ally of progressive reform. Consequently, executive power was refurbished in a way that was compatible with the objectives of programmatic liberalism, and administrative reform was intended to insulate reformers and reforms from the presidential election cycle. By executive orders issued with authority granted by the 1939 Executive Reorganization Act, most of the emergency programs of the New Deal were established as permanent institutions. Moreover, the Roosevelt administration obtained legislative authority in the 1940 Ramspeck Act to extend civil service protection over New Deal loyalists who were brought to Washington to staff the newly created welfare state.[57] New Deal civil service reform, therefore, did not replace politics with administration, nor did it replace patronage practices with civil service procedures dedicated to "scientific management"—to what Herbert Kaufman has called "neutral competence."[58] Rather, it transformed the political character of administration. Previously, the choice was posed as one between politics and spoils, on the one hand, and nonpartisan, nonpolitical administration on the other.

The New Deal celebrated an administrative politics that denied nourishment to the regular party apparatus but fed instead an executive department oriented toward expanding liberal programs. As the administrative historian Paul Van Riper has noted, the new practice created another kind of patronage, "a sort of intellectual and ideological patronage rather than the more partisan type."[59]

In this sense, the New Deal realignment prepared the ground for an administrative constitution that would protect reforms and reformers from future contests of opinion. The Democratic Party triumphed as a party of administration, dedicated to subordinating partisanship to enlightened government. Interestingly, FDR chose the 1940 Jackson Day dinner, a party event, to herald a less partisan future. To establish the right mood, FDR went so far as to invite the Republican leaders to the Democratic celebration, an invitation they declined. In his address, Roosevelt observed that the independent vote was on the increase, that party loyalties were becoming less significant, and that "the future lies with those wise political leaders who realize the great public is interested more in government than in politics."[60] The fate of the modern presidency, then, was not predicated on popular leadership alone. Its future was allied to a policymaking state in which partisanship and debate were subordinated to programmatic rights and the delivery of services associated with those rights.

Breaking the Two-Term Tradition

The Ramspeck Act and its aftermath point to the importance of FDR's defiance of the two-term tradition. Indeed, Roosevelt's success in inspiring and managing the recasting of the executive might not have happened had he not taken the extraordinary step of running for a third term in 1940. Congress might have been willing to resist the Ramspeck Act had it been championed by a "lame duck" but found it difficult to forestall a popular president during an election year, especially on an issue trumpeted by the Roosevelt administration and the press as an assault on the spoils system.[61]

The approach of war gave Roosevelt the opportunity to stand for an unprecedented third term, which in turn enabled him to use this legislation to secure civil service protection for New Deal loyalists in the federal bureaucracy. The decision to try for a third term was in truth, however, made during the woeful beating Roosevelt suffered in the 1938 elections. "They are already casting lots for the cloak of the Master," White House aide Thomas Corcoran told Roosevelt that summer. But while Democratic leaders were already discussing FDR's possible successor, the White House was planning his precedent-shattering try for a third term. Apparently a decision was made by Corcoran and other New Dealers in July 1938 that the salvation of the New Deal required that Roosevelt run again. No liberal could get the Democratic nomination in 1940, they concluded, except for Roosevelt, and they were determined to draft him.[62]

The White House bid for a third term, unlike the purge campaign, was hidden from public view, but it was no less energetic and was perhaps better organized. In important respects, Roosevelt's nomination in Chicago in July 1940 reversed the bitter defeats the White House suffered during the Seventy-fifth Congress and the 1938 primary elections. Despite spirited competition from Farley and Vice President John Nance Garner (the first time an incumbent vice president challenged his "chief" for a party's nomination), Roosevelt was easily renominated. "For the first time since 1932 Franklin Roosevelt was in absolute command of the party," *Time* magazine reported after the convention. "The purge that had failed in 1938 was being carried through in 1940."[63]

But the "purge" of 1940 did not secure the liberalism of the Democratic Party. Indeed, Roosevelt did not take over the party in shattering the two-term precedent; instead, his domination of the 1940 Democratic convention confirmed the displacement of party politics by executive administration. As his aide Ernest Cuneo put it, FDR had "pistol-whipped" the Democratic Party chieftains into nominating him for a third term and into accepting Secretary of Agriculture Henry Wallace, a militant liberal with virtually no support in the Democratic organization, as his running mate. That the secretary of agriculture did not even have the delegation of his home state, Iowa, behind him testified to his complete disconnection from the party organization.[64] Nevertheless, the Democratic delegates grudgingly ratified the president's choice, sobered by the warning of his surrogates in Chicago that FDR would not run unless Wallace were nominated. It is little wonder, then, that in spite of FDR's nomination and the election to a third term as the Democratic standard-bearer, Samuel Lubell's postmortem on the 1940 campaign bespoke of a New Deal—not a Democratic—triumph: "The Republicans do not know what hit them; the Democrats, certainly, as distinguished from the New Dealers, do not know what they hit the Republicans with. The New Deal aimed at a bloodless revolution. In 1940 it went a long way toward accomplishing it."[65]

The New Deal Goes to War

The economic crisis that dominated Roosevelt's first two terms was displaced in the third by the approach and then the outbreak of the Second World War. The old saw of the historical literature on the New Deal is that the national security state displaced domestic reform, that the economic constitutional order had to be abandoned to unite the nation and mobilize for war.

But, as Jytte Klausen argues in this volume, "Dr. Win the War" did not eclipse "Dr. New Deal." Indeed, the condition of total war gave Roosevelt the authority he needed to shape further the reconstructed executive as an agent of New Deal policies. Woodrow Wilson had put business leaders such as Bernard Baruch in charge of industrial mobilization during World War I. In contrast, FDR scuttled the business-backed War Resources Board (WRB), formed in 1939, which recommended the appointment of a single individual to control mobilization, a czar with extraordinary power who would, presumably, be chosen from among industry's managerial leaders. Baruch, who had directed the War Industries Board (WIB) in the Great War—directing the defense industry, setting priorities, and fixing prices—pressed the WRB's plan on Roosevelt. But Roosevelt had no intention of turning power over to industry or one of its leaders. The Nye Committee investigation of 1934 had confirmed that munitions manufacturers and bankers had profited handsomely from World War I. Even though the Senate investigation could not lay these excess profits directly at the feet of the WIB, "New Dealers dreaded regulation written and administered by big businessmen that might favor great corporations." Roosevelt promoted partnerships with business in public enterprises such as electric generation, but as Jordan Schwarz has shown, FDR's disbanding of the WRB testified to his insistence that defense preparations be directed from cabinet departments. "If they needed any emergency setup, he would originate it in the White House and make it consonant with New Deal principles."[66]

This is not to suggest that Roosevelt led a well-coordinated planning effort during the war that efficiently melded war production and liberal reform. His success in centralizing power in the White House came at the expense of systematic coordination of a nationwide mobilization effort. As Barry Karl has argued, Roosevelt's reluctance to delegate authority to industrialists also "blocked the tendency of his industrial administrators to centralize production in a way that would turn the process of post-war conversion into a bonanza for the country's largest industries."[67] By the same token, FDR's unwillingness to turn war production over to industrial leaders ensured that New Deal liberalism would not be lost amid the exigencies of war. Roosevelt staffed many key positions during World War II with New Dealers who were committed to his perception of the nation's needs. With such loyal New Dealers as Harold Smith, who headed the Bureau of the Budget, and Chester Bowles, who directed the Office of Price Administration, playing key roles in industrial mobilization, the Roosevelt revolution and the war effort were combined so as to establish the government's responsibility for the welfare of the American people irrevocably.

The change was more than economic; Roosevelt's leadership elevated this new government responsibility into a new creed. The condition of total war not only accelerated the flow of power to the executive but also strengthened Roosevelt's moral authority, thus giving him the opportunity to root the New Deal vision of a good society more securely in American soil. World War II "mobilized most of the society and as a consequence, the number of people who worried over issues of obligation was broad and diverse," Robert Westbrook has written. It was also the "first American war to follow the consolidation of mass culture and social science," thus the common themes of FDR's rhetoric may more readily have influenced widely shared attitudes about politics and government.[68]

The power of New Deal Liberalism's influence on American political culture was suggested symbolically in 1943 when Norman Rockwell illustrated the "freedom from want" on the cover of the *Saturday Evening Post*. This revealed, FDR enthused, "the plain, everyday truths," "the staunchly American values" contained in the new understanding of rights that he hoped to make a permanent part of the American political heritage.[69]

The Four Freedoms

The freedom from want was first pronounced in FDR's annual address to Congress on January 6, 1941. The principal message of the speech was not the need for domestic reform but the growing crisis abroad. In the face of this crisis, Roosevelt had effectively ended America's stance of neutrality by executive order in the destroyers-for-bases deal with Great Britain, which paved the way for the United States to send fifty naval destroyers to help Great Britain in its desperate battle with Nazi Germany. But the administration's Lend-Lease program, which was announced in FDR's State of the Union Address, proposed aid in a form that required congressional authorization. Equally important, FDR saw the crisis in Europe as an opportunity to engage the Congress and the American people in a great debate about both America's role in the world and the profound changes in the national government's domestic responsibilities. Thus, in a dramatic peroration defining the "four essential freedoms" that his policies aimed to secure, Roosevelt spoke of the need to inoculate the United States from the mounting threat of tyranny abroad with political and economic reforms that had become the sine qua non of "a healthy and strong democracy." To the traditional freedoms of speech and religion, Roosevelt added the freedom from fear, dedicated to "a world-wide reduction of armaments to such a point and in such a fashion that no nation will be in a position to commit an act of physical aggression against any neighbor," and the freedom from want, the commitment "to economic understandings which will secure to every nation a healthy peace-time life for its inhabitants."[70] These four freedoms, depicted in Norman Rockwell's illustrations, soon became, as David Kennedy has written, "a sort of shorthand for America's war aim." More to the point, "they could be taken too, especially the concepts of freedom from want and fear, as a charter for the New Deal itself."[71]

Critics have charged that Roosevelt's celebration of a rights-based welfare state squandered the opportunity presented by the war to fuse New Deal Liberalism with a sense of *public* responsibility. Nor did artists such as Rockwell challenge the nation's obsession with privacy and rights. Rockwell's artistic renditions of the New Deal, popular as they were, Westbrook argues, did little to remedy the defects of Roosevelt's virtues. By depicting the Four Freedoms in private terms, in illustrations that celebrated the home life and family, Rockwell merely reflected, if he did not compound, FDR's failure to strengthen the American sense of mutual obligation. Westbrook argues that this failure was most significant with respect to Rockwell's depiction of the freedom from want. This was the most controversial of the war aims proclaimed, he acknowledges, "because it introduced into the reciprocal relationship between the liberal state and its citizens the obligation of the state to provide and protect a minimal level of subsistence for the individuals who compromise it." But, Westbrook laments, this was not conveyed in Rockwell's painting:

> The painting portrayed a Thanksgiving dinner for which an extended family has gathered (and to which the viewer is invited). This was intended to convey the message that Americans are fighting to protect the opportunities they had, as Americans, to provide for the material needs of themselves and their families. Here Roosevelt's most controversial "freedom" was rendered not, as Henry Wallace would have had it, as the foundation of a Global New Deal in which every child was guaranteed a quart of milk a day, but rather as the defense of the familial surfeit of a peculiarly American holiday.[72]

Rockwell, it must be said, was not immune to such criticism. To be sure, he took some comfort from the delight FDR expressed concerning the illustrator's ability to translate his rhetoric into American folklore. But more telling, he feared, was the criticism from oversees. "The Europeans sort of resented it because it wasn't freedom from want," he confessed in his autobiography, "it was overabundance, the table was so loaded down with food." So viewed as an expression of American excess, Rockwell lamented, his illustration of economic rights would not have "any wallop."[73] Noting Rockwell's artistic angst about his own work, Westbrook finds FDR's unstinting praise for it curious. That FDR did not shun Rockwell's illustrations, Westbrook concludes, confirms the president's limited vision, his "implicit contention that freedom from want was something that the New Deal had secured for Americans who now wished to extend it to the rest of the world."[74]

Westbrook's criticism of the Four Freedoms stems from a deeper cultural criticism, one that laments the impoverishment of liberalism and champions other—nonliberal—traditions in American life that may foster a sense of community. Michael Sandel has made this argument most strongly, denigrating the New Deal for corroding a competing "republican" ideology that emphasizes community and political participation.[75]

The importance of competing and alternative ideologies in American political culture notwithstanding, Roosevelt understood the reformist potential of the liberal tradition better than have most scholars.[76] More to the point, FDR deliberately exploited this potential to bring about important changes in American political life. Indeed, his celebration of

Lincoln suggests that FDR believed that true reform in the United States came not by ex cathedra lectures to the American people about the immorality of "rights talk" but rather, as Lincoln put it, from "appeals to their better angels," from vital debate and resolution about the true meaning of their rights.[77] Indeed, all previous political realignments in American history involved presidential leadership that engaged the people in a great contest of opinion about constitutional principles, about those things—the Declaration, the Bill of Rights, and constitutional forms—that are the essence of community in the United States.[78]

In truth, as the Commonwealth Club Address suggests, Roosevelt's political genius was to recognize not just the promise but also the limits of the Declaration of Independence for his day—to comprehend how the New Deal could transform American political culture without seeming to do so. The Four Freedoms speech and his reaction to Rockwell's paintings reveal how Roosevelt hoped the war might abet him in this enterprise. Of the four freedoms, Roosevelt in his 1941 State of the Union Address devoted the most attention to freedom from want. As Rockwell noted, the famous peroration of FDR's address was stated in such exalted and universal terms as to risk sounding "platitudinous."[79] But FDR took particular care to give concrete form to freedom from want. "The basic things expected by our people of their political and economic systems" were, he insisted, "equality of Opportunity for youth and for others," "jobs for those who can work," "security for those who need it," "the ending of special privilege for the few," "the preservation of civil liberties for all," and "the enjoyment of the fruits of scientific progress in a wider and constantly rising standard of living."[80]

Pace Westbrook, FDR made clear his understanding that these economic rights had not been secured by the New Deal but remained its exalted yet practical aspiration. A passage he added to the speech called for the expansion of Social Security and unemployment insurance, widening the opportunities for medical care, and developing "a better system by which persons deserving or needing gainful employment may obtain it." These economic obligations did not weaken or deflect attention from America's duties abroad, FDR maintained. Rather, they strengthened the nation's resolve by "making its people conscious of their individual stake in the preservation of democratic life in America."[81]

That Roosevelt had been talking since the Commonwealth Club Address about the importance of redefining the social contract, of creating

an "economic constitutional order," indicates that the pronouncement
and elaboration of the freedom from want were not frivolous. Clearly the
approach of war caused him to think more boldly about the possibilities
of constitutional change. FDR's ardent but opportunistic New Deal allies encouraged him in this posture. Neither the four freedoms nor the
appeal for the enlargement of domestic reform was included in the first
draft of the Lend-Lease speech. Their incorporation and elaboration in
subsequent drafts were due in no small part to the timely intervention of
Secretary of Interior Harold Ickes.[82] Ickes called Roosevelt's attention
to a new book by Samuel Grafton, *All Out,* which contained a defense
of economic rights from a "very surprising source," the *Economist.*[83] Like
Grafton, Ickes was pleasantly taken aback by the "better sections" of
the British press advocating for an "economic bill of rights," which was
Roosevelt's term, not that of the *Economist.* But the magazine did recognize the need for Great Britain, even in the midst of its desperate fight
against Nazi Germany, to draw up a "modern Bill of Rights, whereby the
citizen is guaranteed not only his personal liberties but the minimum of economic welfare and security that will enable him to enjoy those liberties."[84]

This new understanding of rights was no mere afterthought but integral to the war's success, according to the editorial, titled "Dynamic Democracy." The "obligations of the citizens to the community" demanded
by war compelled the community to consider that it had "greater obligations to its citizens." By promising its individual men and women not
only their personal liberties but also "minimum standards of housing,
food, education, and medical care," the *Economist* argued, Great Britain
and other free nations would serve a dual purpose: democracies would
give their citizens a greater stake in their own countries, and in doing
so, they would take the wind out of Hitler's sail by demonstrating that
the need was "not to throw overboard the old liberal principles, but to
supplement them."

It is not surprising that Ickes's letter had an important influence on
Roosevelt's Four Freedoms address. Grafton's book and the *Economist*
essay endorsed, albeit implicitly, a position FDR had been arguing since
his first quest for the White House. Roosevelt glimpsed from this new
confirmation how the international challenges he faced need not dilute
his reform program. Indeed, the abandonment of American neutrality in
1940 made more urgent the need to redefine the social contract. The
time was right, as the *Economist* put it, for "nailing our democratic col-

ors to the mast and reinforcing our own faith in the principles to which
we adhere." To be sure, these ideas were being debated seriously in Great
Britain, which did not have the same deep-rooted cultural antipathy to
statism that had hobbled the New Deal's forward march. Yet a strikingly
similar editorial had appeared in the *New York Post* the day before Ickes
penned his letter to Roosevelt.[85] In truth, as FDR must have realized, the
call for a rights-based welfare state, the goal of "supplementing" the liberal tradition, prescribed by the *Economist,* may have been more appropriate, at least at the level of doctrine, in the United States than in Great
Britain. As T. H. Green's attention to duties suggests, English political
culture was more amenable to nonliberal social democratic remedies for
economic insecurity.

The ruminations in the British and American press encouraged Roosevelt to pronounce the "new" Declaration that was anticipated by the
1936 Democratic platform; the ability of Norman Rockwell to translate
the New Deal creed into understandable American folkways appeared to
sanctify this new understanding of rights. "This is the first pictorial representation I have seen of the staunchly American values contained in the
rights of free speech and free worship," Roosevelt enthused, "and our
goals of freedom from fear and want." That Rockwell had so engagingly
and successfully combined pictorial representations of traditional rights
and New Deal programmatic ambitions suggested to Roosevelt that he
had gone far, despite the bitter defeats of his second term, in persuading
the American people to recognize a new understanding of self-evident
truths, to accept New Deal principles as irrevocably interwoven with
American ideals and aspirations.[86]

Indeed, Roosevelt was not simply a passive observer of Rockwell's interpretations. His administration played a critical part in supporting the
celebrated illustrator's efforts, welcoming him to the White House for
"a sketching visit" and orchestrating the Four Freedoms War Bond
Show, which visited several major cities in the country during the summer of 1943.[87] The White House sponsorship of Rockwell's project was
rewarded handsomely, as its extraordinary success played an important
part not only in supporting the war effort but also in identifying the New
Deal principles of freedom from fear and freedom from want with deeply
ingrained values of American life.[88]

Given his desire to "supplement" rather than transcend the liberal
tradition, FDR believed that Rockwell's depiction of these principles in

ways that celebrated the home life reinforced rather than diminished them. The representation of economic freedom as the bountiful celebration of Thanksgiving was an effective way to connect private and public values, for it showed the joy of an extended family, the primary relationship that has traditionally linked America's generations. It had been this very linkage that Roosevelt and his New Deal allies built on in establishing Social Security as a new programmatic right.

Moreover, Rockwell's illustration showed three generations celebrating a *civic* holiday. Significantly, Thanksgiving became a national holiday slowly, finding acceptance only in the wake of civil insurrections and reform struggles that tortuously forged a nation. At the beginning of the twentieth century, Thanksgiving, as a distinctly American holiday, was considered an introduction to American values for the millions of immigrants then entering the country. In the face of the Great Depression at home and the threat of tyranny abroad, Roosevelt recognized this unique holiday, combining civic and private virtues, as an opportunity to appeal to America's fragile sense of national community. As he put it in his Thanksgiving Day Proclamation of 1941, the same year he delivered the Four Freedoms speech, "Let us ask the Devine Blessing on our decision and determination to protect *our way of life* against the forces of evil and slavery which seek in these days to encompass us."[89]

The Second Bill of Rights

Roosevelt gave the most detailed account of the freedom from want in his 1944 State of the Union message, in which he proclaimed a "Second Bill of Rights." It was our duty, he announced, to begin to lay the plans and determine the strategy for winning a lasting peace—a peace that was possible only through a program dedicated to the economic truths that the American people now accepted as self-evident: the right to a useful and remunerative job; the right to earn enough to provide adequate food, clothing, and recreation; the right of every family to a decent home; the right to adequate medical care and the opportunity to achieve and enjoy good health; the right to adequate protection form the economic fears of old age, sickness, accident, and unemployment; and the right to a good education. "All these rights spell security," FDR concluded. "And after this war is won we must be prepared to move forward, in the implementation of these rights, to new goals of human happiness and well-being."[90]

The Second Bill of Rights had its origins in a report of the National Resources Planning Board (NRPB), a White House planning agency, created in pursuance of the 1939 Executive Reorganization Act.[91] Given the task of coming up with a "vigorous and stimulating" statement of Roosevelt's freedom from want, the board suggested that FDR couch his prescription for the renewal of activist government in a new bill of rights. Such an idea would not have appeared novel to Roosevelt, of course, who had seen this idea debated in the British and American press during his preparation of the Four Freedoms speech.

Still, FDR must have been pleasantly surprised at how well this idea was received by the American people. Just as Rockwell's illustrations suggested the penetration of New Deal values into American political culture, so newly developed polling techniques appeared to confirm that the American people had begun to embrace a new understanding of rights. The radio enabled FDR to cultivate public opinion; the development of polling offered him the opportunity to circumvent his party and the Congress in taking the measure of public opinion. Especially interested in the people's reaction to the NRPB's report on the Second Bill of Rights, which the president made public in March 1943, the Roosevelt administration commissioned the respected pollster Hadley Cantril to investigate public reaction to "The NRPB Report and Social Security." The NRPB worked closely with Cantril, helping his polling organization, the Office of Public Opinion Research, to frame the questions for two national surveys to be taken two weeks after FDR had announced the board's blueprint for the postwar political economy. Cantril's polls showed that the American people were strongly supportive of the idea of an economic bill of rights. When asked to characterize the report, some respondents chose to describe it as "too much like Communism" (23 percent) or "Washington bureaucracy bidding for power" (29 percent), but a far greater number of those surveyed, Democrats and Republicans alike, indicated that they believed the report was best described as reflecting the "duty of government to provide for the needy" (79 percent). Large numbers of those sampled also expressed support for more tangible goals such as the government guaranteeing adequate health care and remunerative employment.[92]

The work of the NRPB was scorned by Congress, which eliminated the agency's funding during the summer of 1943. But the elimination of the planning agency did not deter Roosevelt. Encouraged by polls that showed that the people were on his side and urged on by Office of Price Administration director Chester Bowles, FDR was determined to send a "blast" to a Congress dominated by a conservative coalition of Republicans and southern Democrats. But his real audience was the American people, who still had not heard a full-dress exposition of the Second Bill of Rights.[93] Thus, the self-evident truths of the economic constitutional order, first pronounced in the 1936 Democratic platform, did not simply constitute a political strategy to win votes. They were now formally delineated and clearly allied with the New Deal dedication to strengthening national administrative power.

In the debates that followed Roosevelt's Second Bill of Rights speech, Barry Karl has noted, "critics of the idea of a new conception of 'rights' would ask what the term was being stretched to encompass." Did the president's pronouncement of new rights suggest, for example, that someone who could not get a job would be entitled to sue in a court of law?[94] Constitutionalists would claim that economic rights had no historical status. Even New Dealers hedged; after all, sanctifying government programs as formal constitutional rights appeared to violate the New Deal faith in administrative discretion.

As his rejection of the proposal to hold a constitutional convention to bring about administrative reform suggested, Roosevelt too was skeptical about the benefits of constitutional change. Throughout the struggles for judicial and executive reform, he had rejected plans that called for formally amending the Constitution. In private communications and public discourse he consistently defended the statutory avenue to institutional reform on the grounds that the problem was not the Constitution but the "manner in which it had been interpreted."[95] FDR also considered the pursuit of formal constitutional change impractical. "The reason for the elimination of the amendment process was to me entirely sufficient," he wrote Felix Frankfurter after the announcement of the court-packing plan: "to get two-thirds of both Houses of this session to agree on the language of the amendment which would cover all of the social and economic legislation, but at the same time, not go too far would have been difficult." Furthermore, Roosevelt warned, to engage in the sort of protracted struggle that would be necessary to get an appropriate amendment would fail to address the pressing demands of a profound domestic crisis.[96]

The rejection of the amendment process went beyond practical considerations, however. Equally important, the New Deal understanding of the Constitution was not a legalistic one. Alexander Hamilton had argued in *Federalist* 84 that a bill of rights was not necessary to buttress the integrity of the Constitution, warning that the codification of particular liberties would tend both to denigrate the federal government's discretion and to tempt it to usurp powers—"to prescribe proper regulations" concerning the protection of these liberties.[97] So Roosevelt feared it would be with the Second Bill of Rights. To transmute this understanding into a formal legal document would deny New Dealers the discretion to administer programs prudently, would bind the economic constitutional order in a legal straitjacket. Committed to "programmatic rights," to a pragmatic administration of the economy and society, the New Deal revolution sought to emancipate the national government from the demands of formal constitutionalism. "The Constitution," FDR insisted in his address celebrating its 150th anniversary, "was not a Lawyers Contract." More to the point, the Constitution had to be remade so that constitutional *policy* displaced formal constitutional obligation.[98]

To be sure, some New Dealers were intrigued by the prospect of treating the economic bill of rights as a formal constitutional program. In urging Roosevelt to make these new rights the centerpiece of his 1944 State of the Union Address, Chester Bowles cautioned that they "should not *necessarily* . . . be adopted into the Constitution, although that idea should be studied." The most important objective, Bowles concluded, was to articulate "a program which everyone can understand, and will bring to all men in our Armed Forces and to millions of men, women, and children here at home, new hope for the future that lies ahead."[99]

These new programmatic rights were never ratified as constitutional amendments, but as Bowles anticipated, the idea of a new bill of rights resonated with the American people. FDR returned to the Second Bill of Rights during the 1944 presidential election, making it the principal theme of his most important campaign address.[100] Beyond the 1944 election, the new bill of rights became the foundation of political dialogue, redefining the role of the national government. Although Congress rejected the NRPB's plans for postwar America, it did enact the GI Bill, which entitled veterans to home and business loans, unemployment compensation, and subsidies for education and training. This legislation did not provide the broad security and employment programs that Roosevelt championed, but as Ronald Story's essay in this volume shows, "the sheer number of veterans—the sheer magnitude of the war—meant that it was bound to have a major social impact."[101]

In the wake of the Roosevelt revolution, nearly every important public policy was propounded as a right, purporting to confer constitutional status on such programs as Social Security, Medicare, and food stamps. The new social contract heralded by Roosevelt thus marks the beginning of the so-called rights revolution—a transformation of the governing philosophy of the United States that has brought about major changes in American political institutions. With the advent of the New Deal political order, an understanding of rights dedicated to limiting government gradually gave way to a more expansive understanding of rights, requiring a relentless government identification of problems and the search for methods by which these problems might be solved.[102]

Conclusion: Rights, Rhetoric, and Limits of Presidential Leadership

For the past sixty years we have been struggling to come to terms with the legacy of the New Deal. In forging an alliance between rights and national administration, Roosevelt did not abolish the obstacles to the creation of a centralized state. The defeats Roosevelt suffered during the Third New Deal did not prevent him from strengthening executive administration; abetted by the exigencies of total war, FDR's plans for consolidating the modern presidency were successful. But clothed in the garb of constitutional propriety, opponents of the New Deal were able to preserve the independence of the courts and the Congress to influence the details of administration.[103]

In truth, Roosevelt himself was somewhat diffident in his support for centralized administration. The New Deal order created new obstacles to statist ambitions. Once viewed as entitlements, New Deal programs became autonomous islands of power that would constrain presidents no less than had localized parties. As Martha Derthick has written about the Social Security program, its architects "sought to foreclose the options of future generations by committing them irrevocably to a program that promises benefits by rights as well as those particular benefits that have been incorporated in an ever expanding law. In that sense they designed social security to be uncontrollable."[104] Little wonder that Republican presidents, even ardently conservative ones such as Ronald Reagan, often felt as though they were relegated to managing the liberal state.[105]

Still, the expansion of national administrative power that followed the New Deal realignment did not result in the form of national state that Roosevelt and the architects of the modern presidency had hoped for— one that established regulation and social welfare policy that could be expressions of national unity and commitment. Karl has argued that Americans continue to abhor, even as they embrace, national administrative power.[106] As Roosevelt's second term revealed so dramatically, they rejected the New Deal state, although they supported many of its programs. Unlike Roosevelt's efforts to mobilize support for the First and Second New Deals, his institutional program polarized the nation. Persuading the people to modify their understanding of rights was one thing; convincing them to accept executive dominion was quite another. Roosevelt sought to circumvent the American antipathy to the expansion of national administration by rooting his idea of enlightened administration in the fertile soil of rights. But his successes in this regard left New Deal programs exposed not only to the interference of Congress and the courts but also to the "public" interest groups that formed to protect these programs. Consequently, particular programs such as Social Security and Medicare have achieved popular support, but New Deal Liberalism was never defined and defended in such a form that could withstand the rights-based claims of favored constituencies.

At the end of the day, Americans have formed a love-hate relationship with the national state, a profound ambivalence that seeks refuge in forms of participation, such as the direct primary, referendum, and initiative, that expose national and state governments to the uncertain fortunes of mass public opinion. The direct form of popular rule championed by the Progressive Party of 1912 became newly relevant in the 1960s and 1970s, as reformers attempted to recast the administrative state as an agent of democracy. For all the failures these reformers experienced, their call for "participatory democracy" would have an enduring influence on politics and government. Unwilling to embrace or reject the entitlement state, the country has increasingly supported reforms to give the "people" more control over it.[107]

Ultimately, the public's uncertainty about the state forged on the anvil of the New Deal realignment follows from a development in which a national administrative apparatus and activist public philosophy were grafted onto a rights-based constitutional system and political culture. Charged with the stewardship of this "uneasy state," as Karl calls it, presidents have attempted to use the tools of the modern presidency, rhetoric and administration, to form new, more personal ties with the public. Caught between the Scylla of bureaucratic indifference and the Charybdis of the public's demands for new rights, the modern presidency has evolved, or degenerated, into a plebiscitary form of politics that mocks the New Deal concept of "enlightened administration" and exposes citizens to the sort of public figures who will exploit their impatience with the difficult tasks involved in sustaining a healthy constitutional democracy. As the shifting fortunes of the Clinton presidency dramatically illustrated, the New Deal freed the executive from party politics, but at the cost of subjecting it to fractious national politics within the Washington beltway and volatile public opinion outside it.

The New Deal and its legacy for politics and government in the United States invite us to consider a dilemma as old as the Republic: How can a state that is expansive and powerful enough to protect our rights provide for an active and competent citizenry? In the nineteenth century, Americans sought answers to this dilemma in a natural rights version of liberalism that "erred" on the side of localism. Born of the Jeffersonian and Jacksonian support for local self-government, traditional party organizations and newspapers rectified the Constitution's insufficient attention to the civic matters. But there was no "golden age" of parties. Progressive and New Deal reformers had good reasons to view localized political parties and the provincial liberties they upheld as an obstacle to economic, racial, and political justice.

By the same token, the administrative constitution spawned by programmatic liberalism, which weakened political parties, has "erred" on the side of centralization. Having created a nation, the New Deal's legacy is a more active and better-equipped state—the national resolve to tackle such problems as forced segregation at home and communism abroad—but one without adequate means of common deliberation and public judgment, without the means to sustain the vitality of its civic culture. This is the modern dilemma of America's extended republic—this is the central challenge that the New Deal has left at the dawn of a new century.

Notes

1. Arthur Schlesinger Jr., "Rating the Presidents: Washington to Clinton," *Political Science Quarterly* 112, 2 (1997): 179–90.

2. This phrase comes from Robert Eden, in his response to Eldon Eisenach's criticism of the New Deal for vulgarizing progressive political thought. See Eisenach, "Pragmatic Democracy and Constitutional Government: Comments on Robert Eden," and Eden, "Reply to Eisenach," both in *Studies in American Political Development* 8 (Fall 1994): 409–22 and 423–26, respectively.

3. James MacGregor Burns, *Roosevelt: The Lion and the Fox, 1882–1940* (New York: Harcourt, Brace and World, 1956), 375, 380. Scholarly diminution of FDR's popular leadership contrasts strikingly with the treatment of Woodrow Wilson. For Richard Hofstadter, Roosevelt appeared "more flexible and a cleverer politician than Wilson, . . . but less serious, less deliberate, and less responsible" (Hofstadter, *The American Political Tradition and the Men Who Made It* [1948; New York: Random House, 1989], 455).

4. Sidney M. Milkis, *The President and the Parties: The Transformation of the American Party System since the New Deal* (New York: Oxford University Press, 1993). See also "Franklin D. Roosevelt, Progressivism, and the Limits of Popular Leadership," in *Speaking to the People: The Rhetorical Presidency in Historical Perspective,* ed. Richard Ellis (Amherst: University of Massachusetts Press, 1998).

5. See especially Jeffrey Tulis, *The Rhetorical Presidency* (Princeton: Princeton University Press, 1987), and James Ceaser, *Presidential Selection: Theory and Development* (Princeton: Princeton University Press, 1979), esp. chap. 4. Tulis and Ceaser view Woodrow Wilson as the founder of the rhetorical presidency and thus the patriarch of modern executive leadership. Whereas the founders scorned popular presidential leadership, Wilson provided the most important theoretical and practical lessons that transformed the executive into a leader of public opinion. From this perspective, FDR was not a regime builder; rather, his presidency is to be understood as operating within, and in certain respect vulgarizing, a progressive regime that was formed during the first two decades of the twentieth century.

6. Both FDR quotes found in FDR to Ray Stannard Baker, March 20, 1935, President's Personal File 1820, Roosevelt Papers, Franklin D. Roosevelt Library, Hyde Park, New York.

7. Ernest Cuneo, "The FDR Drama," no date, box 82, folder JAF (James A. Farley), pre-1932, Ernest Cuneo Papers, Roosevelt Library.

8. Work on the "rhetorical presidency" tends to confound the art of public persuasion with plebiscitary politics. Jeffrey Tulis's depiction of the "modern" presidency suggests that presidents have come to speak to the public routinely and without a prudential understanding of the executive's duty to educate, not simply to arouse, popular opinion (Tulis, *The Rhetorical Presidency*). This distinction between the traditional and the modern presidency overlooks the popular leadership allied to party politics in the nineteenth century. More to the

point, an examination of presidential leadership of public opinion calls for a distinction between rhetoric, which is essential to democratic leadership, and plebiscitary politics, which, as Alexander Hamilton warned, flatters the people only "to betray their interests" (Alexander Hamilton, James Madison, and John Jay, *The Federalist Papers,* ed. Clinton Rossiter [New York: New American Library, 1999], 400). Through rhetoric, as Thomas Pangle has observed, "the wisdom that is politically possible and the consent that is politically necessary are combined and elevated, under the somewhat distant guidance of philosophy" (Pangle, *The Ennobling of Democracy* [Baltimore: Johns Hopkins University Press, 1992], 129). For a treatment of Roosevelt's rhetoric in this more classical sense, see Halford R. Ryan, *Franklin D. Roosevelt's Rhetorical Presidency* (New York: Greenwood, 1988).

9. Felix Frankfurter to Franklin Roosevelt, August 9, 1937, box 210, Papers of Thomas Corcoran, Manuscript Division, Library of Congress, Washington, D.C.

10. This view of Roosevelt is similar to Stephen Skowronek's. See his *The Politics Presidents Make: Leadership from John Adams to Bill Clinton* (Cambridge: Harvard University Press, 1997), esp. chap. 7. Skowronek views Roosevelt as a "reconstructive" leader, who like Jefferson, Jackson, and Lincoln shattered the politics of the past, orchestrated the establishment of a new coalition, and enshrined their commitments as the restoration of original values, thereby "resetting the very terms and conditions of constitutional government" (39). I place more emphasis on FDR's rhetoric and view these ideas as more fully embedded in institutions and policies than does Skowronek. But I share his view of FDR's leadership as the principal agent in the transformation of American politics and government during the 1930s. For a discussion of the differences between Skowronek's understanding of FDR's reconstructive leadership and the view of Roosevelt's contribution that informs this chapter, see Sidney M. Milkis, "What Politics Do Presidents Make?," *Polity* 28, 3 (1995): 485–96.

11. Hofstadter, *American Political Tradition,* 411–12.

12. James Farley, memorandum, December 20, 1934, Cuneo Papers, box 82, folder 1934.

13. Franklin D. Roosevelt, "A Tribute to Abraham Lincoln to be Read on His Birthday," January 25, 1936, in *The Public Papers and Addresses of Franklin D. Roosevelt,* ed. Samuel I. Rosenman, 13 vols. (New York: Random House, 1938–50), 5:68.

14. Walter Lippman, *Essays in the Public Philosophy* (Boston: Little, Brown, 1955), 98–99.

15. Roosevelt, *Public Papers and Addresses,* 1:751–52.

16. Berle's draft, written with the assistance of his wife, Beatrice, can be found in the "Commonwealth Club" folder, box 18, Berle Papers, Roosevelt Library. The change in wording that appears in the final version of the speech is consistent with the themes that Berle meant to convey in his draft. Indeed, the substitution of "enlightened administration" for "manager" was probably prompted by Berle's September 19 wire to Raymond Moley, alerting the presi-

dent's party that the speech had been airmailed that day. In outlining the address, Berle's telegram read: "Fundamental issue today adaption old principles to new and probably permanent change in economic conditions which can only be done by *enlightened government*" (telegram, Berle to Moley, September 19, 1932, box 15, Berle Papers, emphasis added).

17. Roosevelt, *Public Papers and Addresses,* 1:752.

18. Theodore Roosevelt, *The Works of Theodore Roosevelt,* 26 vols. (New York: Scribner's, 1926), 20:414.

19. Theodore Roosevelt and his political allies were quite conscious about rethinking Hamiltonian principles. In sending Herbert Croly's *Promise of American Life* to TR, the progressive jurist Learned Hand wrote, "I hope that you will find in it as comprehensive and progressive a statement of American political ideas and ideals as I have found. I think that Croly has succeeded in stating more adequately than anyone else,—certainly of those writers whom I know,—the bases and prospective growth of the set of political ideas which can be fairly described as Neo-Hamilton, and whose promise is due more to you, as I believe, than to anyone else" (Hand to Roosevelt, April 8, 1910, Learned Hand Papers, Harvard University Law School).

20. "A Contract with the People," platform of the Progressive Party, adopted at its first national convention, August 7, 1912, Progressive Party Publications, 1912, Theodore Roosevelt Collection, Houghton Library, Harvard University.

21. "Progress and the Constitution," editorial *Nation,* November 7, 1912, 424. On the Progressive Party campaign of 1912 and its legacy, see Sidney M. Milkis and Daniel Tichener, "'Direct Democracy' and Social Justice: The Progressive Party Campaign of 1912," *Studies in American Political Development* 8 (Fall 1994): 282–340.

22. Herbert Croly, "The Future of the State," *New Republic,* September 15, 1917, 182.

23. Herbert Croly, *Progressive Democracy* (New York: Macmillan, 1914), 15; John Dewey, "Individualism, Old and New," reprinted in *John Dewey: The Later Works, 1925–1953,* ed. Jo Ann Boydston, (Carbondale: Southern Illinois University Press, 1984), 5:41–123.

24. John Dewey, *Liberalism and Social Action* (New York: G. P. Putnam's, 1935), 26.

25. T. H. Green, "Lecture on 'Liberal Legislation and Freedom of Contract,'" in *T. H. Green Lectures on the Principles of Political Obligation,* ed. Paul Harris and John Morrow (Cambridge: Cambridge University Press, 1986), 210.

26. Dewey, *Liberalism and Social Action,* 93.

27. H. M. Kallen, "Salvation by Intelligence," review of *Liberalism and Social Action,* by John Dewey, *Saturday Review,* December 14, 1935, 7.

28. John Dewey, *The Public and Its Problems* (New York: Henry Holt, 1927), 208, 211.

29. A passage from Machiavelli's *Discourses* suggests the significance of Roosevelt's contribution to progressive reform: "He who desires to reform the government of a state, and wishes to have it accepted and capable of maintaining it-

self to the satisfaction of everybody, must at least retain the semblance of the old forms; so that it may seem to the people that there has been no change in the institutions, even though they are entirely different from the old ones" (Niccolò Machiavelli, *The Prince and the Discourses* (New York: Modern Library, 1950), chap. 25, 182.

30. Roosevelt, *Public Papers and Addresses,* 1:756.

31. For a discussion of the 1860 Republican platform fight, see Marc Landy and Sidney M. Milkis, *Presidential Greatness* (Lawrence: University Press of Kansas, 2000), chap. 5.

32. "Democratic Platform of 1936," in *National Party Platforms,* ed. Donald Bruce Johnson (Urbana: University of Illinois Press, 1978), 360. For evidence of FDR's role in drafting the platform, see the materials of the President's Secretary File, no. 143, "Democratic Platform" folder, Roosevelt Library. Also see Burns, *Roosevelt,* 271–78.

33. *New York Times Magazine,* February 23, 1936, 3, 24.

34. "Republican Platform of 1936," in Johnson, *National Party Platforms,* 365. It was Hoover, rather than the Republican presidential nominee, Alfred Landon, governor of Kansas, who formulated the Republican case against the New Deal. Landon, who had bolted the party in 1912 to support the Bull Moosers, represented a much less fundamental challenge to New Deal principles and policies. Ronald Rotunda, "The Liberal Label: Roosevelt's Capture of a Symbol," in *Public Policy,* ed. John D. Montgomery and Albert O. Hirschman (Cambridge: Harvard University Press, 1968), 17:399.

35. Roosevelt, *Public Papers and Addresses,* 5:238. The phrase "economic royalists" was Stanley High's. Since December 1935 he had urged Roosevelt "to redefine the New Deal in those fundamentally American terms in which the Cosmopolitan [*sic*] speech first defined it." In doing so he suggested comparing the battle for an economic constitutional order with "various American crises—beginning with the Tory record in the revolution and following the Tory thread right on down through our history to the present." How well such a historical comparison would reveal, High enthused, "the New Deal as the real Americanism." Memorandum, Stanley High to Stephen Early, December 22, 1935, box 35, Franklin D. Roosevelt, 1935 (October to December) folder, Farley Papers. Obviously, High meant to refer to the Commonwealth Club Address.

36. Rotunda, "Liberal Label," 400.

37. The Works Progress Administration (WPA) was not created during the first hundred days; it was established in January 1935 as the successor to the First New Deal's Federal Emergency Relief Agency. Thus, the WPA was set during the interregnum between the First and Second New Deals, but its organization and policies were characteristic of the emergency legislation of the former period. See William Leuchtenburg, *Franklin D. Roosevelt and the New Deal, 1932–1940* (New York: Harper and Row, 1963), chaps. 6, 7.

38. Joseph Harris, "Outline for a New York Conference," April 8, 1936,

Papers of the President's Committee on Administrative Management, Roosevelt Library.

39. For an overview and critique of work on the Third New Deal, see John W. Jeffries, "A Third New Deal? Liberal Policy and the American State, 1937–1945," *Journal of Policy History* 8, 4 (1996): 387–409.

40. Stephen Skowronek, *Building a New American State: The Expansion of National Administrative Capacities, 1877–1920* (Cambridge: Cambridge University Press, 1982).

41. Felix Belair Jr., "Roosevelt Drives for Completion of the New Deal," *New York Times,* August 16, 1938, sec. 4, p. 3.

42. Louis Brownlow, final edited manuscript, vol. 2, chap. 30 ("We Report to the President"), p. 20, Louis Brownlow Papers, John F. Kennedy Library, Boston, Massachusetts.

43. Luther Gulick, "Politics, Administration, and the New Deal," *Annals* 169 (September 1933): 64.

44. Louis Brownlow, in a 1943 memorandum, reflected on this objective of executive reorganization: "We must reconsider critically the scholarly assumption, which has almost become a popular assumption, that the way to produce unity between legislative and executive is to take steps toward merging the two. . . . In direct opposition to this assumption and these proposals, it may be suggested that the objective to be sought is not to unify executive and legislature, but to unify governmental policy and administration" (Brownlow, "Perfect Union," January 27, 1943, appendix to Official Files 101 and 101b, pp. 38–39, Roosevelt Library).

45. *Report of the President's Committee on Administrative Management* (Washington, D.C.: Government Printing Office, 1937), 53.

46. *Congressional Record,* 75th Cong., 3d sess., April 8, 1938, 83, pt.5:5121.

47. Josh Lee to FDR, June 22, 1938, President's Personal File 1820, Roosevelt Papers, Roosevelt Library.

48. Significantly, the two Supreme Court cases that triggered the dispute between Roosevelt and the judiciary were *Humphrey's Executor v U.S.,* 295 US 602 (1935) and *A.L.A. Schechter Poultry Corp. et al. v United States,* 295 US 553 (1935), both of which imposed constraints on the administrative authority of the president. William Leuchtenburg notes that FDR's angry reaction to the *Humphrey* decision, which denied Roosevelt the right to remove a commissioner from an independent regulatory agency, is misunderstood as an arbitrary act of retaliation in the face of a personal blow from the Supreme Court. In fact, it was "a rational attempt to enable the presidency to emerge as the central institution to cope with the problems of the twentieth century world" (Leuchtenburg, "The Case of the Contentious Commissioner: *Humphrey's Executor vs. U.S.,*" in *Freedom and Reform,* ed. Harold M. Hyman and Leonard W. Levy (New York: Harper and Row, 1967), 312.

49. Rotunda, "Liberal Label," 404; *New York Times,* September 3, 1938, 1.

50. James Farley, *Jim Farley's Story: The Roosevelt Years* (New York: Whittlesey House, 1948), 146.

51. Ernest Cuneo, "The Eve of the Purge," p. 24, unpublished manuscript found in box 111, Cuneo Papers.

52. Raymond Clapper, "Roosevelt Tries the Primaries," *Current History,* October 1938, 17.

53. William H. Meier to James Farley, December 23, 1938, Official File 300 (Democratic National Committee), Roosevelt Papers.

54. Felix Frankfurter to FDR, August 9, 1937, box 210, Franklin D. Roosevelt, 1937, folder, Corcoran Papers, and FDR to Frankfurter, August 12, 1937, microfilm reel 60, Felix Frankfurter Papers, Manuscript Division, Library of Congress, Washington, D.C.

55. Whereas the 1937 proposal would have delegated plenary administrative authority to the president, subject only to congressional veto by joint resolution, an action that in turn could be vetoed by the president, this bill made the president's plans of reorganization subject to veto by concurrent legislation, which was not subject to veto by the chief executive. In addition, the 1939 act exempted twenty-one independent agencies from the president's reorganization power, including the important independent regulatory agencies. Also missing from the bill were controversial measures such as the modernization of the Civil Service System, the renovation of accounting procedures, and the creation of new departments of government. Still, the legislation was similar to the final amended version of the 1937 recommendations that the House defeated in April 1938. Moreover, the 1939 act marked an important turning point, whereby the Congress recognized for a time the president's authority to control administrative management. As one member of the Brownlow Committee staff would write many years later, "Its passage converted the immediate 1938 defeat into a victory over the long term and laid the basis for [an] extraordinary series of administrative reforms." Herbert Emmerich, *Federal Organization and Administrative Management* (Birmingham: University of Alabama Press, 1971), 134. For a more detailed account of the fight for administrative reform, see Milkis, *President and the Parties,* chaps. 5, 6.

56. This argument is developed more completely and documented in Milkis, *President and the Parties,* esp. chaps. 6–11.

57. The Ramspeck Act authorized the extension by the president of the merit system rules to nearly two hundred thousand positions previously exempted by law. Roosevelt took early advantage of this authorization in 1941 and by executive order extended the coverage of civil service protection to the point where about 95 percent of the permanent service was included. Leonard White, "Franklin Roosevelt and the Public Service," *Public Personnel Review* 6 (July 1945): 142.

58. Herbert Kaufman, "Emerging Conflicts in the Doctrines of Public Administration," *American Political Science Review* 50, 4 (1956): 1057–73.

59. Paul Van Riper, *History of the United States Civil Service* (Evanston, Ill.: Row, Peterson, 1958), 327.

60. Roosevelt, *Public Papers and Addresses,* 9:28.

61. Roosevelt's popularity was not damaged substantially by the controver-

sial policies of the Third New Deal. To be sure, those policies alienated conservative Democrats in Congress; however, the president's popularity among rank-and-file Democrats was considerably greater than with those in Congress. Even before the Nazi invasion of Holland, Belgium, and France in May 1940, which greatly increased popular support for a third term, polls of Democrats in the hinterlands revealed considerable support for Roosevelt's renomination. See Bernard F. Donahue, *Private Plans and Public Dangers* (Notre Dame: University of Notre Dame Press, 1965), esp. chap. 4.

62. Ernest Cuneo, "Tommy the Cork: A Secret Chapter of American History," p. 3, box 110, Thomas Corcoran file, Cuneo Papers.

63. *Time,* July 25, 1940, 11.

64. Cuneo, "Tommy the Cork," 7.

65. Samuel Lubell, "Post-Mortem: Who Elected Roosevelt?" *Saturday Evening Post,* January 25, 1941, 9–10.

66. Jordan Schwarz, *The New Dealers: Power Politics in the Age of Roosevelt* (New York: Knopf, 1995), 311; see also Barry Karl, *The Uneasy State* (Chicago: University of Chicago Press, 1983), 209–210.

67. Karl, *Uneasy State,* 211. The position taken here departs from Alan Brinkley's argument that in the end, New Deal war mobilization followed the World War I model. See Brinkley, *The End of Reform: New Deal Liberalism in Recession and War* (New York: Knopf, 1995), 189. Roosevelt's administration of war was far more unwieldy and thus less dependent on business than Wilson's. More to the point, in giving Roosevelt the opportunity to run for a third and fourth term and to expand his administrative authority, the war helped to rescue the New Deal. On this point, see Schwarz, *New Dealers,* 308–42.

68. Robert B. Westbrook, "Fighting for the American Family: Private Interests and Political Obligation in World War II," in *The Power of Culture: Critical Essays in American History,* ed. Richard Wrightman Fox and T. J. Jackson Lears (Chicago: University of Chicago Press, 1993), 197–98.

69. Roosevelt to Rockwell, February 10, 1943, Roosevelt Papers.

70. Roosevelt, *Public Papers and Addresses,* 9:671–72.

71. David M. Kennedy, *Freedom from Fear: The American People in Depression and War, 1929–1945* (New York: Oxford University Press, 1999), 469–70.

72. Westbrook, "Fighting for the American Family," 204.

73. Norman Rockwell, as told to Tom Rockwell, *Norman Rockwell: My Adventures As an Illustrator* (New York: Harry N. Abrams, 1988), 315.

74. Westbrook, "Fighting for the American Family," 204 n. 15.

75. Michael J. Sandel, *Democracy's Discontent: America in Search of a Public Philosophy* (Cambridge: Harvard University Press, Belknap Press, 1996), esp. chaps. 8, 9.

76. For a critical analysis of Sandel and others who have identified competing cultural traditions in American political history, see Mark Hulliung, "Republicanism, Liberalism, Illiberalism: An American Debate in French Translation," *Tocqueville Review* 22, 2 (2000): 109–32.

77. This term was coined by Mary Ann Glendon, *Rights Talk* (New York:

Free Press, 1985). She offers an important intellectual and public service by stimulating debate about the danger of setting too many rights apart form political life. My criticisms are directed not at her exploration of the controversy over rights but at the substantial body of contemporary criticism that singles out individualism and an obsession with rights as a fatal disease of American democracy.

78. This idea is developed more fully in Landy and Milkis, *Presidential Greatness.*

79. Rockwell, *Norman Rockwell,* 312.

80. Roosevelt, *Public Papers and Addresses,* 6:71.

81. Ibid., 670–71.

82. Ickes to Roosevelt, December 27, 1940, Roosevelt Papers. The Four Freedoms speech was prepared carefully, requiring seven drafts. These drafts, along with Roosevelt's contribution to them, can be found in the speech files of the Roosevelt Library. For a good secondary source on the preparation of the address, see Samuel I. Rosenman, *Working with Roosevelt* (New York: Harper and Row, 1952), 256–63.

83. Samuel Grafton, *All Out: How Democracy Will Defend America* (New York: Simon and Schuster, 1940), 68.

84. Quotations here and in the two following paragraphs from "Dynamic Democracy," editorial, *Economist,* August 3, 1940, 145–46.

85. "The New Order," editorial, *New York Post,* December 26, 1940; see also Rosenman, *Working with Roosevelt,* 265. As Grafton was a columnist for the *Post,* the similarity between the *Economist* and *Post* editorials may not have been entirely coincidental.

86. Roosevelt to Rockwell, February 10, 1943, Roosevelt Papers (emphasis added).

87. Norman Rockwell to Stephen Early, May 6, 1943, Roosevelt Papers; Stuart Murray and James McCabe, *Norman Rockwell's Four Freedoms: Images That Inspire a Nation* (Stockbridge, Mass.: Berkshire House, 1993), 55–92.

88. Roosevelt's cultural accomplishment was recognized by many of his opponents, who lamented Rockwell's complicity with the president. As one critic wrote to the famous illustrator, "The Four Freedoms guaranteed by the 'Bill of Rights' are Freedom of Religion, Freedom of Speech, Freedom of the Press, Freedom of Assembly. When President Roosevelt or Vice President Wallace speak of 'the 4 freedoms' they are talking about something of their own invention. . . . By freedom from want and fear they mean that if the people will give up their independence and do what the government tells them, the government will take care of them. . . . Why don't you make pictures of the American Freedoms instead of the New Deal Freedoms?" T. R. Grant to Rockwell, cited in Murray and McCabe, *Norman Rockwell's Four Freedoms,* 67.

89. "Thanksgiving Day Proclamation," November 8, 1941, in Roosevelt, *Public Papers and Addresses,* 10:482 (emphasis added).

90. Roosevelt, *Public Papers and Addresses,* 13:40–41.

91. On the NRPB and its legacy, see Patrick D. Reagan, *Designing a New*

America: The Origins of New Deal Planning, 1890–1943 (Amherst: University of Massachusetts Press, 1999).

92. Oscar Cox to Hadley Cantril, May 3, 1943; Hadley Cantril to Oscar Cox, April 30, 1943; Memorandum, Hadley Cantril to David Niles, James Barnes, and Oscar Ewing, April 30, 1943; "Public Opinion: The NRPB Report and Social Security," Office of Public Opinion Research, April 28, 1943, all in box 100, Lend-Lease Files, Oscar Cox Papers, Roosevelt Library. On the Roosevelt administration's use of polls, see Robert Eisenger and Jeremy Brown, "Polling as a Means toward Presidential Autonomy: Emil Hurja, Hadley Cantril, and the Roosevelt Administration," *International Journal of Public Opinion Research* 10 (1998): 239–56, and Theodore Lowi, *The Personal President: Power Invested, Promise Unfulfilled* (Ithaca: Cornell University Press, 1985), 62–66.

93. The Cantril report on the NRPB suggested the need for such an address. The NRPB report's influence on the public was ephemeral, and its recommendations for expanding social welfare policy were likely to be ignored unless somebody "took the trouble to tell the people what broadening Social Security means to them." Noting that "all signs point to the basic faith of people in our ability to build a better world," the Cantril report boldly proclaimed that "everything will go to the leader who will fight aggressively for goals the people want and think they can get" ("Public Opinion," 3–4, 10). Roosevelt was less certain that an address would elicit strong public support for strengthening the economic constitutional order; nevertheless, in response to a similar importunity from Louis Brownlow, he wrote: "I think it is a good idea to sound such a note. . . . and I am going to try my hand at it. Of course, times now are very different from 1932 or even 1936. The weakness and many of the social inequalities of 1932 have been repaired or removed and the job now is, first and foremost, to win the war. . . . However, even now we must look ahead and lay plans for the kind of America we want to see after the peace has been made." Roosevelt attached the letter to a note for Samuel Rosenman, asking him to prepare a draft speech, dedicated, as Brownlow urged, to "realizing the Four Freedoms." Brownlow to Roosevelt, December 14, 1943; Roosevelt to Brownlow, December 29, 1943; and Memorandum, FDR to Samuel I. Rosenman, December 28, 1943, in President's Personal File 1820, Roosevelt Papers.

94. Karl, *Uneasy State*, 221.

95. The conversations concerning the "court-packing" plan between FDR and his attorney general, Homer Cummings, recorded in the latter's diary, offer important clues to FDR's views on constitutional change. For example, see the Diaries of Homer Stille Cummings, December 26, 1936, no. 6, pp. 185–94, Homer Cummings Papers, Manuscripts Department, University of Virginia Library, Charlottesville.

96. Roosevelt to Frankfurter, February 9, 1937, microfilm reel 60, Felix Frankfurter Papers.

97. Alexander Hamilton, James Madison, and John Jay, *The Federalist Papers* (New York: New American Library, 1961), 513–514.

98. "The Constitution of the United States Was a Layman's Document, Not

a Lawyer's Contract," address on Constitution Day, September 17, 1937, Washington, D.C., in Roosevelt, *Public Papers and Addresses,* 6:357–67.

99. Bowles to Samuel Rosenman, "Outline of a Suggested Home Front Speech by Mr. Roosevelt," box 1, Bowles, Chester folder, Samuel Rosenman Papers, Roosevelt Library York (Bowles's emphasis).

100. Memorandum, Roosevelt to Samuel I. Rosenman, October 2, 1944, President's Personal File 1820, Roosevelt Papers; "We Are Not Going to Turn the Clock Back, Campaign Address at Soldiers' Field, Chicago, Illinois," October 28, 1944, in Roosevelt, *Public Papers and Addresses,* 13:369–78. Roosevelt told his aides that he wanted to make the Chicago address "a well reasoned resume of his political and economic philosophy." See Rosenman, *Working with Roosevelt,* 495.

101. Not surprisingly, Cantril's survey results in "Public Opinion: The NRPB Report and Social Security" showed stronger popular support for expanding social welfare benefits for soldiers than for the general public. "Tie the idea of social security to the problem of returning soldiers," he urged. "This will command the support of a tenth more of the electorate than proposals without this context" (9).

102. On the "rights revolution" and its legacy for governing institutions, see R. Shep Melnick, *Between the Lines: Interpreting Welfare Rights* (Washington, D.C.: Brookings Institution, 1994), and Marc Landy and Martin Levin, eds., *The New Politics of Public Policy* (Baltimore: Johns Hopkins University Press, 1995).

103. By the 1960s, R. Shep Melnick argues persuasively, Congress and the courts had seized much of the president's administrative power (Melnick, "The Politics of Partnership," *Public Administration Review* 45 [November 1985]: 653–60).

104. Martha Derthick, *Policymaking for Social Security* (Washington, D.C.: Brookings Institution, 1983), 417.

105. On the New Deal and the Reagan "revolution," see Milkis, *President and the Parties,* chaps. 10, 11.

106. Karl, *Uneasy State,* 225–39.

107. This point is developed more fully in Sidney M. Milkis, *Political Parties and Constitutional Government: Remaking American Democracy* (Baltimore: Johns Hopkins University Press, 1999), chap. 5.

Presidential Party Leadership and Party Realignment

FDR and the Making of the New Deal Democratic Party

Marc Landy

The New Deal party realignment created arguably the most dominant political party in American history. Between 1936 and 1999 there have been only two years in which the Democrats have been entirely out of power at the national level. At all other times they have controlled at least one house of Congress and/or the presidency. Between 1936 and 1968 they controlled the presidency seven out of nine times and both houses of Congress for all but four years. I contend that this remarkable partisan achievement was made, not born. It was the product of FDR's great party leadership.

Franklin D. Roosevelt's political achievement is not without irony, for, as Sidney Milkis has shown, he was no great lover of the party system of which he became the master manipulator.[1] He cut his political teeth as an adversary of political machines. He enjoyed strong support from progressive Republicans and often supported them as well. But one need not love war to be a great warrior. FDR so assiduously built the Democratic Party for the same reason Woodrow Wilson prosecuted World War I. Wilson fought a "war to end war." FDR built a party to end partisanship.[2] The mighty New Deal Democratic Party was the political weapon he needed to defeat those who opposed his programmatic ambitions. Once the administrative state he envisaged was in place, such grand partisanship would no longer be either necessary or even possible. As Milkis has described, administration would replace partisanship as the defining force in public affairs.[3] To a considerable extent this has come to pass. Parties no longer play the crucial role in political life that they once did. Nonetheless, the strength and endurance of the New Deal party over a span of two generations is an achievement worthy of serious examination. FDR built a great and sturdy partisan edifice, even if it was not built to last forever.

Coalitions and Parties

The very phrase "New Deal coalition," which has become synonymous with the Democrats' success, partially obscures the nature of that success. A coalition is not a party. No party can thrive which lacks a large support coalition, but unless it succeeds in forging a direct set of loyalties between the citizen and the party itself, it cannot endure. "Coalition" implies transience. If a coalition does not serve the interests of a particular member, that member departs. The repeated success of the Democrats, particularly between 1936 and 1968, implies far greater stability. Although loyalists may depart for a given election (Democrats in 1952, Republicans in 1964), they show great reluctance actually to change their affiliation. On important occasions, Democratic voters chose to stick by their party against the wishes of interest group leaders. Unionists, for example, resisted John L. Lewis's demand that they vote Republican in 1940. In 1948, white southerners, for the most part, resisted the racist and sectionalist appeals of the Dixiecrats to remain in the Democratic fold.

FDR's achievement is further obscured by his own ambivalence about it. He was not a full-fledged party man in the mold of Martin Van Buren. Rather his great ambition, as Milkis has so convincingly depicted, was to create a party to end party.[4] He hoped that once the Democrats, along with their liberal Republican allies, had built a solid administrative state, the need for party and its attendant seaminess and corruption would disappear and parties might even whither away. To an important extent, FDR got his wish. The administrative state has indeed survived all political challenge, including the remarkable Republican assault of the 104th Congress. And the Democratic Party is not what it was in its heyday. But no political edifice lasts forever. The party that FDR built proved remarkably long-lived, and therefore much can be learned by studying its architecture.

To build the party, FDR had to figure out how to expand its base without causing it to crack. Expansion came by mobilizing support among new segments of the electorate. Cohesion was maintained by ruthlessly purging those leaders of both the new and the old elements of the support coalition who were unwilling to subordinate their aims to those of the party.

Bridges and Purges

FDR harbored no illusions about his victory in 1932. It was neither a partisan nor a personal triumph but rather a repudiation of the incumbent. He was surely aware that, after a brief taste of Democratic rule, the Republicans and the Republican-leaning independents who voted for him simply because his name was not Herbert Hoover would be ready to return to the GOP fold. Because the Democrats had been the minority party, he could not rely simply on rousing the troops to defeat the Republicans. His task was to lift the Democrats out of the residual status they had occupied since the Civil War—winning the White House only when economic depression or partisan fratricide destroyed the Republican chances of winning.

Roosevelt's strategy for party expansion centered not on the conversion of Republicans but rather on the introduction into the national political arena of those who had been on the sidelines—Catholics, unskilled workers, and the mass of the unemployed—many of whom were too young to have developed deep partisan roots.[5] These missionary forays posed a grave threat to party unity because of the deep resentment they inspired among those who were already in the national Democratic congregation. Anti-Catholic sentiment had threatened to destroy the party in 1924 and had driven a multitude of Democrats to vote Republican in 1928.[6] The American Federation of Labor (AFL), the voice of organized skilled labor, had declared itself adamantly opposed to the mobilization of unskilled workers undertaken by John L. Lewis and his Committee for Industrial Organization (CIO).[7] Traditional Democrats, adhering to the party's long-standing commitments to balanced budgets and states rights, were outraged by the massive federal expenditures that FDR undertook to ensure all able-bodied Americans a job.[8]

FDR's success in enlarging the party without dividing it stemmed in large measure from attributes of the political character he had established well before his election as president. One might argue that he was uniquely well positioned to bridge these chasms. Roosevelt's credentials as an old-fashioned Democrat were unimpeachable. His roots lay in the agrarian, conservative, reform-minded party that predated both the immigrant urban machine and rural populism. His father had been a close friend of Grover Cleveland and had bolted the party in protest against Bryan's monetary heresy. FDR had first made a name for himself in politics by fighting Tammany Hall. Given his expertise in the policy areas of agriculture and conservation, Roosevelt's designation as the party's vice presidential candidate in 1920 was viewed as a victory for western, rural, and agrarian elements of the party.[9]

In 1924 he took what would prove to be a crucial step. At the Democratic Convention in New York City, which would later drag on for more than one hundred ballots, this gentrified upstate New York Episcopalian placed the name of a Catholic from the Lower East Side in nomination for the presidency of the United States.[10] He repeated the gesture in 1928 and thus became the only prominent Protestant politician in America whose philo-Catholicism was indisputable. The year 1928 witnessed a massive increase in the participation rate of Catholic voters, and the Democrats were the beneficiaries.[11] FDR moved swiftly to reinforce this bond by acting to end Prohibition as soon as he took office in 1932. His stature in the Catholic community was so great that in 1936 neither the vituperative opposition of Al Smith himself nor that of numerous other notable Catholic laymen, especially the radio priest Father Coughlin, could make any dent in the Catholic vote for FDR.[12]

FDR minimized defections among the "dry," rural Protestant wing of the party by continuing to give vigorous support to those policies, other than Prohibition, which comprised its reform agenda. His opposition to Tammany continued unabated. By encouraging a second Democrat to enter the 1933 New York mayoral race, he ensured the victory of the anti-Tammany Republican-Fusion candidate, Fiorello La Guardia.[13] He made the plight of the farmer the number one issue on the recovery agenda. The Agricultural Adjustment Act was the greatest accomplishment of his first year in office. He also continued the battle that he had launched as governor of New York against the arch enemy of rural America, the public utilities. His vigorous support for conservation likewise remained unabated. He reduced opposition to his work programs by emphasizing that they were temporary responses to a national emergency. His budget cuts in 1938 demonstrated that this was not mere hypocrisy. He also replaced the dole with work programs, many of which—most notably the Civilian Conservation Corps and rural roads program—were of direct benefit to those most suspicious of federal "boondoggle."

In those instances where conciliation failed, harsher methods were imposed. The purge effort of 1938 was aimed specifically at conservative Democrats who had proclaimed their unshakable opposition to the New Deal. FDR's failure to unseat Millard Tydings of Maryland and Walter George of Georgia in the Democratic senatorial primaries has served to obscure other successes, most important, in New York, where representative John O'Connor, chairman of the Rules Committee and an anti–New Deal Tammany Hall congressman, was beaten by a pro–New Deal challenger whose primary campaign was orchestrated by FDR's political lieutenant, Ed Flynn, of the Bronx.[14]

Perhaps the most important race of the year was in Kentucky, where Alben Barkley, who had just recently become majority leader of the Senate and had done so with FDR's backing, was being challenged in the Democratic primary by the popular incumbent governor A. B. "Happy" Chandler. Chandler was a superlative campaigner and had the support of a well-oiled statewide political organization fueled by gubernatorial patronage. Barkley countered by welding the county Works Progress Administration (WPA) organizations into an active political machine, thus pioneering a new form of federally assisted party organization that proved too strong for Chandler.[15]

Purges were not reserved for conservatives. FDR was equally ruthless toward those of his supporters who would not subordinate their own claims for the good of the party. In this way Huey Long and John L. Lewis, the two most talented politicians in America after Roosevelt, were destroyed politically. Long had been a vociferous supporter of FDR for the 1932 nomination. But as senator he led the attack on the New Deal from the left, claiming that it was a set of ill-designed halfway measures that did not speak to the essential issue of sharing the wealth. Although others, such as Senators Robert La Follette Jr. of Wisconsin and Senator Bronson Cutting of New Mexico, made similar criticisms, only Long possessed the rhetorical and organizational skills necessary to lead a successful challenge to FDR's claim to represent the interests of the "have-nots." FDR responded to this challenge by attacking Long's Louisiana political base. He removed all federal patronage from Long and distributed it among his enemies. He turned a deaf ear to Long's demand that his vital role in securing FDR's nomination be acknowledged and rewarded. Thus Long's political future was destroyed even before the intercession of an assassin's bullet.[16]

The political importance of the hundreds of thousands of unskilled workers who flocked to the CIO banner during the early New Deal was magnified by their concentration in the midwestern states of Ohio, Michigan, and Illinois, which possessed large numbers of electoral votes and were traditional Republican bastions. Their national leader, John L. Lewis, was a registered Republican who had supported Herbert Hoover in 1932. After obtaining FDR's grudging support of section 7a of the National Industrial Recovery Act, which endorsed the right of workers to organize, Lewis became an avid New Deal supporter. He trumpeted the news to every mine shaft and steel mine that FDR personally wanted them to organize. This was hardly FDR's intent, but in view of the extraordinary partisan opportunity that Lewis's organizing campaign offered, he refrained from disavowing the claim. The response to Lewis's invocation of presidential support was overwhelming. In less than two years, hundreds of thousands of new members joined the CIO.[17]

FDR's support for the Wagner Act, which actually provided a mechanism for enforcing the promise contained in 7a, was even more grudging than for the earlier pro-labor bill. In fact, he remained neutral until it became clear that Senator Robert Wagner's masterful legislative leadership was certain to secure its passage regardless of what the president did.[18] Nonetheless, FDR signed the bill. In the 1936 campaign he accepted enormous campaign contributions from the CIO and proclaimed himself the friend of organized labor.[19]

FDR's relations with John L. Lewis and the rest of organized labor represent a dramatic but by no means the only example of his ability simultaneously to expand his party's support coalition and to subordinate the claim of any particular element of that coalition to primacy. In the wake of the 1936 triumph, Lewis embarked on new organizing efforts in the steel industry which proved particularly violent and disruptive. Sensing that the public had grown weary of such confrontations, FDR announced his neutrality in the dispute, declaring a plague on both "houses," union and industry. Lewis's response stands as one of the greatest of all scornful public utterances: "Labor, like Israel, has many sorrows. Its women weep for their fallen, and they lament for the future of the children of the race. It ill behooves one who has supped at labor's table to curse with equal fervor and fine impartiality both Labor and its adversaries when they become locked in deadly embrace."[20]

FDR responded to this attack with an equally eloquent silence. In a fashion similar to his treatment of Long, he failed to consult Lewis concerning key Labor Department appointments, conferring instead with AFL leaders whose contribution to the 1936 campaign effort had been far less substantial. Most infuriating of all, he deprived Lewis of his place as labor's spokesman within the councils of the administration. This coveted role was given to Lewis's second in command, Sidney Hillman, whom the president felt he could count on to be loyal and trustworthy. In May 1940, as the war in Europe was raging, FDR appointed Hillman to be labor's representative to the National Defense Advisory Council. He thus made Hillman the voice of labor in the war effort without even consulting Lewis in advance.[21]

In the wake of these slights, Lewis announced his support of Wendell Willkie in the upcoming election and threatened to resign as head of the CIO if the workers repudiated him. The image of FDR as the "friend of labor," which Lewis himself had done so much to create, could not be readily undone. Despite Lewis's pleadings, industrial workers stood by FDR. Lewis resigned his office and was never again to play a significant role in Democratic Party politics. The lesson of his demise was not lost on the next generation of national labor leaders, most notably Walter Reuther and George Meany, who chose to accept labor's subordinate status within the party.

The 1936 Election

The overarching importance of the 1936 election in achieving this realignment cannot be measured simply by the size or even the composition of the vote for FDR. The real measure of the accomplishment lay in FDR's ability to make use of the campaign to translate his great personal popularity into means for strengthening the party. This effort took several forms, from the strictly procedural to the highly symbolic.

The South had long resisted efforts to alter the party rule which stipulated that a presidential aspirant had to obtain two-thirds of the votes of convention delegates to win the nomination. This two-thirds rule gave the South a virtual veto over the choice of the nominee. The rule was also favored by the other large cohesive bloc within the party—the heads of the urban "machines"—who likewise viewed it as a means for the exercise of veto power. This rule was responsible for the 1924 debacle and provided a continuing threat to the ability of a party majority to work its will.

FDR recognized that the threat posed by the two-thirds rule would grow greater as the party grew increasingly heterodox and would undermine its ability to put forth candidates who appealed to the new and growing sectors of the party's support coalition. He therefore determined to make use of his standing with his party, as well as his ironclad control of the 1936 convention, to abolish the rule and have candidates nominated by a simple majority. The delegates who assembled in Philadelphia for the purpose of engaging in a love feast were hardly in a mood to deny their beloved president this request.[22] Even the southern and urban delegations swallowed it. Southern opposition to New Deal policies in general and those perceived as pro-black in particular increased significantly after 1936.[23] This rule change could not have been accomplished at any subsequent convention without a bitter and divisive battle that might have led to a much larger defection of southern delegates than that which occurred in 1948. Yet one could hardly imagine the nomination of either Harry Truman or John F. Kennedy if the rule had remained in place.

From a partisan standpoint, FDR's rhetorical strategy was of even greater significance. Through public speech, he was able to crystallize the terms of debate between the two parties in a manner that riveted the attachment of those who had been leaning toward the Democrats. The pattern was set in the acceptance speech he gave at the Democratic Convention in Philadelphia.[24] Rather than rehearse his administration's accomplishments and take credit for the recovery, he chose instead to castigate the opponents of the New Deal in terms that were harsh and provocative. His depiction of the opponents of the New Deal as "economic royalists" provided a clear focal point for the anger that ordinary people felt toward those whom they held responsible for the economic devastation they had experienced. They rejoiced as he rallied against the forces of darkness: speculators, bankers, and bosses.

Roosevelt's images were carefully chosen to reinforce his theme, inspired by the host city, that 1936 would end "economic tyranny" as

1776 had ended political tyranny; thus his choice of metaphors: "privileged princes of the economic dynasty," "this new industrial dictatorship," "new kingdoms . . . built upon concentration of control of material things." This was not a class-based message but a promise to overthrow a monarchy in the name of the commoners. In a nation where virtually everyone fancies himself or herself a commoner, the breadth of the appeal was enormous. More to the point, FDR was providing a means for partisan identification based on a powerful and enduring political passion—the hatred of privilege. Affluent though they have become, few current descendants of those who applauded these words in 1936 consider themselves to be members of the elite. Roosevelt's words continued to grip them for at least another thirty years.

Like his decision to oppose the two-thirds rule, FDR's rhetorical bellicosity in 1936 represented a masterpiece of timing. This manner of speaking did not characterize his campaign rhetoric in either previous or subsequent campaigns. Adopting it was a strategic decision geared to the maximum advantage of temporary political conditions. As Samuel Beer has argued, the electorate of 1936 was uniquely susceptible to such an appeal. The moral and intellectual bankruptcy demonstrated by the business community in the years since 1929 had created public revulsion toward the captains of industry and finance which was as strong as it was transitory. Beer depicts how FDR worked on his acceptance speech while listening to the proceedings of the 1936 Democratic Convention on the radio. Hearing the crowd's reaction to other speakers, he sensed a growing mood of belligerence. Almost at the last minute he cast aside a milder version of his text and quickly dictated the "economic royalist" version.[25]

These same themes were repeated periodically throughout the campaign, most notably in the culminating speech of the campaign delivered to a tumultuous crowd in New York's Madison Square Garden on October 31. In that speech FDR declared that government by the "organized money" that the New Deal had unseated was as dangerous as government by an "organized mob."[26]

At no time other than 1936 could FDR have counted on both business and labor to react to his rhetoric in ways that would reinforce rather than undermine its political impact. By 1940 the business community had acquired a certain sophistication in coping with Roosevelt and the New Deal, as reflected in its support of Wendell Willkie for the Republican nomination. But the business community of 1936 was still reeling from the depredations inflicted on it by a politician whom it perceived as not only hostile to its interests but traitorous to his class as well. Its blistering attacks against "that man" cemented the notion in the popular mind that FDR was the people's champion. Why else would those who were to blame for the misery that had befallen them heap such calumny on him? Indeed, FDR's own depiction of Andrew Jackson serves as a succinct description of his own good fortune in this regard: "The beneficiaries of the abuses to which he put an end pursued him with all the violence that political passion can generate. But the people of his day were not deceived. They loved him for the enemies he had made."[27]

The success of FDR's strategy depended on Lewis's support. By 1937 John L. Lewis was prepared to challenge FDR's claim to being the worker's friend, but not so in 1936, when he was placing all the CIO's political resources at the service of the reelection campaign.[28] Thus he deprived himself of the opportunity to use his unrivaled capacity for sarcasm to remind workers of how uncertain an ally FDR actually was. Had Lewis wished to do so, he could have pointed out to them how difficult it was to reconcile the FDR who sat on the sidelines during the Wagner Act debate and who acquiesced in the antilabor tilt adopted by the National Recovery Administration with the FDR who claimed to be leading a frontal assault on economic tyranny. The votes of unionized workers, even if halfheartedly cast, would still have won FDR the 1936 election, but the stage might have been set for significant worker defections during the ensuing four years. If the 1936 victory had not so deeply riveted the loyalties of union workers, one could imagine how skillfully the CIO chief might have exploited FDR's subsequent "evenhandedness" toward labor disputes, as well as the devastating 1938 recession and worker fears of intervention in the war in Europe, to crack the New Deal coalition and lead the Democrats to the left.

To take the full measure of FDR's accomplishment, consider that since his death, six presidents have run for reelection. Two lost. None of the four victors was able to translate victory into any significant congressional inroads. All four faced Congresses controlled by the opposition party during their entire second terms. During this period, the most impressive combination of presidential and congressional landslide, comparable in magnitude with 1936, occurred in 1964 when Lyndon Johnson wrapped himself in the shroud of John Kennedy. But 1964 did not renew Democratic power for the long term; instead, it was the beginning of the end. The midterm election of 1966 reduced Democratic congressional majorities to below their 1964 levels, and two years later the Republicans regained the presidency, launching a twenty-four-year period of Republican presidential dominance.

The most intriguing comparison to 1936 is 1984. Arguably, the opportunity for realignment was much greater in that year than in any of the other reelection years. By then President Ronald Reagan had regained the popularity he had lost during the recession of 1982, and the boom of 1984 lent great credibility to the admonition he issued during the depth of the recession to "stay the course." Although Walter Mondale was no Alf Landon, he was a perfect foil for Reagan. Mondale's long history of loyal party service and his close ties to the Democratic Party establishment made him ripe for caricature as the creature of an ossified Democratic Party, composed of "special interests"—organized labor, the teachers unions, and the major civil rights organizations. Despite his relative youth, he, not Reagan, was perceived to be the representative of the old ways, while Reagan, whose jauntiness and charm belied his age, appeared to be the candidate of youth and change.

But unlike FDR, Reagan was not prone to exploit his victory. He did not try to make the election meaningful in partisan terms. His 1984 campaign was a marvel of antipartisanship. The theme was "morning in America." Congressional Republicans, eagerly grasping after Reagan's coattails, were hard put to claim that they were more "pro-morning" than their Democratic adversaries who were obstinate in their refusal to register a preference for the afternoon. FDR's theme song, "Happy Days Are Here Again," was played at the Republic Convention, and on the stump, Reagan made countless references to FDR, Truman, and even JFK. He talked of America's "rendezvous with destiny" and described how "surprisingly difficult" it had been for him to leave the Democratic Party. Only in the waning days of the campaign, when it was too late to matter, did he appeal to voters to support the rest of the Republican ticket.[29] Reagan did indeed win in a landslide, losing only Minnesota and the District of Columbia and garnering 59 percent of the popular vote.[30] But the GOP made no perceptible dent in the huge Democratic House majority and actually lost seats in the Senate.[31]

History provides no natural experiments. One will never know for sure whether President Reagan could have achieved a Republican realignment in 1984 had he chosen to try, although the circumstances appeared propitious. His reluctance to do so, despite his enormous personal popularity, helps to place Roosevelt's accomplishment in better perspective. FDR could have taken Reagan's path, choosing to secure his own victory at the cost of the party's fortune. Depression-weary Americans might have welcomed a frothy nonpartisan campaign full of praise for Abraham Lincoln, not to mention cousin Theodore Roosevelt. Great politics is risky politics. FDR put himself at risk and garnered great political reward. The extraordinary birth and development of the New Deal party coalition is a worthy reminder of the role that leadership plays in partisan change.

Notes

1. Sidney M. Milkis, *The President and the Parties: Transformation of the American Party System since the New Deal* (New York: Oxford University Press, 1993), esp. 28, 44–51.

2. FDR was not the first great politician to conceive of his partisan ambitions this way. Jefferson had much the same view. He was opposed to the political party in principle and justified his role as leader of the Democratic Republicans on the grounds that such a party was necessary to defeat the party in power. Then it would be possible to restore constitutional governance, obviating the need for further partisan strife. See Marc Landy and Sidney M. Milkis, *Presidential Greatness* (Lawrence: University Press of Kansas, 2000).

3. Milkis, *President and the Parties,* 11.

4. Ibid., esp. 102–4.

5. Kristi Andersen, *The Creation of a Democratic Majority, 1928–1936* (Chicago: University of Chicago Press, 1979). Evidence for this proposition appears throughout the book. See esp. 122.

6. David Burner, *The Politics of Provincialism: The Democratic Party in Transition, 1918–1932* (Cambridge: Harvard University Press, 1986), 103–41, 179–216.

7. Philip Taft, *The A.F.L. from the Death of Gompers to the Merger* (New York: Harper and Brothers, 1959), 172–80.

8. James T. Patterson, *Congressional Conservatism and the New Deal: The Growth of the Conservative Coalition in Congress, 1933–1939* (Lexington: University Press of Kentucky, 1967), 13–31.

9. Burner, *Politics of Provincialism,* 63.

10. Matthew Josephson and Hannah Josephson, *Al Smith: Hero of the Cities* (Boston: Houghton Mifflin, 1969), 311–13.

11. Burner, *Politics of Provincialism,* 230.

12. Samuel Lubell, *The Future of American Politics* (New York: Harper and Brothers, 1951), 50.

13. Lyle W. Dorsett, *Franklin D. Roosevelt and the City Bosses* (Port Washington, N.Y.: Kennikat Press, 1977), 51–52.

14. Ibid., 65–66.

15. Glenn Finch, "The Election of U.S. Senators in Kentucky (the Barkley Period)," *Filson Club Historical Quarterly* 45 (1971): 286–96.

16. T. Harry Williams, *Huey Long: A Biography* (New York: Knopf, 1970), 636–38, 795, 812–13.

17. For a broader discussion of this relationship, see Marc Landy, "FDR and John L. Lewis," in *Modern Presidents and the Presidency*, ed. Marc Landy (Lexington, Mass.: Lexington Books/DC Heath, 1985), 105–12.

18. J. Joseph Huthmacher, *Senator Robert F. Wagner and the Rise of Urban Liberalism* (New York: Atheneum, 1968), 189–90.

19. Melvyn Dubofsky and Warren Van Tine, *John L. Lewis: A Biography* (New York: Quadrangle/New York Times Book Company, 1977), 252.

20. Ibid., 323.

21. On Sidney Hillman and his relationship with FDR and John L. Lewis, see Matthew Josephson, *Sidney Hillman: Statesman of American Labor* (Garden City, N.Y.: Doubleday, 1952), 381–502.

22. See the account of the rules change in Milkis, *President and the Parties,* 69–72.

23. Patterson, *Congressional Conservatism.*

24. *The Public Papers and Addresses of Franklin D. Roosevelt,* ed. Samuel I. Rosenman, 13 vols. (New York: Random House, 1938–50), 5:230–36.

25. Samuel Beer, "Two Models of Public Opinion: Bacon's New Logic and Diotima's Tale of Love," *Political Theory* (May 1974): 174–78.

26. Roosevelt, *Public Papers and Addresses,* 5:568.

27. Ibid., 5:197.

28. Dubofsky and Van Tine, *John L. Lewis,* 323–30.

29. Gerald Pomper et al., The Election of 1984: Reports and Interpretations (Chatham, N.J.: Chatham House, 1985), 28–30, 72, 78, 159.

30. Ibid., 60.

31. Ibid., 113.

The "Boss"

Franklin Roosevelt, the Democratic Party, and the Reconstitution of American Politics

Jerome M. Mileur

Americans have never greatly admired politics or politicians, yet as a nation we were founded on politics, not merely as a method of governance but also as that public activity which best protects the liberty our Constitution was designed to secure. Indeed, the Constitution was the work of politicians, and their blueprint for a government incorporating separated powers, federalism, and individual rights built the activity of politics into their new construction as the only way to make it habitable for a free people.[1] Our greatest public figures have been our most accomplished politicians, masters in the arts of politics, high and low. What marks their greatness is not that they were above politics, or outside it, but that they used it, in all of its vulgarity, to good and even great purposes. Franklin Roosevelt may not have been as cynical as Willie Stark, the Huey Long figure in Robert Penn Warren's *All the King's Men*, who believed that good had to be made out of "badness" because "there isn't anything else to make it out of."[2] But FDR knew he had to work with and within the politics of his times, and he well understood that James Madison's admonition "Men are not angels" meant that he had to use this politics to convert the raw material of private interests into public good.[3] Thus, as Abraham Lincoln distributed the patronage essential to nineteenth-century politics while he prosecuted a war to save the Union and end slavery, Franklin Roosevelt did likewise to accommodate big-city bosses and southern Bourbons, who were central to his efforts both to restore prosperity to a nation beset by depression and to secure liberty in a world threatened by tyranny.

The great politician is not merely a master of tactics, a manipulator of people and opinion, though he or she is that—and FDR excelled in these ways—but is more importantly a master of strategy who sees larger possibilities and brings his or her skills to bear on the realization of these greater purposes. Like his greatest predecessors, Thomas Jefferson and Lincoln, Franklin Roosevelt was centrally concerned with the place and role of the national government in the American constitutional system, but where Jefferson sought to limit it and Lincoln to call it to a higher purpose, Roosevelt sought to revolutionize it, bringing it into the lives and homes of millions of Americans for whom the national government had been at most a remote enterprise. Each of them succeeded, reconstructing party politics through a new public philosophy and program of government backed by a new arrangement of forces in the electorate; in doing so, each reconstituted American politics itself.

The New Deal was a great political achievement wrought by a great politician. Calling him a "prime specimen of Aristotle's political animal," Albert Romasco argues that Roosevelt "can best be understood as a complete, thoroughgoing political being, a man who saw his world through cultural lenses that were politically tinted and who, consequently, understood and dealt with both people and issues from a consistent, political frame of reference."[4] If not ideological, Roosevelt's program was purposeful: it aimed initially at economic recovery and then at stability, the first requiring an expansion of the federal role in the economy and the latter an enhanced managerial capacity for the nation's chief executive. That his achievement entailed compromises—half a loaf where the true believers wanted the whole loaf—attests not to a weakness of leadership but instead, especially in the context of his consistent and revolutionary purpose, to the importance of *political* leadership in a constitutional system designed for precisely such leadership. And it produced, George McJimsey argues, "a transforming moment in the history of American politics and government."[5]

The Education of a Politician

Jesse Jones described Franklin Roosevelt as "a total politician."[6] Indeed, few, if any, presidents since the founding generation entered the White

House with the wealth and variety of governmental and political experience that Franklin Roosevelt brought with him. He had served one term in the New York state senate, to which he won reelection in 1912 but chose instead to move to Washington to join the administration of Woodrow Wilson as assistant secretary of the navy. He retained that post through Wilson's two terms. In 1920, he had been on the Democratic national ticket as the vice presidential running mate of James M. Cox. He had been a member of the Democratic state central committee in New York, who as a delegate to national conventions made nominating speeches for New York governor Al Smith in both 1924 and 1928. He had served consecutive two-year terms as governor of New York before becoming president in 1933. And his immediate classroom for it all was the largest and one of the most complex two-party states in the nation, one fraught with intraparty factionalism, as well as intense interparty competition.[7]

In 1910, anticipating the retirement of the Republican incumbent, the Democratic Party organization of Dutchess County, New York, which includes the Roosevelt home in Hyde Park, recruited FDR to run for the state senate, as much for his name as anything. When the incumbent chose not to retire, Roosevelt decided to challenge nonetheless and went on to win in a district that had not elected a Democrat since before the Civil War. The party organization easily managed his nomination, but he ran as a "good government" candidate, opposed to "bossism" and appealing to "independent thinking voters."[8] Roosevelt mounted an energetic campaign, covering the district in the only automobile available; working long hours; meeting large numbers of voters individually; perfecting techniques of public speaking, including the phrase "my friends"; and relying heavily on other Democrats who knew voters across the district.

Upon entering the senate, he joined an insurgent group of Democrats opposed to Tammany's nominee for the U.S. Senate and became leader of an extended fight with the New York City Democratic machine. Eventually, he supported a second Tammany nominee, but in the course of the struggle FDR had gained national attention and strengthened himself in his district and among Progressives in general. Roosevelt continued to champion clean government but also supported his party through patronage appointments to minor offices, cleared with his district party officials, which he saw as "vitally important" if there was to be any party organization. He also supported party spoilsmen in legislation designed to place Democrats in public positions held by Republicans. Roosevelt saw these measures as "justified by the partisan acts of the Republicans while in power."[9] His struggles with Tammany also led often to vacillation on questions, as he puzzled over how to balance the many interests affected by his actions.

Roosevelt's progressivism was largely political at first, concerned with the direct election of U.S. senators, municipal home rule, and the direct primary, while his policy interests centered primarily on agriculture. But he embraced a broader program of social and economic reform as he moved through his term. He backed a shorter workweek, workman's compensation, factory legislation, and other labor-related reforms. In addition, the many reports and studies that he read made him much more aware of social problems, leading him to support the expansion of welfare and of public education and the establishment of old-age pensions. He also came to respect many from Tammany, especially fellow legislators Bob Wagner and Al Smith, with whom his public career would intersect often over the next thirty years and whom he saw as having a concern for social justice much like his own.[10] From newspaper reporters lobbyists, and others, he learned the political trade in dealing with everything from issues and publicity to handling constituents and party leaders. He was, James MacGregor Burns writes, "learning the craft of parliamentary politics with remarkable speed," adding, "Above all, he learned the lesson that democratic politicians must learn: that the political battle is not a simple, two-sided contest between opposing parties or between right and wrong, or between regulars and irregulars, but . . . a many-sided struggle that moved over broad sectors and touched many interests."[11]

Some of the lessons were blunt, as in 1914 when Roosevelt ran for the U.S. Senate as an anti-Tammany candidate and was defeated by the Democratic Party machine. But they were also quickly learned, as FDR almost immediately sought rapprochement with the New York organization, being a featured speaker at its July 4 celebration in 1917. Tammany also viewed him as a prospective "unity" candidate for governor in 1918, but he chose instead to remain in Washington.[12] From his legislative experience, Roosevelt had come to appreciate the value of strong parties when they were organized around a socially conscious progressive program of government, but he remained opposed to those organized primarily for the control and distribution of the "spoils" of office.

He came also to appreciate that not all bosses were corrupt and to respect Charles Murphy, who headed Tammany from the first decade of the twentieth century until his death in 1924. He most likely did not share Wagner's view that Murphy's Tammany was "the cradle of American liberalism," but Roosevelt did call Murphy the "strongest and wisest leader" of Tammany in generations, "a genius who kept harmony" and who "helped accomplish much in the way of progressive legislation and social welfare in our State."[13]

As 1912 approached, Roosevelt met with Woodrow Wilson, his choice for the Democratic presidential nomination that year, and became an early leader of the Wilson campaign in New York. Once again, FDR ran afoul of Tammany, which preferred Champ Clark, Speaker of the House of Representatives. He lost his bid to be a delegate to the national party convention in Baltimore but went anyway and with others set up a campaign operation that lobbied delegates to back Wilson. When Wilson won the nomination, Roosevelt again challenged Tammany, organizing the Empire State Democracy, an organization that paralleled the regular state party organization, but soon abandoned it to focus on his own reelection.[14] With Wilson's election, FDR happily accepted appointment as assistant secretary of the navy, the number two position under Secretary Josephus Daniels. A "shrewd and adroit politician," Daniels, a Bryanite, had played an important role in securing the nomination for Wilson and, like Louis Howe, was to serve as a political check on the "brash, overly self-confident, and overly ambitious" Roosevelt, in whom Daniels saw great potential.[15]

The assistant secretary was responsible for the day-to-day administration of naval affairs across the nation and abroad, from installations and the fleet through contracts for shipbuilding to relations with military and civilian personnel.[16] The position not only introduced Roosevelt to the internal culture, administrative practices, and many constituencies of a large bureaucratic organization but also schooled him in how to deal with powerful national interests, such as organized labor, and with political leaders, congressional as well as executive, foreign as well as domestic. While it was the secretary's responsibility to maintain good working relations with the president and members of Congress, FDR dealt with both executive and legislative figures on a host of matters and, as Burns observes, showed a "quick mastery of the political dimensions of his job" and a "capacity for political administration."[17]

Roosevelt, who loved ships and the sea, was an admirer of Admiral Alfred Thayer Mahan, the great advocate of naval power, and FDR seized opportunities to champion Mahan's theories. He seized as well on opportunities for publicity and travel to inspect U.S. naval installations and to meet with local officials and the press to discuss issues of the day as they pertained to the navy and larger matters. With the coming of World War I, Roosevelt witnessed the effects of national emergency on federal administrative capacities. He also traveled abroad to deal with routine administrative and diplomatic matters, meeting too with leading English and French officials and politicians, Winston Churchill among them. His tenure was not without controversy, especially after 1918 when the Republicans regained control of Congress and launched investigations into the administration's wartime activities which produced some seemingly serious charges against Roosevelt that came to nothing in the end.

His years in Washington expanded Roosevelt's perspectives on politics and the administration of national government. He came to know Louis Brandeis, Felix Frankfurter, and others who were to play important roles in his subsequent political life. It was a time of reform in Washington, as Wilson pressed his New Freedom program, and FDR was there to observe both the president's party leadership with the Congress and the administrative, political, and other constraints on a chief executive seeking to exercise first national and then international leadership. He recognized especially the president's limited capacity for managerial control over administration, particularly the budget, and he began to practice an "unorthodox administrative style," managing information as assistant secretary with care and secrecy, playing officials off against one another, shifting positions from one meeting to the next, sowing confusion but "conserving power."[18] In sum, he received, as Alonzo Hamby notes, "a firsthand training in the use of governmental power to create a feeling of national purpose," and he came to appreciate both the human and the political dimensions of administration.[19] In 1920, as the Wilson years were coming to an end, FDR flirted with the idea of running for the U.S. Senate, but before any decision was made he went to San Francisco as a delegate to that summer's Democratic national convention, where he "enjoyed a good deal of influence" as a member of the Wilson administration.[20] It was a tumultuous affair, but on the forty-fourth ballot James M. Cox of Ohio won the nomination for president. A reform governor but not identified strongly with Wilson, Cox tapped Roosevelt, whom he had never met, to be his vice presidential running mate, chosen for his name, his association with the Wilson administration, and as coming from the nation's then largest state.[21] Tammany boss Murphy was cool to the idea but agreed that New York would nominate his less-than-favorite son.[22] Cox and Roosevelt decided to make the League of Nations the central issue of their campaign, much as President Wilson desired, but there proved to be little public enthusiasm for the issue. FDR campaigned extensively across the Pacific and Rocky Mountain West, as well as through New England and New York, widening his contacts with Democratic party leaders.

The Republicans behind Warren Harding swept to victory with 60 percent of the popular vote, and for the first time in a decade, Franklin Roosevelt was out of public office. In the loss, however, as Hamby observes, FDR had become one of the future hopes of the party. "He alone," Hamby writes, "emerged from the debacle in a position of strength, possessing greater public recognition than any and having obtained a first-hand knowledge of the structure of the Democratic party."[23] Roosevelt had established himself as a progressive in New York politics and as a nationalist and internationalist in Washington. He was a solid, though at times independent, party man who had entered into a peaceful coexistence with Tammany. Following his campaign, Roosevelt undertook an initiative in national party building, urging the Democratic National Committee to strengthen its organizational capacities by maintaining a full-time headquarters, developing more effective fundraising methods, and convening regular conferences involving the rank and file in developing a common party program.[24] His suggestions were ignored, but FDR was clearly emerging as a national figure within the party—then came polio.[25]

The polio, which struck in the summer of 1921, was an extremely painful as well as paralyzing illness. Once diagnosed, doctors were initially optimistic that Roosevelt would recover, but despite enormous efforts on his part, he never regained the full use of his legs and was thereafter able to walk only with the use of heavy braces and the assistance of others. "The evidence is," Burns writes, "that Roosevelt's illness did not alter but strengthened already existent or latent tendencies in his personality."[26] Moreover, it did not diminish his interest in politics but, if anything, Burns concludes, "made him want to be more active, more involved." In some ways, his disability was politically advantageous, for it enabled Roosevelt to avoid candidacy for public office in a decade that was dismal for Democrats.[27] Louis Howe and Eleanor Roosevelt shouldered much of the burden of maintaining his political viability, but FDR too threw himself into an extensive correspondence with friends and party leaders around the country.

After 1920, Mrs. Roosevelt became more and more active in professional and political women's organizations. In the first years of the decade, she became associated with Marian Dickerman of the Todhunter School for Girls in New York City. In 1924 Governor Al Smith recruited her to work with the state party's women's division, headed by Nancy Cook. She, Cook, and Dickerman made political organizing tours around New York, setting up units of the women's division to educate and mobilize the newly enfranchised vote for the Democratic Party. With FDR incapacitated, Mrs. Roosevelt came more and more, Frank Freidel writes, "to speak for her husband and to act as his eyes and ears at political meetings" and rapidly became "one of the most effective women Democratic leaders during the 1920s."[28]

Franklin Roosevelt made his public reentry into politics in 1924 as a delegate to the Democratic national convention, where, with help, he walked to the podium, smiled broadly, gestured vigorously, and gave an eloquent nominating speech for Al Smith, dubbing the New York governor the "happy warrior." The convention was a disaster for the Democrats, who wrangled through two weeks and 103 ballots before nominating John W. Davis. It was, however, a triumph for Roosevelt, whose personal magnetism and energy impressed delegates, diverting attention from his physical disability. FDR played almost no role in the fall campaign, in which the Democratic candidate won less than 30 percent of the popular vote in a three-way race with the Republican Calvin Coolidge and the Progressive Robert La Follette. Following Davis's defeat and at Howe's urging, Roosevelt bypassed the Democratic National Committee and wrote to several thousand state and local party officials, including all the convention delegates, urging reforms of the national party like those he had proposed four years earlier and asking for suggestions to strengthen the party at all levels. His letter drew several hundred positive responses and gave FDR insights into the condition of the Democratic Party at the state and local levels across the country. But his initiative was seen as a threat by national party leaders, especially those in Congress, and nothing more came of it. "His almost single-handed effort to rejuvenate the party," Burns writes, "gave him a harsh lesson in the internal power arrangements of the Democratic party."[29] Still, the initiative once more brought him to the attention of Democrats at the grass roots, added to his growing card file of friends and potential allies across the country, and maintained his standing as a national party leader.

In 1926 Roosevelt declined nomination for the U.S. Senate but continued to conduct an extensive political correspondence. Two years later, Al Smith was again a candidate for the presidency, taking an early lead and winning a first-ballot nomination. Franklin Roosevelt once more placed his name before the Houston convention, speaking over national radio networks for the first time. Sensing the potential of this new technology, Roosevelt "aimed his nominating speech less at the delegates than at the enormous audience throughout the country."[30] To strengthen the ticket in New York, Smith, with an assist from Mrs. Roosevelt, persuaded a reluctant Roosevelt, who felt it would be a Republican year, into running for governor. With the ever present and loyal Louis Howe joined now by Democratic state chairman James Farley, Tammany boss from the Bronx Ed Flynn, and Samuel Rosenman, and with his wife galvanizing the women's vote, FDR threw himself into the race, traveling the state by rail and auto and delivering thirty-three major speeches, as well as numerous minor ones, in a frantic three-week campaign. Defying a national GOP tide that swept Smith under by a margin of almost 3 to 2 in the popular vote, FDR pulled out victory, winning by 25,000 votes of the more than 4 million cast. The win was secured by Tammany's Ed Flynn, whose election night phone calls upstate threatened investigations in Republican areas where polls were slow to report.

Roosevelt took charge of the governorship.[31] He replaced prominent Smith allies, which led to a growing estrangement between the two, whose friendship had been political but whose social differences were considerable. In his first two years FDR established himself as a progressive governor, more interested in agricultural and public power questions than his predecessor had been. Through Farley as traveling salesman and organizer, Roosevelt sought to pump life back into the largely moribund upstate Democratic party organization. He had come to appreciate the importance of party; leadership and ideology were of no great value without an organization to produce a vote. Rosenman, Roosevelt's aide, put it succinctly: "You have to get the votes first—then you can do the good work."[32] Moreover, Roosevelt believed that his program and the party organization must be integrated and that both had to be strong to win elections; as Freidel notes, he "kept firm control over both his administration and the party organization."[33] Roosevelt also continued to speak directly to the voters over radio, in part because most newspapers were Republican and could not be relied on to print news releases from the administration.

As governor of the nation's largest state, Roosevelt drew national attention, but in a time of Republican prosperity, prospects for the presidency seemed remote. This changed with the stock market crash in October 1929. At first, FDR shared the general view that prosperity would soon return and was cautious in dealing with the depression, but by 1931, as unemployment continued to grow, he abandoned this conservatism and became one of the strongest proponents of government action to restore prosperity. He had won a landslide reelection in 1930 to a second term as governor, and he no doubt felt this gave him a stronger hand politically. His analysis of the causes of depression began to echo former Progressive attacks on concentrations of corporate wealth and power. He appealed to the "forgotten man," promoting broad-ranging program of emergency relief, unemployment insurance, and old-age benefits, though he continued to have misgivings about public works programs, fearing that they would produce dangerous deficits. "No other governor in the nation," Kenneth Davis writes, "had moved so directly and forcefully into relief activity," which drew national attention to his differences with Hoover.[34] Ultimately, Roosevelt came to the belief that nothing less than unprecedented federal intervention could reverse the direction of the economy.

Roosevelt's campaign for the presidential nomination in 1932 began almost immediately after his triumphant reelection as governor. He was widely thought to be the Democrat most likely to get the party's nomination, and Farley set out on a cross-country trip, meeting with Democratic leaders from the Midwest to the Far West, laying the groundwork for FDR's candidacy and trying to nail down a first-ballot win. Old Progressives, especially Burton K. Wheeler and George Norris in the Congress, were among the first to endorse Roosevelt's candidacy, but the campaign organization itself drew most heavily on New Yorkers and former Wilsonites.[35] As the depression deepened and the economy sank lower, the party's presidential prospects rose, prompting other candidates to consider the race. The most threatening of these was Al Smith, whose candidacy four years earlier had broken the hold of the South on the selection of the party's nominee. As a northern, big-city, working-class, machine "pol," the son of Irish Catholic immigrants, Smith had mobilized a vast new "ethnic" vote in support of his candidacy. In city after city across the North, the Democratic vote grew in 1928, often dramatically, as in Boston, where it almost tripled.[36] It was the first time that the nation's twelve largest cities had cast a majority of their presidential ballots for a Democrat.[37] Though beaten decisively, Smith had laid the electoral foundation for a new Democratic Party.

Roosevelt knew that opposition to his nomination could come from the big-city machines across the Northeast and the Midwest. His on-again, off-again relationship with Tammany, as well as the distance that had grown between him and Al Smith, made FDR suspect in the eyes of the urban bosses, all of whom were of recent immigrant stock and knew that Roosevelt was not one of their "own kind." The political problem, moreover, was not just that Democratic Party machines dominated the big cities in New York, Illinois, New Jersey, Massachusetts, and other states north of the Mason-Dixon line but also that the rural areas in those states were dominated by well-oiled Republican Party machines. Thus, electorally, Roosevelt had no way around the Democratic Party machines; he could not appeal to any significant independent constituency in these states. At the same time, FDR knew that the bosses, political pragmatists to the core, would support a likely winner.[38]

Strategically, this led Roosevelt in two directions: (1) to look to the West and the South as the initial bases of support for his nomination, and (2) to seek a quick victory by using the primaries and endorsements to demonstrate his widespread appeal.[39] This strategy would marginalize the bosses and leave them in the position of having to find someone on whom they could agree to stop FDR. As a first step, James Farley traveled west to line up support for Roosevelt, whose strategy was to align the Midwest, West, and South against the Northeast.[40] As 1932 dawned, FDR moved easily through a succession of early primary victories. But his successes came to an abrupt end in Massachusetts, where Smith overwhelmed him by a margin of 3 to 1. Roosevelt recovered in Pennsylvania, winning with 56 percent of the vote to Smith's 43, but fell again in California, this time to House Speaker John Nance Garner, losing by almost ten percentage points and finishing only narrowly ahead of Smith, who was third. A week later, he was again beaten by Smith, this time in New Jersey by a margin of nearly 2 to 1. With Illinois and Ohio now supporting favorite sons and the New York delegation split with Tammany backing Smith, the Roosevelt campaign arrived in Chicago with a majority of convention delegates in its camp, but not the two-thirds required for nomination. It appeared that FDR's place in history might be as the second Democrat in the century to have a majority of the delegates but be denied the nomination, the other being Champ Clark in 1912, whom Roosevelt had helped to defeat in favor of Wilson.

Farley, Roosevelt's convention manager, flirted briefly with but abandoned the idea of trying to change the party's two-thirds rule to a simple majority. Roosevelt led through the first three convention ballots, but his total vote did not increase significantly and some of his supporters, especially in the South, began thinking about another candidate. At this point, with Roosevelt's blessing, Farley cut the deal that offered the vice presidency to Garner, which brought both California and Texas into the ranks of Roosevelt delegates and won nomination for the ticket. FDR thus owned much to the South, the party's power center before Smith's 1928 nomination, and to the West, but less to the Northeast and the Midwest, which were, ironically, to be the core of the electoral coalition that was to be among his greatest legacies to the Democratic Party. Roosevelt asserted his new leadership dramatically, breaking with the past by accepting the nomination in person and doing so, Kenneth Davis writes, "in the most dramatic possible fashion, descending upon Chicago, godlike, out of the heavens."[41]

Entering the presidential contest as the favorite, Roosevelt for the most part ran a cautious race, conscious that only he could beat himself. After calling for a "new deal" in his acceptance speech at the Democratic national convention, his campaign adhered to conventional economic appeals for a balanced budget and to such issues as agriculture with which he was most comfortable from his years in public office. FDR did promise a more active assault on the causes and, especially, the consequences of depression, and his Commonwealth Club Address, delivered in late September, presented his plans in broadly philosophic terms. He argued that the new challenge was "administering" the resources of the nation and called on the heads of industry and finance to "work together to achieve a common end," to sacrifice private advantage to the common good, adding that "the task of government in its relation to business is to assist the development of an economic declaration of rights, an economic constitutional order. This is the common task of statesman and businessman. It is the minimum requirement of a more permanent safe order of things." The "high contract" into which the American people had entered, Roosevelt reminded his listeners, was for liberty and the pursuit of happiness, and government—he called it "political government"—had the responsibility to maintain the balance between interests necessary to protect this. This might entail restrictions on property as "needful," "not to hamper individualism but to protect it," for these were the "new terms of the old social contract." Roosevelt went on to victory in November in an election that was more a rejection of Herbert Hoover and the Republican Party than it was a vote for Roosevelt, a rejection perhaps of the old terms of the social contract but no clear embrace of FDR's new terms.[42]

Thus, Roosevelt entered the White House with a rich two-decade education in one of the most demanding political academies in America. He was by then, as Richard Hofstadter observes, "a seasoned professional politician who had learned his trade straddling the terrible antagonisms of the 1920's, was thoroughly at home in the realities of machine politics and a master of the machine techniques of accommodation."[43] He had experienced politics in different branches and on different levels of government, from inside and outside public office, in calm and in crisis, on state, national, and even international planes. He had an extensive national network of friends and supporters; had mastered the "outside" game, the techniques of mass appeal, as well as the "inside" one of bluff and bargain; and knew the strengths and limitations of party and program, of political organization and candidate, in both winning office and governing. He knew interest-group politics, administrative politics, and the news media. Roosevelt had, in short, mastered the politics of his time and, as president, would use it in all its myriad forms, virtuous and vulgar, to fight in turn economic depression and political authoritarianism—and to win. He had formulated the elements of a program to deal with the depression and had also assembled key players on the "team" that would move to Washington with him: political aides Howe, Farley, Flynn, and Rosenman; policy advisers Frances Perkins, Henry Hopkins, and Henry Morganthau; "brain trusters" Raymond Moley and Rexford Tugwell; personal secretaries Marguerite "Missy" LeHand and Grace Tully; and his wife, Eleanor.

The "Boss" Goes to Washington

Franklin Roosevelt thus entered the White House with, arguably, the best political preparation of any president since the founding generation of Americans. His schooling in the socially and economically diverse politics of New York State and City had taught him both the changing demographics of the nation's population and the importance and potential of his political party as an instrument of effective governance. He understood the possibilities of a politics of compromise in a system of durable and pragmatic interests. He knew the job of a chief executive in American government, the limits of power in the office as well as the potential, the necessity for bargaining but also the need to frame issues to shape negotiations. He knew especially the critical importance of a principled but not dogmatic leadership that both defined the purpose of his administration and made the realization of that purpose possible. He was an aggressive consumer of political ideas and views but surrounded himself with men and women whose views had been tested in the combat for public office. For him, elections and public opinion were the measures of the possible, and while the possible could be stretched by the desirable, he knew it could not be broken. He understood what Al Smith meant in describing politics as the art of the second best and what James Farley meant in saying that in politics the shortest distance between two points is a curved line. His national service in the Wilson administration, his run for the vice presidency, his two terms as governor, and his association with state and national Democratic Party committees had reinforced his belief in the centrality of party to governance and had also underscored the personal qualities of political leadership, the latter magnified by the model of his cousin Theodore Roosevelt's tenure in the Oval Office. All these lessons came together, for better and otherwise, in FDR's presidency.

Roosevelt's political training was put to the test soon after his election to the presidency in 1932. He began assembling the team he needed, many of whom simply moved from Albany to Washington with him, while others were drawn from party ranks and from the private sector. Roosevelt organized "teams" through which to govern; he ruled these with authority, integrity, wisdom, and political guile. Roosevelt's political skills were tested publicly in the interregnum, when President Herbert Hoover asked repeatedly that the president-elect join him in various statements and declarations about policy. Roosevelt demurred that Hoover was still the nation's chief executive and should act on his own, thus leaving himself unencumbered and free to act on his own when the time came. And act he did.

In office, Roosevelt governed initially as a party leader in the tradition of the early Wilson. Working principally through James Farley, a member of his cabinet as postmaster general as well as chairman of the Democratic National Committee, FDR courted party leaders across the country from urban bosses to southern agrarians and western progressives, involving them in the administration of federal programs and rewarding them with the traditional patronage. "His strategy for enlisting them," McJimsey writes, "was to create programs that brought tangible benefits to their constituents" in the belief that "policies that improved people's lives would translate into voter loyalty" and into loyalty to Roosevelt's New Deal program as well.[44] He also worked closely with his party's leaders in Congress. Politically, FDR had promised bold action, and from his first day in the White House, he undertook one initiative after another, drawing widely on congressional and other sources and even co-opting congressional initiatives as his own. "All of the major legislation of his first term," McJimsey adds, "was a product of presidential and congressional interaction, with Roosevelt following the lead of Congress as often as he led."[45] "Despite the talk of a rubber stamp Congress," E. Pendleton Herring writes, "a scrutiny of President Roosevelt's relations with Capitol Hill shows more manipulation than control. Diplomacy, bargaining, intrigue, persuasion, cajolery, threats, promises, flattery," Herring concludes, "these have been his tools."[46] Still, it was Roosevelt who took the political lead, with the public and Congress alike, for he knew and relished the job of the democratic politician. "The line between leading and following is sometimes a thin one," Dexter Perkins writes, adding: "A successful politician does not develop his policies out of thin air. He catches the drift of opinion; he seeks to anticipate the inevitable; he sometimes allows his hand to be forced and sometimes speaks out boldly. He understands and uses the personal ambitions, antagonisms, and aspirations of those with whom he must work; he gives a little here and gains a little there. All these things were true of F. D. R. He knew that he was the leader of a democracy; he knew that he had to act with the concurrence of Congress to accomplish results; he knew that he had to reconcile conflicting wills and conflicting interests in the evolution of policy."[47]

The political style of Roosevelt in drafting and promoting legislation was to build a team that involved a wide range of expert and often
conflicting opinion drawn from Congress, his administration, interest groups, and the academy. The very first piece of New Deal legislation—the banking bill—evinced the Roosevelt style. It was drafted
by Wilson Wyatt of the Federal Reserve Board with the assistance of
Hoover appointees in Treasury, as well as Roosevelt's treasury secretary designate William Woodin and presidential aide Raymond Moley,
then revised substantially by Senator Carter Glass before being swept
through both houses of Congress and signed by the president. Both
the Agricultural Adjustment Act (AAA) and the National Industrial
Recovery Act (NIRA), which embodied the approach to recovery set
forth in the Commonwealth Club Address, brought all the relevant
private interests to the drafting table, along with congressional and administration leaders, to devise the legislative initiatives and administrative strategies of the early New Deal. The Tennessee Valley Authority, inspired by Republican senator George Norris's long interest
in the potential of the region but largely of FDR's design, brought together those interested in hydroelectric power, low-cost fertilizer, and
flood control behind a plan that linked industry, agriculture, and conservation interests on a grand scale. On the other hand, securities legislation and much labor legislation sprang largely from the Congress and
were, for the most part, simply embraced by the White House.

The novelty of the Hundred Days was not in the originality or coherence of the legislation. Most of the ideas that became law had been dis-
cussed for some time, and there was no overarching plan. Indeed, the
economic effect of some programs was inflationary, whereas that of others was deflationary. The novelty lay instead in the sheer volume of measures and the new role for the federal government that sprang from them
through Roosevelt's political adroitness. In the end, almost every aspect
of American social and economic life was touched by this whirlwind of
lawmaking. The AAA made the federal government a partner with the
farmer in the management of crops and production; the NIRA did the
same in business and industry. There seemed to be something for everyone in the new cooperative commonwealth as Roosevelt initially envisioned it. The crisis of depression and the large Democratic majorities in
both houses of Congress invited and facilitated federal initiatives, but
Roosevelt's success, both legislative and administrative, in the First and

Second New Deals lay also in his political style of leadership. He was able to bring diverse interests together, focus them piecemeal on specific problems, and hold them together to forge policy.[48] And he was willing to use patronage and traditional political methods, as well as radio and the newer political methods, in his pursuit of recovery.

Roosevelt's political skills were tested again midway in his first term in 1935 when the Supreme Court invalidated the National Industrial Recovery Act, which was the cornerstone of FDR's recovery program. More than any other program, the NIRA embodied Roosevelt's ideal of a cooperative commonwealth. The National Recovery Administration (NRA), created by the act, sought to "unite capital and labor" by bringing their representatives together on public boards organized by industry to set production and labor market rules to be administered by the NRA.[49] Roosevelt reacted angrily to the Court's ruling, declaring it, Burns writes, a "horse and buggy decision" that made "national action, collective action, the great partnership" impossible.[50] He abandoned the strategy of bringing competing interests to the table to make rules by which they would be governed, moving away, as McJimsey observes, "from 'nation' solutions toward 'group' solutions and to a definition of citizenship that included identification with a social group."[51] While not wavering from his goal of economic recovery, Roosevelt moved politically to an expansion of the regulatory state and of federally protected "positive" rights.[52]

With the NIRA unconstitutional, FDR threw the weight of his administration behind passage of Senator Robert Wagner's National Labor Relations Act (NLRA), which restored and strengthened provisions in the NIRA guaranteeing the right of workers to organize and bargain collectively with management through unions of their own choosing and, in addition, created a new federal tribunal, the National Labor Relations Board (NLRB), to enforce these rights. Roosevelt was a latecomer to support of the Wagner bill and was, for that matter, David Kennedy notes, "a rather diffident champion of labor, especially of organized labor unions."[53] FDR saw the bill as the most promising way available to increase the purchasing power of workers as consumers, not their political power as unionists. He also saw it as "urgently necessary" for industrial peace once the Court had invalidated the labor provisions of the NIRA.[54] The NLRA created a juridical rather than a cooperative relationship between unions and management. "No legislation of the New

Deal period," Perkins notes, "met with more determined opposition than the Wagner Act."[55] As business criticism of the administration escalated and cooperation declined, Roosevelt resolved that the NLRB would enforce workers' rights.

The burst of legislation in the summer of 1935 that began with passage of the Works Progress Administration, then accelerated with the Wagner Act, moved the New Deal in new political directions. The Social Security Act, with its range of entitlements for the young, those with infirmities, the elderly, and families, became law. Long an idea embraced by the administration, it would subsequently become a centerpiece of the new arrangement of "positive" rights, but at the time of its passage it was for FDR primarily a way to strengthen and secure the purchasing power of groups at the social and economic margins of American life. But perhaps nothing better exemplified the new politics of the New Deal than Roosevelt's wealth tax bill, which enacted levies on inheritances, estates, gifts, corporate incomes and dividends and also increased income tax rates for the wealthy. It was a master political stroke, answering Roosevelt critics on the left—Huey Long, Father Charles Coughlin, and Doctor Francis Townsend—and, at the same time, punishing his business antagonists on the right.[56] It defined the sides in the struggle for recovery and made clear on whose side FDR stood.

But if recovery was the first item on Roosevelt's agenda, not far behind it was his desire to reconstruct the Democratic Party as the nation's liberal party. It was to be the political vehicle through which the New Deal—its ideals and programs—would be secured as the framework for American politics well beyond his time in office. "Before assuming the presidency," McJimsey writes, "Roosevelt had been a party man who sought ways to strengthen the party's organization and focus its program."[57] It was a cause he had taken up immediately after the 1920 presidential campaign, and one he had pursued through the decade of the 1920s. Yet, Roosevelt's quick success in legislation was not matched by success in remaking the Democratic Party. He moved with greater ease and certainty in the more structured and national realm of Congress and the bureaucracy, where political relations were clearer, than in the more fluid and decentralized one of electoral politics. In governing, a leadership of principle and national purpose could frame issues more effectively and produce change more quickly, but not so with party leadership, in which old habits and localism held sway. Nothing could have prepared

Roosevelt fully for the kaleidoscope of national politics, in which, unlike the more settled politics of New York State, ideology, partisanship, culture, and regionalism intersected and overlaid one another in subtly shifting patterns and in which the growing number and influence of business, labor, farm, and other groups continually reworked the political calculus.[58] Western progressives had limited experience dealing with urban progressives such as Robert Wagner who were culturally and politically a different breed; rural and small-town members of Congress had little experience or sympathy with the burgeoning diversity of nationalities that comprised the nation's cities; southern Democrats and other party conservatives had no wish for a larger or more intrusive federal role in the government and politics of their states; and so it went.

Roosevelt was supremely self-confident but clearly seems to have overestimated his chances of effecting a two-term makeover of the Democratic Party. Opposition to FDR grew within his party during his first term, as southern Democrats regularly defected on legislation dealing with unions and labor conditions. More conservative Democrats such as Al Smith and John W. Davis joined the anti–New Deal American Liberty League, while populist Democrats, such as Long and Father Coughlin, challenged from the left. In his second term and despite his landslide reelection, opposition to FDR became open, evident in part in his break with prominent southern Democrats and in part because his lame-duck status encouraged others, including his vice president and postmaster general, to maneuver to be his successor. In the end, Roosevelt trumped this opposition with a third and then fourth term, did reconstruct the Democratic Party, though not perhaps in the way or with the consequences he anticipated at the outset, and changed the constitution of American national politics more profoundly than any president other than Jefferson and Lincoln.

The Reconstruction of Party

In 1884 the Reverend Samuel Dickinson, a Presbyterian minister, speaking at a rally for Republican presidential candidate James G. Blaine, branded the rival Democrats as the party of "rum, Romanism, and rebellion." In 1932 the party Franklin Roosevelt was chosen to lead was much the same party, except that rum and Romanism had triumphed over rebellion in 1928, when the urban Catholicism of the "wet" Al

Smith captured the party nomination, forcing the southern Bourbons into the background. In this book, Marc Landy argues that Roosevelt's great political achievement was to wed the elements of his electoral coalition to the Democratic Party. In 1932, however, it was FDR who wed himself to the Democratic Party; the new elements came together four years later. Through his first four years in office, Roosevelt added significantly to this collection of forces to build what Landy calls, electorally, one of, if not *the,* greatest political party in American political history. Not only did this party take FDR to three reelection victories, but it also carried an embattled Harry Truman back to the White House in 1948, did likewise for John Kennedy in 1960, and has cast shadows across national politics ever since.

This new coalition spoke for different interests. Unlike earlier reform movements, which Richard Hofstadter argues responded to "the needs of entrepreneurial classes or of those who were on the verge of entrepreneurship," the New Deal addressed itself to the needs of the unemployed and to the demands of a rising and increasingly powerful labor movement. It also raised new issues, as essays in this volume attest. Where earlier movements had seen government as a threat to individual liberty and thus viewed it in largely negative or preventive terms, the New Dealers argued that governmental action designed to place a solid material foundation under the individual did not destroy freedom but rather made it more possible. As Sidney Milkis argues in this volume, "New Deal Liberalism was the foundation on which a full-scale partisan realignment arose." Where earlier reformers had celebrated the competitive order, seeking only, in Hofstadter's view, "to clear the way for new enterprises," New Dealers sought a positive role for the state in managing the economic well-being of the nation.[59] The New Liberalism lay behind the new solutions urged by Roosevelt, which in turn brought different forces into active support of the Democratic Party.

Roosevelt also entered the White House with a definite conception of how a political party should be built. Like Woodrow Wilson, he believed that a party should be organized around a program of governance. Owing to his experience in New York State and Washington politics, Roosevelt's notion of a strong party was one integrated on three levels of thought and action: (1) it must embody a clear public philosophy, such as the New Liberalism, (2) it must espouse policies and programs consistent with this philosophy, and (3) it must enlist a coalition of interests and groups which embrace the party philosophy and programs and which are capable of generating the electoral support required to carry them into practice. Unlike Wilson, FDR was not greatly concerned with the design of a *party system,* though he did believe that the two national parties should be built around different philosophies and programs, one liberal and the other conservative; that they should compete for the favor of the electorate on this basis and be sufficiently disciplined to make good on their promises if elected; and that they should be held "responsible" by the electorate for a failure to translate their promises into action.[60] Roosevelt was interested primarily in establishing a politically coherent national Democratic Party strong enough to secure the New Liberalism as *the* public philosophy in American politics, *not* as a contestable point of view but as a permanent frame that would define liberalism and conservatism and within which electoral battles would be fought in the future. To a remarkable degree, he achieved this end, in part, as Milkis details in this volume, through administrative reform and a rights-centered strategy but also, as Landy suggests, by changing significantly the constituent groups that made up the national Democratic Party.

The political vehicle of the New Deal was the electoral coalition forged by Franklin Roosevelt. It was a coalition cast largely in economic terms. The problems in response to which it arose were essentially those of the Great Depression—unemployment, despair, and a loss of confidence in the economic system—and the groups it united were primarily the "have-not" groups' of the nation: the poor, the working class, the family farmer, and the small businessperson. The programs it championed were broadly those of the social welfare state. It was in many respects the urban machine—Tammany Hall—writ large, whose constituents were largely from the margins of American life, drawn together by social service programs with FDR as the "boss" of a new and national party "machine." In this way Roosevelt and the New Deal transformed the Democrats from an ideologically fragmented grouping of regional and religious interests into a powerful liberal party that spoke to the economic concerns of middle- and lower-class Americans and in doing so both realigned party politics and reconstituted national politics. It relegated the Republicans to minority standing in the two-party struggle and restored the Democrats to the status of majority party for the first time since the Civil War.

This political reconstruction of the Democratic Party was achieved through a multidimensional dynamic. An academic debate has persisted on the question of whether it was the product of conversion or mobilization, and while the evidence is strong that the latter was more important, both dynamics were at work.[61] But there was a third dynamic as well, namely, the turning away of old partisans. It was the political equivalent of what the legendary baseball executive Branch Rickey called "addition by subtraction." Players of great individual talent did not necessarily make for a winning team, and Rickey regularly dealt them away, much as Roosevelt was willing to "subtract" conservative Democratic leaders in the North and the South to build a more liberal "team." The voting blocs that Roosevelt attracted to the party, which came ultimately to dominate the national Democratic Party, were a function of both mobilization and conversion, and the position of these groups in the party was strengthened by the subtraction of older forces. It was a dynamic that accorded with Roosevelt's belief that strong party organization had to be built around a clear philosophy and program of governance.

The Democratic Base

The South was part of the early Roosevelt coalition and had been critical to his nomination. It had always been an important part of the Democratic Party from the days of Jefferson and Jackson, but following Reconstruction it became more and more a one-party Democratic region—the so-called Solid South. Moreover, after the 1890s, when the radical "western" populism of William Jennings Bryan frightened the more conservative Grover Cleveland Democrats in the Northeast and splintered the party, the South became the single most powerful faction within the party. By the 1920s, however, its dominance was being seriously challenged by the urban North, where immigration had transformed politics. The 1928 nomination of Al Smith, a first-generation American who hailed from the sidewalks as well as the Statehouse of New York, marked the effective end of the southern veto over the party's presidential selection process, yet the region remained powerful within the Democratic Party, both for its electoral vote and the seniority of its members in Congress.

In 1932 Roosevelt swept all the states of the Old Confederacy, four of them with over 90 percent of the vote and three others with over 80 percent. Indeed, all the southern states backed FDR in each of his pres-

idential races, always by overwhelming though diminishing margins after 1932. Yet, southern Democrats had many misgivings about New
Deal programs, especially those that centralized greater authority and
power in the national government. Roosevelt's congressional majorities
were so great in his first term that southerners could be impediments
but rarely obstructionists. Nonetheless, FDR recognized that, in the
long run, the South posed a serious challenge to his desire for a liberal
Democratic Party capable of carrying his reform program beyond his
administrations. In 1936, on Roosevelt's initiative, the Democratic national convention abolished its rule requiring a two-thirds vote of the
delegates for the party's presidential nominations. On the party books
since the 1830s, the two-thirds rule had given the South a veto over
Democratic presidential candidates, and its elimination reduced the
region's power dramatically. This was followed in 1937 by Roosevelt's
"court-packing" plan, which struck at the last bastion of conservatism
in the national government, the Supreme Court, and by the Brownlow Commission report that called for greatly enhancing the managerial capacities of the White House. Both were seen by many southern
Democrats as giving too much power to the president and as supporting a political philosophy and program that threatened localism and
states' rights.

The breach between FDR and southern Democrats burst into the
open in the "purge" campaign of 1938, in which Roosevelt campaigned in party primaries for the defeat of several Democratic members of Congress from the Deep South and the border states. The electoral success of younger southern congressmen sympathetic to the
New Deal, Lister Hill of Alabama and Claude Pepper of Florida among
them, had led Congress to enact the Fair Labor Standards Act in 1938,
which no doubt encouraged FDR to undertake the purge.[62] Despite
some successes, Roosevelt lost the fight to cleanse his party of its Dixie
recalcitrants, and from the loss there emerged in Congress a "conservative coalition" of southern Democrats and midwestern Republicans
who united to block any further New Deal initiatives. Having failed to
remove conservatives from the leadership of the Democratic Party in
Congress and faced with the two-term precedent for presidents, FDR
appeared to many in 1938 to be more of a dead than a lame duck, and
the purge campaign might properly be seen as a rather desperate attempt to fix the Democratic Party before his time in office expired.[63]

Roosevelt's decision to seek a third term clearly had its roots in the 1938 campaign.

Meanwhile, the South drifted more and more away from the national Democratic Party, especially on the issue of civil rights, though more generally on that of federal power. Some southern states split openly with the national party in the Dixiecrat revolt of 1948 but could not prevent the election of Democrat Harry Truman as president. In the 1950s, the border states gave majorities to Republican Dwight Eisenhower, while the Deep South went to the GOP and Barry Goldwater in 1964. The Civil Rights and Voting Rights Acts passed in the 1960s at the behest of Democrat Lyndon Johnson led more white southerners to shift their partisan loyalties in national politics. In 1972 the South was solid once more, only this time it was for the Republican Richard Nixon.

In the 1930s the big cities of the Northeast and the Midwest emerged as the new center of power in the Democratic Party. It was the "revolt of the cities," Samuel Lubell argues, which moved dramatically from Republican to Democrat, that formed the cornerstone of the Roosevelt revolution.[64] The Republican hold on the nation's twelve largest cities was broken in 1928 by Al Smith, who carried them by a margin of just over two hundred thousand votes. Four years later, Roosevelt swept these same cities by almost nine times that plurality. Moreover, these cities were growing rapidly as immigration remained high in the early decades of the twentieth century, in addition to which there was an internal migration of population from farm to city after World War I, including for the first time large numbers of African Americans moving north and west from the South. In the 1930s the urban North, heavily populated by Catholic working-class ethnic minorities and organized politically by Democratic Party machines fueled with patronage, was the key to success in presidential politics, for command of the big cities usually meant command of the big electoral states as well.

The Roosevelt presidency provided urban Democrats with their first taste of national power, as he brought the children of immigrants into his administration as none before him had. No ethnic group was more prominent in or had longer association with the Democratic Party than the Irish, whose allegiance antedated the Civil War.[65] Through the latter decades of the nineteenth century, they came to dominate big-city Democratic Party machines in New York, Chicago, and elsewhere, as well as factional politics in such cities as Boston. But their influence was almost wholly local; they were not prominent in national politics. Indeed, William Shannon concludes that the "most important Irishman in the federal government prior to the New Deal was Joseph Tumulty, private secretary to Woodrow Wilson."[66] The presidential candidacy of Al Smith in 1928 reinforced the partisan predisposition of the Irish, increased their participation, and also attracted other ethnic minorities from southern and eastern Europe—the "newer races," as Boston's James Michael Curley called them—into the ranks of Democrats. Irish support for the Democrats was overwhelming and cut across all class lines.[67] In 1932 Roosevelt expanded some, though not greatly, on Smith's achievement and then brought Irish Catholics into highly visible positions in his administration. James Farley joined the Roosevelt cabinet as postmaster general and also served as chairman of the Democratic National Committee, the latter a position filled thereafter by a succession of Irish Democrats into the 1950s from Robert Hannegan to J. Howard McGrath.[68] Thomas G. "Tommy the Cork" Corcoran was among FDR's closest advisers in the White House, writing speeches, drafting laws, working with members of Congress and the press, recruiting talent for the New Deal administration, and fielding task forces to deal with special problems. Edward Flynn, the Tammany boss from the Bronx, was also a frequent adviser to FDR and troubleshooter in the White House. In addition, Frank Murphy was appointed governor-general to the Philippines in 1933, returned to serve one term as governor of Michigan from 1937 to 1938, after which he was named to Roosevelt's Cabinet as attorney general and in 1940 appointed to the Supreme Court. Joseph P. Kennedy was another highly visible Irish appointment, first as chairman of the Securities and Exchange Commission and later as ambassador to England. The prominence of Irish Catholics continued through the administration of Harry Truman, who was himself a product of the Kansas Democratic organization headed by boss Tom Pendergast.

From his years in New York State politics, Roosevelt was at once comfortable and his own man in dealing with the party's urban machines. As Shannon observes, "Unlike Grover Cleveland and Woodrow Wilson, his two Democratic predecessors in the period since the Civil War, he [Roosevelt] was able to tilt with the Irish machines as a reformer, cooperate with—and make use of—them as a party leader, and all the while look beyond them to encourage rebels and outsiders in the Irish community who did not fit the traditional machine stereotypes." Shannon adds that "because of the Democratic Party's success and the hospitable atmosphere of the New Deal, the Irish for the first time were able to develop their talent for politics and public service at the national level."[69] This continued into the Truman years, though Roosevelt was more inclined to pick and choose whom to embrace among local Democratic bosses than was his successor.[70] The New Deal added to Irish support for the party, especially among younger voters, and the support was not diminished by FDR's public breaks with Smith, Farley, Kennedy, and Boston's colorful James Michael Curley. Much as he did with southern Democrats, Roosevelt treated the Irish vote as securely Democratic, retaining those Irish Americans in his administration who supported his liberal-nationalist New Deal program at home and, later, his interventionism abroad, but he had no compunction about "subtracting" those who did not.[71]

Mobilization: The Dormant Democrats

The great political "creation" of the New Deal—and perhaps its greatest social "invention" as well—was "big labor." There had, of course, been a labor movement in the United States for over a century and an American Federation of Labor (AFL) for a half century before Franklin Roosevelt became president. But the AFL, dominated by craft unions, had long resisted or, at best, equivocated on a larger social or economic role for government. Its president, Samuel Gompers, whose political credo called for supporting labor's friends and opposing its enemies regardless of party, championed a union shop strategy that concentrated on the private sector, preferring a business unionism in which labor bargained directly with employers over the conditions of work, unencumbered by government regulation. He feared that government intervention would weaken the labor movement by encouraging workers to look to government rather than to unions to deal with their problems. But the hostility of the courts to labor's interests and a growing opposition to unions among employers early in the twentieth century led Gompers and the AFL into a flirtation with the Bryan campaign in 1908 and later with the Wilson presidency, but never into an embrace of the Democratic Party.[72] From the outset, however, the New Deal sought to strengthen the legal position of unions, first in the National Industrial Recovery Act and later, successfully, in the Wagner Act of 1935. FDR's colleague from the New York senate, Robert Wagner, now a U.S. senator, led the fight for union recognition and for labor reforms generally; he had to rally an often hesitant Roosevelt behind his initiatives, which were to become some of the most significant legislation of the New Deal years.[73]

The political response of the older trade unions in the AFL remained cautious, tied still to the volunteerist principles of Gompers, but not so an emerging industrial union movement that formed within the AFL as the Committee (later Congress) of Industrial Organizations (CIO). Leaders of the CIO threw themselves enthusiastically behind Franklin Roosevelt and the New Deal. The CIO launched a successful fight to unionize the nation's mass production industries: automobile, steel, rubber, chemical, coal mining, garment, and others. "Perhaps the most significant aspect of the labor movement in the New Deal period," Milton Derber notes, "was its growth and expansion."[74] From fewer than 3 million members in 1933, union membership grew to 8 million by 1933, 4 million belonging to CIO unions. The greatest increases were among miners and garment workers, whose industries that had been organized for some time. But even more important gains, Jong Oh Ra argues, occurred "among factory workers, service workers, and other groups that had been substantially outside union ranks."[75] The organizing success of CIO unions provoked a bitter response from many of the older trade unions, which first tried to raid the new unions and then expelled them from the AFL.

Many of the leaders of the CIO unions came from socialist backgrounds, leading them to be more sympathetic than older AFL trade unionists to both the specific social programs of the New Deal and the need for positive government to counter social and economic injustices. Moreover, the nature of industrial unionism reinforced this predisposition to politics, as the mass basis of organization lent itself more readily to collective action than did the more individualistic and independent basis of organization in the craft unions.[76] In addition, the CIO was in a sense born of politics, for the presence of a friendly administration in Washington—one, as Nelson Lichtenstein notes in this volume, that was an advocate for labor—facilitated its organizing efforts. Finally, the membership of CIO unions was generally of even lower social and more marginal economic status—more vulnerable to the impersonal forces of the marketplace—than were the older trade unionists, and consequently, government was simply more important to them as an ally.

The CIO unions mobilized behind FDR, creating a new force that brought votes, campaign workers, money, and a social consciousness to the Democratic Party.[77] The New Liberalism espoused by Roosevelt was championed by this new phalanx of labor. By the early 1940s, many CIO leaders had a growing influence within the Democratic Party, leading the AFL to follow its offspring into a more active partisan politics and generally into the Democratic Party as well. The craft unions, however, while accepting the reforms of the New Deal, never fully shared its more liberal impulses. On the whole, they remained more conservative than their industrial counterparts—more "pragmatic," less "ideological"—and their entry into the party coincided roughly with the turn of the New Deal to the right. The 1955 merger of the AFL and CIO enabled organized labor to speak with a single voice in national politics, one by then consistently Democratic but also more moderate and, socially, less ideological. By the late 1950s, with the influence of the South in decline, organized labor ranked with the big-city organizations as the major centers of power within the party. There was, to be sure, a sizable overlap in the two constituencies.

Women constituted another bloc of voters that Franklin Roosevelt and especially his wife, Eleanor, had worked to organize and mobilize since ratification of the Nineteenth Amendment in 1920.[78] With FDR incapacitated, Mrs. Roosevelt came more and more to represent her husband at public events and political meetings and began to emerge as an effective Democratic party leader and a strong voice for social justice for women and workers.[79] In these years Mrs. Roosevelt brought many people to meet with her husband, to engage his intellect and spirit, among whom were Maude Schwartz and Rose Schneiderman from the Women's Trade Union League. Schooled in the history and theory of the trade union movement, they helped FDR to understand the exploitation of workers, especially women, and why unions were critical to improving the unhealthful working conditions of the sweatshops. While Roosevelt, in Perkins's opinion, was "well disposed" toward labor, it was through meetings like these that he came to "understand with real detail the purpose of the movement."[80]

In 1924 Governor Al Smith recruited Mrs. Roosevelt to work with the state party's women's division, headed by Nancy Cook. She, Cook, and Marian Dickerman made repeated political tours around the state organizing local units of the women's division to educate and mobilize the newly enfranchised vote for the Democratic Party. Conscious of the importance of the women's vote to the party, FDR "took seriously the new Democratic women" and encouraged his wife's development as a political figure in her own right. In his 1928 gubernatorial bid, Roosevelt especially encouraged the recruitment of women in rural, upstate counties, where Republicans were strong, in the belief that their prominence as Democrats would elevate the image of the party and enhance its chances.[81] His victory was due in part to his ability to run more successfully in Republican areas than was usual for a Democrat.

In the 1932 presidential contest, Roosevelt again encouraged the party to be aggressive in pursuing the women's vote. Mary "Molly" Dewson, head of the Democratic National Committee's Women's Division, led the charge, focusing on issues, such as the high cost of electricity, that were of immediate interest to housewives. FDR commissioned a flyer that compared electricity costs for household appliances in New York and Canadian cities, and Dewson, a tireless campaigner, kept her staff busy writing letters to Democratic women workers around the country urging them to circulate the material. In 1936 Roosevelt again centered attention on winning the support of women. In his speeches, Perkins notes, he appealed "to their moral sense" and to their "faith in community life and in social good." He recognized that women's votes had increased during the New Deal, was "insistent that the Democratic National Committee should give a generous appropriation to the Women's Division," and was pleased that the "campaign literature put out by the women had a wider and more effective circulation than anything else issued."[82]

From his years as assistant secretary of the navy, when he supported a Women's Bureau in the Department of Labor to set standards for female workers in the war industries, through his term as governor of New York and in the White House, Roosevelt supported programs to protect working women. The New Deal also took initiatives to ease the lives of housewives. The Rural Electrification Act of 1935, for example, brought cheap electricity into American homes, which may have done more to transform the everyday lives of women in rural areas than any single piece of federal legislation, before or since, liberating them from the harsh and onerous chores of housekeeping, providing them with time for leisure.[83] The Women's Division of the national Democratic Party proved to be not only an energetic campaign organization but also among the strongest and most consistent supporters of Roosevelt's New Liberalism.

In addition to the success of the New Deal in mobilizing unionized workers and women, more was at work among the nation's poorer, nonunionized agricultural workers and manual laborers—the "working stiffs," as John Dos Passos called them affectionately—and that "something more" was Franklin Roosevelt himself. From the Pathé News in movie theaters, fireside chats on radio, and photographic essays in popular magazines to the voting booth where turnout reversed a thirty-year decline, the story was the same: hundreds of thousands of Americans felt their lives had been touched and improved by the programs of the alphabet agencies—the CCC (Civilian Conservation Corps), PWA (Public Works Administration), WPA (Works Progress Administration), FERA (Federal Emergency Relief Administration), TVA (Tennessee Valley Authority)—that made the national government an immediate and positive presence in their daily lives. The New Deal also took the federal government into new areas of public policy, such as housing, that brought the American Dream closer to great numbers of Americans. The Home Owners' Loan Corporation saved family homes from foreclosure, casting the federal government in the role of protector of ordinary citizens against the financial interests, while the Federal Housing Administration lent money directly to individuals for home construction, setting standards for builders and regulating interest rates. The devotion of the mass of lower-status Americans to FDR is evident in accounts of their experiences. Families of modest income found new recreation facilities in public parks, with playing fields and swimming pools, lodges and picnic areas, built by federal agencies. For them, Roosevelt and his government gave both hope and tangible goods, which made grim times more easily borne, and these families felt a personal tie to him as they had to no other president.[84] They said "thanks" through the ballot box as well as in the volumes of personal correspondence that flooded the White House.[85]

Conversion: The New Democrats

The most dramatic political conversion in the 1930s was among black Americans. Historically, the black vote in America had belonged to the party of Lincoln, but in 1936 it shifted dramatically to Roosevelt. Before World War I, the black population was concentrated overwhelmingly in the South. In the first decade of the twentieth century, major cities in the

upper North—New York, Chicago, Boston, Cleveland, and Detroit—
had negligible black populations, 2 to 4 percent of the whole, while the
population in cities of the lower North—St. Louis, Cincinnati, Pittsburgh, and Philadelphia—was only slightly larger. After the war, however, black migration to the North and the West began in earnest, owing
especially to the prospect of better-paying jobs in manufacturing,
slaughterhouses, and other industries. By the 1930s this population had
grown well into double digits in most of the large northern cities, with
vibrant and growing middle-class communities in New York, Chicago,
and elsewhere. Like the European immigration of the nineteenth and
early twentieth centuries, this black migration created a new electorate
strategically located in cities across the North. Politically, black voters remained Republicans, in part as their birthright, though the GOP had
largely taken their vote for granted, but also because the Democratic
Party machines, dominated by the Irish, were less welcoming to them
than to white immigrants from southern and eastern Europe.

The depression hit black populations in the North (and the South) far
harder than it did the white population, yet African Americans in 1932
remained loyal to the Republican ticket. Influential newspapers, such as
the *Chicago Defender, New Amsterdam News,* and *California Eagle,* endorsed the reelection of President Hoover and urged their readers to stay
true to their heritage. There were exceptions, the most notable being
Robert Vann, editor of the *Pittsburgh Courier,* who endorsed FDR and
backed his candidacy with repeated editorials. African Americans had
little reason to support the Democratic Party in 1932: it was still the
party of the white South, its platform contained little for blacks, and the
candidates were a patrician for president, whose great-grandfather had
owned slaves, and a Texan for vice president. Roosevelt repeatedly expressed his belief that all Americans should be treated alike, but it was
election rhetoric all too familiar to blacks, who had heard the same from
the GOP for years with little effect. In the cities of the North, the African
American vote went overwhelmingly to the Republicans by margins of 7
and 8 to 1. Only in New York City did the Democrats win a majority of
the black vote, and then by the narrowest of margins.[86]

Support for the New Deal and Roosevelt built slowly among African
Americans. They benefited from jobs and relief programs, but the continuing rhetoric of opportunity and equality did not result in any legislative initiatives in the area of civil rights. From time to time, Roosevelt

did consult on racial matters with black leaders, such as Walter White of the National Association for the Advancement of Colored People (NAACP), with whom he agreed that relief should come before desegregation, especially in the South, and that there should be no discrimination against blacks in federal jobs programs. The track record of the administration was mixed with respect to the latter. Harold Ickes was most supportive, and the Tennessee Valley projects were generally integrated. But Harry Hopkins handled the race question "gingerly" in his various public works programs, and there were documented cases of discrimination in both relief and public works programs, especially in the South. In addition, the military remained segregated.[87]

FDR also appointed blacks to positions in his administration, mainly as advisers in federal agencies and departments. Indeed, as Nancy Weiss reports, Roosevelt brought "a larger group of talented black men and women" into government "at significantly higher positions than ever before" and "positioned black people for the first time to work from within the government to influence federal policies" that affected race.[88] Their numbers were such that a "black cabinet" arose whose members were important symbolically to the Democrats but also served as visible representatives of the administration. Robert Weaver, for example, later a member of Lyndon Johnson's cabinet, presented the administration's case to the 1937 NAACP convention: almost four hundred thousand blacks were employed on WPA programs (20 percent of total jobs); 10 percent of CCC enrollment was black; the PWA had built schools for blacks in the South and housing for them in the North; ten thousand black children attended WPA nursery schools daily; and thirty-five thousand black students were in high school and college through the National Youth Administration.[89] Mrs. Roosevelt played an important role in winning African American support for the Democrats, encouraging the black cabinet but also meeting with blacks in all walks of life, being photographed with them, bringing black artists and glee clubs to the White House, regularly pressing the issue of racial justice within the administration, and coming to be seen as a genuine friend of black Americans.[90]

For all the symbolism of a black presence in the Roosevelt administration and White House, it was jobs and relief that drew African Americans to support for the Democrats, coupled with an all-out political effort in 1936 to win their backing. For the first time, there was an evident black presence at the Democratic national convention, as twelve states sent black delegates or alternates. One session opened with an African American minister giving the convocation, and a black congressman was among those who made seconding speeches for FDR's renomination. Some forty African Americans, many of them Republicans, formed the Good Neighbor League to campaign actively for Roosevelt, especially among labor and religious groups. The Democratic National Committee also made a concerted effort to win black support. The party's Colored Division, largely a token before, was mobilized to provide speakers and distribute literature. Political advertising and articles were placed in black newspapers and magazines; films to promote the success of WPA and other New Deal programs included shots of African Americans; a CCC camp with black officers was opened; a new chemistry building at Howard University, a PWA project, drew national attention when FDR came to dedicate it; and millions of photographs were distributed of Mrs. Roosevelt with blacks. Members of the black cabinet, among them Mary McLeod Bethune, campaigned for the Democrats; ministers and labor leaders encouraged black support for Roosevelt; and even the Roosevelt's maid, Lizzie McDuffie, went on the stump to tell about the president's personal relationship with his African American employees. Some black newspapers endorsed the Republican Alf Landon, but most backed FDR, and officials of long-established black organizations, such as the NAACP, announced their support for the Democrat.[91]

On election day Roosevelt won with 60.8 percent of the popular vote, the largest plurality in history, but he won by an even greater margin among black voters in most of the cities of the North. The key to his victory, Weiss asserts, "lay in economics rather than race" and in the political determination of Roosevelt to include blacks as part of the New Deal and the liberal program for which it stood.[92] Black support in 1936 did not lead to any civil rights initiatives by the New Deal, but blacks were rewarded in economic terms in the second Roosevelt administration, and the Democratic Party continued to pay careful attention to the African American vote. By the 1944 campaign, Democratic National Committee chair Robert Hannegan was urging party leaders at the state and local levels to register blacks and get them to the polls, and the Truman administration subsequently put civil rights on the national party agenda.[93]

African Americans were not the only group converted to the Democratic Party by Franklin Roosevelt. In 1936, as Morton Keller notes in this volume, over 90 percent of the children of newcomers—Italians, Poles, and others—voted for Roosevelt. Many Jewish voters were among them, abandoning their Republican allegiances to ally with the New Deal. In the two decades before World War I, over 2 million Jewish immigrants entered the United States, most of them refugees from the prejudice and poverty of eastern Europe. New York became home to many, while others settled in Boston, Philadelphia, and Chicago where by the 1920s they had become a significant part of the ethnic mix in these cities. Many Jews, especially those who were better off, became Republicans, attracted in part to the party in office during the years of their heavy migration and by its reformist impulses, but also because they encountered anti-Semitism in local Democratic Party machines.[94] The depression, however, severed the loyalty of working-class Jews to the GOP. In 1932 Roosevelt carried lower-class Jewish precincts in Boston, for example, by margins of 4 to 1, while losing in upper-middle-class precincts. By 1936 he carried the Jewish vote as a bloc, often with more than 90 percent of the vote. As with other ethnic and racial groups, Jews had played a visible role in the first term of the New Deal, but the Jewish attraction to Roosevelt and the Democrats was largely economic.[95] The idealism of the New Liberalism and World War II solidified the Jewish vote in the Democratic Party, where its significance has been greater than its numbers.

It was then Roosevelt's skills as a politician, honed through two decades of politics in New York and the nation, that enabled him through patronage, program, the management of public opinion, and the symbolic used of politics to reconstruct the Democratic Party as a vehicle, however imperfect, for his New Liberalism. A master of the patronage game, he used it to reward those in the traditional bases of the party—the South and the urban North. He drew organized labor into an open embrace of the party through legislative initiatives, such as the Wagner Act that gave unions the right to organize and bargain collectively, as well as those regulating working conditions—wages, hours, health, and safety—and insuring against unemployment and old age. Family farmers, small business owners, women, and minorities were likewise attracted to the New Deal by its programs. African Americans, attracted by relief, housing, and other New Deal programs, were courted aggressively in 1936 with all the resources from patronage to publicity that the reelection campaign could muster. For the first time, Catholics and Jews, as well as some women, were given politically important and highly visible roles in both the Roosevelt White House and the Democratic National Committee, while African Americans were scattered throughout the administration in secondary and advisory roles. All were symbols of an administration prepared to share national power with groups largely excluded from it in the past. But above all, Roosevelt knew that, in a time of crisis, the American people wanted a government that understood their plight, spoke to their fears, and was on their side. Through regular meetings with the press, his fireside chats, the jobs and relief programs of the New Deal, and his public visibility and energetic leadership, ordinary Americans rallied to Roosevelt. His personal popularity was high, widespread, and proved to be an enormous electoral asset. A master of the political game both inside and outside his party and government, FDR, despite frustrations in Washington, rebuilt the Democratic Party nationally, recast the role and scope of the federal government, and ultimately remade the politics of the nation.

The Reconstitution of Politics

As a period of realignment, the 1930s differs in many ways from the Progressive Era: they produced a new partisan majority in the nation built on a new governing philosophy and transformed the social and professional character of government itself.[96] The New Deal also differed markedly from Progressivism in its reformist enthusiasms. The rallying cry of the latter was to restore popular rule. It marched to the drumbeat of democracy, seeking a purer form of popular rule through reform of the political parties, lobbying, and political money and the advocacy of nonpartisan local government, as well as a more direct role for citizens in their governance through the initiative and referendum, the recall, and the direct election of U.S. senators.[97] There was no analogous impulse in the New Deal. There can be no doubt that the programmatic innovations of the Roosevelt years had consequences for the party system. Milkis makes a persuasive case in this volume and elsewhere that the construction of an administrative state with the presidency at its center was central to FDR's reform program and that this had the effect of diminishing the role of party in staffing and managing the federal government.[98] Similarly, the rights-centered justifications for the New Deal matured in ways that weakened deliberative processes, which in turn weakened parties and encouraged a politics by "other means."[99] The Democratic Party and the two-party system that emerged from the New Deal were, to be sure, different from those which Roosevelt inherited in 1932, but the changes were derivative: they were the product of changes in the sides and the terms of the party battle and not of self-conscious reform of the parties as institutions.[100]

But perhaps the most striking difference between the Progressive Era and the New Deal as periods of realignment is the role played by political elites and the mass electorate in each. Political change in the Progressive Era was almost wholly the product of elites working within and upon the major parties; it was not the result of dramatic changes in partisan loyalties at the grass roots. After two decades of struggling toward reform, followed by world war, the electoral coalitions of the two major parties in their general outlines remained much as they had been in 1900, with the Republicans sustained as the nation's normal majority party. While the nation and its electoral system were changed by the enthusiasms of reformers and construction was begun on a new national state, the composition and character of the two major parties remained much the same. No fundamental rearrangement of forces occurred in the political bases of the two major parties. Progressives were evident in the ranks of the Republicans but were a minority in a party dominated by its Old Guard. Populists and some Progressives had joined the Democrats but were the minority in a party still controlled by its southern faction.[101] The shift associated with the New Deal, on the other hand, grew out of major changes in the partisan loyalties of the mass electorate. It was in the mobilization of new voters, the subtraction of others, and the conversion of yet others that the New Deal reorganized the lines of party combat in 1936 and redefined the battle around the role and responsibilities of the new liberal national state.

Franklin Roosevelt's reconstitution of party and politics in America was designed for its time and place. Its significance and greatness lie in its durability. Ultimately, however, time and place have been its enemies. Roosevelt's hostility to southern conservatives in his party, manifest in the purge campaign of 1938, ripened in the presidential wing of the national party and bore fruit in the mid-1960s with the passage of the Civil Rights and Voting Rights Acts, as well as in affirmative action and other policies. The white South, a portion of which marched out of the 1948

Democratic convention in protest of a civil rights plank and again in 1960 over the seating of the Mississippi Freedom Democrats, completed its journey in 1972, when the South was solid for the first time since it went for Roosevelt in 1944, only this time for the Republican Richard Nixon.[102] This southern secession, as FDR anticipated, made the Democrats an ideologically more coherent liberal party facing an ideologically more coherent conservative Republican Party, but it has also erased the advantage that Democrats held in presidential elections in the decades immediately following the New Deal.

The electoral power of the Democratic Party of Roosevelt has also been eroded by the great movements of population from the North and the Midwest to the West and the Southwest. In 1932, when FDR won election, states in the Northeast, Mideast, and Midwest, as defined by the U.S. census, cast 55.8 percent of the electoral vote for president. By 1992, when the Democrat Bill Clinton won, these states held only 44.4 percent of the votes in the Electoral College.[103] The West, especially California, has become the new power in presidential politics, and it is a region whose political history and heritage differs from that of both the old North and the old South.[104] Within the industrial states of the North, the movement from city to suburb since World War II has likewise changed the calculus of presidential politics. In 1932 in Illinois, the City of Chicago cast about half the popular vote statewide; in 1992 it accounted for only about 20 percent. In 1932 in Massachusetts, the City of Boston was home to about a quarter of all voters in the Commonwealth; in 1992 suburban Middlesex County cast almost three times as many votes as Boston. The pattern repeats itself in all the old industrial states that were critical to the New Deal Democratic Party. The new suburban voter, moreover, is less interested in party, more focused on candidates, and less dependent directly and tangibly on government and politics.[105] For the party of Roosevelt and the politics he bequeathed, demography has indeed been destiny.

Roosevelt had entered the presidency as a party man, intent on making the Democrats the party of liberalism, and through one term he governed as a party leader. He saw his triumphal reelection in 1936 as a massive popular endorsement for his New Liberalism, though it seems in retrospect more an endorsement of FDR than of his philosophy. In January 1937, given the precedent of a two-term limit for presidents, Roosevelt was a lame duck, which may have weighed more heavily in the thinking of his fellow Democrats than did his landslide reelection. He ran into immediate problems with Congress, losing the vote for his "court-packing" proposal and, with it, his image of invincibility. An economic downturn, brought on in part by the fiscal conservatism of his administration, further tarnished his image and left him more vulnerable. To this was added the rejection by Congress of his executive reorganization bill, a proposal that enabled his foes to lump him with communist and fascist leaders in Europe as part of a new authoritarianism that claimed popular support while undermining political freedom.

The "purge" campaign of 1938, which the public agreed with but thought would fail, was a product of Roosevelt's frustration with his party and a last valiant but ill-conceived effort to make it over as the nation's liberal party.[106] In the short run he failed, but in the long run he succeeded. The newer forces that his presidency had converted or mobilized to support the Democratic Party in the 1930s came to dominate the party by the 1960s. But for Roosevelt, with time of the essence and no obvious successor at hand, the gamble on these untested forces was too great, and he was persuaded—if persuasion were required—to fall back on the single greatest political resource of the New Deal, Franklin Roosevelt himself. The decision to seek a third term was not an isolated one but part of a more general strategy to secure the New Deal and the New Liberalism on which it rested in the absence of a strong liberal party. Through the Ramspeck Act, as Milkis notes, FDR locked many New Dealers into their administrative positions in the national government by covering them with civil service protection, thus making the government, if not the Democratic Party, a carrier of New Deal Liberalism.

World War II was the proximate justification for a third term and enabled Roosevelt to extend his campaign to secure the future of the New Deal. Unlike World War I, which was fought in the name of democracy, World War II was prosecuted in the name of freedom. It was in this context that Roosevelt shifted political gears from reliance on party to rights as the means to secure the New Deal. The four freedoms and the economic bill of rights embodied his new conception of "positive" rights, the primary beneficiaries of which were many of the new constituencies—workers, minorities, women—that FDR had brought into the Democratic ranks. Consistent with the goals set forth in his Commonwealth Club Address of 1932, this new strategy departed from the old in the means by which the goals of the New Deal were to be achieved. Roo-

sevelt, as his brain truster Rexford Tugwell observed, had a "bulldog determination concerning objectives and a completely contrasting flexibility concerning means."[107] Rather than bringing diverse interests together in political communities to devise and implement policy through
deliberative processes, FDR's new strategy was to establish new rights for
individuals that it was government's responsibility to enforce. Milkis is
correct to locate the origin of the so-called rights revolution, which began in earnest in the mid-1950s, in Roosevelt's resort to rights rather
than party as a more solid grounding for the New Liberalism. It was, of
course, the new forces FDR recruited to the Democratic Party, especially
African Americans and women, who led this revolution. Having helped
to win a war to secure freedom, they now sought to share equally in the
benefits of that freedom, and they capitalized on Roosevelt's expanded
understanding of rights to change the nation's politics dramatically.

But FDR's reconstitution went further: it placed the presidency at
the center of American national politics as it had never been before.
The president became a "party" unto himself. The modern candidate-
centered campaigns were, in many ways, born with Roosevelt and have
simply been advanced by changes in communications technologies, especially television, and by party and election reforms of the 1970s and
1980s. This has produced not only a plebiscitary presidency but also a
plebiscitary Congress, governors, and state legislatures. It is, on the one
hand, the triumph of Progressivism and, on the other, the nightmare of
the Founders. Nor has the new politics been kind to its maker, for it has
exposed the presidency, now a much bigger political prize, to a relentless
scrutiny, partisan and professional, that subjects its occupant to criticisms
of personal as well as official activities. This has both diminished the
stature of the office and encouraged widespread public cynicism about
all aspects of public life. This was not the aim of the Progressives, the
Founders, or, for that matter, Franklin Roosevelt.

Roosevelt's successes are so many and so large that no criticism will
or should reduce his standing as one of the nation's two or three greatest presidents. But among his failures, the most notable may be one he
shares with the Progressives: the failure to build a political infrastruc-
ture sufficient to sustain the new national state. There is, however,
greater irony in Roosevelt's failure than in that of the Progressives, for
FDR was a man of politics, a politician who mastered and admired the
activity and clearly aimed in his early years in the presidency to secure

his program on a solid political foundation. That he turned away from this in his latter years in office is perhaps a testament to the constitutional difficulties in forging a national political structure of the type he sought. Much is written about the effects of the separation of powers on the American party system, but in the end it was federalism that Roosevelt could not overcome.

Notes

1. John P. Roche, "The Founding Fathers: A Reform Caucus in Action," *American Political Science Review* 55 (December 1961): 799–816.

2. Robert Penn Warren, *All the King's Men* (New York: Random House, 1946), 272–73.

3. On presidents in their times, see Stephen Skowronek, *The Politics Presidents Make—Leadership from John Adams to George Bush* (Cambridge: Harvard University Press, 1993).

4. Albert U. Romasco, *The Politics of Recovery: Roosevelt's New Deal* (New York: Oxford University Press, 1983), 5.

5. George McJimsey, *The Presidency of Franklin Delano Roosevelt* (Lawrence: University Press of Kansas, 2000), 120.

6. Jesse H. Jones with Edward Angly, *Fifty Billion Dollars* (New York: Macmillan, 1951), 260.

7. In 1908 Franklin Roosevelt told his fellow law clerks in a New York City firm that he would win election to the state legislature, then become assistant secretary of the navy, governor, and president. Ironically, his only failures as a candidate for public office were the two exceptions to this progression: his candidacy for the U.S. Senate in 1914 and for vice president in 1920.

8. In the same year, cousin Theodore made his return to New York politics by attacking Republican "bossism" and winning the GOP gubernatorial nomination for Henry L. Stimson on this platform. For an account of FDR's years in the New York senate, see James MacGregor Burns, *The Lion and the Fox* (New York: Harcourt Brace Jovanovich, 1956), chap. 2.

9. Party spoilsmen sponsored so-called ripper bills, an example of which was one that abolished the Republican-staffed Bronx Sewer Commission and gave the Democratic governor power to appoint a new one. J. Joseph Huthmacher, *Senator Robert F. Wagner and the Rise of Urban Liberalism* (New York: Atheneum, 1968), 25.

10. James Farley and Louis Howe were others whom Roosevelt came to know in his Senate years who were to play prominent roles in his subsequent political life well into his presidency.

11. Burns, *Lion and the Fox,* 41, 43.

12. See Alonzo L. Hamby, *Liberalism and Its Challengers* (New York: Oxford University Press, 1985), 18.

13. Quoted in Charles LaCerra, *Franklin Delano Roosevelt and Tammany Hall of New York* (New York: University Press of America, 1997), 61. See also Huthmacher, *Robert F. Wagner,* 35–36.

14. Roosevelt fell ill during the campaign and brought in Louis Howe, an Albany newspaperman, to run it for him, beginning a close and lifelong political association between the two men. On this relationship, see Alfred B. Rollins Jr., *Roosevelt and Howe* (New York: Alfred A. Knopf, 1962).

15. The descriptions are from Kenneth S. Davis, "No Talent for Subordination: FDR and Josephus Daniels," in *FDR and the U.S. Navy,* ed. Edward J. Marolda (New York: St. Martin's, 1998), 3, 10. A North Carolinian, editor of the *Raleigh News and Observer,* Daniels had served in the Grover Cleveland administration and was to serve in FDR's as ambassador to Mexico. Carroll Kilpatrick, in compiling an anthology of correspondence between Daniels and Roosevelt, writes that there was something of a "father-son" relationship between them. Kilpatrick, *Roosevelt and Daniels: A Friendship in Politics* (Chapel Hill: University of North Carolina Press, 1952), 5.

16. Ironically, senatorial consent for Roosevelt's appointment was given by James O'Gorman of New York, a Tammany man who had been the "compromise" choice for the U.S. Senate in 1910 following the FDR-led insurgency against the machine's first nominee. O'Gorman apparently consented to the nomination with little enthusiasm, while New York's other senator, the Republican Elihu Root, warned Daniels that Roosevelts always had to ride in the front seat.

17. Burns, *Lion and the Fox,* 50, 51.

18. Wlado Heinrichs, "FDR and the Admirals: Strategy and Statecraft," in Marolda, *FDR and the U.S. Navy,* 116, 117.

19. Hamby, *Liberalism,* 18. The one sour experience in these years was Roosevelt's unsuccessful bid in 1914 for New York's U.S. Senate seat, when he lost in the primary, rebuffed again by the forces of Tammany despite having been a reliable source of federal patronage to New York Democrats.

20. Burns, *Lion and the Fox,* 72.

21. Cousin Theodore Roosevelt had died the year before, and the Democrats apparently hoped to pick up some support from Progressive Republicans with another Roosevelt on the national ticket.

22. Charles LaCerra suggests that Roosevelt's nomination resulted from a scheme hatched by Tammany leaders to rid themselves of him. Expectations were that the Republicans would win the fall elections and as part of the national ticket FDR would go down to defeat and into oblivion. See LaCerra, *Roosevelt and Tammany Hall,* 56–58.

23. Hamby, *Liberalism,* 18.

24. On FDR as party leader, see Sean J. Savage, *Roosevelt: The Party Leader, 1932–1945* (Lexington: University of Kentucky Press, 1991).

25. Unknown to the public, Roosevelt had suffered another political "affliction" in this time, as his affair with Lucy Mercer, which threatened his marriage, had begun in 1919. From this, Eleanor emerged as less a wife and more of an in-

dependent public figure whose work with women's organizations and, later, with blue-collar workers and minorities proved a great source of political strength and ideological leverage during FDR's presidency.

26. Burns, *Lion and the Fox,* 89. Many have noted that, in the early 1920s, FDR lacked a certain maturity and personal authority. One commentator writes that Roosevelt did not have "the inner resources—the strength of character, the moral courage—that are necessary to lead a great nation in moments of desperate crisis," but adds that it was his experiences in that decade which gave him "the composure, the confidence, the energy, and the character" for the presidency. David F. Trask, "FDR at War: 1913–1921," in Marolda, *FDR and the U.S. Navy,* 16.

27. Burns notes that Roosevelt "was able again and again to use his disability as an excuse for not taking part in political activities he wished to avoid" (*Lion and the Fox,* 9). Similarly, Frank Freidel writes, "Roosevelt profited politically from being disabled during the years of Republican prosperity. . . . It removed him temporarily from contention for office and allayed the suspicions of potential rivals" (Freidel, *Franklin D. Roosevelt: A Rendezvous with Destiny* (Boston: Little, Brown, 1990), 51.

28. Freidel, *Franklin D. Roosevelt,* 49.

29. Burns, *Lion and the Fox,* 95.

30. Freidel, *Franklin D. Roosevelt,* 53. Always alert to technologies and their political uses, Roosevelt made extensive use of newsreel and film in his 1930 run for governor.

31. On Roosevelt as governor, see Kenneth S. Davis, *FDR: The New York Years, 1928–1933* (New York: Random House, 1985), and Bernard Bellush, *Franklin D. Roosevelt as Governor of New York* (New York: Columbia University Press, 1952). The latter argues that the "seeds of the New Deal" were planted by Al Smith (ibid., 282).

32. Quoted in LaCerra, *Roosevelt and Tammany Hall,* 59. LaCerra suggests that, while Roosevelt continued to work with Tammany, he also tried to curb its power. His appointment of Bronx Democratic Party boss Edward Flynn as secretary of state raised him to a position of importance equal to the new boss of Tammany, George Olvany, thus dividing control of the organization (ibid., 69–70).

33. Freidel, *Franklin D. Roosevelt,* 57.

34. Davis, *FDR,* 242.

35. See Arthur M. Schlesinger Jr., *The Crisis of the Old Order* (Boston: Houghton Mifflin, 1957), 277–80.

36. See J. Joseph Huthmacher, *Massachusetts: People and Politics* (Cambridge: Harvard University Press, 1959), esp. chap. 6, and Gerald H. Gamm, *The Making of New Deal Democrats: Voting Behavior and Realignment in Boston, 1920–1940* (Chicago: University of Chicago Press, 1986), esp. chaps. 6, 7. Al Smith captured 50.2 percent of the Massachusetts popular vote to become the first Democrat *ever* to win a majority of the Bay State vote for president.

37. Samuel Lubell, *The Future of American Politics* (Garden City: Doubleday

and Company, 1951), chap. 3. Smith lost a number of traditionally Democratic cities in the South and the Southwest, and his vote was smaller as well in cities with large Lutheran populations, reflecting their unease with his Catholicism.

38. The bosses were not the only threat to Roosevelt's nomination. Conservative leaders in the party, including its 1924 presidential nominee, John W. Davis, and national party chairman, John Raskob, sought to block his candidacy. See Davis, *FDR*, 199–200, and Schlesinger, *Crisis of the Old Order*, 282–83. FDR confronted their challenge directly, using a speech to the 1931 Governors Conference to present views on the depression and the need for government planning that drew a sharp distinction between himself and both President Herbert Hoover and the conservative Democrats. "State and national planning," Roosevelt told the governors, "is an essential to the future prosperity, happiness and very existence of the American people," Schlesinger, ibid., 281.

39. Roosevelt may have speculated briefly on reforming the Democrats as a progressive party based on an alliance of the South and the West but was reluctant to move too quickly in this regard because he thought progressives "too individualistic," "good fighters, but not good soldiers." See McJimsey, *Presidency of Franklin Delano Roosevelt*, 21.

40. On the West in Roosevelt nomination and general election campaigns, see Richard Lowitt, *The New Deal and the West* (Bloomington: Indiana University Press, 1984), chap. 1.

41. Davis, *FDR*, 306. See also Skowronek, *Politics Presidents Make*, 288–95.

42. Franklin D. Roosevelt, "Commonwealth Club Address," in *Free Government in the Making*, ed. Altheus Thomas Mason and Gordon E. Baker, 4th ed. (New York: Oxford University Press, 1985), 666–72.

43. Richard Hofstadter, *The Age of Reform: From Bryan to FDR* (New York: Alfred A. Knopf, 1959), 305.

44. McJimsey, *Presidency of Franklin Delano Roosevelt*, 131.

45. Ibid. For a brief account of the "wheeling and dealing" in the Hundred Days, see Michael Barone, *Our Country: The Shaping of America from Roosevelt to Reagan* (New York: Free Press, 1990), chap. 10. On Roosevelt's use of patronage through the Hundred Days, see E. Pendleton Herring, "American Government and Politics," *American Political Science Review* (February 1934): 65–83. James Farley had about 150,000 patronage jobs to fill in 1933, roughly one-fifth of all federal jobs. One of his tests was "FRBC," that is, "For Roosevelt before Chicago."

46. E. Pendleton Herring, *The Politics of Democracy* (New York: W. W. Norton, 1940), 218. James L. Sundquist agrees, arguing that Democratic leaders in Congress had moved toward more activist government before 1932, responding to "forces demanding change" that had captured the party by 1932 and that these forces also controlled Roosevelt after 1932. "If Roosevelt led his party and the people," Sundquist concludes, "he was also led by them" (Sundquist, *Dynamics of the Party System*, rev. ed. [Washington, D.C.: Brookings Institution, 1983], 206–7, 211).

47. Dexter Perkins, *The New Age of Franklin Roosevelt, 1932–45* (Chicago:

University of Chicago Press, 1957), 9. See too Hamby, *Liberalism and Its Challengers,* 74.

48. McJimsey, *Presidency of Franklin Delano Roosevelt,* 53.

49. Perkins, *New Age,* 35.

50. Burns, *Lion and the Fox,* 85.

51. McJimsey, *Presidency of Franklin Delano Roosevelt,* 85.

52. The New Liberalism that evolved from the early New Deal was grounded in an extension of the concept of individual rights from the traditional "negative" protections in the Bill of Rights to "positive" guarantees of government services. See John Dewey, *Individualism Old and New* (New York: Capricorn Books, 1962). In the Commonwealth Club Address, Roosevelt had spoken of the need for an economic bill of rights to supplement the constitutional guarantees, but his notion of a cooperative commonwealth took legislative precedence in the early years of the New Deal. It may have been that FDR expected his economic bill of rights would be written into the Constitution through court decisions, which to a substantial degree it was beginning in his second term. This might explain the intensity of his anger toward the Supreme Court, with its "nine old men," as well as the secrecy that attended his surprise court-packing proposal at the start of his second term. In his third term, after entry into World War II, the economic bill of rights and the four freedoms moved to center stage as justifications for the war effort as well as for domestic initiatives.

53. David M. Kennedy, *Freedom from Fear: The American People in Depression and War, 1929–1945* (New York: Oxford University Press, 1999), 297. See also Burns, *Lion and the Fox,* 217–18.

54. Ibid., 273.

55. Perkins, *New Age,* 39.

56. Burns argues that "the main reason for the new posture was the cumulative impact of the attacks from the right," adding that this was no hard ideological turn to the left but rather payback time to business and other groups that had abandoned the New Deal. See his *Lion and the Fox,* 225–26.

57. McJimsey, *Presidency of Franklin Delano Roosevelt,* 148.

58. Both Skowronek, *Politics Presidents Make,* and McJimsey, *Presidency of Franklin Delano Roosevelt,* note the effects of the growing pluralism of American life on the Roosevelt presidency, but where Skowronek finds it hemming him in, McJimsey sees Roosevelt as its master.

59. Hofstadter, *Age of Reform,* 303.

60. See Austin Ranney, *The Doctrine of Responsible Party Government* (Urbana: University of Illinois Press, 1962), esp. chap. 3.

61. Kristi Andersen, *The Creation of a Democratic Majority, 1928–1936* (Chicago: University of Chicago Press, 1979). James Sundquist argues that conversion and mobilization are present in every realignment, and he is surely correct insofar at the New Deal realignment is concerned. See Sundquist, *Dynamics of the Party System,* 37, 229–39.

62. Freidel, *Franklin D. Roosevelt,* 280–81. Previous presidents in the twentieth century had attempted to purge members of Congress with whom they did

not agree. William Howard Taft tried to defeat four Progressive Republicans and lost in each case. In contrast, Woodrow Wilson tried to defeat five conservative Democrats and succeeded in four of the cases. Taft appealed to public opinion, whereas Wilson enlisted the help of local party organizations. Like Taft, FDR sought to purge southern Democrats by appealing to public opinion but lost. In New York, like Wilson, he worked through the party organization, enlisting the help of Bronx boss Ed Flynn in the campaign against John O'Connor, and he won. See Austin Ranney and Willmoore Kendall, *Democracy and the American Party System* (New York: Harcourt, Brace and World, 1956), 286–89.

63. McJimsey notes that the "major result" of the purge campaign was "to illustrate the limits of party reform" (*Presidency of Franklin Delano Roosevelt*, 148). Freidel also observes that FDR's ability to lead his party in Congress had diminished as he had exhausted much of his store of both goodwill and patronage in his first four years (*Franklin D. Roosevelt*, 223).

64. Lubell, *Future of American Politics*, 30.

65. New York's Tammany Hall, for example, was organized shortly after the inauguration of George Washington as president and between 1846 and 1850 attracted large numbers of Irish immigrants, who rose to its leadership with the fall of Boss Tweed in the 1870s. See Daniel Patrick Moynihan, "The Irish of New York," in *American Ethnic Politics*, ed. Lawrence H. Fuchs (New York: Harper and Row, 1968), esp. 78–83.

66. William V. Shannon, *The American Irish* (New York: Macmillan, 1963), 328.

67. Edgar Litt writes that the "two most important facets of this [Irish] behavior have been sustained Democratic partisanship and strong opposition to many noneconomic 'liberal' policies, even though these policies have often been products of the Democratic party's liberal coalition." He cites also Nathan Glazer and Daniel Patrick Moynihan's observation in their *Beyond the Melting Pot* (Cambridge: MIT Press, 1963) that the Irish loyalty to the Democrats was "an ethnic and religiance alliance, as much as an economic one," to which they add, "Irish businessmen hated Roosevelt much as did other businessmen, but with the special twist that they felt it was their own political party, overcome by alien influences, that was causing the trouble." See Litt, *Beyond Pluralism: Ethnic Politics in America* (Glenview: Scott, Foresman and Company, 1970), 128. See also Gamm, *Making of New Deal Democrats*, 137.

68. Roosevelt had also appointed Senator Thomas Walsh of Montana to his first cabinet as attorney general, but Walsh died two days before FDR's inauguration.

69. Shannon, *American Irish*, 327.

70. See Lyle W. Dorsett, *Franklin D. Roosevelt and the City Bosses* (Port Washington, N.Y.: Kennikat Press, 1977).

71. Roosevelt's internationalism, seen by many Irish as too pro-British, led to some defections from the party in 1940 and 1944, as had been the case with Irish support for the Democrats and for the League of Nations after World War I.

72. On the AFL's attitude toward government and its commitment to private sector strategies in dealing with employers, see David Brian Robertson,

Capital, Labor, and State: The Battle for American Labor Markets from the Civil War to the New Deal (New York: Rowman and Littlefield, 2000), esp. chaps. 3–5.

73. Many of the New Deal programs came originally from the Congress and were embraced by Roosevelt. Even suggestions of Republican congressmen were taken by FDR and are remembered as part of his New Deal: Senator George Norris, Republican from Nebraska, was the great champion of what became the massive flood control and land use program overseen by the Tennessee Valley Authority, while Republican senator Arthur Vandenberg of Michigan initially proposed creation of the Federal Deposit Insurance Corporation as a way to secure bank accounts of Americans.

74. Milton Derber, *Labor and the New Deal* (Madison: University of Wisconsin Press, 1957), 3.

75. Jong Oh Ra, *Labor at the Polls* (Amherst: University of Massachusetts Press, 1978), 21.

76. Craft or trade unionists—carpenters, plumbers, electricians, and so on—had a skill to sell, whereas industrial unionists did not. Historically, this had led the former to associate themselves with the entrepreneurial and competitive tradition of small businesspeople and to seek private labor market, not governmental, solutions for their working conditions.

77. The first political action committee (PAC) in American politics was the CIO-PAC, established in the late 1930s. Ironically, it was in an effort to secure the legality of union PACs in the reforms of the Federal Election Campaign Acts, enacted after Watergate in the mid-1970s, that language was adopted which opened the legal door to corporate PACs as well.

78. See McJimsey, *Presidency of Franklin Delano Roosevelt,* chap. 7.

79. Freidel, *Franklin D. Roosevelt,* 49.

80. Perkins, *New Age,* 310.

81. Freidel, *Franklin D. Roosevelt,* 50.

82. Perkins, *New Age,* 136, 121.

83. See Robert A. Caro, *The Years of Lyndon Johnson: The Path to Power* (New York: Alfred A. Knopf, 1982), 504–11.

84. The intensity of popular support for Roosevelt was evident in 1936 when the *Baltimore Sun,* traditionally a Democratic newspaper, urged its readers not to reelect FDR. It aroused "a storm of protest," Jo Ann Argersinger writes, "including an unprecedented number of letters to the editor and citywide boycotts of the paper." Petitions of protest were circulated accusing the *Sun* of having "gone Benedict Arnold" and of having a "Herbert Hoover type of mind." See Argersinger, *Toward a New Deal in Baltimore* (Chapel Hill: University of North Carolina Press, 1988), 187–88.

85. The nation's intellectual community was another group that rallied to support the New Deal. Far fewer in number than members of unions or the unorganized poor, the nation's intellectuals, from universities, law, and journalism, were of greater significance in the leadership of the New Deal, staffing its new agencies of governance and publicizing its achievements in the news media.

86. The pollster Samuel Lubell is quoted by Nancy Weiss as reporting that

blacks "defected in smaller numbers in the 1932 election than did any other group of Republican voters." See Weiss, *Farewell to the Party of Lincoln* (Princeton: Princeton University Press, 1989), 29.

87. Antilynching legislation also continued to be bottled up in the Congress. Roosevelt quite frankly did not want to challenge southern Democrats who chaired major committees, especially in the Senate, where the filibuster was an additional deterrent.

88. Weiss, *Farewell to the Party of Lincoln,* 136.

89. Joseph P. Lash, *Dealers and Dreamers* (New York: Doubleday, 1988), 488. The WPA was the third largest employer of African Americans in the nation. See McJimsey, *Presidency of Franklin Delano Roosevelt,* 103.

90. Mrs. Roosevelt drew national attention to the cause of racial justice when she resigned her membership in the Daughters of the American Revolution in 1939 when the organization denied the use of its hall to black singer Marian Anderson. She helped to arrange and attended Anderson's subsequent performance at the Lincoln Memorial.

91. The extent of the Democratic campaign for black support in 1936 is detailed by Weiss in *Farewell to the Party of Lincoln,* 192–205.

92. Weiss writes: "Despite the fact that Roosevelt had done very little for blacks as a racial minority, he had managed to convey to them that they counted and belonged. In the light of inattention from previous administrations, even the limited racial recognition of the New Deal seemed to many black Americans to be a token of hope" (ibid., 210–11). The political import of relief is evident in the fact that 80 percent of WPA workers voted Democratic in 1936, and the implication of this for the black vote is apparent in the fact that the WPA was the third largest employer of African Americans (McJimsey, *Presidency of Franklin Delano Roosevelt,* 103, 105).

93. Ralph Goldman, *Search for Consensus: The Story of the Democratic Party* (Philadelphia: Temple University Press, 1979), 184.

94. See Lawrence H. Fuchs, "American Jews and the Presidential Vote," in *American Ethnic Politics,* ed. Fuchs (New York: Harper and Row, 1968), 50–76.

95. See Gamm, *Making of New Deal Democrats,* chap. 2.

96. While Franklin Roosevelt drew lessons in political leadership and public policy from the earlier reformist period, he did not draw great numbers of old Progressives into its ranks, save those associated with the Democrat Woodrow Wilson's New Freedom administration. Some younger, second-generation Republican Progressives, such as Harold Ickes, Henry Wallace, and Charles Merriam, found work in the New Deal, while some older Republican Progressive warhorses in Congress, George Norris and Robert La Follette among them, backed many of Roosevelt's initiatives, but they were the exceptions and not the rule. See Otis L. Graham Jr., *An Encore for Reform: The Old Progressives and the New Deal* (New York: Oxford University Press, 1967).

97. Indeed, the Progressive Era is commonly associated with those of Jacksonian democracy in the 1820s and 1830s and participatory democracy in the 1960s and 1970s as distinguished from other realigning periods, such as the

New Deal, the Civil War, and the Jeffersonian era. Samuel Huntington depicts the former as "creedal passion periods" in which reforms sought to bring political institutions into greater harmony with the ideals upon which the nation was founded. See Huntington, *American Politics and the Promise of Democracy* (Cambridge: Harvard University Press, 1981). For similar treatments that deal with party reforms, see Austin Ranney, *Curing the Mischiefs of Faction* (Berkeley: University of California Press, 1975), and James Ceaser, *Presidential Selection* (Princeton: Princeton University Press, 1979).

98. See Sidney M. Milkis, *The President and the Parties: Transformation of the American Party System since the New Deal* (New York: Oxford University Press, 1993).

99. Benjamin Ginsberg and Martin Shefter argue that bureaucracy and the courts have largely displaced elections as the arenas of political combat in America. See Ginsberg and Shefter, *Politics by Other Means* (New York: Basic, 1990). On the impoverishing effects of a rights-based politics on deliberative institutions and processes, see Mary Ann Glendon, *Rights Talk* (New York: Free Press, 1991).

100. Indeed, the most significant party reform in the New Deal years was the 1936 repeal of the Democrats' two-thirds rule, which made it impossible ever again for a candidate favored by a majority of the delegates to be denied the party's nomination and thereby nationalized the party's presidential selection process.

101. The restoration of the Old Guard Republicans in the 1920s did bring to power a new and tougher business conservatism with little sympathy for unions and also a party with less of a nationalist outlook on politics than in the past, which provided the immediate ideological backdrop for FDR's campaign to convert the Democrats to liberalism. See John Gerring, *Party Ideologies in America, 1828–1996* (New York: Cambridge University Press, 1998), esp. chap. 4.

102. On the rise of Republicanism in the South, see Alexander P. Lamis, *The Two-Party South* (New York: Oxford University Press, 1984). On the new role of the South in presidential politics, see Earl Black and Merle Black, *The Vital South* (Cambridge: Harvard University Press, 1992).

103. The census defines the Northeast as New England plus New York; the Mideast as Delaware, Maryland, New Jersey, Pennsylvania, West Virginia, and the District of Columbia; and the Midwest as Illinois, Indiana, Michigan, Minnesota, Missouri, and Ohio. Most of the gains in electoral votes are concentrated in three states: California, Florida, and Texas. The border states and Deep South have actually lost electoral votes since 1932, casting 19.3 percent of the total then and 18.3 percent in 1992.

104. The electoral vote of Texas and Florida has grown significantly since World War II, but that of the old South—Dixie and the border states—has not changed.

105. Behind the decline of both the industrial states and the older cities is the changed character of the economy. As jobs moved away from the mass production industries and into the service and professional sectors, membership in

the old industrial unions dropped sharply and, with it, their muscle in national politics. Today, white-collar unions of teachers and service workers unions and government employees unions rival the craft and industrial unions as the voice of labor, and they often speak a language different from their older brethren.

106. Roper poll, August 1938 (Roper Center, University of Connecticut, Storrs, Conn.). Text of question: "In a recent fireside talk, President Roosevelt proposed that old party lines be disregarded and that the liberals of all parties unite to support liberal candidates for Congress. Do you think this is a good or bad idea?" Good, 47 percent; bad, 24 percent; don't know, 29 percent. Second question: "Do you think this is likely to happen?" Yes, 30 percent; no, 34 percent; don't know, 35 percent. After the fall election, however, Americans thought the failure of the purge campaign was good. Roper poll, November 1938. Text of question: "Do you think it was a good thing or a bad thing that certain Senators who were recently opposed by President Roosevelt in his so-called purge attempt were renominated?" Good thing, 46 percent; bad thing, 11 percent; don't know or (volunteered) don't care, 8 percent.

107. Quoted in Bernard Sternsher, *Rexford Tugwell and the New Deal* (New Brunswick: Rutgers University Press, 1964), 121.

Politicized Unions and the New Deal Model

Labor, Business, and Taft-Hartley

Nelson Lichtenstein

The "labor question" stood at the heart of New Deal politics. But New Deal politics also defined what would come to constitute the scope and meaning of that social issue. During the first third of the twentieth century, American progressivism gave a twofold layering to the relationship between labor and capital. First, and most pervasive, the laborite reform of industrial capitalism required the democratization of work and authority in shop, office, mine, and farm. Here New Dealers recast the discourse generated by decades of social debate, both reformist and revolutionary, which sought to bring "industrial democracy" to an abode heretofore governed by the ancient laws of property, as well as the ethnicized social structures of a world deeply shaped by authority, deference, and cultural tradition.

The 1935 Wagner Act was a radical legislative initiative because it sought to democratize the world of work in order to counterbalance the "industrial autocracy" that had been the preoccupation of social reformers since the 1880s. Collective bargaining, wrote Harvard's Sumner Slichter, the interwar dean of American labor economists, is a method of "introducing civil rights into industry, that is, of requiring that management be conducted by rule rather than by arbitrary decision."[1] To Slichter and even more so to a new generation of laborite New Dealers, "industrial jurisprudence" stood at the heart of a democratic system of work site constitutionalism. "Before organization came into the plant, foremen were little tin gods in their own departments," declared a 1941 United Automobile Workers (UAW) shop steward's handbook. "With the coming of the union, the foreman finds his whole world turned upside down. His small time dictatorship has been overthrown, and he must be adjusted to a democratic system of shop government."[2]

But the reconfiguration of the labor question was about more than shop floor governance, and this brings us to the second great reform generated by the New Deal. The Wagner Act was designed not only to bring industrial democracy to the factory but also, through a system of economic empowerment, to raise the living standards and purchasing power of the working class as a whole. Robert Wagner, Leon Keyserling, Gardner Means, Paul Douglas, and other "underconsumption" theorists wanted a broad, upward shift in working-class purchasing power, a Keynesian prescription that made the interests of the new unions, the only prospective institution then capable of policing industry-wide wage standards, largely synonymous with those of the nation as a whole.[3]

We have commonly come to think of this project as entailing a system of collective bargaining in which a body of workers organize a trade union, which in turn bargains with an employer or group of employers to raise workers' wages and resolve other grievances. Such was the ostensible ideology and purpose of the Wagner Act itself. But such a voluntary, privatized system of collective bargaining never existed during the first decade after the passage of that law. Indeed, from 1933 until 1947, collective bargaining was a highly politicized process that routinely put unionists, capitalists, and government labor relations experts in the Oval Office, the halls of Congress, and the chambers of the Supreme Court. Not only did the state provide material aid in helping workers organize themselves against the wishes of most private employers, but equally important, the government played a decisive role in the outcome of the bargaining that took place between the parties in every crisis that put the relationship between workers and capitalists in the headlines during the years that followed.[4]

As Sidney Hillman, founder of the political action committee (PAC) of the Congress of Industrial Organizations (CIO), put it in 1943, American workers "can no longer work out even their most immediate day-to-day problems through negotiations with their employers and the terms of their collective agreements. Their wages, hours, and working conditions have become increasingly dependent upon policies adopted by Congress and the National Administration."[5]

Employers hated this politicized system of labor relations. In 1947 they sought to end it—or at the very least to limit its scope and reduce its potency—with a thorough revision of the Wagner-era labor law. In this essay I explore their worldview in order to understand how advocates of the Taft-Hartley Act saw the relationship between the state, the unions, and the labor question at a moment when the New Deal system was still very much in ascendance. I focus here on the opponents of that system, not only because they were the eventual winners, but also because the story of New Deal–era class relations is one that pivots on the extent to which employer groups could reprivatize industrial relations, thus taking the "labor question" out of the realm of politics and returning it to the far more favorable terrain of personnel management, grievance arbitration, "free" collective bargaining, and the world of the firm-centered welfare state.

The Contested Meaning of Taft-Hartley

The 1947 Taft-Hartley Act was, in Daniel Bell's apt phrase, "essentially a definition of power."[6] But as pathologists of the New Deal's aging and death, we might ask: Did the Taft-Hartley law simply ratify an emerging industrial orthodoxy, or did it inaugurate a new era of class relations that was qualitatively different from that which had gone before? Most historians and legal scholars have tended toward the view that Taft-Hartley merely codified a preexisting set of relationships. These commentators describe a pluralist system of industrial relations that was forged in the era after 1938 when collective bargaining became increasingly routinized and when, from both a political and an ideological perspective, the opportunities available to the labor movement and its liberal allies were increasingly constrained.

Such a proposition holds considerable weight, and not only among those consensus-era academics and industrial relations practitioners who emphasized the growth and stability of the unions in the decade or so after the law's passage. Writing in the late 1950s, Joseph Shister, one of the nation's most prominent industrial relations scholars, concluded that "ten years of experience under the Taft-Hartley Act have made one point crystal clear: it is certainly not a 'Slave Labor Law' and it has certainly not destroyed trade unionism and collective bargaining." By 1958 union membership has "risen by over three million—which is hardly symptomatic of a labor movement in the process of disintegration."[7] His judgment was soon endorsed by a generation of pluralists, including Derek Bok and David Feller, who thought the Taft-Hartley reform of the Wagner Act did little to disestablish a large and durable union presence within the American polity.[8]

Scholars influenced by the late New Left have also tended to downplay the import of Taft-Hartley, if only because they saw the Wagner Act itself as inherently statist. Thus Christopher Tomlins asserted that "the Taft-Hartley Act . . . proved much less of a break with the past than has usually been assumed." Writing in 1985, he argues that while the Republican-dominated Congress did seek "to limit the influence of entrenched labor organizations . . . the ambitions of some of its proponents to go further than this and overthrow the model of labor relations established in the United States after 1940 remained unfulfilled."[9] Even George Lipsitz, one of the most imaginative of the postmodern, post–New Left historians, thought that Senator Robert Taft's commitment to a system of collective bargaining, enshrined in the final version of the law, "demonstrated the essentially moderate nature of the bill, its congruence with prior legislation, and the limited nature of the conservative critique."[10] More recently, the political scientist David Plotke asserted that "Taft-Hartley did not lead to a sweeping reduction in union power." Indeed, Plotke argues that the 1947 law was "distinctively favorable to labor, given the long-standing resistance of business to unions."[11]

But a number of questions are left begging. First, what precisely was the "model of labor relations" that the Taft-Hartley Act sought to reform? Here we must distinguish between a legal, administrative framework put forward under the Wagner Act and modified over time by the courts, the War Labor Board, and the National Labor Relations Board, and the actual model of highly politicized union growth and economic bargaining that emerged from twelve years of ideological combat, political organization, state building, and union growth.

I contend that the proponents of the Taft-Hartley Act sought far more than the mere reform of the labor law; instead, their effort was part of a larger contestation in which the entire structure of the political economy and the postwar political culture had been put into play. Taft-

Hartley advocates saw the law as but a proxy for a much larger social and political project whose import extended well beyond the recalibration of the "collective bargaining" mechanism. Indeed, the Taft-Hartley law stands like a fulcrum on which the entire New Deal order teetered. Before 1947 it was possible to imagine a continuing expansion and vitalization of the New Deal impulse. After that date, however, labor and the Left were forced into an increasingly defensive posture.

The Specter of "Industrial Slavery"

One way to approach the meaning of Taft-Hartley is to consider the language by which its contemporary proponents and detractors evaluated its consequences. If the act proved so moderate and inconsequential, then why did such passionate rhetoric accompany the legislative battle of 1947? Why did President Truman expend such political capital in a vain effort to veto the law and then make its reform, if not its outright repeal, the single most important domestic plank in his 1948 election campaign? The language of politics has a meaning and a weight that merits analysis on its own terms. Indeed, the half-century-old rhetoric still blisters with a passion that cannot be ignored: "slavery," "servitude," "freedom," "liberty," and "redemption" were the words both opponents and supporters of the Taft-Hartley Act hurled at each other.[12]

Labor's denunciation of the law as one of "slave labor" is well remembered. After the Congress passed the act in May 1947 but before enactment over President Truman's veto, CIO president Philip Murray glimpsed an abyss of totalitarian repression unfolding before the nation. "Where in the name of God is our country going?" he asked his colleagues on the CIO executive board. "You have read these stories of what is happening in Europe," he continued. "I venture to the assertion that if that bill becomes law, in the course of time under its operation . . . the trends are and the powers have so decreed, that we should have a type of Fascist, capitalistic control over the lives of men, women, and children."[13] As a devout Roman Catholic, Murray declared the law "conceived in sin."[14] Meanwhile, CIO counsel Lee Pressman, a secular Jew of left-wing sympathies, offered his own ethical judgment: "When you think of it merely as a combination of individual provisions, you are losing entirely the full impact of the program, the sinister conspiracy that has been hatched." In giant rallies of protest and petition, both the

American Federation of Labor (AFL) and the CIO unfurled huge ban-
ners denouncing Taft-Hartley as a "Slave-Labor Law."[15]

Labor's charge that Taft-Hartley was a "slave labor" statute raised an
immediate outcry from the law's proponents. In response, George
Meany, then secretary-treasurer of the AFL, welcomed the opportunity
to defend the proposition that the new law was a step toward involun-
tary servitude. In a speech delivered a few months after its passage,
Meany declared that Taft-Hartley "completely demolishes the natural,
organic development which is collective bargaining, and substitutes,
instead, what at best is paternalistic statism, and at worst, out and out
dictatorship." Meany went out of his way to assert that Taft-Hartley
amounted to a kind of industrial slavery, which he evaluated according
to the democratic promise of the 1914 Clayton Act. To Meany, that law
had declared that "the labor of a human being is not an article or commodity of commerce." In contrast, Meany contended that the Taft-
Hartley Act's restrictions on trade union use of the boycott, as well as its
more general efforts to limit the spread of unionization, made more difficult the equalization of wages and conditions among firms that competed with each other within the same industry. Labor costs would
therefore be put back into play, pitting worker against worker in a downward spiral that would transform human labor into a mere commodity
and workers into chattel. Quoting the great anti-injunction jurists,
Oliver Wendell Holmes and Louis Brandeis, Meany argued that any governmental restrictions upon the right to refuse work "reminds one of in-
voluntary servitude."[16]

Employer and conservative rhetoric was equally apocalyptic. Virtually
all corporate executives argued for a reform of the Wagner Act, not to
coolly rebalance the industrial scales but to stave off what they saw as a
bureaucratic, near totalitarian, collectivist disaster. Thus did Eugene E.
Wilson, the vice-chairman of United Aircraft Corporation, warn that unless the power of a laborite New Deal was stanched, "Christian freedom
will give way to atheistic slavery, cooperation to compulsion, hope to
fear, equality of opportunity to privilege, and the dead hand of bureaucracy will close the throttle on progress."[17]

The House Committee that reported a Taft-Hartley revision in the
spring of 1947 used rhetoric of a similar sort. The draconian reform of
the labor law was essential because the unamended Wagner Act had created a situation whereby "the American working man has been deprived

of his dignity as an individual. He has been cajoled, coerced, intimi-
dated. . . . His whole economic life has been subject to the complete
domination and control of unregulated monopolists. He has on many
occasions had to pay them tribute to get a job. . . . In short, his mind, his
soul, and his very life have been subject to a tyranny more despotic than
one could think possible in a free country."[18]

Such sentiments were not simply those of "brass hat" industrialists or
congressional reactionaries but also resonated widely among the literate
public. The *Saturday Evening Post* published essays that routinely turned
union leaders into "bosses," "czars," "barons," "dictators," and "lords,"
while relegating the rank and file to the status of "serfs" and "slaves."[19]
And F. A. Hayek's *Road to Serfdom*, which the University of Chicago
first published as an academic tome in 1944, was selling hundreds of
thousands of copies each year by the end of the decade.[20]

Why did American managers, executives, and business-oriented conservatives feel so oppressed by the New Deal and the Wagner Act at a
moment when in every other industrialized democracy, social and political structures were being put in place which institutionalized a postwar
settlement characterized by corporatist bargaining structures, the
growth of trade unions, and an expansion of the welfare state? When the
Taft-Hartley Act was passed in June 1947, the Labour Government in
Great Britain was preparing to nationalize the coal and steel industries,
the Scandinavians were well on their incremental way toward the further
consolidation of tripartitism, and the Western-zone Germans, now re-
covering from the shock and disorganization of total defeat, were beginning to discuss a model of industry governance which put the idea of
codetermination at its ideological and industrial center.[21]

In the United States many trade unionists sought to put such models
on the postwar agenda, but American industrialists repudiated these visions as either Stalinism or servitude. These business executives saw the
emergence of such a corporatist, regulatory state, backed by a powerful
labor movement, as the essence of "creeping socialism." "Americans
have failed to comprehend the magnitude of the challenge to free enterprise," declared Chamber of Commerce president William Jackson in
a Milwaukee speech in January 1947. "Despite the extent of nationalization in England and France, in Argentina and Spain and the expanding domain of Soviet Communism, we tend to console ourselves with
the thought that it can't happen here."[22]

American Exceptionalism, Management Style

Since the early years of this century, scholars and journalists have devoted much ink to explain why the American working class is "exceptional" when compared with the ostensibly more radical and class-conscious workers of Europe and Latin America. But as the remarks of Jackson and other business executives illustrate, the most "exceptional" element in the American system of labor-capital relations is the hostility managers have shown toward both the regulatory state and virtually all systems of worker representation. Thus, business support for the National Recovery Administration's system of state-supervised cartelization collapsed by 1935, even before the Supreme Court declared such a regulatory scheme unconstitutional. And despite much wishful historiography, no well-organized "corporate liberal" cohort of enlightened managers supported either the Wagner Act or the Social Security Act, the two linchpins of New Deal social reform.[23]

Social scientists have devoted much effort to categorization of business sentiment in terms of the labor policy pursued by each firm. As early as 1948 C. Wright Mills divided conservative business sentiment along an axis that counterpoised an antiunion, entrepreneurial set of "practical conservatives" from their oligopolistically organized, internationally minded, "sophisticated" brethren. Since then, historians and political economists have merely refined Mills's typology. In the late 1960s scholars identified a set of New Deal–era "corporate liberal" businessmen who advocated unionism as a stabilizing feature of the industrial landscape. Still later some historians emphasized the importance of the business "realists" who, during the 1940s, came to accept a well-constrained collective bargaining regime. Meanwhile, many scholars have counterposed both the corporate liberals and the realists to the entrepreneurial reactionaries of the South and the West who have uncategorically rejected collective bargaining.[24]

But this typology collapses when it comes to Taft-Hartley. During the immediate postwar era, the business community found no room for defenders of an unamended Wagner Act. The voice of the corporate liberals, never very loud in any event, was almost entirely absent, while the so-called realists in auto, steel and other sectors of unionized manufacturing were often among the most ideologically driven of all those calling for a revision of the Wagner Act. They demanded not only sharp curbs on union political activism but also the destruction of supervisory unionism, the elimination of the union shop, and the abolition of industry-wide bargaining. Thus even Averell Harriman, FDR's former secretary of commerce and one of the New Deal's "tame" millionaires, denounced John L. Lewis as a "labor boss" repugnant even to the most liberal elements of the business community. "Labor power has grown to the point where we find one man defying the government and recklessly tearing down the life of his nation," Harriman told a 1946 National Association of Manufacturers convention, thus affirming the conventional business wisdom of the day.[25]

Business hostility to trade unionism and to the state structures that supported it had three historic sources. The first arose out of a profound commitment to what most in business saw as their historic, inherent managerial prerogatives. The second reflected the relatively decentralized, hypercompetitive structure of many key industries, and the third arose out of the economic transformations generated by fifteen years of depression and war.

The tradition of American management was one of self-confidence and autonomy. In sharp contrast to their counterparts in Britain or Germany, American capitalists had presided over economic institutions that were of both continental scope and vast revenue long before the rise of a powerful state or the emergence of overt class politics. In every other industrializing nation, a strong bureaucratic state either preceded or emerged simultaneously with that of the multidivisional firm, but this pattern was inverted in the United States. Although the government famously aided railroad development in the nineteenth century, such assistance and regulation proved the exception rather than the rule when it came to the great industries of the second industrial revolution: steel, chemicals, automobiles, rubber, food processing, chain stores, and movies. Thus, throughout the era of U.S. industrialization, from the Civil War to the 1920s, the most critical decisions about the direction of American economic development were in private hands.[26]

This legacy made business managers hugely jealous of their prerogatives when they confronted both the new unionism and the New Deal. Indeed, American executives first began to use the term "free enterprise" to describe the American capitalist system in the 1930s. Such nomenclature reflected an effort, however crudely put, to distinguish U.S. conditions from those of Europe, where the state, the gentry, and the unions constrained entrepreneurial activity and regulated the labor market. Moreover, such a definition of U.S. capitalism highlights the desperate sense of individual autonomy America's captains of industry sought to rescue from both the New Deal and the new unions. To them, this dual threat represented a Europeanized collectivism, because even the limited constraints imposed by America's mixed social welfare regime seemed radical. As Alfred Sloan of General Motors analogized at the end of World War II: "It took fourteen years to rid this country of prohibition. It is going to take a good while to rid the country of the New Deal, but sooner or later the ax falls and we get a change."[27]

In addition, American business never enjoyed a successful system of self-regularization or cartelization, often characteristic of Europe and the Far East. The American market was of continental magnitude and regional variation. Despite much talk of giant trusts and industrial oligarchy, the U.S. system was one of "disorganizational synthesis," a revealing phrase coined by the historian Colin Gordon. Ironically, the historic conservatism of the American labor movement, which celebrated firm-centered bargaining and eschewed independent political action, exacerbated this competitive disorder. Thus American employers never came to see a system of collective bargaining as a "lesser evil" when compared with Continental socialism or British labor politics. Indeed, American capitalists saw even the most narrowly focused brand of unionism as highly detrimental to their "prerogatives" because the shop-centered thrust of such unionism ensured that labor costs were unlikely to be distributed evenly among competitors. In France, Germany, and Great Britain, industrial cartels and associations arose naturally out of the insularity and class cohesion of their leading industrialists. But in the United States, the regional competitiveness endemic to the industrial archipelago gave ambitious entrepreneurs the opportunity to undercut trustification and managerial cooperation. Thus, in the United States the very disorganization of the capitalists put a premium on keeping labor costs flexible, production techniques plastic, and unions weak.[28]

Finally, nearly a generation of depression and war had forced Americans to confront the transition of economic power from small, local interests to private and public bureaucracies of national scope. New Deal statism and union egalitarianism were tied to White House intellectuals and university planners whose interests lay with urban machines, ethnic minorities, organized labor, and northern blacks. Meanwhile, almost a third of a million small business firms folded during World War II, more than 10 percent of all those existing at the end of the 1930s. Manufacturing companies with fewer than one hundred workers saw their proportion of total output drop from more than a quarter to less than a fifth. The loss of autonomy particularly threatened small-town bankers, merchants, manufacturers, and others in the "old" middle class. Thus trade union leaders were routinely denominated as "union bosses" and "labor skates" because their power was a fundamentally illegitimate transgression against the decentralized producer republic that still retained a powerful imaginative grasp on the minds of so many entrepreneurs and professionals whose social roots lay with the Protestant bourgeoisie. For these citizens and others, an intrusive federal government symbolized the daily threat to individual and traditional values.[29]

Given these ideological propensities and structural imperatives, we can understand the horror with which the vast bulk of American business confronted the New Deal and its allies within the suddenly powerful industrial unions. During the years after 1933, the social and organizational ingredients for a corporatist reconstruction of U.S. capitalism may well have been in place. American trade unionism reached European levels of density, labor leaders were ushered into the White House for top-level conferences with their industrial counterparts, and unionism had a real impact on the political consciousness of 35 percent of the entire American electorate.

Politicized Bargaining and U.S. Corporatism

The economic power wielded by American trade unions was by its very nature political power, for the New Deal had thoroughly politicized all relations between the union movement, the business community, and the state. The New Deal differed from previous eras of state activism not only because of the relatively more favorable political and legislative environment it created for organized labor but also, perhaps even more importantly, because the Roosevelt government provided a set of semipermanent political structures within which vital economic issues were negotiated between unions and employers. Capitalism seemed both unstable and parochial, so it needed guidance from the state, whatever the immediate interests of individual entrepreneurs and managers.[30]

Thus from 1933, when the new Roosevelt administration pulled together the National Recovery Administration (NRA), until 1946, when the consumer/populist Office of Price Administration (OPA) finally collapsed, all the key bargains in all the principal U.S. industries were ultimately determined by a set of state institutions that collated wages, prices, profits, and union status. Although neither the legal nor the administrative structures of the American state could long sustain the NRA's grand corporativist ambitions, the Blue Eagle had a lasting impact. As Ellis Hawley and Colin Gordon have shown, labor, management, and the state sought to reproduce key elements of the NRA social bargain in several industries, especially those characterized by intense competition and strong trade unions. The United Mine Workers pushed Congress to enact the Guffey Coal Act to replace the NRA codes, the teamsters were instrumental in framing the new Motor Carrier Act that ended wage chiseling, while the newly powerful airline pilots helped make the Civil Aeronautics Board a reality in 1938.[31]

The 1938 Fair Labor Standards Act was a far weaker statute than Sidney Hillman would have wished, but like the NRA industry codes, it sought to socialize—make society-wide—the key wage and hour bargains negotiated by the unions, chiefly in the needle trades and textiles, and thereby extend them to those labor-intensive, low-wage sectors of the economy where collective bargaining had not established even a tentative foothold. Moreover, the politicization of collective bargaining took root even among the mass production oligopolies where management remained hostile to any sort of state regulation of the labor question. Thus Michigan's New Deal governor, Frank Murphy, played a crucial role in the final stages of the General Motors sit-down strike.[32] And in the steel industry, White House intervention was taken for granted in every set of negotiations after the CIO won recognition from U.S. Steel and the other big producers. Beginning in 1941, the price of steel and the rate of pay enjoyed by the workers in that industry was set not at a Pittsburgh bargaining table but in a Washington office hosted by government policymakers. Indeed, the successive appearances of a powerful set of New Deal regulatory agencies—seemed to signal that, in the future as in the past, the fate of organized labor and, by extension, the fortunes of capital would be determined as much by a process of politicized bargaining in Washington as by the give-and-take of contract collective bargaining.[33]

As a result the United States seemed to advance toward the kind of labor-backed corporatism that would later characterize social policy in northern Europe and Scandinavia. Corporatism of this sort called for government agencies, composed of capital, labor, and "public" representatives, to substitute their decisions for the "chaos" of the market. In this system highly organized social "blocs" struck periodic economic bargains through a process of political negotiation, usually industry-specific but in some extraordinary instances society-wide. Corporatism of this sort placed capital-labor relations within a highly centralized context, where representatives of the contending "peak" organizations bargained politically for their respective constituencies.[34] In the New Deal–era United States, such corporatist arrangements, involving the Business Advisory Council, the National Association of Manufacturers, the AFL, and the CIO, as well as key government policymakers, became increasingly formalized. It was therefore almost politics as usual when, in November 1945, President Truman convened a tripartite conclave of all the major labor and business organizations to set postwar wage policy and determine the power and prerogatives of unions and management in the postwar era.[35]

Corporatist policymaking reached its apogee during World War II. Although the prestige and power of big business grew during that conflict, the politicization of U.S. labor relations proved decisive in raising the living standards of millions of workers, as well as adding to the organizational power of the union movement. The War Labor Board (WLB), for example, socialized much of the trade union movement's prewar agenda, thus making such elements of the wage bargain as seniority, grievance systems, vacation pay, night-shift supplements, sick leave, and paid meal times standard "entitlements" for an increasingly large section of the working class. Likewise, the government-enforced World War II wage formulas, although bitterly resisted by the more highly paid and well-organized sections of the working class, had enough loopholes and special dispensations to enable low-paid workers in labor-short industries to bring their wages closer to the national average. Black wages rose twice as rapidly as white under this regime, and weekly earnings in cotton textiles and in retail trade increased about 50 percent faster than in such high-wage industries as steel and automobiles.[36] By the onset of postwar reconversion, WLB wage policy was explicitly egalitarian. "It is not desirable to increase hourly earning in each industry in accordance with the rise of productivity in that industry," declared a July 1945 memorandum. "The proper goal of policy is to increase hourly earnings generally in proportion to the average increase of productivity in the economy *as a whole*."[37]

Politicized bargaining of this sort demanded of the trade unions an organic amalgamation of strike action, organizing activity, and political mobilization. Thus, the new unions born in the 1930s represented a qualitative break with both the "job conscious" unionism celebrated by Selig Perlman and the shop syndicalism associated with the Industrial Workers of the World. Although radical intellectuals such as Daniel Bell and Dwight Macdonald now criticized the bureaucratization and statification of the industrial unions, American business saw this same growth of labor power, worker solidarity, and state capacity as a potent threat. With all wartime work disputes routinely handled by a set of powerful public bodies, millions of workers understood that their resistance to management authority had attained a kind of social legitimacy. By the end of the war, business was desperate to reprivatize the relationship between management and labor by eviscerating the sanctions that a wartime government had tacitly conferred on worker activism and union political ambitions.[38]

Postwar Conflict

Two auto industry conflicts in the months following the collapse of Japan helped crystallize a managerial determination to transform the legal and political framework through which they battled their class adversaries. In August 1945 a two-month strike erupted at the Kelsey-Hayes Wheel Corporation, which supplied brake shoes and other parts to Ford and Chrysler. Now long forgotten, this strike of forty-five hundred Detroit workers encapsulated all that managers thought had gone wrong in the New Deal system of labor relations. By 1945 a social revolution had transformed Kelsey's shop practice and workplace culture as a cohort of second-generation immigrants and African American migrants achieved power within the factory.[39]

No formal contract existed between the union and Kelsey management, but these workers defended their prerogatives in a near constant series of battles with shop supervisors. During the war there had been some fifty-one wildcat walkouts, many directed against foremen who failed to respect the authority wielded by union stewards. "We made broad concessions for labor peace," Kelsey president George Kennedy told the House committee drafting the Taft-Hartley Act, "but we did not get peace."[40] Although the UAW opposed such unsanctioned walkouts, the union's defense of a strong shop stewards system, combined with a combative ideology, nevertheless legitimated such militancy. Shop militants ridiculed, shunned, and sometimes forced uncooperative foremen out of the factory. Indeed, Kelsey foremen were incapable of carrying out the disciplinary tasks mandated by top management, and in response an overwhelming majority joined an independent supervisory union, the Foreman's Association of America (FAA), whose membership spread like wildfire throughout heavy industry at the end of World War II.[41]

The Kelsey strike sought the reinstatement of key shop leaders fired by Kennedy, whose desperate attempt to win back a measure of shop discipline had kept the Kelsey factory in a high state of tension for nearly six months. Lasting for forty-five days, the Kelsey strikers defied the War Labor Board, top UAW officers, company management, the governor of Michigan, and the Detroit police. Halting vital auto parts production, the strike nearly closed Ford's giant River Rouge complex and put on layoff almost one hundred thousand workers. The amazing solidarity exhibited by these workers made the Kelsey stoppage front page news for more than a month, foreshadowing the giant industry-wide wage strikes that would soon put millions of workers on the picket line and shut down entire cities in a wave of general strikes later in 1946 and 1947.[42]

An account of the strike occupied seventy-five pages in the hearings conducted by a House of Representatives committee in early 1947. "The outstanding weakness in the labor field today is the lack of union responsibility and the complete lack of any laws compelling or even encouraging responsibility," George Kennedy told the committee that would help write the Taft-Hartley Act. "Severe penalties, such as loss of bargaining rights by the union, loss of jobs by the men and fines should be imposed for illegal strikes."[43]

Working-class insurgency from below was soon matched by labor's strategic offensive from above. During the fall and winter of 1945–46 the UAW struck General Motors (GM) for 113 days. Led by Walter Reuther, the union sought a 30 percent increase in wages without a rise in the cost of cars. GM denounced the demand as un-American and socialist, but in reality Reuther was merely seeking to put some backbone into the Truman administration's effort to sustain price controls and working-class living standards during the crucial demobilization era. As Reuther put it, "The fight of the General Motors workers is a fight to save truly-free enterprise from death at the hands of its self-appointed champions."[44]

The General Motors response was predictable but also indicative of the stakes, as seen from the highest levels of corporate power: "America is at the crossroads! It must preserve the freedom of each unit of American business to determine its own destiny. . . . The UAW-CIO is reaching for power. . . . It leads surely toward the day when union bosses . . . will seek to tell us what we can make, when we can make it, where we can make it, and how much we can charge."[45] George Romney of the Automobile Manufacturers' Association exaggerated but slightly when he personalized the darkest fears of American capital: "Walter Reuther is the most dangerous man in Detroit because no one is more skillful in bringing about the revolution without seeming to disturb the existing forms of society."[46]

To conservatives, this kind of mobilization from below, legitimated by governmental policy from above, reached its most frightening dialectic in the power briefly wielded by the Office of Price Administration. The OPA was another one of the late New Deal's great mobilizing bureaucracies that helped build a powerful administrative state. Like the National Labor Relations Board (NLRB) and the Fair Employment Practices Commission, the OPA's effectiveness depended on the organized activism of huge numbers of once voiceless individuals. Both labor and the Truman administration believed the continuance of OPA price regulations essential to the success of an orderly and progressive reconversion of the economy. In 1945 the OPA employed nearly seventy-five thousand and enlisted the voluntary participation of another three hundred thousand, mainly urban housewives, who checked the prices and quality of the consumer goods regulated by the government. Chester Bowles, OPA chief and a spirited New Deal liberal, called the volunteer price checkers "as American as baseball." Many merchants denounced them as a "kitchen Gestapo," but the polls found that over 80 percent of all citizens backed OPA price-control regulations. In response, the National Association of Manufacturers (NAM) poured as much money into anti-OPA propaganda as it would later spend on agitation for Taft-Hartley. The association called OPA an agency leading to "regimented chaos," an oxymoronic phrase that nevertheless captured business's fear of a powerful state whose regulatory purposes are vitalized by an activist, organized citizenry.[47]

The Taft-Hartley Act was enacted twice. In 1945 and 1946 labor's political and ideological defeat set the stage for the legislative passage of Taft-Hartley twelve months later. By October 1945, the Kelsey-Hayes strikers were isolated and their strike leaders permanently fired. The kind of rank-and-file militancy exemplified in their struggle never won a legitimizing public voice in the debates that led up to passage of the Taft-Hartley Act, not even from the most left-wing of top union leaders. Then in 1946 the failure of the Reutherite wage-price program at General Motors, combined with the collapse of price controls later that summer, represented a defeat for the kind of politicized economic bargaining that American business found so anathema. When an inflationary spiral during the summer and fall of 1946 seemed to discredit both union power and the Rooseveltian state, 10 million working-class voters remained at home. The result was a Republican sweep in the fall and the election of the Eightieth Congress that put the containment of union power and the reprivatization of collective bargaining at the top of its agenda.[48]

The Restoration of Managerial Authority

With the enactment of Taft-Hartley, American managers once again took the offensive, successfully regaining much of their authority in shop and office, while establishing the larger political conditions that would transform the unions into little more than ghettoized interest groups. The devil, however, is always in the details, which is why the conservative effort to transform the entire political economy depended on what at first glance seem like mere technicalities in the labor legislation that would sweep through the Congress in the spring of 1947. To understand the structural import of the new Taft-Hartley law, three elements of the managerial agenda require some elaboration: the destruction of unionism among foremen and first-line supervisors; the elimination of communist influence from the trade unions; and the effort, unsuccessful at the time, to curb industry-wide bargaining.

Section 2(3) of the Taft-Hartley Act, which excluded supervisors from coverage under the National Labor Relations Act, proved the single most powerful weapon crafted by labor's opponents under the new law.

The organization of supervisory employees, usually into unions of their own, represented one of the most important sociopolitical phenomena of the late New Deal. With the rise of mass production and bureaucratic rationality, first-line supervisors had become both a linchpin in the production process and an anomalous "man in the middle" buffeted from below and above by militant workers and the managerial quest for efficiency and control. The Foreman's Association of America claimed neutrality in the "ceaseless struggle between ownership and wage labor," but it functioned like a trade union and allied itself with the CIO.[49] Theodore Iserman, the Chrysler attorney who played a key role in drafting the House version of the Taft-Hartley Act, recognized that "solidarity of labor is not by any means an empty phrase, but it is a strong and active force." He estimated that supervisory unionism might soon win recognition in between 20 and 50 percent of all workplaces.[50]

Shifting its stance to accord with industrial reality, both the WLB and the NLRB sustained the unionization of foremen. In its March 1945 *Packard* decision, the board used the same criterion advanced by the FAA in distinguishing first-line supervisors from top management: they were employees under the Wagner Act because they did not set policy. The next year the board went further and ruled in a case involving coal mine supervisors at the Jones and Laughlin Steel Company: foremen could not be barred from membership in a rank-and-file union if the employees' freedom of choice under the Wagner Act were not to be abridged. By 1946 the FAA held a collective bargaining contract at the Ford Motor Company and had won NLRB elections at scores of midwestern manufacturing facilities.[51]

To America's top managers, supervisory unionization spelled industrial anarchy, which was the language they used to describe union control of the shop floor work environment. "We must rely upon the foremen to try and keep down those emotional surges of the men in the plants and urge them to rely on the grievance procedure," argued a Ford Motor Company spokesman. "If we do not have the foremen to do that, who is going to do it?" Seniority rights, grievance procedures, and union representation by first-line supervisors were subversive because if lower-level managers felt less threatened by orders from above, then the immense social and psychological pressures generated from below would surely turn them into unreliable agents of corporate power. Hence the corporate recourse to the military analogy. "Picture if you can the confusion of an army in the field," asserted a Detroit machine shop executive, "if the non-commissioned officers were forced to listen to the commands of the men in their ranks as well as those of their superior officers." Argued Kelsey's George Kennedy, "If the foremen are taken away from management, how can management effectively operate its plants?"[52]

Foreman organization, however, did not just threaten to weaken management authority at the point of production; it also eroded the vitality of corporate ideology in society at large by shattering the unitary facade of management and opening the door to a much larger definition of what constituted a self-conscious working-class identity. "The Foreman Abdicates" ran a *Fortune* headline in 1945, but the larger issue was whether the lower middle class—clerical workers, sales personnel, store managers, bank tellers, engineers, and draftsmen—would also abandon their identification with the corporate order. "Where will unionization end?" asked GM's Wilson. "With the vice presidents?"[53] The *Legislative History* of the Taft-Hartley Act put it this way: "Supervisors are management people. . . . It seems wrong, and it is wrong, to subject people of this kind, who have demonstrated their initiative, their ambition, and their ability to get ahead, to the leveling process of seniority, uniformity and standardization."[54] The deunionization of the first-line supervisors and their forced-draft conscription back into the managerial realm was therefore essential to the reghettoization of the union movement and the victory of management all along the white-collar frontier.

The magnitude of labor's defeat on the issue of supervisory unionism has become clearer with each passing year. Through the 1940s and even into the next decade, top executives feared their own supervisors as the potent allies of a well-organized, working-class insurgency. In response, managers demanded supervisory "loyalty," but few executives actually defined such an attitude in an aggressively antiunion fashion. But in the 1970s and 1980s the very conditions that once made first-line supervisors vulnerable to rank-and-file influence—their daily contact, rapport, and sociological affinity—have given managers and antiunion consultants the incentive to conscript this stratum as the shock troops who are thrown into the antiunion battle at the first hint of an organizing campaign. In the 1950s the NLRB often protected supervisors who refused to report to top management the union activities of their subordinates, but the erosion of the standard by which the courts judged employer interference in the free exercise of employee rights has also stripped supervisors of this protection. When labor's organizing activities threaten a union-free company today, standard operating procedure requires that management call a meeting of all first-line supervisors to threaten or fire those who resist implementation of the antiunion strategy. As one labor organizer noted, once managers "make it a point to frighten the supervisors," the supervisors "turn around and frighten the employees."[55]

Anticommunism

If the elimination of supervisory unionism is today a largely forgotten episode in the politics of Taft-Hartley, then the anticommunist thrust of the law—including section 9(h), which required all trade union officials to sign an affidavit asserting they were not communists, by organizational affiliation or belief—looms large in our historical imagination. This clause generated enormous bitterness among trade unionists of all political colorations, touched off a civil war within the CIO, and generated more than a decade of litigation that marginalized scores of union leaders even as leftists and civil libertarians waged a long and ultimately successful legal battle to overturn the prohibition.

The clause was obnoxious to contemporary unionists because it inscribed in the law a class distinction and a stigma that even the most anticommunist trade union officials found repugnant. Only trade unionists had to sign such an affidavit, not employers. Thus denunciations of the clause came not only from the left but from such veteran anticommunists as John L. Lewis, who hated the CIO leftists, and Max Zaritsky of the hatters union, who had purged his organization of communist influence twenty years before. Lewis, who labeled Taft-Hartley "the first ugly, savage thrust of Fascism in America," pulled six hundred thousand miners out of the AFL rather than sign the affidavit, while Zaritsky, who filed in September 1947, put his signature to the affidavit "with a feeling of revulsion for the trend of thought that has forced this foreign procedure on American labor."[56]

Given such laborite hostility and the subsequent damage the anticommunist clause wreaked upon the unions, one might have expected much advocacy, from the ranks of employers and congressional conservatives, for the insertion of this clause into the final bill that became the Taft-Hartley Act. But the issue figured hardly at all, in either the rhetoric of those businessmen who championed Taft-Hartley or in the testimony offered at the exhaustive congressional hearings on the bill in February and March 1947. Such silence speaks volumes, for these were the very months in which the president of the United States established a federal loyalty review board and enunciated the Truman Doctrine, which may well be taken as the moment that the U.S. government declared an ideological cold war against the Soviets.

Two reasons account for this curious silence surrounding passage of Taft-Hartley's anticommunist clause. First, the enormous legal and ideological warfare touched off by the clause was a function not so much of the Right persecuting the Left—which was true enough—but of a civil war within the ranks of labor and its liberal allies that long antedated Taft-Hartley. The UAW, the International Ladies Garment Workers Union (ILGWU), the United Mine Workers (UMW), and several other important unions had already put anticommunist provisions in their constitutions. Section 9(h) added a new front in this battle but was not essential to the prosecution of this particular civil war. More important, business leaders believed that when it came to bargaining issues or shop floor militancy, the distinction between communists and their more conventional trade union counterparts was rather slim. "Nothing is more dangerous than to assume that those who today attack 'Communists' within their union, and who are in consequence unthinkingly labeled 'right-wingers,' are *ipso facto* believers in private enterprise or in our form of government," warned Stuart Ball, counsel for Montgomery Ward, late in 1946. He asserted further that "it is not necessary to pin the label of 'Marxist' upon a labor leader to prove that what he believes is incompatible with our basic political and economic beliefs."[57]

Even the most prominent representatives for American business sometimes downplayed the communist role in U.S. labor strife in order to strike a blow at this more important target. Thus in January 1947, when U.S. Chamber of Commerce president William Jackson spoke in Milwaukee, the bitter, Communist-led Allis-Chalmers strike in that city was nearly a year old. But Jackson went out of his way to attack not the Communists but a pair of anticommunists, "the Reuthers and Philip Murrays," whom he characterized as "extreme elements" who are "today exploiting their authority and monopoly position as recklessly as industrial barons did in the earlier stage of the country's history."[58] In textiles, retail trade, shoemaking, and tobacco, business played the anticommunist card to keep its workplaces union-free. But the real issue was always unionism, not communism.[59]

Unionists understood this dynamic, but by 1947 the labor movement had become overwhelmingly reliant on the state. Although both the AFL and the CIO initially favored a boycott of Taft-Hartley, such a nullification would also deprive them of access to the NLRB, to bargaining unit election procedures, and to what protections the labor law still afforded them against antiunion employers. The Communists, who were influential in unions representing about a million workers, were sacrificed to the cold war's growing requirement for political orthodoxy, both at home and abroad.[60]

Section 9(h), therefore, did more than eliminate a politically vulnerable left-wing. The main thrust of the anticommunist clause was directed toward that depoliticization of all the unions demanded by even the most sophisticated elements of the business community. During the 1940s such anticommunist liberals as Walter Reuther correctly attacked the Communists as "counterfeit revolutionaries" because so much of their politics—like the support they offered to the no-strike pledge during World War II—was really a function of their ideological allegiance to Soviet power.[61] But the American Communists were not simply creatures of that foreign power. Instead, the tragedy of their demise lay in the organic relationship held by U.S. Communists to so much that characterized midcentury social liberalism: opposition to the cold war, trade union militancy, the defense of civil liberties, protofeminism, and, above all, the movement for the liberation of African Americans. This trade union Left represented an anchor for many of these movements, thus whatever the meaning of their Soviet romanticism, the elimination of the Communists from so much of American political life fatally diminished the role that the trade unions would play in the emergence of the civil rights movement and the New Left just a decade later.[62]

"Monopoly Unionism"

The final element of the Taft-Hartley Act that requires inspection is a section of the law that was not enacted, at least not in 1947. This was a ban on "industry-wide bargaining" or, as its advocates liked to put it, on "monopoly unionism." Fred Hartley's House committee actually drafted such a provision, which would have made far more difficult the centralized negotiation of multiplant or multifirm collective bargaining contracts, but in the Senate, Robert Taft knew that such a provision was a "killer amendment," and he stripped it away in the House-Senate conference.[63]

Most historians see this conflict, as well as its resolution, as reflective of the divergent interests of two sectors of capital. On the militant right stood those smaller firms, often family-owned and labor intensive, who battled the unions in highly competitive sectors of the economy. Their interests were not always the same as the nation's larger, oligopolistically structured enterprises that were quite willing to allow trade unions to take wages out of competition. In this story, Taft's Senate victory represented the growing power of the monopolistic firms, which sacrificed the interests of their smaller, more competitive cousins to a larger industrial relations stability. Although big business had the market power to pass on to consumers the burden of higher wages, smaller firms were heavily penalized in this process. Not only did they have to pay these higher prices, but they then discovered that their workers also demanded pay levels commensurate with those won by firms whose high productivity and pricing leverage enabled them to absorb the higher labor costs.[64]

But if one listens to business rhetoric during the Taft-Hartley debate, one finds a distinct counternarrative, and not only among the oppressed class of entrepreneurs and family firms. American business executives universally opposed industry-wide bargaining because they saw it leading inexorably to the kind of class solidarity, politicized bargaining, and governmental intervention from which they were trying to escape. They were convinced that industry-wide bargaining would generate a wage-price spiral, inflation, and a public demand that the federal government establish a permanent set of wage-price-profit guidelines. Thus Charles Wilson of General Motors argued: "If labor monopolies are permitted on an industry-wide basis, employer cartels to match them are thereby made inevitable, and the product of this situation in the end will require state control of both. This is the Nazi-Fascist-Communist pattern."[65]

Ira Mosher, who headed the National Association of Manufacturers, led a business group whose membership tilted well toward the family firm and the competitive sector enterprise. He therefore attacked the "labor monopoly" and favored single-plant bargaining relationships, because "human relations in industry as in the home are intimate and personal, varying from plant to plant and from company to company. . . . The unique employment conditions of a given plant should not be forced into patterns established by a few labor leaders in meetings with a few industry representatives."[66]

Mosher advocated the destruction of industry-wide bargaining, the evisceration of union solidarity, and the depoliticization of unionism. He asserted that "when you combine a secondary boycott with industry-wide bargaining and the closed shop, you have, in a few men, the power to absolutely wreck the whole country." Mosher attacked industry-wide bargaining first and foremost, because he recognized that when the unions shut down an entire industry they also had the leverage to bring the state in on their side. Indeed, the destruction of this politicized regime stood at the very top of the NAM agenda, followed by a ban on the secondary boycotts and supervisory unionism.[67]

Without the destruction of monopoly unionism, "practical operating problems are neglected and social philosophies and ideologies are emphasized. . . . In short there is a marked tendency in such circumstances to emphasize the 'class struggle' and to argue and fight for political ends." Mosher predicted that "government intervention can become a habit, leading to regulation of wages, hours and other conditions of employment and also of prices. In short when government intervenes in labor relations, the economy is on the highway to nationalization and competitive productive enterprise is on the way out."[68]

Ira Mosher's forecast proved accurate in spirit, if not in the details. The industry-wide collective bargaining that characterized the steel, automobile, trucking, rubber, coal, and transport industries did sustain what some scholars have described as a system of mesocorporatism, or pattern bargaining. Business grudgingly accepted such economic coordination throughout the 1950s and 1960s, but as David Stebenne has demonstrated in his outstanding biography of Arthur Goldberg, they gave to the "labor-management accord" of those years a highly qualified allegiance. The United Steelworkers felt compelled to strike the industry at almost every contract renewal between 1946 and 1959. In 1962, when President Kennedy and Arthur Goldberg, his new secretary of labor, actively tried to politicize these industry-wide bargaining arrangements by putting into place a set of wage-price guideposts, the steel industry precipitated a major confrontation with the White House. Kennedy forced U.S. Steel and other big firms to rescind an initial round of price increases, but the political fallout was so severe that no Democratic president ever initiated such a direct confrontation with industry again.[69]

Industry-wide bargaining proved to be far from the wave of the future imagined by either its friends or foes. The growth of competitive industry in the nonunion South and in the entrepreneurial West provided the economic and political basis for a full-scale assault on this model and a turn toward the conception advanced in Fred Hartley's House committee. The issue reemerged on the national political agenda ten years after the passage of the law, during the deep recession of 1957–58, which put the first real squeeze on competitive-sector firms since the Roosevelt recession of twenty years before. Here we find the dramatic rise of a Republican Right, whose distinguishing characteristic was its unqualified rejection of industry-wide wage bargaining. Conservatives launched a new assault on the union shop, even in such northern states as Ohio and California. They denounced both Walter Reuther and Jimmy Hoffa as "labor bosses," and the antiunion Right found a champion in Republican senator Barry Goldwater, who got his political start in Phoenix by successfully mobilizing his fellow retailers on behalf of Arizona's 1948 "right-to-work" law. By the end of the 1950s he was declaring industry-wide bargaining "an evil to be eliminated" and Walter Reuther "a more dangerous menace that the Sputnik or anything Soviet Russia might do in America."[70]

Industry-wide bargaining finally collapsed in the early 1980s, presided over by Goldwater's most successful ideological heir. One cannot link the concession bargaining of those years directly to passage of the Taft-Hartley law, but taken as a whole, the 1947 labor statute established the structural framework that made such a bargaining debacle possible. As a consequence, the American republic is today in the midst of a truly daring experiment: can an industrial democracy maintain viable parliamentary institutions and a healthy civic life in the absence of a minimally powerful trade union movement? Given the demise of the idea of industrial democracy, the atrophy in our party politics, the legacy of a generation-long era of wage stagnation, and the insecurity that stalks the American workplace, this issue remains open to debate. And if so, then labor's proposition of 1947 is still viable: Taft-Hartley was indeed a "slave labor law."

Notes

1. Sumner H. Slichter, *Union Policies and Industrial Management* (Washington, D.C.: Brookings Institution, 1941), 1.

2. International Education Department, UAW-CIO, *How to Win for the Union: A Discussion for UAW Stewards and Committeemen* (Detroit: UAW-CIO, 1940), 8.

3. Colin Gordon, *New Deals: Business, Labor, and Politics in America, 1920–1935* (New York: Cambridge University Press, 1994), 194–224; Theodore Rosenof, *Economics in the Long Run: New Deal Theorists and Their Legacies, 1933–1993* (Chapel Hill: University of North Carolina Press, 1997), 19–52; Steven Fraser, *Labor Will Rule: Sidney Hillman and the Rise of American Labor* (New York: Free Press, 1991), 260–77; and, more generally, Meg Jacobs, "The Politics of Purchasing Power: Political Economy, Consumption Politics, and American State-Building, 1909–1959," Ph.D. diss., University of Virginia, 1998.

4. Among the recent labor histories that explicate this experience, see Melvyn Dubofsky, *The State and Labor in Modern America* (Chapel Hill: University of North Carolina Press, 1994), 107–95 passim; Robert H. Zieger, *The CIO, 1935–1955* (Chapel Hill: University of North Carolina Press, 1995), 177–90, 212–27; and Nelson Lichtenstein, *The Most Dangerous Man in Detroit: Walter Reuther and the Fate of American Labor* (New York: Basic, 1995), 154–84, 220–47.

5. Quoted in Fraser, *Labor Will Rule*, 503.

6. Daniel Bell, "The Taft-Hartley Fumble," *Fortune*, May 1949, 190.

7. Joseph Shister, "The Impact of the Taft-Hartley Act on Union Strength and Collective Bargaining," *Industrial and Labor Relations Review* 11 (April 1958): 250.

8. Derek Bok, "Reflections on the Distinctive Character of American Labor Laws," *Harvard Law Review* 84 (April 1971): 1394–1463, and David E. Feller, "A General Theory of the Collective Bargaining Agreement," *California Law Review* 61 (May 1973): 663–856.

9. Christopher Tomlins, *The State and the Unions: Labor Relations, Law, and the Organized Labor Movement in America, 1880–1960* (New York: Cambridge University Press, 1985), 251.

10. George Lipsitz, *Rainbow at Midnight: Labor and Culture in the 1940s* (Urbana: University of Illinois Press, 1994), 170.

11. David Plotke, *Building a Democratic Political Order: Reshaping American Liberalism in the 1930s and 1940s* (New York: Cambridge University Press, 1996), 257.

12. Historians of labor and social class have become particularly attuned to the rhetoric of politics and the discourse of debate. See, for example, Leonard R. Berlanstein, *Rethinking Labor History: Essays on Discourse and Class Analysis* (Urbana: University of Illinois Press, 1993); Bryan Palmer, *Descent into Discourse* (Philadelphia: Temple University Press, 1990); and Michael Kazin, *The Populist Persuasion: An American History* (New York: Basic, 1995), esp. 285–86.

13. David L. Stebenne, *Arthur J. Goldberg: New Deal Liberal* (New York: Oxford University Press, 1996), 62.

14. CIO, *Proceedings of the Ninth Constitutional Convention,* Boston, October 13–17, 1947, 22.

15. Ibid., 186, 189.

16. George Meany, "The Taft-Hartley Law: A Slave Labor Measure," in *Vital Speeches of the Day* 14 (December 1, 1947): 122, 120.

17. As quoted in Elizabeth Fones-Wolf, *Selling Free Enterprise: The Business Assault on Labor and Liberalism, 1945–60* (Urbana: University of Illinois Press, 1994), 22.

18. William Walker, "The Taft-Hartley Law Preserves the Freedom of the Worker," in *Vital Speeches of the Day* 14 (December 1, 1947): 123.

19. As quoted in Lawrence Richards, "The Culture of Anti-Unionism, 1943–1963" (1998), unpublished seminar paper in Lichtenstein's possession.

20. For a discussion of the impact of Friedrich von Hayek's *The Road to Serfdom,* see Alan Brinkley, *The End of Reform: New Deal Liberalism in Recession and War* (New York: Alfred A. Knopf, 1995), 157–61.

21. Charles S. Maier, "The Two Postwar Eras and the Conditions for Stability in Twentieth-Century Western Europe," in *In Search of Stability: Explorations in Historical Political Economy* (New York: Cambridge University Press, 1987), 153–84; Anthony Carew, *Labour under the Marshall Plan: The Politics of Productivity and Marketing of Management Science* (Detroit: Wayne State University Press, 1987); Guido Baglioni and Colin Crouch, eds., *European Industrial Relations: The Challenge of Flexibility* (London: Sage, 1990), 127–53.

22. See "Threat to Capital Held U.S. Menace," *New York Times,* January 14, 1947, 8.

23. See, generally, Sanford Jacoby, "American Exceptionalism Revisited: The Importance of Management," in *Masters to Managers: Historical and Comparative Perspectives on American Employers,* ed. Jacoby (New York: Columbia University Press, 1991), 173–200; David Vogel, "Why Businessmen Distrust Their State: The Political Consciousness of American Corporate Executives," in *British Journal of Political Science* 8 (January 1978): 45–78; and Gordon, *New Deals,* 5–34.

24. C. Wright Mills, *The New Men of Power: America's Labor Leaders* (New York: Harcourt, Brace and Company, 1948), 223–50; Howell John Harris, *The Right to Manage: Industrial Relations Policies of American Business in the 1940s* (Madison: University of Wisconsin Press, 1982), 23–40; Thomas Ferguson, "Industrial Conflict and the Coming of the New Deal: The Triumph of Multinational Liberalism in America," in *The Rise and Fall of the New Deal Order,* ed. Steven Fraser and Gary Gerstle, (Princeton: Princeton University Press, 1989), 3–31.

25. Harriman quoted in Lipsitz, *Rainbow,* 169–70.

26. This paragraph relies heavily on Vogel, "Why Businessmen Distrust Their State," 45–78; see also Jacoby, "American Exceptionalism Revisited," 173–200.

27. Sloan quoted in Joshua Freeman et al., *Who Built America? Working People and the Nation's Economy, Politics, Culture, and Society* (New York: Pantheon, 1991), 472.

28. Gordon, *New Deals,* 35–86.

29. See, especially, David Horowitz, *Beyond Left and Right: Insurgency and the Establishment* (Urbana: University of Illinois Press, 1997), 159, 203, and also Leo Ribuffo, "Why Is There So Much Conservatism in the United States and Why Do So Few Historians Know Anything about It?" *American Historical Review* 99 (April 1994): 409–49.

30. This perspective is advanced most forcefully by Theda Skocpol and Kenneth Finegold, "State Capacity and Economic Intervention in the Early New Deal," *Political Science Quarterly* 97 (Summer 1982): 255–78. A useful critique may also be found in Peter Swenson, "Arranged Alliance: Business Interests in the New Deal," *Politics and Society* 25 (March 1997): 66–116.

31. Ellis Hawley, *The New Deal and the Problem of Monopoly: A Study in Economic Ambivalence* (Princeton: Princeton University Press, 1966); Louis Galambos and Joseph Pratt, *The Rise of the Corporate Commonwealth: United States Business and Public Policy in the Twentieth Century* (New York: Basic, 1988), 114–26; James P. Johnson, *The Politics of Soft Coal: The Bituminous Industry from World War I through the New Deal* (Urbana: University of Illinois Press, 1979), 5, 219; Gordon, *New Deals*, 97–121; Isaac Cohen, "David L. Behncke, the Airline Pilots, and the New Deal: The Struggle for Federal Labor Legislation," Labor History 41 (February 2000): 47–66.

32. Fraser, *Labor Will Rule*, 391–96; Sidney Fine, *Frank Murphy: The New Deal Years* (Chicago: University of Chicago Press, 1979), 300–325.

33. Stebenne, *Goldberg*, 45–77 passim; Ronald Schatz, "Battling over Government's Role," in *Forging a Union of Steel: Philip Murray, SWOC, and the United Steelworkers*, ed. Paul Clark, Peter Gottlieb, and Donald Kennedy (Ithaca: ILR Press, 1987), 87–102. For contrasting discussions of the way in which state functions accommodated and influenced the new labor movement, see Theda Skocpol, "Political Response to Capitalist Crisis: Neo-Marxist Theories of the State and the Case of the New Deal," *Politics and Society* 10 (1980): 155–201, and Tomlins, *The State and the Unions*, 197–328 passim.

34. Philippe Schmitter, "Still the Century of Corporatism?" in *Trends toward Corporatist Intermediation,* ed. Schmitter and Gerhard Lehmbruh (Beverly Hills, Calif.: Sage, 1982); Wyn Grant, ed., *The Political Economy of Corporatism* (New York: Cambridge University Press, 1983); Leo Panitch, *Working-Class Politics in Crisis: Essays on Labor and the State* (London: Verso, 1980), 132–86; and Ronald Schatz, "From Commons to Dunlop: Rethinking the Field and Theory of Industrial Relations," in *Industrial Democracy in America: The Ambiguous Promise,* ed. Nelson Lichtenstein and Howell John Harris (New York: Cambridge University Press, 1993), 87–112.

35. But Truman's long-awaited labor-management conference was a failure because business executives recognized that any such state-sponsored corporatism put them at a disadvantage. See Andrew Workman, "Manufacturing Power: The Organizational Revival of the National Association of Manufacturers, 1941–1945," *Business History Review* 78 (Summer 1998): 279–301.

36. Nelson Lichtenstein, "From Corporatism to Collective Bargaining: Or-

ganized Labor and the Eclipse of Social Democracy in the Postwar Era," in Fraser and Gerstle, *New Deal Order,* 125.

37. Quoted in Craufurd Goodwin, *Exhortation and Controls: The Search for a Wage Price Policy, 1945–1971* (Washington, D.C.: Brookings Institution, 1975), 13.

38. Howard Brick, *Daniel Bell and the Decline of Intellectual Radicalism: Social Theory and Political Reconciliation in the 1940s* (Madison: University of Wisconsin Press, 1986), 102; see also Nelson Lichtenstein, "America's Left-Wing Intellectuals and the Trade Union Movement," in *Proceedings, Industrial Relations Research Association* (Madison: University of Wisconsin Press, 1998).

39. Rosa Lee Swafford, *Wartime Record of Strikes and Lockouts, 1940–1945* (Washington, D.C., 1946), 20–21; Nelson Lichtenstein, *Labor's War at Home: The CIO in World War II* (New York: Cambridge University Press, 1982), 223–24.

40. House Committee on Education and Labor, "Testimony of George Kennedy," *Amendments to the NLRA,* 80th Cong., 1st sess., February 20, 1947, 1069.

41. Lipsitz, *Rainbow,* 100–102; Nelson Lichtenstein, "'The Man in the Middle': A Social History of Automobile Industry Foremen," in *On the Line: Essays in the History of Auto Work,* ed. Lichtenstein and Stephen Meyer (Urbana: University of Illinois Press, 1989), 153–89.

42. Swafford, *Wartime Record,* 21; Lichtenstein, *Most Dangerous Man in Detroit,* 224; Lipsitz, *Rainbow,* 101–3.

43. House Committee, "Testimony of George Kennedy," 1071.

44. I offer a discussion of this strike in Lichtenstein, *Most Dangerous Man in Detroit,* 220–47; quotation on 220.

45. Ibid., 230.

46. Ibid., 230.

47. Meg Jacobs, "'How about Some Meat?' The Office of Price Administration, Consumption Politics, and State Building from the Bottom Up, 1941–1946," *Journal of American History* 84 (December 1997): 910–41; National Association of Manufacturers, "Would You Like Some Butter or a Roast of Beef?" (newspaper advertisement), reproduced in Jacobs, "How about Some Meat?" 935; Horowitz, *Beyond Left and Right,* 112.

48. James Boylan, *The New Deal Coalition and the Election of 1946* (New York: Garland, 1981), 151–67; Joel Seidman, *American Labor from Defense to Reconversion* (Chicago: University of Chicago Press, 1953), 233–44; Jacobs, "How about Some Meat?" 940–41. Even such unionists as Walter Reuther, who had been among the most outspoken corporatists and planning advocates, made a rhetorical about-face. After the Republican congressional sweep he adopted much of the language of the anti–New Deal Right, now urging "free labor" and "free management" to join in solving their problems or a "superstate will arise to do it for us." Still later, after the Taft-Hartley restrictions were in place, Reuther put the issue even more bluntly: "I'd rather bargain with General Mo-

tors than with the government. . . . General Motors has no army" (quoted in Lichtenstein, *Most Dangerous Man in Detroit*, 261).

49. Among the classic essays on this subject are F. J. Roethlisberger, "The Foreman: Master and Victim of Double Talk," *Harvard Business Review* 23 (1945): 283–98, and Donald E. Wray, "Marginal Men of Industry: The Foreman," *American Journal of Sociology* 54 (1949): 298–301. See also Lichtenstein, "'Man in the Middle,'" 153–89.

50. House Committee on Education and Labor, "Testimony of Theodore Iserman," *Amendments to the NLRA*, 80th Cong., 1st sess., March 7, 1947, 2710–11.

51. Charles P. Larrowe, "A Meteor on the Industrial Relations Horizon," *Labor History* 2 (Fall 1961): 259–87; Virginia A. Seitz, "Legal, Legislative, and Managerial Responses to the Organization of Supervisory Employees in the 1940s," *American Journal of Legal History* 28 (January 1984): 218–35.

52. Lichtenstein, "'Man in the Middle,'" 177–78; House Committee, "Testimony of George Kennedy," 1074.

53. "The Foreman Abdicates," *Fortune*, September 1945, 38.

54. Quoted in Seitz, "Legal, Legislative, and Managerial Responses," 230.

55. Charles T. Joyce, "Union Busters and Front-Line Supervisors: Restricting and Regulating the Use of Supervisory Employees by Management Consultants during Union Representation Election Campaigns," *University of Pennsylvania Law Review* 135 (January 1987): 453–93; quotation on 464.

56. Robert H. Zieger, *John L. Lewis: Labor Leader* (Boston: Twayne, 1988), 163–67; Louis Stark, "CIO to Follow AFL on Anti-Red Order," *New York Times*, September 11, 1947, 9.

57. Stuart Ball, "A Balance of Power: The Prerequisite to True Collective Bargaining," *Vital Speeches of the Day* 13 (March 1, 1947): 303.

58. "Threat to Capital Held U.S. Menace," *New York Times*, January 14, 1947, 8.

59. Fones-Wolf, *Selling Free Enterprise*, 53–55; Timothy Minchin, *What Do We Need a Union For? The TWUA in the South, 1945–1955* (Chapel Hill: University of North Carolina Press, 1997), 32–47; and Barbara Griffith, *The Crisis of American Labor: Operation Dixie and the Defeat of the CIO* (Philadelphia: Temple University Press, 1988).

60. See Mary Sperling McAuliffe, *Crisis on the Left: Cold War Politics and American Liberals, 1947–1954* (Amherst: University of Massachusetts Press, 1978), 33–47; Harvey A. Levenstein, *Communism, Anti-Communism, and the CIO* (Westport, Conn.: Greenwood, 1981), 208–29; and Ellen Schrecker, "McCarthyism and the Labor Movement: The Role of the State," in *The CIO's Left-Led Unions*, ed. Steve Rosswurm (New Brunswick: Rutgers University Press, 1992), 139–57.

61. Sidney Lens, *The Counterfeit Revolution* (New York: Beacon, 1952), 1–12.

62. Studies that see U.S. communism largely as the Stalinist product of Soviet foreign policy include Theodore Draper, *American Communism and Soviet*

Russia (New York: Viking, 1960); Irving Howe and Lewis Coser, *The American Communist Party: A Critical History* (New York: Praeger, 1957); and Harvey Klehr, John Earl Haynes, and Fridrikh Igorevich Firsov, *The Secret World of American Communism* (New Haven: Yale University Press, 1995). Social and labor historians of the current generation recognize the weight of Moscow's heavy hand, but most also assert the complex, indigenous sources of communist influence within the United States during the 1930s and 1940s. See, for example, Michael Honey, *Southern Labor and Black Civil Rights: Organizing Memphis Workers* (Chapel Hill: University of North Carolina Press, 1993); Maurice Isserman, *Which Side Were You On? The American Communist Party during the Second World War* (Middletown: Wesleyan University Press, 1982); and Robin Kelley, *Hammer and Hoe: Alabama Communists during the Great Depression* (Chapel Hill: University of North Carolina Press, 1990). For an exhaustive, balanced survey, see Ellen Schrecker, *Many Are the Crimes: McCarthyism in America* (New York: Little, Brown, 1998).

63. Harry Millis and Emily Clark Brown, *From the Wagner Act to Taft-Hartley: A Study of National Labor Policy and Labor Relations* (Chicago: University of Chicago Press, 1949), 382–87; James T. Patterson, *Mr. Republican: A Biography of Robert A. Taft* (Boston: Houghton Mifflin, 1972), 352–66.

64. Lipsitz, *Rainbow*, 160; Plotke, *Building a Democratic Political Order*, 233–36.

65. C. E. Wilson, "Problems Industry Faces: The Months Ahead," *Vital Speeches of the Day* 13 (January 1, 1947): 181. The language of the Wagner Act's preamble dealing with wages and business depressions was actually deleted from Rep. Fred Hartley's draft of the new labor law. See Daniel J. B. Mitchell, "Inflation, Unemployment, and the Wagner Act: A Critical Reappraisal," *Stanford Law Review* 38 (April 1986): 1071.

66. House Committee on Education and Labor, "Testimony of Ira Mosher," *Amendments to the NLRA*, 80th Cong., 1st sess., March 7, 1947, 2683.

67. Ibid., 2691. But note that the elimination of communists from union leadership found no place on the legislative agenda of this right-wing business organization.

68. Ibid., 2685.

69. David Stebenne, *Arthur J. Goldberg*, 279–315; Walter Heller, *New Dimensions of Political Economy* (Cambridge: Harvard University Press, 1966), 42–47; Irving Bernstein, *Promises Kept: John F. Kennedy's New Frontier* (New York: Oxford University Press, 1991), 133–37.

70. Barry Goldwater, *The Conscience of a Conservative* (Shepherdsville, Ky.: Victor Publishing, 1960), 56; Lichtenstein, *Most Dangerous Man in Detroit*, 347; Rick Perlstein, *Before the Storm: Barry Goldwater and the Unmaking of the American Consensus* (New York: Hill and Wang, 2001), 17–68; Gilbert Gall, *The Politics of Right to Work: The Labor Federations as Special Interests, 1943–1979* (New York: Greenwood, 1988), 83–128.

Competition and the New Deal Regulatory State

Donald R. Brand

The reformers who reshaped American politics in the first half of the twentieth century believed in progress. The history of humanity was the story of people's development from primitive origins to civilization, and the history of the United States was the story of our development from frontier anarchy to an increasingly modern state and society. For progressives it was a mistake to turn to the past for moral and political guidance, for this was to chain a morally superior modernity to the cruder standards of our ancestors.

This historicist mentality accounts for the decline in reverence for the American founding. Charles Beard's debunking of the Framers as a self-interested, propertied elite who sought to stem the tide of democracy resonated strongly with progressive values. Those who come last see the furthest and judge the best. Moreover, the past was replete with wars and struggles to overcome economic scarcity, and these facts shaped the moral horizon of our ancestors. The future, on the other hand, held the promise of peace and plenty, and this vista permitted a revaluation of values. In this new moral dispensation the role of competition and the virtues associated with it would appear in a new light. The exemplary entrepreneur of the nineteenth century appeared to progressives as a selfish impediment to universal prosperity. Progress had transformed the virtues associated with competition into vices, and this moral and political agenda came to fruition in the anticompetitive spirit of New Deal economic regulation.

The anticompetitive spirit of the New Deal has been obscured by a linguistic sleight of hand. Reformers of the first two decades of the twentieth century were sufficiently self-conscious of the centrality of the concept of progress in their thinking that they adopted the name "Progressives" to describe themselves. Historians ratified the reformer's self-image by referring to these decades as the Progressive Era. By the 1930s, however, this felicitous nomenclature had disappeared. One of Franklin Roosevelt's most notable contributions to the political success of progressivism was to change its name. With his encouragement, progressives became "liberals," co-opting the term that defenders of the natural rights of man had previously used to describe themselves.[1] Adopting the term "liberal" allowed progressives to present themselves as faithful heirs of the American political tradition and defused the charge of radicalism, but the new usage of the term was also fundamentally misleading, for these repackaged progressives still took their bearings from their claims about the direction of historical development rather than from the natural rights horizon properly associated with liberalism. This rhetorical ploy also masked the anticompetitive implications of their understanding of progress, but those implications can nevertheless be ascertained by an analysis of New Deal economic thought.

Franklin Roosevelt's Commonwealth Club Address, his most ambitious attempt in the 1932 presidential campaign to summarize his political views, demonstrates both his basic reliance on the concept of historical progress and the policy commitments implicit in that concept. Roosevelt begins this speech by describing America as "in the process of change and development," affirming that "we can still believe in change and in progress." Progress, however, depends on a realistic assessment of our history *and* our current situation. When progressive reformers confronted the potential threat posed to equal opportunity by the growth of corporate power, their initial response was to try to dismantle that power through antitrust laws and trust-busting. Roosevelt criticizes this policy as an attempt "to turn the clock back" and "to return to the time when every man owned his individual small business." For Roosevelt, political actors define themselves by their orientation toward the future and the past, not in relationship to some transhistorical standard such as nature or natural rights.[2]

Our political history is presented as the clash between two parties, each the outgrowth of principles that are partial and thereby defective.

The founder of the first party is Alexander Hamilton, who was committed to a strong central government and a vigorous executive but also, Roosevelt alleges, distrustful of democracy. Hamilton "believed that the safety of the republic lay in the autocratic strength of its government" and "that the destiny of individuals was to serve that government." The founder of the second party was Thomas Jefferson. Jefferson, FDR argues, was committed to democracy and rights but was also distrustful of the only agent capable of guaranteeing those rights in the modern context: the centralized, energetic state. Jefferson feared "the encroachment of political power on the lives of individuals," but with the development of modern corporations, Roosevelt claims, it is the abuses of corporate power, not government power, that provide the greatest cause for concern. Progress beyond the American founding is both necessary and possible through a marriage of Hamiltonian and Jeffersonian traditions that incorporates the strength of each and abandons the elements in each that have retarded progress. Progressives were committed to a centralized democratic state.[3]

Progress is also possible in economic affairs, but its fruits had thus far largely eluded the working men and women of America. The industrial revolution, FDR continued, had awakened "the dream of an economic machine, able to . . . bring luxury within the reach of the humblest . . . and to release everyone from the drudgery of the heaviest manual toil." The reality, however, is that many citizens had not benefited, though "our industrial plant is built." With the triumph of industrialization, "equality of opportunity as we have known it no longer exists." Under these new circumstances "a mere builder of more industrial plants . . . is as likely to be a danger as a help," and "the day of the great promoter of the financial Titan . . . is over." The challenge is no longer creating wealth but distributing and administering it.[4]

In the new economic order competition will give way to cooperation. Rather than dismantle large corporations, the business elite will be encouraged and required to assume a responsibility for the common welfare commensurate with their power. In "enlightened industries" the competitive struggle has been transcended as the business elite "endeavor to limit the freedom of action of each man and business group within the industry in the common interest of all." If cooperative arrangements effected through trade associations are threatened by the competitive practices of "the lone wolf . . . whose hand is against every man's" and who "declines to join in achieving an end recognized as being for the public welfare," and if this lone wolf "threatens to drag the industry back to a state of anarchy [i.e., back to a competitive market]," then government "may properly be asked to apply restraint."[5]

The continuity between Progressives and New Dealers revealed by this speech is evident in their shared faith in progress and in the implications this faith in progress has for the value placed on economic competition. This new understanding of competition is critical for understanding the New Deal response to the Great Depression. According to New Deal reformers, the Great Depression was not a temporary aberration in the growth of national wealth associated with capitalism; it revealed emergent failures in markets as mechanisms for allocating economic resources in modern times. Mass production industrial techniques had laid the foundation for a transition from scarcity to abundance *if* social, economic, and political institutions could adapt to these new conditions. The New Deal "progressives" claimed it was inexcusable that the inherited and obsolete market-based order was producing chronic imbalances between supply and demand.[6] Overproduction was purportedly evident in the collapse of prices and the waves of bankruptcies as too many goods chased too few consumers. Underconsumption was attributed primarily to the low wages that reputedly prevailed in laissez-faire capitalism because, it was alleged, competitive pressures forced businesses to cut costs by depressing wages.

While progressives ostensibly targeted only laissez-faire capitalism, their criticism of the existing economic order was broader than they generally either recognized or acknowledged.[7] Roosevelt, for instance, did not repudiate competition but argued that the goal of the New Deal was only to limit it. Competition was "useful up to a certain point *and no further.*" But Roosevelt insisted that restoring the primacy of social considerations required that "cooperation must begin where competition leaves off and cooperation is as good a word for the new theory as any other."[8] What is striking about this formulation is that Roosevelt is *not* saying simply that actual markets often fall short of the competitive ideal and that alternative forms of control are called for where competitive restraints on business behavior are ineffective. For him, as for progressives in general, the failure of the market was more fundamental: laissez-faire capitalism had become morally repugnant. Unfettered competition legitimated selfishness and a ruthless disregard for one's fellow citizens.

Progressives were trying to establish new forms of community and to in-
still appropriate virtues in the citizenry. Their writings are filled with references to duties, obligations, and responsibilities, not with celebrations
of individual economic opportunity. Like all moralists, progressives had
a deep and abiding hostility to corruption and a strong commitment to
justice, which they often referred to as fairness. For progressives, cooperation was conducive to fairness.

Thus the progressive critique of the market should not be confused
with the more narrowly tailored criticism of market failures that has become a staple of contemporary economic analysis. Whereas economic
analysis at the end of the twentieth century begins from the assumption
of scarce resources and difficult choices in allocation, the New Dealers
began from the premise of abundance. Competition as a spur to growth
was not needed if overproduction and maldistribution were the problems; instead, competition came to be viewed as a disruptive force that
subverted the possibilities for social and economic cooperation.

Other New Dealers went even further in their rhetoric. The most
forthright rejections of competition are found among Roosevelt's early
brain trust: Raymond Moley, Rexford Tugwell, and Adolf Berle. The
brain trusters were committed to economic planning and to collectivism
because they believed it would be economically disastrous to use antitrust laws to break up big corporations and return to a competitive market composed of many smaller businesses.[9] Raymond Moley contrasted
a "chaotic competitive system" that produced "sweatshops, child labor,
rackets, ruinous price cutting, a devastated agriculture, and a score of
other blights even in the peak year of 1928" with the possibilities of "cooperative business-government planning." Planning would allow "the
whole people to enjoy the benefits of mass production and distribution."[10] His model of cooperative business-government planning was the
War Industries Board from 1917 to 1919, which became the template
for the National Recovery Administration.

Rexford Tugwell was the most radical proponent of a collective alternative to the market. Tugwell asserted that even businesspeople "have
learned that competition, in most of its forms, is wasteful and costly," a
conclusion he inferred from their propensity to avoid competition by
forming cartels or monopolies.[11] He insisted that relying on the profit
motive to determine investment decisions was "unnatural" and contrary
to "security, order and rationality": "From what I know of human na-

ture I believe that the world awaits a great outpouring of energy so soon as we shall have removed the dead hand of competitive enterprise that stifles public impulses and finds use only for the less effective and less beneficial impulses of men. When industry is government and government is industry, the dual conflict deepest in our modern institutions will be abated."[12]

The third member of the brain trust triumvirate, Adolf Berle, also rejected competition. Berle considered competition anachronistic in a world of large corporations, because oligopolists cooperate with one another rather than compete in setting prices. With Gardiner Means, Berle was coauthor of *Industrial Prices and Their Relative Inflexibility* in which they sought to demonstrate that in many modern industrial sectors prices were determined administratively rather than through competitive market mechanisms. In this new economy, ownership of firms through stocks had become divorced from managerial control, and the behavior of firms was no longer determined exclusively by the profit motive and the external cues of a competitive marketplace. Means echoed Berle in asserting that "modern industrial organization" had "destroyed the free market."[13] Since markets were obsolete, the only remaining question was who would set prices, an unaccountable business elite or our elected leaders? Insisting on democratic controls, Berle welcomed an age of democratic collectivism and rational planning.

On the other hand, New Dealers who drew their progressive inspirations from Louis Brandeis seemed more respectful of competition but more worried about bigness. Brandeis had been Woodrow Wilson's most influential adviser on antitrust policy, and he continued to shape progressive thought about markets from his seat on the Supreme Court. Brandeis embraced competition as long as it was "fair"; he wanted to use federal antitrust policy only to prevent "unfair" competition. The anticompetitive tendencies in his principles, his rhetoric notwithstanding, become manifest when the distinction between fair and unfair competition is examined more closely.[14]

Brandeis believed that large corporations had gained an unfair competitive advantage over their smaller rivals, and he consistently railed against "the curse of bigness."[15] Big firms had market power. They could force suppliers to sell to them at discounted prices that were not available to their smaller rivals. Thus, Brandeis argued, when big firms undersold smaller firms, driving the latter out of business, their ability to do so was not rooted in economies of scale and true economic efficiency but in power. Rather moralistically, he also emphasized the role of unfair trade practices and predatory pricing in the elimination of small firms. Only in a few cases of natural monopoly were size and efficiency linked. The proper goal of antitrust policy was to break up big firms or to prevent them from using their power "unfairly" to drive competitors out of business. Brandeis described the just order he envisioned as "industrial democracy."[16]

One problem with Brandeis's analysis was that economies of scale were more significant and widespread than he acknowledged, and thus the only way to protect small business from the competitive advantages of big business was to limit or suppress competition.[17] Thomas Mc-Craw has argued that Brandeis never recognized that protecting competitors (small business) was not the same thing as protecting competition and he thus continued to use the rhetoric of fair competition to support anticompetitive policies. The problem, however, is more fundamental. Brandeis's main concerns were political, not economic. He was not simply mistaken about which policies were most conducive to achieving economic efficiency; rather, he valued small business because he believed it provided the economic preconditions for a viable democratic polity.

Identifying the political character of Brandeis's concerns sheds new light on his reflections on competition. For him, economic institutions were to be judged by their effects on the character of our citizenry. Citizens have an obligation to put the national interest before personal interest, and for this to happen they must feel strong bonds of solidarity with one another. Genteel rivalry might not undermine the spirit of cooperation requisite for citizenship, but full-blooded competition would encourage an ignoble self-interested individualism. Thus Brandeis's "fair competition" resembled cooperation far more than it did competition.

The clearest indication of the limits of Brandeis's commitment to competition was his support for the fair trade movement, which sought legislation to protect local retailers from the competition of chain stores and discount houses. The legislative agenda of this movement eventually triumphed in the New Deal with the passage of the Robinson-Patman Act and the Miller-Tydings Act.[18] But Brandeis's reservations concerning competition were also evident in his attempts to promote worker participation in corporate management. Industrial democracy would replace competitive relations between labor unions and capitalists with cooperation based on shared interests. Brandeis never embraced socialism as an alternative to competitive capitalism because socialism implied centralized control of economic relations by a large bureaucratic state, and Brandeis's suspicion of large organizations extended from big business to the big state. Nevertheless, the reformed capitalism championed by Brandeis claimed to serve the interests of all because it was based on the same ideal of cooperation that inspired socialism. As Brandeis noted in his analysis of the sources of labor unrest, "It seems to me that the prevailing discontent is due perhaps less to dissatisfaction with the material conditions, as to the denial of participation in management, and that the only way to avoid Socialism is to develop cooperation in its broadest sense."[19]

Business and Competition

Ideology is not the only factor that explains New Deal hostility to competition. The New Deal was a populist political coalition that rallied the owners of small businesses, farmers, and blue-collar workers against big business. All these groups shared the perception that they were victims of the existing competitive marketplace and of the large corporations that dominated some markets, and they demanded reforms that would dampen competition and thereby protect their economic interests. Industries composed of small businesses have been a particularly fertile breeding ground for demands for government-sponsored cartelization. Labor favors anticompetitive policies because a less competitive environment relaxes business opposition to wage increases. At the same time, these groups also feared regimentation and a loss of autonomy through the expansion of the regulatory state, with the result that they have often been ambivalent about the growth of federal regulation even when their general response was supportive.

In identifying the anticompetitive policies that can be attributed to the New Dealers, one must distinguish the anticompetitive proclivities of New Dealers from those of big business, which was not part of the New Deal coalition. Big business can have powerful interests in restricting competition. Even if the size of a large firm is an indication that it has been competitively successful (and this is not always the case), its market position is constantly threatened by new rivals. Moreover, profit margins in a competitive marketplace are lower than they would be under monopoly or cartelized oligopoly.

Nevertheless, big business's preferred options for limiting competition generally differed from those favored by the New Dealers and their small business and labor constituencies. Big firms were frequently found in oligopolistic industries with a small number of big firms. Collusive agreements can be effective on a voluntary basis in an oligopolistic industry where firm behavior consistent with cartel agreements is easier to police. Government involvement is unnecessary and unwanted. In less concentrated industries it is easier for smaller and medium-size firms to cheat unobtrusively on cartel agreements, which then tend to unravel as enforcement breaks down. In industries with a large number of small to medium-size firms, anticompetitive agreements can be effective only if they are enforced by government.[20]

With these considerations in mind, I now turn to three areas of New Deal regulatory reform to demonstrate that the regulatory state established in this period often had an anticompetitive bias; that the anticompetitive character of these reforms was shaped by the ideological commitments of New Dealers and the economic interests of progressive constituencies; and that the reforms were generally opposed by big business.

The National Recovery Administration

The National Recovery Administration (NRA), established by the National Industrial Recovery Act of 1933 (NIRA), was a brief but bold experiment with corporatist national planning. It was the keystone of Roosevelt's efforts to promote economic recovery in the early New Deal and one of the most ambitious regulatory regimes ever attempted in peacetime in American history. New Dealers had hoped that the NRA, approved on an experimental basis for only two years, would lead to a fundamental and permanent restructuring of the American economy, providing a third path between the extremes of socialism and laissez-faire capitalism. Industries were encouraged to join together and draft codes of fair trade competition that, if approved by government supervisors, would become legally enforceable codes prohibiting a new class of economic crimes such as cutting prices below costs. Over 550 codes covering industries representing 90 percent of the industrial production of the

United States were implemented. The NRA insignia, the Blue Eagle, became a new symbol of patriotism and was displayed by an overwhelming majority of American businesses.

The outcome of this massive corporatist experiment is not a matter of serious dispute. Far from eliciting a patriotic spirit of cooperation that would mitigate differences between economic interests, the NRA became a battleground focusing and intensifying clashes of economic interest. Small and middle-size businesses fought with big businesses for control of the code authorities and the contents of the codes. Section 7a of the NIRA had guaranteed labor the right to organize and bargain collectively, but the battle over the interpretation and implementation of this provision turned 1934 into one of the most strike-filled years in American labor history.[21] This politicization of economic conflict was a primary factor in the political failure of the NRA.

When cooperation did occur, it was generally through the establishment of cartels that operated at the expense of the consumer. The economist Michael Weinstein has estimated that "the codes eliminated a potential 8 percent average annual increase in real output (and a 15 percent reduction in the number of individuals who were unemployed during the NRA period)" and that "NIRA-induced diminution of real wealth (due to the inflationary consequences) was responsible for a 6–11 percent reduction in annual GNP during the two years of the NIRA codes."[22] The NRA was a public policy failure because the anticompetitive ethos it institutionalized impeded economic growth and recovery. What remains to be determined is the source of this anticompetitive spirit. Was it derived from the New Deal and its constituents, or was it from big business?

One factor contributing to the formation of cartels under the umbrella of the NRA was the ideological orientation of the progressives who were supervising its implementation. Hugh Johnson was the NRA administrator, a position he secured based on his role on the War Industries Board (WIB) during World War I. The WIB had many similarities to the NRA. Despite stints as a businessman, Johnson had never been enamored of competition. He frequently coupled such pejorative adjectives as "unfair" or "destructive" to the term when he described the state of the American economy. Arguing that capitalism had brought the nation close "to collapse and ruin," he proposed a balanced economy under "government supervision" as a replacement for "the murderous doctrine of savage and wolfish individualism, looking to dog-eat-dog and devil take the hindmost."[23]

Donald Richberg, who was second in command at the NRA as its general counsel and who subsequently replaced Johnson as NRA administrator, shared Johnson's skepticism toward a free-market economy. "The truth is that no man of any political intelligence and economic vision has been able to defend the existing economic order since the World War laid bare its utter inadequacy and its insane consequences." For Richberg, the depression was the death knell of the old order, and he demanded a new social order based on the "democratization of industry."[24] The "democratization of industry" implies a far more radical restructuring of economic life than would a regulatory state committed to maximizing consumer welfare, the more modest goal embraced by economic theory today.

The progressive inspiration of the NRA has frequently been overlooked because, superficially, it resembled a corporatist alternative proposed by corporate liberals in the big business community. Even before the Great Depression these corporate liberals had advocated coordination of economic decision making among firms through strong trade associations and greater cooperation with government. Some corporate liberals also encouraged the unionization of labor to encourage collaboration between labor and management. After the Great Depression, Gerald Swope, executive director of General Electric, formalized this preference for cooperation over competition in a proposal for industrial self-government called the Swope Plan.[25]

Despite some similarities between the Swope Plan and the NRA, the inspiration for the NRA was not corporate liberalism. Swope's proposal was a scheme for industrial *self*-government, and the role assigned to government was therefore modest. Swope wanted the federal government to relax antitrust laws to permit greater cooperation among businesses, but he did not want government to use the trade association network to impose government plans on business. When the regulatory role played by government in the NRA departed sharply from the role he had envisioned in his plan, he became a critic and called for the replacement of the NRA with a more voluntary approach that would substitute coordination through an expanded U.S. Chamber of Commerce for compulsory planning by a government agency.[26]

Swope's disaffection with the NRA was not idiosyncratic. When the

NIRA came up for reextension in 1935, the Chamber of Commerce and the National Association of Manufacturers opposed it. Both organizations were influenced by big business leadership. That their rejection of the NRA reflected the posture of big business is evident also in the vigorous opposition of the American Liberty League to the NRA, as well as to many other New Deal programs. The American Liberty League was a newly formed organization that represented the interests of some of America's largest firms. Even the seemingly more conciliatory Business Advisory Council, an informal council of big business leaders who advised the Commerce Department, was demanding fundamental changes in the NRA, changes that would have transformed it into a system of industrial self-government.

To the extent that there was interest group support for an extension of the NRA, it came from small and medium-size businesses and from organized labor—that is, the New Deal political coalition. In bituminous coal, retail selling, and cotton textiles, there was strong business support for an NRA-type program. These were all industries composed of small to medium-size firms in highly competitive markets. When the Supreme Court declared the NRA unconstitutional in *United States v. Schechter Poultry Corporation* (1935), leaders in all these sectors sought legislation to re-create mini-NRAs just for their industries.[27] While there was some small business dissatisfaction with the NRA, it arose most often from the enforcement problems encountered by code authorities rather than from a fundamental hostility to the aims of the program. A poorly enforced code allowed competitors who cheated to gain a competitive advantage and penalized the law-abiding. Lacking market power, firms in these industries were induced to accept government regulation to mitigate market competition.[28]

The American Federation of Labor (AFL), which had added more than nine hundred thousand new members during the NRA period, also supported an extension of the NRA. Because NRA codes had to include a section recognizing the right of labor to organize and bargain collectively, the AFL appreciated the opportunities provided by the federal recognition of labor rights. Labor support for the NRA cooled markedly when Hugh Johnson allowed company unions to vie with AFL unions for recognition rights and then allocated representation proportionately to voting strength in labor elections, but even then the AFL did not simply repudiate the NRA. Instead, it demanded winner-take-all elections that would have more effectively delegitimized company unions, a demand that was realized with the passage of the Wagner Act. But the AFL still strongly preferred the NRA to the legal environment that had preceded it.

This pattern of support and opposition for its extension is strong evidence that the NRA was dominated by progressive New Dealers, because it was benefiting New Deal constituencies. The anticompetitive features of the NRA, which were inextricably part of the original conception of the program, mirrored the anticompetitive spirit of the New Deal. Admittedly, such progressives as Brandeis were opposed to the NRA. Indeed, Brandeis joined in the majority opinion of the Supreme Court in the Schechter decision that struck down the NRA as an unconstitutional delegation of congressional power and an improper extension of federal regulatory power over intrastate commerce. Brandeis's opposition, however, arose from his concern that the NRA was a vehicle for collusion between big business and big government rather than from reservations about its anticompetitive effects or its impact on economic efficiency.

Transportation Sector

The transportation sector, encompassing railroads, trucking, maritime shipping, and airlines, provides numerous examples of the anticompetitive orientation of New Deal business regulation. Declining profits and layoffs in these industries were described by New Dealers as the inevitable consequences of "excessive" or "cutthroat" competition. Regulatory solutions were developed which often claimed to do no more than mitigate competition and make it fairer, but the tendency of this regulatory regime was to suppress competition altogether. Transportation regulation generally adopted some form of rate setting combined with barriers to entry to reduce competitive pressures on established rates.

In the case of trucking, "excessive" competition was attributed to the ease of entry into the industry. The industry had numerous independent or wildcat truckers who owned a single truck and would drop prices below the more profitable levels desired by established firms in order to attract additional business. In the case of railroads, "excessive" competition was a problem because capital-intensive firms with high fixed costs were constantly tempted to cut prices to increase their volume of business. In maritime shipping, excessive competition had an international dimension, as higher-cost but subsidized American shippers struggled to compete with subsidized foreign firms. Because the New Dealers discovered excessive competition in a variety of market structures, some of which were not confined to the transportation industries, the logic of the New Deal analysis was that excessive competition was a widespread feature of a modern capitalist system.[29]

The New Dealers looked to government to address the problems plaguing the transportation industries. The Emergency Railroad Transportation Act, passed in 1933, provided for joint government-business coordinating committees to achieve greater efficiencies through the pooling of resources and the elimination of "unnecessary" duplicate services spawned by competition.[30] The Motor Carrier Act of 1935 gave the Interstate Commerce Commission (ICC) regulatory powers over interstate trucking. Licensing and entry controls were established for common and contract carriers, and the ICC was authorized to fix maximum and minimum rates.[31] The Merchant Marine Act of 1936 created a Maritime Commission, provided subsidies for American companies to meet foreign competition, and established regulatory controls over wages and executive salaries, shipping rates and routes, trade practices, industrial structure, and profits.[32] The Air Mail Act of 1934 and the Civil Aeronautics Act of 1938 established entry, route, and price controls for the emergent airline industry.[33] In all these industries the characteristic legislative solution imposed anticompetitive regulatory controls.

Furthermore, the legislative histories of these measures confirm their progressive credentials even if business interests also played a role in the drafting process. The progressive wing of the Democratic Party had established solid control of Congress in the 1932 election and would retain that control until the 1938 elections. While there were elements in the dominant coalition that were not ideologically progressive, they were not in control of the legislative agenda. Conservative southern Democrats had essentially ceded control over national economic policy to Roosevelt and the progressives in tacit exchange for state control over race relations. Forces opposed to the progressive agenda could block legislation occasionally, but they could not enact measures actively opposed by progressives. In addition, each of these measures proved acceptable to the Roosevelt administration, for none was enacted over Roosevelt vetoes, and some, such as the Emergency Railroad Transportation Act, were drafted at the administration's behest.

Joseph Eastman directed the transportation task force that had drafted the Emergency Railroad Transportation Act. He had been an ICC commissioner before Roosevelt tapped him to become the federal coordinator of transportation, the regulatory czar of transportation in the New Deal. He was a pillar of the reform regulatory establishment. Eastman recognized that "there are impressive evidences that competition is a stimulus to alert, aggressive management," but he also insisted that monopoly "may lead to an indifferent and unprogressive management."[34] In the case of railroads, which were the original object of his regulatory zeal, he did not believe that competitive forces were strong enough to encourage efficiency, and he distinguished himself from those who "set great store upon competition."[35]

Eastman had reached this conclusion after his experiences with railroad regulation and control during World War I. The federal government had taken over the railroads when private industry failed to provide efficient coordination of services, jeopardizing the war effort. When the war ended, Eastman opposed proposals to return the railroads to their private sector owners. He asserted that "the roads should continue in the possession and control of the nation" to assure the availability of low-cost capital, to avoid high rates, to provide for efficient consolidation, and to improve labor relations.[36]

Despite his claims of pragmatism and sensitivity to the particularities of industrial structure, Eastman's preference for government ownership of railroads influenced his regulatory posture toward other industries in the transportation sector. He became an advocate of planning, writing to Felix Frankfurter in 1933 that "disinterested students know that the theory [of private enterprise] is to a very considerable extent fallacious and the results are not what they should be."[37] As his responsibilities expanded to encompass trucking and inland waterways, he championed an aggressive regulatory agenda that relied on government-enforced rules rather than competition to control business behavior.

Business responses to Eastman's regulatory initiatives provide further evidence that the anticompetitive thrust of New Deal regulation was a policy preference determined by reformers and their constituencies. Ever since the owners and managers of large railroads were condemned as "robber barons" by nineteenth-century reformers, they had been targeted for further regulatory scrutiny by each new generation of reformers. Not surprisingly, these oligopolistic firms opposed the New Deal regulatory state and preferred private cooperation to government regulation to relieve competitive pressures. The Association of American Railroads, which was formed in 1934, became the coordinating agency for the industry, which proceeded to undercut labor support for regulation by promising unemployment compensation for laid-off workers. When the Emergency Railroad Transportation Act came up for reextension in 1936, it died in committee after both management and unions expressed opposition.

The response of the trucking industry, composed of small and medium-size firms lacking market power, was very different. These New Deal constituents realized that a trucking cartel was impossible without government help owing to the large number of trucking firms and the ease of entry into the industry. Association was further impeded by clashes of interests dividing common carriers, contract carriers, and private truckers. Five percent of all trucking firms were common carriers that offered their services to the public at large and therefore were legally obliged not to discriminate among shippers. Common carriers, which were further subdivided into regular route and irregular route firms, had somewhat different interests from the 85 percent of truckers who were private carriers. Private carriers were nontrucking businesses who used trucks to transport their wares in the course of their other business activities. Finally, the remaining 10 percent of the trucking industry was composed of contract carriers who were principally in the business of transportation but did not offer their services to the public at large. Contract carriers served specific shippers with specialized needs.

Under the NRA all truckers had been encouraged to join a national trade association and draft a code of fair trade practices that would mitigate competition in an equitable manner for all the interests in the industry. However, the industry could not reconcile its diverse interests. Only after prolonged negotiations and great prodding from government officials was the American Trucking Association (ATA) formed and a code of fair trade competition agreed on. Soon thereafter the NRA was declared unconstitutional.

Into the vacuum caused by the collapse of the NRA stepped Joseph Eastman. Eastman persuaded the ATA to support what became the Motor Carrier Act of 1935. Ostensibly, this was a shift away from the self-regulation emphasized by the NRA and toward a form of public regulation, but the change was less dramatic than it seemed. Eastman had developed an administrative style of consultation and compromise with those he was regulating, and the Motor Carrier Act included a clause directing the ICC to work with industry organizations. Eastman's administration of the Motor Carrier Act improved enforcement over that of the NRA, but the substantial continuities in regulatory approach between the two periods provide additional proof that the anticompetitive NRA orientation was not an isolated aberration in the New Deal regulatory regime. The support of small and medium-size trucking firms for this regulatory regime, moreover, especially when contrasted with the opposition of the big-business railroads to a more expansive government role, provides further justification for affixing the label "progressive" to this regulatory order.

The creation of the Civil Aeronautics Board (CAB) provides an additional example of the New Deal regulatory approach. Airline regulation is significant both because it occurred late in the New Deal, at a time when the anticompetitive NRA approach had purportedly been abandoned, and because the decision to create a new, independent regulatory agency, rather than entrust airline regulation to the ICC, provided an opportunity for reformers to develop regulations in an emergent industry without being unduly influenced by the legacy of railroad regulation. This opportunity was squandered, however, because the agency established the same forms of price controls and barriers to entry as had characterized the general New Deal regulatory approach. This outcome suggests that the anticompetitive impulses of the New Deal were indeed intrinsic to its fundamental spirit.

Banking

The anticompetitive spirit of banking reform was not as pronounced as that in the NRA and in transportation regulation, but it is important for understanding the significant institutional reforms of the banking sector that were introduced in the New Deal. The wave of bank failures brought on by the depression threatened the nation with financial chaos, and the first objective of government action was necessarily to make the banks solvent and restore public confidence. As was generally the case with such recovery measures, however, the New Dealers also incorporated reforms intended to change permanently the character of the banking system so as to prevent future collapses. The executive proclamation of a national bank holiday and the enactment of the Emergency Banking Act of 1933 and the Glass-Steagall Act of 1933 were all early New Deal responses to the banking crisis. The most frequently noted reform to emerge from this period was the creation of the Federal Deposit Insurance Corporation (FDIC). The presupposition for providing federal insurance for deposits, though, was regulation of banking practices that would prevent banks from failing in the first place. Such a regulatory framework would help to avoid costly FDIC bailouts.[38]

One example of banking regulations that exposed the anticompetitive presupposition of New Deal economic thinking was that establishing price controls for checking and savings accounts. The Banking Act of 1933 prohibited the payment of interest on demand or checking accounts and allowed the Federal Reserve Board to regulate the interest rates paid on savings accounts for banks that were members of the Federal Reserve system. These controls were extended to nonfederal reserve banks that were nevertheless insured under the FDIC by the 1935 Banking Act. Reformers' reasons for doing so illuminate their beliefs about markets and the causes of the Great Depression.[39]

New Dealers laid considerable blame for the Great Depression on the speculative lending policies of banks. Franklin Roosevelt referred to bankers as "unscrupulous money changers" who had caused incalculable misery by gambling with "other people's money."[40] Bankers, it was charged, had conveyed the savings of hardworking Americans into the hands of Wall Street speculators, who then defaulted on these loans when the Great Crash burst their speculative bubble. While Roosevelt exploited widespread moral outrage in reaction to anecdotes of greed and exploitation, he and his fellow progressives also saw a systemic failure lurking behind moral malfeasance. Banks were driven to make loans to Wall Street speculators by a competitive marketplace in which depositors flocked to banks offering the highest interest rates. Because riskier loans provided higher rates of return and greater bank profits that could then be used to pay higher interest rates and attract more customers, the progressives assumed that the marketplace encouraged banks to make unsound loans. The regulatory solution was to use price controls to prohibit banks from competing for deposits.

The Banking Act of 1933 also prohibited national banks from establishing branches on a statewide basis unless state laws allowed state banks to do so. This significant restriction on branch banking prevented national banks under most circumstances from competing with local banks. Banking reform was in this way preserving competitors, which were often small, inefficient banks, rather than encouraging competition. The rationale for this anticompetitive restriction was vintage Brandeis. Progressives insisted that local banks under local control would deal more humanely with those who defaulted on loans. Roosevelt had embraced this principle while still governor of New York, when banking reform was on that state's political agenda: "We must by law maintain the principle that banks are a definite benefit to the individual community. That is why a concentration of all banking resources and all banking control in one spot or in a few hands is contrary to a sound public policy. We want strong and stable banks, and at the same time each community must be enabled to keep control of its own money within its own borders."[41]

The anticompetitive thrust of banking regulation in 1933 provides the backdrop against which the great battles over the Banking Act of 1935 are to be understood. The banking reform agenda of the New Deal had not been exhausted by the spate of legislation in 1933. The structural precondition for New Deal regulation of banks was the establishment of an institutional framework in which government regulators had the power to control the behavior of private banks. The most influential New Dealers in this policy arena rejected the most radical alternative to the current system: the nationalization of banking. Nevertheless, they did insist on further centralization of power within the federal reserve system and on strengthening the policy instruments at the Federal Reserve Board's disposal for controlling bank behavior. This agenda was substantially realized with the enactment of the Banking Act of 1935, which reduced the power of bankers and enhanced the power of government over the Federal Reserve Board (FRB) and over the regional reserve banks. It also granted the FRB control over the new Federal Open Market Committee with its important powers to influence the reserve requirements and lending policies of member banks. The anticompetitive presuppositions of New Deal reformers made it probable that those new powers would be used to dampen competition rather than to intensify it.

As was the case with the NRA and regulation in the transportation sector, anticompetitive regulations in the banking sector cannot be attributed to the cartel aspirations of big business. The legislative history of the Bank Reform Acts of 1935 make this particularly clear. Progressive elites driven by an ideological agenda made common cause with small and medium-size banks opposed to the dominance of Wall Street to enact this reform. The eastern banking establishment opposed the reforms.

The controversial provisions in the 1935 banking bill were in Title II, the section that dealt with the extension of government control over banking by increasing presidential appointments while reducing slots reserved for bankers in the composition of the Federal Reserve Board. Title II also centralized regulatory powers in the hands of the FRB. James Warburg, chairman of the Bank of Manhattan and a pillar of the eastern banking establishment, testified before congressional hearings that he was "unequivocally opposed" to Title II. He considered Title II so fundamentally flawed that it would be unacceptable even if modified. Winthrop Aldrich, president of the powerful Chase National Bank, similarly spoke for most of Wall Street when he condemned Title II, arguing that "this is not liberalizing the Federal Reserve System. It is making it over into an instrument of despotic authority."[42] The leaders of the banking community warned that monetary policy would become the plaything of partisan politics if Title II were not dropped from the bill.

To the extent that the administration garnered support from bankers, it came from western and rural bankers who resented Wall Street dominance. A. P. Giannini of California's Bank of America disputed Warburg's testimony, arguing that "however typical his attitude may be taken as that of the New York banker it by no means represents the attitude of many bankers outside New York. . . . Personally I would rather that this power be exercised by a public body in the public interest than by the New York banking fraternity."[43] Giannini's comments confirmed the assertions of Democratic representative Thomas Ford that "some of the leading bankers of the West that I have talked with are in favor of it."[44]

Opponents of the administration's bill eventually succeeded in watering down Title II, most notably by providing safeguards against partisan presidential control of the FRB. But the modifications had more to do with the pique of Senator Carter Glass, who despite his august status as the Senate expert on banking had been excluded from the drafting of the bill, than it did with Wall Street opposition to the bill. Even in its revised form, Wall Street was virtually unified in opposition to the measure.

While the centralized control over banking established by this bill had the potential to strengthen a market economy by correcting what most economists would identify as market failures, New Deal rhetoric and legislation reveal a more anticompetitive agenda.

The Banking Act of 1935 did not satiate the New Dealers' regulatory zeal. In 1938 Roosevelt requested legislation that would further restrict bank holding companies to prevent bank monopolies. Although this bill was not enacted in 1938, largely because Congress had become more conservative and was increasingly hostile to New Deal initiatives, it was regularly reintroduced in Congress until 1956, when the Bank Holding Company Act became law. This act can properly be described as part of the New Deal legacy. Like other New Deal measures, the Bank Holding Company Act is distrustful of markets and the logic of competition. This law closed a loophole in such earlier anticompetitive banking laws as the National Banking Act of 1863 and the 1927 McFadden Act. Those laws had protected small local banks from competition by branch offices of large national banks, thereby inhibiting the development of interstate banking and large banks that reaped the rewards of economies of scale. National banks partially circumvented these restrictions through the development of holding company bank networks, but the Bank Holding Company Act required state approval for bank holding companies to acquire or charter a bank in a state other than the one that served as their headquarters. There were virtually no state authorizations for expansion of bank holding companies between 1956 and the early 1980s.[45]

Renewing Faith in Markets and Competition

New Deal regulation of transportation and banking and the comprehensive regulation of the economy under the NRA exemplify the anticompetitive character of much New Deal regulation. Moreover, this list is illustrative, not exhaustive. The New Deal approach to regulation of agriculture in the Agricultural Adjustment Act provided for price supports and output controls for a number of crops, as well as for the dairy industry. There were far too many agricultural producers for cartelization to be a feasible strategy without the aid of government. But New Dealers convinced that excessive competition was the cause of economic distress in this sector proved all too willing to provide the requisite subsidies and coercion. Similarly, the Guffey Coal Acts established price floors and output restrictions for bituminous coal.

Comparable policies were sought unsuccessfully with some administration support in cotton textiles, lumber, the apparel trades, and anthracite coal. The Natural Gas Act of 1938 established the legal foundation for control of natural gas prices, although this did not become effective until 1954 when legal ambiguities were resolved by the Supreme Court. The Robinson-Patman Act and the Miller-Tydings Act protected small retailers from the competition of larger retailers and chain stores by limiting price discrimination (that is, restricting quantity discounts available to larger stores) and by allowing resale price–maintenance agreements.

The New Deal frequently limited competition in economically inefficient ways, but it did not give up on competition and markets altogether. The followers of Brandeis, in particular, continued to espouse competitive ideals even though their hostility to bigness impoverished their conception of competition. When the Brandeisians were influential, regulation could enhance competition or detract from it depending on the specific regulatory problem being addressed. When Wright Patman, whom Jordan Schwarz has aptly described as "the last Brandeisian," championed small retailers by cosponsoring the Wright-Patman bill, the results were anticompetitive.[46] When Ben Cohen and Tommy Corcoran set to work drafting securities regulations that would protect investors from dishonestly advertised stocks and from insider trading, the results were pro-competitive and market strengthening.

There is, however, a paradox worth noting about securities regulation, which is arguably the greatest regulatory triumph of the New Deal. Although the Securities and Exchange Commission (SEC) has established a reputation for effectiveness and efficiency in regulating the stock market and many of the abuses that were the target of New Deal reforms have been corrected, the larger Brandeisian agenda of reducing the market power of big business has remained unfulfilled. Ironically, the reforms of the stock market which Brandeis inspired may have transformed it into an efficient instrument for the further consolidation of American business through mergers and leveraged buyouts. In addition, an unanticipated consequence of stock market reform is that it has become disproportionately expensive for small companies to comply with the exacting registration requirements for listing stocks on the New York Stock

Exchange, a continuing concern despite repeated efforts by the SEC to remedy the problem.

The Brandeisians were not the only New Dealers who might have had second thoughts about the consequences of New Deal securities regulation. Such planners as Rexford Tugwell had hoped that the New Deal would be a stepping-stone to government control of investment decisions. For Tugwell, the public good as determined by technical experts in government, rather than private profit, should determine the allocation of capital. Market-strengthening securities reforms like those enacted by the New Deal reduced the likelihood that the United States would embrace planning.

Neither the Brandeisians nor the planners could properly appreciate New Deal securities reform despite the pride some members of the former group displayed in this accomplishment. This would suggest that the deepest failure of the New Deal was conceptual and ideological rather than practical. The New Dealers failed to understand that scarcity remained the foundation of economic life and that this fact had different implications for the proper role of competition in the rational organization of society than those they embraced.

Once the New Deal regulatory order was institutionalized, it developed its own internal logic and regulatory momentum. Agencies generally extended their regulatory reach in an incremental fashion from the forties until the late 1970s. If new problems arose, Congress would authorize additional regulations. In the 1960s the regulatory focus shifted from issues of monopoly and fair trade practices to concerns about consumer protection, preservation of the environment, and worker health and safety. The courts also dramatically expanded their role in supervising regulatory agencies. As significant as some of these changes in the character of the regulatory state were, they did not challenge the premises of New Deal regulation.

Beginning in the late 1970s, however, the New Deal regulatory regime was challenged. Reformers committed to deregulation dismantled much of the New Deal regulatory framework in transportation and banking. The Airline Deregulation Act of 1978 abolished the CAB and its controls over rates, routes, and entry for airlines. The Motor Vehicle Act of 1980 partially deregulated trucking by limiting ICC controls that had originally been granted by the Motor Carrier Act of 1935. The Depository Institutions Deregulation and Monetary Control Act of 1980 removed restrictions on interest-bearing checking accounts. Finally, and most recent, in 1999 Congress dismantled Glass-Steagall Act regulatory restrictions that separated commercial and savings banks from investment banks. The Financial Services Act (1999), which also dismantled restrictions stemming from the Bank Holding Company Act, permits commercial banks, securities houses, and insurers to compete with one another. For years economists had been criticizing regulations in these sectors as inefficient and recommending a more market-oriented approach, although in doing so they seldom recognized that they were implicitly repudiating a major component of the New Deal regulatory state.[47] In retrospect this wave of deregulation was as much a repudiation of the New Deal regulatory legacy as the passage of the Personal Responsibility and Work Opportunity Act was a repudiation of the New Deal welfare legacy, but it proved to be far less controversial. In the world of the late twentieth century, where communism had collapsed and planning had been discredited, the distrust of markets and competition exhibited by New Dealers appeared fundamentally misguided.

Notes

The author thanks Steven Teles and Miles Cahill for their assistance.

1. Ronald D. Rotunda, "The Liberal Label: Roosevelt's Capture of a Symbol," in *Public Policy,* ed. John D. Montgomery and Albert O. Hirschman (Cambridge: Harvard University Press, 1968), vol. 17.

2. "The Commonwealth Club Address," in *The Public Papers and Addresses of Franklin D. Roosevelt,* ed. Samuel I. Rosenman 13 vols. (New York: Random House, 1938–50), 1:743–44, 749.

3. Ibid., 745, 749.

4. Ibid., 747, 750–51.

5. Ibid., 752, 755.

6. Ibid., 751–52.

7. Most progressives rejected socialism and therefore described their own economic agenda as an attempt to establish either a middle path between socialism and capitalism or a viable, regulated form of capitalism. However, when regulations include such fundamental departures from market mechanisms as wage and price controls and barriers to entry, then the progressive rhetoric of "reform" should be subjected to critical scrutiny. Saving capitalism from itself by controlling price mechanisms is like saving democracy from the whims of public opinion by depriving the people of the vote.

8. Quoted in Daniel Fusfeld, *The Economic Thought of Franklin D. Roosevelt*

and the Origins of the New Deal (New York: Columbia University Press, 1956), 49; emphasis added.

9. Tugwell asserted that "we [the brain trust] all agreed well enough that collectivism was by now a commitment." Cited in Jordan Schwarz, *Liberal: Adolf A. Berle and the Vision of an American Era* (New York: Free Press, 1987), 79.

10. Raymond Moley, *After Seven Years* (New York: Harper and Row, 1939), 184.

11. Rexford Tugwell, *The Industrial Discipline and the Governmental Arts* (New York: Columbia University Press, 1933), 130.

12. Rexford Tugwell, "The Principles of Planning and the Institution of Laissez-Faire," *American Economic Review* 22, No 1, Supplement, March (1932): 80, 83, 85–86.

13. Ellis Hawley, *The New Deal and the Problem of Monopoly* (Princeton: Princeton University Press, 1966), 293.

14. The most perceptive analysis of Brandeis's economic thinking is Thomas McCraw's "Rethinking the Trust Question," in *Regulation in Perspective: Historical Essays,* ed. McCraw (Cambridge: Harvard University Press, 1981), 1–55.

15. Louis D. Brandeis, *Other People's Money and How the Bankers Use It* (New York: Frederick A. Stokes, 1913), 162–88. See also *The Curse of Bigness: Miscellaneous Papers of Louis D. Brandeis,* ed. Osmond K. Fraenkel (New York: Viking, 1935). As Brandeis colorfully stated his views in a letter to his daughter, Elizabeth Brandeis Raushenbush: "If the Lord had intended things to be big, he would have made man bigger—in brains and character." *Letters of Louis D. Brandeis,* vol. 5 (1921–41), ed. Melvin Urofsky and David Levy (Albany: State University of New York Press, 1978), 527.

16. Brandeis, *Curse of Bigness,* 35–37.

17. On the role of economies of scale in the development of big business and the modern corporation, see Alfred D. Chandler Jr., *The Visible Hand: The Managerial Revolution in American Business* (Cambridge: Harvard University Press, 1977), esp. 372–76.

18. McCraw, "Rethinking the Trust Question," 52. Brandeis had many disciples in the New Deal, but the most important was his friend and protégé Felix Frankfurter. Frankfurter's importance in the New Deal was based on his friendship with Franklin Roosevelt, whom he had gotten to know in World War I when both had served in the Wilson administration. After the war Frankfurter resumed his academic career, and from his faculty position at the Harvard Law School he was ideally situated to inspire his students with Brandeisian progressivism and then channel them into New Deal administrative posts. The Brandeisians trained or recruited by Frankfurer included Ben Cohen, Tommy Corcoran, James Landis, and William Douglas, all of whom played important roles in the development and administration of New Deal regulatory policies.

19. Philippa Strum, *Brandeis: Beyond Progressivism* (Lawrence: University Press of Kansas, 1993), 33–34.

20. Mancur Olson, *The Logic of Collective Action* (Cambridge: Harvard University Press, 1971), 9–16.

21. Charles F. Roos, *NRA Economic Planning* (New York: Da Capo, 1971), 210.

22. Michael Weinstein, *Recovery and Redistribution under the NIRA* (Amsterdam: North Holland, 1980), 30–31.

23. Donald R. Brand, *Corporatism and the Rule of Law: A Study of the National Recovery Administration* (Ithaca: Cornell University Press, 1988), 100.

24. Ibid.

25. Gerald Swope, *The Swope Plan* (New York: Business Bourse, 1931).

26. Brand, *Corporatism,* 129–32.

27. Hawley, *New Deal and the Problem of Monopoly,* 205–25, 247–69; Louis Galambos, *Competition and Cooperation* (Baltimore: Johns Hopkins University Press, 1966), 199–206, 275–79.

28. Brand, *Corporatism,* 102–5, 152–57.

29. This does not imply that the New Dealers had worked out a coherent distinction between excessive competition and healthy competition or between fair competition and unfair competition. As Leverett Lyon noted with regard to the NRA: "There is, in many quarters, an easy-going assumption that it is easy to distinguish between the fair and the unfair, that a mere reference to 'unethical' or 'dishonorable competition' provides in itself the criteria of judging what is 'unethical' or 'dishonorable.' The history of six centuries of common law, the enactment of a large number of federal and state statutes, and the efforts of the Federal Trade Commission have all indicated the fallacy of this view. It has again been demonstrated by the experience of the NRA." Lyon's observation about the problems of the NRA can be extended to the other New Deal programs described in this essay as well. Leverett Lyon, Paul Homan, Lewis Lorwin, George Terborgh, Charles Dearing, and Leon Marshall, *The National Recovery Administration* (Washington, D.C.: Brookings Institution, 1935), 551.

30. Claude E. Fuess, *Joseph B. Eastman* (New York: Columbia University Press, 1952), 211–21, 232–44.

31. William R. Childs, *Trucking and the Public Interest* (Knoxville: University of Tennessee Press, 1985), 119–41.

32. Hawley, *New Deal and the Problem of Monopoly,* 234–39.

33. Ibid., 240–44; Charles S. Rhyne, *The Civil Aeronautics Act Annotated* (Washington, D.C.: National Law Book Company, 1939), 24–30, 41–65.

34. Fuess, *Joseph B. Eastman,* 193.

35. Ibid., 115.

36. Ibid., 98–99.

37. Childs, *Trucking,* 124.

38. A general overview of banking regulation in this period is provided in Helen M. Burns, *The American Banking Community and New Deal Banking Reforms, 1933–1935* (Westport, Conn.: Greenwood, 1974).

39. Milton Friedman and Anna Jacobson Schwartz, *A Monetary History of the United States, 1867–1960* (Princeton: Princeton University Press, 1963), 443–44.

40. In his first inaugural FDR asserted: "Finally, in our progress toward a re-

sumption of work we require two safeguards against a return of the evils of the old order: there must be a strict supervision of all banking and credits and investments, so that there will be an end to speculation with other people's money; and there must be provision for an adequate but sound currency." The phrase "other people's money" is a reference to Louis Brandeis's progressive classic *Other People's Money and How the Bankers Use It*. See "Inaugural Address," March 4, 1933, in Roosevelt, *Public Papers and Addresses*, 2:11–16.

41. Quoted in Fusfeld, *Economic Thought*, 188.

42. Burns, *American Banking Community*, 156.

43. Quoted in ibid., p. 160.

44. Ibid.

45. Michael G. Hadjimichalakis and Krama G. Hadjimichalakis, *Contemporary Money, Banking, and Financial Markets* (Chicago: Irwin, 1995), 359.

46. Jordan Schwarz, *The New Dealers* (New York: Random House, 1993), 285–94.

47. Many economists did not recognize the anticompetitive character of the New Deal because they accepted the capture thesis developed by Marver Bernstein. According to capture theory, regulatory agencies were created to serve the public interest, and they did so until losing regulatory zeal, at which point they were co-opted by powerful business interests. Ignoring the problematic character of regulatory legislation, capture theory attributed the failure of the regulatory state to administrative failures.

Did World War II End the New Deal?

A Comparative Perspective on Postwar Planning Initiatives

Jytte Klausen

Any attempt to grapple with the New Deal's legacy after 1945 must address the difference between planning for scarcity and planning for prosperity. The New Deal was created to address an unparalleled economic crisis. After 1945 the United States experienced unprecedented growth. I contend that war mobilization between 1940 and 1945 did not, as is frequently argued, put an end to the New Deal's commitment to social and economic planning but helped transform it. War mobilization in many respects sustained and "proved" the ideas and assumptions that had informed the New Deal's incipient Keynesianism. The successes of wartime policies (and their failures) allowed an accommodation of what had been a set of policy principles designed for depression and deflation to prosperity and inflation. Contemporary historiography on the New Deal and its legacy suffers, it is argued, from misleading comparisons with an idealized picture of the "social democratic road." Judged against a comparative standard cognizant of the complex history of European planning, the failure of U.S. postwar planning looks less like an anomaly, as attempts to extend wartime planning institutions into peacetime generally failed. When Europeans ultimately found a workable formula for planning, it relied on the involvement of both industry and labor and aimed above all to contain domestic demand for goods and services that had to be paid for in dollars. The mirror image of European dollar shortages was, of course, the U.S. postwar boom. The dollar's hegemony was an impetus for planning in Europe but a hindrance in the United States.

The literature on the role of World War II and the postwar transition in U.S. state development has centered in particular on what has been perceived as two missed opportunities to create a postwar settlement that would have maintained state-centered economic planning. The first is Congress's refusal to allow the National Resources Planning Board (NRPB) to go on after the publication of the board's report in 1943 endorsing presidential planning. The second is the failure of what was originally conceived as the 1945 Full Employment Act. Both policy initiatives had close parallels in Great Britain, the Beveridge Report in the case of the NRPB report and Stafford Cripps's attempt to create industry-wide planning boards known as Industrial Councils in the case of the Employment Act. Conservative critics were the least of the problems facing postwar planners, who having predicted a depression were surprised by the boom. Prosperity further boosted the determination of unions and industry associations to wrest control of wage and price setting away from the state. These posed the more formidable obstacle to the continuation of state controls in peacetime. The prospects for planning in the United States and in Europe diverged, I argue, not in 1945 but by the end the decade, when Europeans were forced by payments crises and dollar shortages to retreat to incomes policy as a means for rationing demand. By way of conclusion, I briefly speculate about the differences that a parliamentary system of government might have made for the durability of the New Deal and the prospects for "real" reform in the United States.

War, State Expansion, and the Post-1945 Settlement

It is a tenet of comparative historical sociology that war mobilization is a cause of state development. Charles Tilly writes on this question, "With a nation in arms, a state's extractive power rose enormously, as did the claims of citizens on their state."[1] The Second World War differed from the wars of the past (and, as it turns out, subsequent wars) in its scope of destruction and domestic resource mobilization. Protected by an ocean that military technology had not yet found a way to cross, the United States was spared direct destruction, but not the transformative effects of military mobilization. Mobilizing for "total war" still enfolded civilian life, and as military needs soaked up productive capacity, civilian and military conscription took over businesses, split up families, and put women to work and children in the care of strangers.[2]

The Allies went to war with a commitment to keep liberal society intact. War mobilization was from the beginning presented as a matter of "system competition" in the many declarations of "war aims" from government and private actors. Lofty promises of how a new postwar order would be better than the past accompanied a demand for sacrifice and toleration of coercive wartime regulations. On the BBC, J. B. Priestley took the lead in promising a "New Jerusalem."[3] Ernest Bevin, a trade union leader of humble origin who was brought into the wartime government to secure union cooperation, promised that socialism at home and "throughout the world" would be the reward for victory.[4] In the United States, the pitch was only marginally less fervent. The Twentieth Century Fund began a "war aims" publication series in 1942 with such titles as *The Road We Are Travelling* and *Goals for America,* both from 1942. If Americans could accept a planned economy in wartime in which unemployment could be eliminated, surely that could also be done in peacetime. The series editor, Stuart Chase, speculated that "in war we are driven by the instinct of self-preservation and by the fire of an aroused patriotism to a unity of purpose and action that no periods of peace have so far equaled. Can peacetime goals generate in us a similar will to do?"[5]

The postwar welfare state, with its emphasis on social minimum standards and government responsibility for full employment, made good on the promises, but scholars have nevertheless argued that the promise to use the new state to "win the war of peace" failed in the United States.[6] Instead of enhancing state capacities, war mobilization between 1940 and 1945 led to the restoration of forces hostile to the state, a restoration that in turn prevented postwar reform and led to the undoing of the achievements and promises of the New Deal.[7] Edwin Amenta and Theda Skocpol summarized the argument when they defined the research agenda for the American political development approach as the question of "why the U.S. failed to forge a national welfare state despite renewed solidarities and increases in federal fiscal capacity brought about by the war."[8]

The thesis of a postwar rollback raises two comparative puzzles. The first is that the post-1945 settlement failed to live up to a trajectory implied by the early New Deal. The second rephrases the exceptionalism thesis by finding U.S. postwar policy lacking compared with the contemporary European approaches to planning and welfare state development. These are separate questions, but sometimes the two perspectives become fused, as in the work of Ira Katznelson, who regards the New Deal as the beginning of a "social democratic road" to reform. In his view, a social democratic alternative was sidetracked in 1945 when "economics replaced political economics, and pluralism supplanted the politics of class."[9] In an article coauthored with Bruce Pietrykowski, Katznelson adds to the argument by suggesting that U.S. Keynesianism was a variant of planning and represented a coherent choice among alternative versions of planning.[10]

Two comparisons are suggested, one to the early New Deal and its "promise" and the other to European social democracy. These are "fuzzy" standards. I agree that choices were made and that U.S. Keynesianism was both "a choice" and different from European approaches. I nevertheless find that the rollback thesis is based on faulty comparative assumptions both with respect to the early New Deal and with respect to postwar European planning policies. What was the essential core of the New Deal, and by what standard may we say that postwar policies were a disappointment? Was it a crisis administration, a social program, or both? Our understanding of the New Deal itself shapes our view of what would have constituted a loyal continuation after 1945. The rigid price-fixing schemes of the code authorities set up under the 1933 National Industrial Recovery Act (NIRA) do not represent a good model for what postwar planning might have been. They would have been of little use in a growth economy and were in any case declared unconstitutional by the Supreme Court in 1935. Moreover, when European postwar planners attempted to impose planning by government agency, roughly modeled on the Codes, they too failed.

An alternative is to regard the New Deal principally as a set of political commitments—that is, as an end rather than a set of specific means.[11] Sidney Milkis has argued, for example, that Roosevelt stood by the aims of the New Deal. He finds that at the core of wartime policies remained a promise of a new economic constitution—the "four freedoms"—that FDR anticipated as early as 1932 in his address to the Commonwealth Club. FDR subsequently renewed the pledge to reform in the 1944 State of the Union Address when he called for an economic bill of rights, a "Second Bill of Rights."[12] This interpretation is close to the understanding of FDR that emerges from the works of such biographers as James MacGregor Burns and Doris Kearns Goodwin, who see his legacy as primarily political.[13]

In one sense, at least, the war indisputably ended the New Deal, namely, by ending the economic crisis that the New Deal was created to address. In the course of a few months in 1940, industrial mobilization for the war effort ended unemployment and an eleven-year-long depression. FDR may even have considered the New Deal over. In a Christmas interview in 1943, he asked reporters to stop using the term to describe his administration. The New Deal, he said, was medicine for a disease that no longer afflicted the country, and war demanded a new set of prescriptions. "Dr. Win the War" had replaced "Dr. New Deal," he said.[14] Where the New Deal had aimed to provide jobs for people in the face of the collapse of private industry and to fix wages and prices to prevent downward spiraling, wartime policies were now put to the task of alleviating labor shortages and controlling inflation, not deflation.

The accomplishments of the New Deal pale in comparison with the social and economic progress of the war years. The per capita gross national product (GNP) declined from $772 to $718 from 1930 to 1935. In 1940, it was $916 and in 1945, $1,293.[15] Growth was also more evenly distributed during the war than before. The personal family income of the poorest 40 percent of the population constituted 12.5 percent of all family incomes in 1929 but rose to 16 percent in 1946. The top 5 percent of the population saw their share of all income decrease from 30 percent in 1929 to 21.3 percent in 1946. Income distribution stabilized after the war, with the top 5 percent taking in 20 percent of all incomes throughout the 1950s. (The picture was not radically altered until the Reagan years, when incomes were redistributed back to the rich.)

War mobilization also allowed corporate profits to bounce back, but with matching increases in wages and farm incomes. Corporate net profits, after taxes, peaked at $12,181 million in 1942, three times what they had been in 1935 and up from a loss of $888 million in 1931. Average annual earnings per full-time employee in manufacturing rose from $1,432 dollars in 1940 to $2,517 in 1945. Based on numbers, the war accomplished much of what the New Deal had aimed to do but could not. In sum, questions about the New Deal's legacy after 1945 must be answered in a context that allows for significant adjustments to the ends and the means of New Deal policies. It is with this reservation in mind that I now return to the question of the demise of the New Deal and the failure of planning in the United States (and in Europe) after 1945.

Wartime Planning and the Postwar Settlement: Comparative Perspectives

United States historians generally agree that policies undertaken during World War I played an important role in shaping New Deal planning policies and public policy philosophies. Consensus has it that war mobilization worked to enhance and modernize the federal state, despite the war's brevity. (The United States entered belatedly in 1917.)[16] Did World War II fail to provide a similar "peace dividend"? The answer is ambiguous. In 1945 it was widely expected—and feared—that this time the war had produced a concentration of state power in the hands of the president and a rollback of federalism that would never recede.[17] Comparativists too have found World War II to be exceptionally important in shaping new state capacities in both combatant and noncombatant countries. Alan Milward's study of core wartime institutions in the Axis as well as Allied countries led him to conclude that war mobilization had a homogenizing effect on states, irrespective of system differences. He notes the similarities between the economic controls and resource mobilization policies put in place in the United States and those established in fascist Japan, Nazi Germany, and liberal Great Britain, even as specific institutional arrangements varied.[18]

In liberal, in contrast to fascist, countries, the creation of extraordinary state powers depended on the consent of courts and other actors to the suspension of peacetime rights. Wartime institutions were based on temporary crisis legislation exempting governments from constitutional restraints. For this reason, Milward contends, wartime planning never did represent a viable model for permanent postwar planning. I have similarly argued elsewhere that while war mobilization produced the concentration and the integration of national interest groups that were a prerequisite for postwar planning, their consent to state-centered planning was contingent and temporary. With the end of the crisis, consent to enlarged state capacities ended too. The success of wartime policies encouraged planning advocates, but planning based on the direct continuation of the crisis institutions to meet peacetime purposes quickly proved unrealistic, in part because state-centered planning was incompatible with interest group autonomy.[19] Hence, the same interest group that the state had nurtured to become a "partner" in the administration of the war economy turned against the state when the war ended.

Scholars who find U.S. planning wanting in comparison with postwar European planning efforts often have an incomplete picture of planning's rocky road in the "success" cases. With peace, unions and business associations that had agreed to wage and price fixing during the war insisted on free wage negotiations—"voluntarism"—and the restoration of associational freedom. The argument that the involvement of business elites in wartime planning was the cause of planning's failure in the United States ignores that when planning succeeded in Europe, it did so only with the collaboration of industry. (France, Sweden, and the Federal Republic of Germany are the important cases. The list illustrates how difficult it is to speak of a "social democratic" model.) From a comparative viewpoint, the inclusion of business elites in wartime controls was an enabling rather than a disabling condition for postwar planning. The integration during the war years accommodated previously hostile business and union elites alike to the state and produced a new template for state-society relations, namely, corporatism.

Wartime planning arguably saved New Deal planning, which had been thrown into disarray by the termination of the National Recovery Administration in 1935, by transforming the means of planning. The war economy "proved" that the government could engage in planning production and consumption and that government debt could be used to finance economic expansion without bringing about the collapse of capitalism or creating runaway inflation. In 1930 the national public debt was $131 per capita. In 1940 it was still only $325, despite the New Deal's use of deficit spending as a remedial tool. The war changed that: in 1945 per capita national public debt was $1,848. The war debt was never really retired, the pronouncements of congressional leaders and President Harry Truman to the contrary. The debt remained stable after the war, as the country simply outgrew it. The war years also proved that redistribution increased consumer demand and was good for the economy, a realization that sustained a new alliance between unions, consumer industries, and agriculture.[20] A new economic policy paradigm emerged that brought academic economists to Washington, D.C., and transformed the economics profession every bit as much as it trans-

formed economic policy. The war ushered in a whole range of new statistical tools for economic forecasting, and a new system of mass income
taxation was created. In that sense, the war provided the bridge to the
New Economics which Keynes had outlined on paper and which the
New Deal had anticipated in objective although not in practice.

The two policy initiatives at the center of debate are "negative" case
studies of what might have been. They are examples of "the road not
taken," to paraphrase Barrington Moore's definition of the role of coun-
terfactuals in comparative theory. The first is a report made public in
1943 from the National Resources Planning Board outlining a comprehensive, albeit somewhat disjointed, program for postwar social and economic reforms. After the publication, Congress refused to reauthorize
appropriations for the agency, and the NRPB shut down. The second
case is the legislation that produced the Employment Act of 1946. The
act was the brainchild of James Patton, head of the National Farmers'
Union, and a number of legislators who hoped to tie the federal government to a statutory obligation to maintain equitably shared economic growth.[21] The Employment Act fell short of the sponsors' original intentions but was hailed as landmark legislation creating a new role
for the federal government in economic management. The act created
the Council of Economic Advisors, but from the perspective of critics
the act was a shadow of what might have been. First I discuss the failures
of both initiatives in a comparative light. I then return to the question of
U.S. postwar "exceptionalism" and consider the question of continuity
and discontinuity between the New Deal and postwar Keynesianism.

The 1943 National Resource Planning Board Annual Report: An American "Beveridge"?

Although published as the NRPB's 1943 *Annual Report,* the document
was actually three separately written reports. The first, *Post-War Plan
and Program,* was a twenty-page sketchy outline of the Keynesian ideas
of Alvin Hansen, a Harvard University economics professor. The second, *Wartime Planning for War and Post War,* was little more than a
summary of the agency's previously published studies. The third, *Security, Work, and Relief Policies,* was written under the direction of a little-
known Columbia University economist, Eveline M. Burns. The longest
of the three, it mixed highly detailed statistical materials with a short and

sketchy outline for a unified social security system administrated by the federal government. Running to more than six hundred pages, it was not easy to read and drew severe criticism for its lack of accessibility. The report had been sent to the president in December 1941, but FDR kept it on his desk until March 1943.

The comparison to the 1942 British "Beveridge Report," which officially was titled *Social Insurance and Allied Services,* got much play at the time. The *New York Times* heralded it as "an American Beveridge."[22] The *New Republic* published a lengthy endorsement, also calling the NRPB report "an American Beveridge Plan" and "a revolutionary answer to the needs of a revolutionary age."[23] The comparison had merit because the two reports had striking similarities. Both held out a promise of new social and economic rights and were published in the depths of the war, when its hardships affected people deeply. Both also aroused criticism for financial excess and administrative overreach.

The legacy attributed to the two reports could hardly be more different, however. The Beveridge Report was initially received coolly by the wartime coalition government, but after the war it was credited with providing the blueprint for the 1945 Family Allowances Act, the 1946 National Insurance Act, the 1946 National Health Service Act, and the 1948 National Assistance Act. Even the 1944 Education Act has been attributed to Beveridge's program. In contrast, the verdict on the NRPB was at first enthusiastic, but in retrospect the board was deemed a dismal disappointment and a harbinger of the general failure of the postwar welfare state in the United States.[24] Beveridge has been called the "father of the postwar welfare state," but his recommendations were never fully realized and many of the ideas credited to him originated in a contemporary debate about planning that involved many contributors. William H. Beveridge was a professor and former director of the London School of Economics. He had been responsible for the planning of food rationing in the previous war and soon made himself unpopular with the coalition government by criticizing the war effort. In June 1941 Ernest Bevin, then minister of labour and national service, put Beveridge in charge of preparing an official report on the consolidation of various insurance programs, hoping that this would keep him out of the government's way.[25] It was intended to have been a minor official report, but Beveridge seized the opportunity to launch his own reform program.[26] Although written in turgid language and filled with tables, the report became a bestseller, particularly after the armed service's propaganda unit distributed it among soldiers at the front, apparently in the mistaken belief that the report expressed the views of the government.

One of the misconceptions of the current debate, encouraged by T. H. Marshall's subsequent reinterpretation of Beveridge's principles in his famous essay on "social citizenship," is that the Beveridge Report intended to give priority to social rights.[27] The Beveridge Report was about social programs because that was what Beveridge had been authorized to write about. But in Beveridge's view, the worst social evil of all was "idleness," a problem that social policy could do little about. Social policy should be designed to eliminate disincentives to work, but the eradication of unemployment was a matter of economic planning. Because the success of the social policy reforms depended on full employment, the latter was to have first priority, and Beveridge promised that a sequel report on full employment would follow shortly after the 1942 report.[28] This was not to be. Beveridge eventually completed the second report without official sponsorship with the help of a staff of young Keynesian economists, but the report, *Full Employment in a Free Society,* was not published until 1945. While writing the second report, Beveridge became acquainted with the New Economics that had emerged from Keynes's work, but in the second report he still recommended a heavy dose of coercive controls modeled on wartime economic regulation. Full employment—by which Beveridge meant a surplus of jobs compared with the number of employees looking for work, a definition that most economists considered highly inflationary and unrealistic—required government control of prices, wages, and production capacity. He also espoused obligatory training schemes for the unemployed and compulsory arbitration of industrial conflicts, all policies that the trade unions vehemently opposed.[29]

In comparison with Beveridge's terse relationship with the government and eventual ostracism, the NRPB was awash in executive support.[30] The 1943 NRPB report was presented as an elaboration of FDR's "four freedoms," and language introduced by the report was reused in FDR's promise of a Second Bill of Rights and reiterated in the 1944 State of the Union Address. Among its recommendations for postwar planning, some big and some small, was that consumer rationing be continued after the war. Some recommendations were little more than bland statements—that "our free enterprise system and economic freedom for the individual will demand consistent assistance from government and a renewed sense of vigilant responsibility on the part of all citizens."[31] Three principles for postwar planning were articulated. One was the principle of executive responsibility for economic stability and full employment. The second called for the creation of a comprehensive "umbrella" program for social security for all segments of society financed by general taxation. The third was the somewhat self-serving idea that a nationwide network of interconnected planning agencies should be set up with an executive planning bureau—supposedly the NRPB—at the apex. The report listed three separate sets of policy objectives: full employment for the "employable," a guaranteed job with fair pay and working conditions, and "equal access" to security, education, health, and "wholesome housing conditions." Legislation on land use planning and continued spending on rural electrification were also recommended. But the most controversial proposal urged "public responsibility" for basic transportation, and tucked away in a section on "promotion of free enterprise" was the proposal that "in some sectors" of the economy "mixed corporations" would be desirable. The list of industries targeted for partial nationalization included aluminum, basic metals, synthetic rubber, chemicals, shipbuilding, and aircraft. The government's wartime investments were used to justify continued public involvement, as was the "strategic" importance of these industries.[32]

The report was the accumulated result of years of work. The board had attracted an eclectic blend of political scientists, economists, and land use planners.[33] FDR's uncle, Frederic A. Delano, was chairman of the board. Charles W. Elliot II, a landscape architect who had worked with Delano on the Capitol Park and Planning Commission, was made director. The central figure on the board was Charles E. Merriam, a political science professor from Chicago.[34] The board had been given the task of developing postwar policies as part of the general "war aims" debate, and a special Postwar Agenda Section was set up, headed by Luther Gulick, a political science professor from Columbia University. Gulick and Merriam had worked together on the 1936 Committee on Administrative Management, or the Brownlow Committee, and were veterans of the battle over the 1939 Executive Reorganization Act. The staff was split up in three divisions, one of which was headed by Eveline Burns, a British labor economist. She had studied at the London School of Economics but declined the comparisons with Beveridge, saying that she had never been a student of his. She was, without doubt, well acquainted with the man and his ideas.[35]

One of the economists associated with the NRPB's work was Alvin Hansen, whose endorsement of fiscal stimulation policies and prominence had earned him the reputation of being the principal representative of Keynesian thinking in the American economics profession. Other postwar Keynesians involved were Paul Samuelson and Herbert Stein.[36] In January 1942 the Agenda Section published a pamphlet written by Hansen, *After the War—Full Employment,* in which he argued that it was the responsibility of government to sustain a high level of demand and proposed deficit spending as the primary tool for government intervention. This pamphlet was subsequently included in a summary version the 1943 *Annual Report* as part of the proposed postwar program. Burns' social security section alluded to historic mission by stating: "For many centuries and in many lands, the problem of social security has challenged the best efforts of man." As the government had been called upon to defend national borders, it continued, government was "now also called upon to guarantee to every citizen the right to his place as a worker and the right to income received under conditions compatible with self-respect when he is unable to work."[37] In contrast to the economic section, the social security section contained relatively precise policy recommendations, but it still failed to provide specific recommendations about how to pay for the proposed reforms.

To the extent that the report gave voice to a coherent perspective on national planning, it was one that stressed efficiency and growth rather than control and redistribution. But there was also a "Trojan horse" quality to the language, which served to infuriate congressional critics. On the one hand, it downplayed the proposals as mere matters of efficiency or "business as usual."[38] On the other hand, the recommendations were also described as "revolutionary" and as inevitable steps in the forward march of history. The NRPB attached no cost estimates to the proposals contained in the report but did estimate that the number of current recipients of public assistance of one kind or another was 22 million people—an improbable number, in my view—and implied that the proposed changes would simply pool preexisting programs. Hence, the report presented a new conceptual understanding of income support by depicting historically heterogeneous programs as parallel efforts that could—and should—be coordinated. The idea that farm income stabilization was in theory no different from income security for those who were unemployed, aged, sick, or disabled hinted at a national minimum income concept and anticipated postwar Keynesian approaches to income stabilization. It was a novel idea at the time.

In tune with the broad conception of social security, the report rejected reliance on earmarked funds for specific programs and endorsed comprehensive, integrated state action. It also hinted at a bridge between economic and social reform, although the connection was at no point made as explicit as Beveridge had done. Fiscal and social policies should be coordinated so as to offset "the wastes and irregularities of operation of uncoordinated private enterprise."[39] Yet the report failed to elaborate the idea and instead simply provided a long list of deserving programs. The thrust of the report was nevertheless more overtly Keynesian than Beveridge's, calling for countercyclical spending where Beveridge preferred direct government controls on prices, wages, and output. The NRPB report also rejected consumption taxes as harmful to growth.[40] Partial funding through payroll taxes and other types of contributory financing was acceptable, but it went to great length to endorse progressive taxation. Part 2 of the report consisted mainly of a detailed description of the NRPB's local offices, their activities, and previous publications.

The differences between the NRPB and Beveridge reports mirrored important differences between the two men behind them. Charles Merriam was the central figure in the NRPB, but he never assumed the public role that Beveridge did. The two shared many characteristics but diverged on their core ideas about the nature of planning. Merriam's vision of national planning was steeped in the municipal planning movement, both philosophically and practically. His principal source of funding for his efforts to build a new political science department at the University of Chicago had come from local communities and municipal planning foundations, including the Commonwealth Club where FDR first launched his ideas about new economic rights.[41] In 1936 Merriam still spoke of "central planning," which he wanted so as to provide a unified leadership for "central and local plans of government, plans of quasi-public agencies, plans of private industry, plans of voluntary associations of a great variety; all these must be related to each other."[42] The NRPB was made out to fit the mold. The agency described itself as the central command at the apex of a national network of planning commissions and "field organizations," but in reality its work was not essential to that of local planning agencies. This was borne out when the demise of the NRPB had little consequence for state-level planning activities.

But what Merriam called central planning was quite different from what Beveridge advocated.[43] In discussions with the British Ministry of Reconstruction about postwar planning, Beveridge made it clear that in his view ownership to the means of production was not "one of the essential British liberties."[44] In the 1945 report, he provided written evidence of his dirigiste views by contending—probably implicitly arguing against Hayek's recently published *Road to Serfdom*—that liberty requires responsibility and that if the British people "are not sufficiently civilized" to accept discipline, they would be "unworthy of freedom."[45] In other words, if associational self-discipline failed to provide a sufficient basis for planning, which he anticipated it would, the government was justified in coercing compliance with objectives and timetables drawn up by civil servants.

Merriam's view of the aims and means of national planning was considerably more in tune with the indirect management tools of modern Keynesianism. He regarded planning as "an organized effort to utilize social intelligence in the determination of national policies" and stressed the role of planners as one of "forecasting."[46] He repeatedly held up Alexander Hamilton's *Report on the Manufactures* from 1791 as a paragon of national planning. As for the role of planners, he wrote, "The planning function is, of course, advisory in its nature, with no power to command or to give orders."[47] National planning should be a matter of acting as a "clearinghouse" for planning carried out at lower levels.

The differences in perspective provide a lens for viewing the strengths and weaknesses of the two reports. The NRPB report lacked the unified—and frankly nationalistic—appeal to a coherent vision of social justice that shaped Beveridge's analysis, emphasizing instead invocations to efficiency, growth, and opportunity. But the substantive ideas about economic planning in the NRPB report were ahead of Beveridge's recommendations in all respects. The early embrace of Keynesian precepts, the emphasis on demand management rather than physical controls, and the stress on planning as a matter of forecasting rather than social control of the economy made the NRPB report a pioneering document. Still, it also contained a depression-era reliance on a public works program, a type of unemployment relief that fiscal stimulation in theory would make superfluous. (And it also reflected a mistaken view of what the immediate postwar priorities would be.) The social security report was more ambitious in scope but much less focused than the Beveridge Report. Whereas Beveridge established the right to a job and security at a level compatible with "prevailing standards in our society," the NRPB listed "self-respect" as the standard against which policy should be measured. The NRPB report never enjoyed the sustained popular attention awarded to the Beveridge Report. There may be many reasons for this difference, among them that the writers of the report never intended to appeal directly to the population the way Beveridge did.

The Press, The Public, and Congress: Reactions to the NRPB

The NRPB led a life of boom and bust. Elevated to presidential think tank in 1940, the agency was generously funded—receiving more money in 1942 than the Bureau of the Budget[48]—and was acclaimed as "path-breaking" in the wake of the 1943 report. Yet Congress abruptly shut down the board by the end of 1943. From a comparative perspective, the controversy aroused by the NRPB report was not unique. Postwar planning reports generally caused discord. In response to the Beveridge Report, Churchill warned, "A dangerous optimism is growing up about the conditions it will be possible to establish here after the war." He continued, "The question steals across the mind whether we are not committing our forty-five million people to tasks beyond their compass, and laying upon them burdens beyond their capacity to bear."[49] In Sweden, where the economist Gunnar Myrdal issued his prospectus for postwar planning and creation of the People's Economy, the head of the Employers' Association, Gustaf Söderlund, who otherwise was favorably disposed toward a new role for government in economic policy, lambasted the plans. "Like the Jesuits," he said, the social democrats were pretending that "the ends justify the means."[50]

Outside Congress, the NRPB report was well received. The press's hyperbolic response was to compare the report with the popular Beveridge Report. Interest group reactions were mixed, though business groups liked enough of the NRPB report to give it some initial support. *Business Week* noted that the promise of tax reductions was "Sugar Coating Plus" and "pleasant reading" but also that most of the suggestions contained in the economic report had "been kicked around for a good many years" and were "debatable."[51] As a result of the NRPB report, postwar planning became even more popular than it had been already. Widespread fears of a postwar recession and happiness with the results produced by the infusion of government money into the economy, industry groups and unions could agreed that they did not want the government to withdraw its involvement overnight. The big remaining question was by what means government involvement should be continued. In December 1943 the Postwar Committee of the National Association of Manufacturers (NAM) called for the quick rollback of war controls and war contracts, but also for policies facilitating increased employment and reconstruction abroad. The association published a number of proposals, including *Can We Avoid a Post-Armament Depression?* in 1941 and *Jobs, Freedom, and Opportunity* in 1943. The group wanted government support for industry but also industry participation in the allocation of that support.

Between 1943 and 1944 the U.S. Chamber of Commerce issued a series of publications on postwar planning under the general title *Postwar Readjustment Bulletins.* When the chamber met in April 1943, opinions were divided on how to respond to the planning offensive. A number of industry representatives, including Fowler McCormick of International Harvester and Beardsley Ruml from Macy's, the department store chain, were supportive. Eric A. Johnston, president of the chamber, went further than most business leaders and supported a corporatist approach to postwar stabilization. When he orchestrated a rapprochement between the chamber and President Roosevelt, Lammot du Pont, from the Du Pont Corporation, led a failed counterattack on Johnston and the chamber's newfound acquiescence to presidential capacities in economic policy making. Interestingly, the issue over which he chose to challenge Johnston's reign was not the NRPB but the renewal of the Trades Agreement Act, which gave the president rather than Congress the power to make agreements. At the meeting, Walter F. George, chairman of the Senate Finance Committee, confronted those within the chamber who were still hostile to planning. It was inevitable, he said, that government responsibility in the economic field was to increase after the war.[52] Senator George's remarks are particularly interesting because he is regarded as a leading figure in the antiplanning faction in Congress owing to his role in shutting down the NRPB. He also chaired the Senate Special

Committee on Postwar Economic Policy and Planning established two days after the publication of the NRPB report.

The unions were slow to respond. In February 1944 the unions organized in the Committee on Industrial Organization (CIO) published a twelve-point program for postwar planning. The CIO Political Action Committee made full employment its first priority and called for government support of industry, higher wages and maintenance of price controls, social security, and special programs for returning soldiers. A "shelf" of public works programs should be prepared in case an economic downturn should occur. But like Congress, the CIO did not like the NRPB's presumption that planning would be a matter of executive power. It proposed instead the creation of a corporatist Industrial Council including representation from industry, labor, and agriculture. Shying away from calling for a nationalization program like those espoused by European trade union confederations, the CIO showed a distinct lack of enthusiasm for state-centered policies and endorsed the NRPB's idea of "mixed corporations" only with caution.

The congressional campaign to shut down the NRPB began in the House in early February 1943. In a Senate roll-call vote, the board was narrowly saved, but with a much reduced budget. House support for a compromise failed to materialize, and the NRPB was shut down. Senator Robert Taft (R-Ohio) spoke for the board's opponents. "Why should the Congress finance a propaganda which is aimed directly at the principles and convictions of a large majority of both Houses of Congress?" He criticized Eveline Burns for being both British and a friend of Harold Laski, whom he accused of being an extreme socialist or perhaps even a communist.[53] Memories of the battle over presidential reorganization fueled the attack on the board, which was suspected of wanting to bring back old wine in new bottles. Rivalry over who should be in charge of planning was another factor, and the board's demise did not end Congress's engagement with postwar planning.[54] On the contrary, both the House and the Senate created high-level committees on planning. Congress's contribution to the postwar planning debate eventually narrowed down to what became the 1946 Employment Act. Before turning to a discussion of this legislation and the comparative accomplishments of European planning advocates, it is useful to speculate about what fate might have befallen the NRPB had its proposals been put in a parliamentary system of government.

Would Party Government Have Saved the NRPB?

Political scientists who grieve over the collapse of a reform in Congress have often wished for another political system. Stephen K. Bailey thus ends his study of the 1946 Employment Act, which began as the 1945 Full Employment Act (FEA), by acknowledging that a sudden change to a British system was impossible but wishing for a stronger president and a stronger party system. Party discipline and presidential leadership would end the power of noisy veto groups—like the group of conservatives that derailed the FEA—and, he argues, enable government in the national interest.[55] There can be no doubt that the U.S. Constitution imposed immediate constraints on planners. The courts, exemplified by the Supreme Court's actions in the case of NIRA, congressional control of the purse, and the difficulties that federalism poses for nationalizing parties are important constraints on state-centered national reform. But the absence of constitutional curbs on executive power in the parliamentary system should not lead one to forget that political constraints are present in those systems as well, most importantly the requirement that the government must at all times possess a majority in the legislature. Governing against a hostile legislature, as FDR did during the war, is not possible. In the British case, party government means that a government always has the votes needed to pass an undiluted reform bill. The straitjacket of the two-party system also virtually guarantees that a reversal of government also means a reversal of policy. It is a system conducive to cycles of reform and repeal. Power is more sweet but opposition also more sour.

In 1945, a new Labour government proceeded to realize its Election Manifesto point by point. Between August 1945 and August 1948, the Bank of England, coal, electricity and gas, communications, railroads, waterways, aviation, and parts of road transportation were nationalized. Within the next two years, the government acted on land use planning (the Town and Country Act), national medical care, and social insurance. Had the NRPB functioned within a parliamentary system of party government, the 1943 report may have served as guidebook for a postwar Democratic government. Had FDR not died in April 1945, he may have acted on the promises in his 1944 State of the Union Address, or as his successor, Truman might have been bound by the party leadership to follow suit. Party discipline and majoritarian government would have relieved the president from worries about a hostile Congress and the Supreme Court. The NRPB report could have continued to be the basis of policy until the next election, on schedule for 1948.

The picture is incomplete. Even with majority government and party discipline, a Democratic president would still have had to deal with unions and industry groups unwilling to let civil servants decide prices, wages, and production schedules in perpetuity. And by the next election, the Republican Party would have skimmed the cream off the postwar reform program—the GI Bill and cheap credit, for example—and left the Democrats to take responsibility for the unpopular parts. The British Conservative Party did exactly that by embracing the social policies put forward by the Labour governments and rejecting unpopular policies associated with the commitment to planning, especially rationing and incomes policy. The result was that the Conservative Party rather than Labour controlled the government for most of the postwar decades. The surprising conclusion of the thought experiment is that under a parliamentary system, the New Deal coalition might well have collapsed in 1948 and the Democratic Party become the minority party decades earlier than it did.

The NRPB program included a number of policies that might have tarred the Democratic Party for a long time—for example, the recommendation that consumer rationing be continued in order to achieve an equitable distribution of goods. The recommendations with respect to physical planning may have imposed national standards on local construction and aroused criticism of bureaucracy. The effect of interest group opposition on voters is also unknown. As it was, the unions reacted to adjustment policies by demanding large wage increases and by going on strike. The number of work stoppages increased radically during the war, but the 1946 strike wave involved nearly 1 million workers for an average of twenty-five days. Had price and wage controls continued, as the NRPB recommended, these workers would have been striking against the government and, by implication, the Democratic Party. In Sweden a 1945 strike among manufacturing workers convinced the Social Democratic government that public ownership inevitably would create a wedge between the government and the workers and, by implication, between the unions and the party. The Democratic Party got a taste of that when in May 1946 Truman seized both the coal mines and the railroads in response to the unions' call for work stoppages in support of wage demands. Likewise, agriculture and industry groups would have had their complaints, pinning the responsibility for various ills on the government.

We do not know if the gloomy or the rosy picture is correct, because both are counterfactual. We do know that voter unhappiness with rationing, industry group resistance to industrial planning, and trade union opposition to wage planning, coupled with the Conservative Party's embrace of part of the postwar social reform agenda, were important factors leading to the Labour Party's political exile from 1951 to 1964.

Keynesianism, Citizenship, and the Postwar Consensus

Support for postwar planning in Europe and in the United States—inside and outside Congress—drew ammunition from several sources. The elimination of unemployment and the rapid expansion of productive capacity caused by war mobilization were taken to be proof of the beneficial role of state direction. Expectations, albeit mistaken, of economic destabilization and social unrest in the wake of demobilization added to the argument for planning. The boom-and-bust cycle from 1918 to 1920–21 was often cited in support for the continuation of wartime controls beyond the cessation of military action.[56] Liberal democracies needed to project a positive and prosperous alternative to totalitarianism, it was universally argued. By 1944 many people were espousing postwar planning for one reason or another. Other agencies, private organizations, and congressional committees picked up the discussion that the NRPB had started. The Twentieth Century Fund identified thirty-three federal agencies involved in postwar planning.[57]

The congressional attack on the NRPB did not put an end to the board's agenda, nor did it discourage Merriam from declaring success. In a special 1944 issue of the *American Political Science Review,* he listed the GI Bill as one of the board's best achievements.[58] The 1944 presidential campaign was dominated by bipartisan appeals to national purpose and reform in the name of citizenship. FDR's 1944 State of the Union Address earlier in the year set the tone. Henry Wallace, who had been replaced by Truman as FDR's running mate, publicly campaigned for a commitment to "sixty million jobs" and the creation of a "Nation's Budget" for a full-employment economy.[59] Thomas Dewey, the Republican candidate, also campaigned for full employment. In his acceptance speech to the Republican Convention, he said: "It would be a tragedy after this war if Americans returned from our armed forces and failed to find the freedom and opportunity for which they fought. This must be a land where every man and woman has a fair chance to work and get ahead. . . . We Republicans are agreed that full employment shall be the first objective of national policy. And by full employment, I mean a real chance for every man and woman to earn a decent living."[60]

The demise of the NRPB left Congress free to contemplate its own ideas about postwar planning. In September 1943 the Senate War Contracts Subcommittee started working on new legislation. The Murray-George Omnibus Contract Settlement Act was introduced in the Senate in February 1944. In March more settlement legislation, the Kilgore Reconversion Bill, was introduced. At the same time, a report on postwar planning prepared by Bernard M. Baruch and John M. Hancock was published.[61] It was widely agreed that demobilization would create a recession and that postwar planning was needed to prevent widespread social and economic dislocation. But there the consensus stopped. No agreement existed on the forms or the extent of planning. The recommendations ranged from short-term proposals to extend the Office of War Mobilization (OWM), the executive agency in charge of coordinating military needs with industrial production within the office of the president, to manage transition problems to sweeping proposals for piggybacking social change on reconversion.

With no role in planning the war, Congress went about planning the peace. By April 1944, the responsibility for working out a compromise between the competing initiatives had been placed in the hands of Senator James Murray (D-Mont.), who went to then senator Harry Truman (D-Mo.) and the author of a competing bill, Senator Harley M. Kilgore (D-W.Va.), for joint sponsorship of a new bill. Whereas previous bills had focused on expanding the Office of War, the new bill created another executive agency in charge of "programs" and responsible for "full employment and full production planning."[62] It also included provisions for an extended federally financed unemployment compensation system. An alternative bill, introduced by Senator George, provided for a temporary and state-controlled unemployment compensation system. In the end, the Senate failed to provide for either unemployment compensation or a new bureau and simply reconstituted the OWM as the Office of War Mobilization and Reconversion (OWMR).

Murray and his staff then tried again to enact postwar stabilization legislation. Murray was on both the Small Business Committee and the Labor and Education Committee, in addition to the War Contracts Subcommittee. Small business and agriculture worried about plunging prices and access to loans and were favorable to the idea of maintaining consumer demand. But they were also concerned about getting squeezed by industry and labor. The bill was drafted by a group that included Gerhard Colm, who had been part of the NRPB endeavor, Walter Salant from the Office of Price Administration (OPA) and representatives from the Bureau of Agricultural Statistics, the National Farmers' Union, and staff from the War Contracts Subcommittee. It was introduced as S.380 on January 22, 1945. The bill required the president to introduce a "national production and employment budget" each year in Congress—called the "national budget"—that estimated the aggregates of the gross product and the share contributed by various actors from state and local governments to consumers and private industry. If a deficit in national activity sufficient to maintain full employment was estimated, the president was required to produce plans for how the federal government could close the gap.

The emphasis on the "national budget" as a planning tool and the statutory commitment to executive action owed much to the ideas articulated by James Patton, head of the National Farmers' Union. Patton wanted to go further and include a statutory commitment to the stabilization of relative incomes. The proposal implied that if farm incomes declined relative to those of industry, for example, the federal government had to take remedial action to raise farm incomes. And although the bill placed responsibility for economic planning with the president, the actual spending power was placed with the congressional Joint Committee on the National Budget. The concept of planning articulated by the bill was a far cry from the presidency as the hub of central planning as envisioned by the NRPB, as well as from the automatic stabilization policies carried out by a president in control of the main economic levers of the economy that eventually evolved.

Small business supported the bill, but apart from the Farmers' Union, other agricultural organizations were divided. The CIO wanted an industrial council rather than a joint congressional committee to be in charge of planning, and the American Federation of Labor (AFL) opposed the bill. Old New Dealers from booming consumer goods industries, such as Eric Johnston, Beardsley Ruml, and Ralph E. Flanders, were supporters, but the new Keynesian economists thought the bill relied too much on statutory mandates and left too little room for economic expertise.[63] Senate hearings on the bill were postponed to August and September 1945.

Truman entered the discussion belatedly in August. FDR's death a few weeks before German surrender had left him with sudden and overwhelming responsibilities for the organization of peace. After the Japanese surrender on August 15 and a gloomy employment prognosis—mistaken though it was—for spring 1946, Truman turned to domestic affairs. After what Alonzo Hamby describes as "forty-eight frantic hours of discussion," Truman went to Congress with his postwar domestic program on August 16.[64] Truman's speech was typical of the outlook at the time, also with respect to two firmly held but fatefully wrong convictions about the nature of the postwar challenges. The first was that a recession was inevitable, and the second, that policy should aim to prevent deflation. Truman supported planning. The war had taught us a great deal about government, he said, continuing: "We shall not be satisfied merely with our prewar economy."[65] The levels of production and income reached during the war years "have given our citizens an appreciation of what a full production peacetime economy can be." Full employment was a "bedrock public responsibility," he concluded, and sought authorization for a range of expansive economic measures.[66]

On September 28 the Senate passed the bill with an amendment introduced by Robert Taft (R-Ohio), a fiscal conservative and staunch opponent of an executive role in planning. It required that expansionary measures be matched "over a reasonable period of time" with increased taxation to prevent a net increase in the national debt. In the House, the bill was assigned to a minor committee dominated by conservatives. Industry groups started lobbying against it. On November 7 the committee voted the bill down and began to write its own bill. When a three-way fight evolved in the House between supporters of the original bill, those who wanted no bill at all, and the committee authors of the new House version, Truman threw his weight behind the committee version, apparently preferring a weaker bill to no bill. He may have thought the matter less than central to his own domestic program or may even have favored the weaker bill on substantive grounds.[67]

The final bill made no mentioning of the "Nation's Budget," created no new Bureau of Programs, and included no mandates tying the president's hands to specific compensatory spending. In less than one thousand words, the act established no bureaucracy and no body of regulation. It mandated that the president give an annual economic report to Congress and created the Council of Economic Advisers which soon would become a meeting place for professional academic Keynesians exercising great caution lest their professional careers be marred by another mistaken economic prognosis. Yet the act reflected a contested paradigm shift in the federal government's role.

The Planning Debates: Keynes versus Keynes

Congressional caprice and presidential inattention played roles in the emasculation of the 1945 bill. It is a mistake, however, to regard the Full Employment Bill as a lost opportunity for state-centered planning. The Patton-Murray proposal called for fixed spending mandates in place of the NRPB's preference for administrative discretion. It reduced the president's role to one of fact-finding while securing Congress's involvement in the process. It was a kind of planning that empowered Congress but left out the economists and the president. It reflected the support of "the third class"—agrarians and small business in the nation's periphery—for federal spending programs but also their skepticism of state power. The proposal echoed with populist ideas about planning, as well as those of the "farmer-worker" alliance of the early New Deal. But conservatives were successful only in defeating a populist ghost. The real victors were the Keynesians who found the emasculated bill sufficiently malleable to allow for a new role for the expert community and a semiautonomous economic presidency pursuing flexible adjustment policies.

Michael K. Brown has taken Ira Katznelson and Bruce Pietrykowski to task for collapsing the differences between the various perspectives on postwar planning and for conflating administrative agencies—notably the NRPB and the Bureau of the Budget (BOB)—with substantive differences in policy.[68] Brown is critical of Katznelson and Pietrykowski's distinction between "fiscalism" and "developmentalism." The terms may not be well chosen, I agree, but the general point is valid that the discussions in 1945 regarded choices between policies that were all in one way or another Keynesian. Disagreements at the time centered on the means of planning rather than the aim. And the resolution of the conflict over means had more to do with practical economic and institutional constraints than with theory. Similar disagreements over the appropriate means for planning can be found in European postwar planning debates, even if the descriptive terms used by Katznelson and Pietrykowski do not translate well. Looming in the background was always the question of *who* was going to be doing the planning.

In Great Britain, the first round of the contest over postwar planning was fought in connection with Stafford Cripps's Working Parties, which were temporary corporatist industry-wide boards modeled on the Code Authorities of the early New Deal. The 1947 Industrial Organization and Development Act aimed to translate the Working Parties into permanent planning agencies—so-called Development Councils—under the authority of the Board of Trade, which at the time was headed by Cripps. They were given the power to develop long-range plans for industrial rationalization, and in the case of some industries they were also charged with the task of making preparations for nationalization. Industry boycotted the councils, and it soon became clear that the kind of planning advocated by Cripps had failed. An alternative trajectory for planning was suggested by the 1944 White Paper on Employment, which linked the attainment of full employment to manipulations of aggregate demand. The White Paper never actually proposed counter-cyclical spending. At the time, the Treasury remained firmly opposed to deficit spending that might lead to permanent increases in public debt. The Treasury, then headed by Hugh Dalton, was concerned that deficit spending would lead to high interest rates. The Treasury's position is often interpreted as an instance of monetarist orthodoxy. This is hardly a sufficient explanation, although the role of agency-specific outlooks in shaping perspectives on planning should not be underestimated. The Labour Party was at the time still committed to a policy of "cheap money," illustrated by Dalton's decision to lower the interest rate on Treasury bills to 0.5 percent in October 1945. The opposition to the Keynesian principle articulated by the White Paper reflected a widespread skepticism within the ranks of the unions and the big working-class parties of what the state could and should do.

In Britain the shift away from "real" planning was complete when the

1949 Economic Survey pronounced budgetary planning the essence of all planning. The annual Economic Survey started out in 1946 and 1947 as statements of the high principles of direct planning but quickly segued into the tradition of Keynesian. Once attention centered on forecasting and economic stabilization aiming to regulate aggregate demand rather than supply-side planning, power shifted within the government from the industrial actuarians in the Board of Trade to the economists in the Treasury. In the four years that passed from 1945 to 1949, the Labour government moved from trying to create a planned economy to the mixed economy. The means and locus of planning shifted accordingly from the nationalization effort and the physical planning overseen by the Board of Trade to income stabilization and budgetary planning conducted by the Treasury.

The Swedish Social Democrats were similarly cautious about deficit spending and committed to low interest rates, and for the same reason. Their economic policy outlook was above all focused on maintaining jobs and wages in the core industries. But because trade unions in general are opposed to government action on wage issues—the exception being low-skilled and poorly organized trades where statutory action was seen as a help rather than a threat—planning involving government timetables and physical quotas and controls was a nonstarter. Given a choice between the economists' automatic indicators and "real" planning based on physical controls, interest organizations fought both at first but chose Keynesianism in the end.

In Britain as in the United States, the shift had much to do with the unanticipated resistance from societal groups to a strong role for the state—and conservative critics waving *The Road to Serfdom* were the least important. The crisis of planning was also inspired by the planners' first big mistake, the "famous Wrong Postwar Forecast," as Paul Samuelson called it.[69] Vast numbers of economists, in both Europe and the United States, using the best available forecasting techniques, predicted that a drop in postwar expenditures would produce deflation and that the arrival of returning soldiers would create unemployment. In both Sweden and Great Britain, the prediction of a postwar recession caused a series of critical policy mistakes—from the lowering of interest rates to stimulation of the money flow—which dangerously fueled inflation and caused immediate currency imbalances because of excessive demand for foreign (mainly U.S.) goods. The result was that the initial effort to decontrol the economy was derailed. In the United States, the wrong forecast also played a role, albeit with a different result. When the Full Employment Act had been introduced in the Senate in January, the economic outlook had been gloomy. By the time of the House floor debates on December 13 and 14, 1945, it had become clear that the economic forecast had been wrong, and opponents of the bill could read letter after letter complaining about labor shortages.

It is not the collapse of postwar planning in the immediate aftermath of peace but what happened next that separates U.S. experience from that of its European counterparts. In Europe the employment situation generally proved better than expected. The resurrection of planning—albeit planning of the Keynesian sort rather than that embodied in the failed Code Authorities and Industrial Councils—took place two years later. It was necessitated by unanticipated dollar shortages and by a balance of payment–induced recession set off by the 1947 sterling crisis and its ripple effects for the rest of Europe. A country's balance of payment is a measure of foreign economic transactions. The balance of payments is like a ledger; it *must* balance. Postwar imbalance problems derived from two sources: Europeans buying more goods for which they needed dollars than Americans buying European goods, and U.S. investments in Europe unmatched by European investments in the United States. The 1947 sterling crisis (and others that followed) resulted from the depletion of British currency reserves and the associated threat of British inability to pay bills abroad. In a system of fixed exchange rates, as the postwar Bretton Woods system, policymakers had little choice but to ration the demand for foreign goods, particularly those which had to be paid for in dollars. The impetus for wage planning derived principally from the need to curb demand in the face of deteriorating trade balances. No comparable constraint worked to sustain planning in the United States, where European shortages competed with domestic demand to fuel economic expansion.

Despite Harold Wilson's 1948 "Bonfire of Controls" and Ludwig Erhard's 1948 currency reform, which also eliminated many wartime trading ordinances, Europeans stuck with "good" controls for more than a decade.[70] Yet the main purpose of the controls was not progressive planning of the sort anticipated by planners a generation earlier. The aim was no longer to distribute scarce consumer goods fairly among the population but to ration scarce dollar resources and prevent the demand for

American goods from eroding the economic position of Europeans. Scarcity is the mother of all planning, and in the United States scarcity was hardly the main problem. The reconversion process proceeded with ease despite predictions to the contrary. Within six months of V-J Day, the control economy had been dismantled. The quickness of the reconversion process was in part due to the military's aversion to maintaining a role in economic management, but the United States also suffered few of the functional and economic constraints that compelled Europeans to maintain rationing and price controls. The surge in consumer demand did not threaten the dollar. The "dollar gap" that worked as a brake on the postwar European economies worked as an accelerator on the U.S. economy.

Certain institutional legacies of the war sustained the social and economic program initiated by the New Deal. Union membership in the United States, as a share of all nonagricultural labor, excluding Canadian membership, rose from 12 percent in 1930 to 13.5 percent in 1935. In 1945 it was 36 percent. The "little-steel" and "big-steel" formulas that eventually guided postwar wage determination were developed under the auspices of the War Labor Board and became another part of the wartime control economy that stuck after 1945. The 1935 Wagner Act sought to put labor relations on a new statutory footing, but the plant certification machinery was not developed until the war years. The certification procedures for union recognition have subsequently had a corrosive effect on American trade unionism, but they were, at the time, developed as a protective mechanism directed against hostile employers and with the support of the unions. The 1947 Taft-Hartley Act imposed new restrictions on union activities, limiting the unions to the pattern-setting bargaining policies that fell far short of the social unionism anticipated by Philip Murray's "social partner" unionism or the Reuther brothers' ideas about a Peace Production Board.[71]

The Taft-Hartley Act has been blamed for the weakness of American unions in later decades. Nelson Lichtenstein concludes, for example, that "if Taft-Hartley did not destroy the union movement, it did impose upon it a legal/administrative straitjacket that encouraged contractual parochialism and penalized any serious attempts to project a classwide political-economic strategy."[72] The question is, of course, if the unions would have done otherwise in the absence of Taft-Hartley. From a comparative perspective, the act seems less important. On the one hand, pattern-bargaining and sectoral unionism provided U.S. workers with great economic gains in the postwar years. It is also the case that the legal restrictions of the act have counterparts in European labor regulations. German unions were curtailed by the 1949 Basic Law's ban on political unionism but emerged nevertheless as an important political force in the postwar years. Outside Great Britain, where the unions succeeded in carving out a protected status under the umbrella of "voluntarism" (the idea that any legal restraints on the unions would violate the principles of a free society), closed-shop arrangements are generally disallowed. Legal restraints on political unionism, closed-shop rules, and striking do not necessarily handicap trade unionism. The difficult history of British unionism suggests that they may even help the unions retain legitimacy and political influence by curbing rogue unionism. Nowhere has this been better illustrated than in Sweden, where striking outside a calendar controlled jointly by the employer and union confederations has been prohibited since 1938. And had Philip Murray's or the Reuther brothers' visions been realized, the unions would have had to accept another set of restrictions, including wage planning and constraints on their bargaining power, all in the name of planned economic development.

Conclusion: Continuities and Discontinuities in Comparative Perspective

The postwar planning debate did not begin or end with the NRPB and the Full Employment bill. The focus in current debates on the "failed" aspects of the postwar agenda occasionally obscures the importance of wartime achievements. In this respect, I agree with Katznelson and Pietrykowski that choices were made. I also find the view that a return to New Deal planning policies was possible but that it was shipwrecked on industrial and conservative opposition lacking an appreciation of the circumstances under which planning *can* succeed. The war introduced a new theoretical paradigm for planning that replaced the stiff controls of the New Deal with fiscal and budgetary planning. In that sense the war saved the New Deal planning agenda.

In a comparative perspective, the shift in the focus of planning does not set the United States apart. When Europeans looked to the early New Deal for inspiration, their proposals failed too. In Sweden, Gunnar Myrdal's People's Economy was based on the creation of Industrial

Commissions responsible for setting up industry-wide planning schedules. In Great Britain, Stafford Cripps called them Development Councils. In France, Jean Monnet went ahead and created the Commission du
Modernization. All were modeled on the Code Authorities created by
the 1933 National Industrial Recovery Act. Ten years after the Supreme
Court ended the experiment in the United States, this particular form
for planning continued to capture the imagination of European planners. With the exception of Monnet's modernization commissions, the
New Deal approach to planning turned out to be equally untenable
across the Atlantic. This is not the place to speculate about why the
French succeeded where others failed, but one obvious explanation is
that the broad outlines of French postwar planning policies were settled
while the country was under military government and union and industry associations were still disabled.

   Postwar "fiscalism" in the United States, to use Katznelson and
Pietrykowski's term, differed from European Keynesianism in several
ways, but so did Swedish Keynesian planning compared with British
"stop-go" stabilization policies and German neoliberal planning. We can
speculate about the "lost" alternative to the "commercial" Keynesianism
practiced by Eisenhower—represented by the idea of the "Nation's Budget," for example—but we can also do so in the case of Sweden, Germany, and Great Britain. Postwar planning failed and then succeeded
only after having been put on new footing. It is wishful thinking to imagine that early New Deal or state-centered planning represented a workable alternative, as some U.S. scholars appear to, with the return to peace
and prosperity. And it was not just because of industrial elites that planning failed. Unions and industry associations were as eager as Congress
was to return to a balance of power with the state that was more favorable to their own organizational and institutional interests.

   Nor is it the case that "real" planning—of the "developmentalist"
kind, to use Katznelson and Pietrykowski's terminology—would have
been possible in the United States without some measure of highly unpopular policies. Again the comparative evidence tells us about the pit-
falls inherent in this approach to planning. General agreement exists, for
example, that the postwar decline of the British economy owed a great
deal to the inability to get the unions to agree to structural planning because that meant government involvement in the determination of
wages. On the other hand, Swedish economic success is attributed to in-

terest coordination between employers, government, and the unions. Some of the unpopular wartime and postwar policies—antistriking provisions, wage controls, and the inclusion of industrial elites in government decision making—were all central to successful planning in postwar Europe.

Europeans do not seem innately more favorable toward planning than Americans. Constitutional differences play an obvious role in enabling or disabling ambitious reform efforts, although not always in predictable ways. National narratives about the legitimacy of the state color the particular language used to discuss the aims and means of planning, but when it comes to civil servants deciding plans for investment and incomes in specific industries, only the poor and the bankrupt will be happy. A comparative perspective on postwar reconstruction policies suggests a highly contextual picture of the trajectories of postwar adjustment with the balance of power between planning proponents and opponents usually working against state-centered planning. When planning succeeded, the reason was either the collapse of civic organizations owing to occupation or a need to ration scarce dollar reserves and prevent inflation. It is important to recognize that the particular European postwar regime described by John Ruggie's notion of "embedded liberalism" had domestic underpinning not only of support for market control but also for liberalization and associational autonomy. If we hope to explain cross-national variations in postwar economic policy regimes, we are probably better served by looking to the functional constraints of the new postwar economic order than to inherited cross-national variations in state capacities. In that case, the domestic consequences of the dollar's hegemonic position in the postwar world economy looms large as an explanation of the fact that the United States achieved less planning and the Europeans achieved more.

Notes

1. Charles Tilly, *Coercion, Capital, and European States, A.D. 990–1992* (Cambridge, Mass.: Blackwell, 1990), 83.

2. The concept of "total war" may be defined as a "functional totality of the politically ordered participation in the war effort of all personal and social forces, the scientific, the mechanical, the commercial, the economic, the moral, the literary and artistic, and the psychological." See Edward S. Corwin, *Total War and the Constitution* (New York: Alfred A. Knopf, 1947), 4. The

classic statement of the thesis of the wartime origins of the welfare state is Richard D. Titmuss, "War and Social Policy," in *Essays on "the Welfare State,"* 3d ed. (London: George Allen and Unwin, 1976). See also my own book *War and Welfare: Europe and the United States, 1945 to the Present* (New York: St. Martin's, 1998).

3. For a description of wartime appeals, see Steve Fielding, Peter Thompson, and Nick Tiratsoo, *"England Arise!" The Labour Party and Popular Politics in 1940s Britain* (Manchester: Manchester University Press, 1995).

4. Broadcast, May 25, 1940, reprinted in Ernest Bevin, *The Balance Sheet of the Future* (New York: Robert McBride and Company, 1940), 51.

5. *Wartime Facts and Postwar Problems* (New York: Twentieth Century Fund, 1943), 2.

6. Theda Skocpol, "The G.I. Bill and U.S. Social Policy, Past and Future," in *The Welfare State,* ed. Ellen Frankel Paul, Fred D. Miller Jr., and Jeffrey Paul, (New York: Cambridge University Press, 1997), 95–115; Alan Brinkley, *The End of Reform: New Deal Liberalism in Recession and War* (New York: Alfred A. Knopf, 1995).

7. Richard Pohlenberg has argued that "the war obliged reformers to grant priority to military objectives" and war mobilization allowed a restoration of industrial elites' domination of policy, in *War and Society: The United States, 1941–1945* (Philadelphia: Lippencott, 1972), 75. In a similar vein, Alan Brinkley contends that World War I was an inspiration for planners but World War II was not, because the wartime state paled in comparison with the accomplishments of the early New Deal. Yet he also concludes that the prosperity produced by the war effort caused "the relegitimation of capitalism," which ended support for planning. See Brinkley, *Liberalism and Its Discontents* (Cambridge: Harvard University Press, 1998), 85, 96. Nelson Lichtenstein regards 1946–48 as a turning point when a strengthened labor movement was beaten back by a hostile Congress using the Taft-Hartley Act as its weapon; see "From Corporatism to Collective Bargaining: Organized Labor and the Eclipse of Social Democracy in the Postwar Era," in *The Rise and Fall of the New Deal Order, 1930–1980,* ed. Steve Fraser and Gary Gerstle (Princeton: Princeton University Press, 1989), 122. Echoing Pohlenberg, Richard Bensel writes that "the war effort reversed the New Deal balance of power" and allowed the restoration of the industrial elite. See his *Sectionalism and American Political Development, 1880–1980* (Madison: University of Wisconsin Press, 1984), 76.

8. Edwin Amenta and Theda Skocpol, "Redefining the New Deal: World War II and the Development of Social Provisions in the United States," in *The Politics of Social Policy in the United States,* ed. Margaret Weir, Ann Shola Orloff, and Theda Skocpol (Princeton: Princeton University Press, 1988), 103.

9. Ira Katznelson, "Was the Great Society a Lost Opportunity?" in Fraser and Gerstle, *Rise and Fall of the New Deal Order,* 192.

10. Ira Katznelson and Bruce Pietrykowski, "Rebuilding the American State: Evidence from the 1940s," *Studies in American Political Development* 5 (Fall 1991): 338. For a criticism, see Michael K. Brown, "State Capacity and Political

Choice: Interpreting the Failure of the Third New Deal," *Studies in American Political Development* 9 (Spring 1995): 187–212.

11. A number of scholars have regarded Congress's elimination of three New Deal programs in 1942 and 1943—the Civilian Conservation Corps, the Works Progress Administration, and the National Youth Administration—as evidence for the rollback thesis; see Amenta and Skocpol, "Redefining the New Deal," 89. But war mobilization had eliminated the need for public works programs. Between 1940 and 1944, 10 million new jobs were created—of which 5 million went to women not previously employed—and by that time unemployment had dropped to 670,000 workers, down from 8 million when the programs were created (U.S. Bureau of the Census, *Historical Statistics of the United States: Colonial Times to 1957* [Washington, D.C.: Bureau of the Census, 1960], 70–71).

12. Sidney M. Milkis, *The President and the Parties: The Transformation of the American Party System since the New Deal* (New York: Oxford University Press, 1993). The full text of FDR's speech is available in Nathan Ausubel, *Voices of History* (New York: Franklin Watts, 1945), 27.

13. James MacGregor Burns, *Roosevelt: The Soldier of Freedom* (New York: Harcourt Brace Jovanovich, 1970), and Doris Kearns Goodwin, *No Ordinary Time: Franklin and Eleanor Roosevelt: The Home Front in World War II* (New York: Simon and Schuster, 1994).

14. Goodwin, *No Ordinary Time,* 481.

15. These figures and the following are calculated on the basis of various tables in Bureau of the Census, *Historical Statistics of the United States: Colonial Times to 1957.*

16. William E. Leuchtenburg, "The New Deal and the Analogue of War," in *Change and Continuity in Twentieth-Century America,* ed. John Braeman et al. (Columbus: Ohio State University Press, 1964), and Ellis W. Hawley, *The New Deal and the Problem of Monopoly: A Study in Economic Ambivalence* (Princeton: Princeton University Press, 1966). Central parts of the first New Deal, the Code Authorities under the National Recovery Administration from 1933 to 1935 and the Civilian Conservation Corps, were modeled on the war controls from 1917 and 1918. See Daniel T. Rodgers, *Atlantic Crossings: Social Politics in a Progressive Age* (Cambridge: Harvard University Press, 1998), 414. At the onset of war in 1940, the New Dealers expected that war would breathe new life into the New Deal. One of them, Adolf Berle, predicted that when the war ended "a great movement of social unrest" would take place, and he laid out a prospectus for extending New Deal planning to world government in his *New Directions in the New World* (New York: Harper, 1940), 1.

17. Corwin, *Total War.*

18. Alan S. Milward, *War, Economy, and Society, 1939–1945* (Berkeley: University of California Press, 1979).

19. Klausen, *War and Welfare,* 233.

20. Karen Orren, "Union Politics and Postwar Liberalism in the United States, 1946–1979," *Studies in American Political Development* 1 (1986): 215–52.

21. In his 1944 State of the Union Address, FDR spoke of the need to "lay plans . . . for the winning of a lasting peace." For a discussion of the address, see Goodwin, *No Ordinary Time,* 485.

22. *New York Times,* March 11, 1943, 1, 12–13. William H. Beveridge went on a speaking tour in the United States in May 1943 at the invitation of the Rockefeller Foundation. He presented "his" report to an American audience and paid a visit to President Roosevelt and the secretary of labor, Frances Perkins (José Harris, *William Beveridge: A Biography* [Oxford: Clarendon, 1977], 427).

23. Bruce Bliven, Max Lerner, and George Soule, *New Republic,* April 19, 1943, 523.

24. Margaret Weir, *Politics and Jobs: The Boundaries of Employment Policy in the United States* (Princeton: Princeton University Press, 1992).

25. Harris, *William Beveridge,* 376.

26. The authors of the NPRB report denied that Beveridge had inspired them, with the argument that their report antedated Beveridge's. Beveridge had outlined his main ideas in two papers that he circulated prior to his report's publication in mid-1941, but the official publication was delayed to December 1942 after the British Actuary estimated that Beveridge's proposals would triple the Treasury's social expenditures. The chronology allows for Beveridge to have inspired some of the NRPB report. See ibid., 394.

27. T. H. Marshal, *Citizenship and Social Class and Other Essays* (London: Cambridge University Press, 1950).

28. Beveridge had hoped that the government would commission him to write the report, but instead Churchill banned all civil servants from assisting Beveridge. See Paul Addison, *The Road to 1945: British Politics and the Second World War* (London: Cape, 1982), 243.

29. For a discussion of Beveridge's ideas about planning, see Klausen, *War and Welfare,* 49.

30. The agency had been created in July 1933 as the National Planning Board under the Public Works Administration. Originally created under the National Industrial Recovery Act, the agency had a perilous life and was saved from extinction twice by the president. It underwent subsequent name changes and was moved into the Executive Office of the President in 1939.

31. U.S. Congress, *National Resources Development: Report for 1943.* Part 1: *Post-War Plan and Program.* Part 2: *Wartime Planning for War and Post War.* Part 3: *Security, Work, and Relief Policies.* 78th Cong., H. Doc. 128 (Washington, D.C.: GPO, 1943), 12.

32. Alvin Hansen, *After the War—Full Employment,* National Resources Planning Board (Washington, D.C., 1943), 30.

33. Lewis L. Lorwin, a trade union economist and an advocate of socialist planning who later went to work for the ILO in Geneva, was economic adviser. His views of planning were in accord with those advanced by British left-wing Keynesians, who worked with Beveridge on his second report from 1945, *Full Employment in a Free Society.* See Lewis L. Lorwin, *Time for Planning: A Social-Economic Theory and Program for the Twentieth Century* (New York: Harper and

Row, 1945). The Agenda Section sponsored dinner parties for planners with a guest list that was a virtual *Who's Who* of New Deal planners. Philip W. Warken lists the following regular participants: Alvin Hansen, Marriner Eccles, Adolf A. Berle, Jerome H. Frank, Lauchlin Currie, Harry D. White, and Leon Henderson. See Warken, *A History of the National Resources Planning Board, 1933–1943* (New York: Garland, 1979), 184.

34. Another member was Wesley C. Mitchell, who resigned in 1935, apparently because of disagreements over the board's role. He was replaced by George F. Yantis, a lawyer from the state of Washington. A history of Merriam's network of planners can be found in Barry D. Karl, *Charles E. Merriam and the Study of Politics* (Chicago: University of Chicago Press, 1974), 250.

35. The comparison with Beveridge irked some people. A memo from the chairman of the Social Security Agency to FDR on the Beveridge Report concluded with the remark, "I am quite confident that we can work out, here in the United States, a more adequate system of benefits which will be simpler and more understandable than the Beveridge program." A similar memo from Eveline Burns to FDR also took pains to portray the NRPB report as superior. The Beveridge Report was narrower, she argued, because it concerned only "income maintenance" and did not include provisions for work. This was only technically true. Beveridge assigned first priority to employment policy but was not allowed to make employment policy recommendations in his initial report from 1942, *Social Insurance and Allied Services,* because the report was the result of a formal inquiry into insurance program consolidation. Burns also pointed out that the flat-rate design proposed by Beveridge would not work in the United States because of geographic differences in income levels. This is an interesting point that merits further discussion because it reflects the awareness on the part of Burns and the NRPB planners that sectionalism and federalism were obstacles to "central" planning. President's Personal File 1820, FDR Papers, Franklin D. Roosevelt Library, Hyde Park, New York. (I am grateful to Sidney Milkis for lending me copies of the files.)

36. Stein was awarded a $25,000 first prize in a competition for "best plan" for postwar employment created by the Pabst Breweries in 1944. Nearly 36,000 people submitted plans for the competition. See Herbert Stein, *A Plan for Postwar Employment.* Pabst Brewing Co. The winning plans in the Pabst postwar employment awards. [1944].

37. U.S. Congress, *National Resources Development,* 1.

38. The NRPB sometimes seemed lost in its own utopia. With scant regard for complications, the economic report declared that "planning for full employment, now under way in the federal government and within individual industries, must be supplemented by local planning in order that local effectiveness of national plans may be assured." Ibid., 32.

39. Ibid., 502.

40. Ibid., 522.

41. Karl, *Charles E. Merriam,* 153. See also Milkis, *President and the Parties,* 44.

42. Charles E. Merriam, *The Role of Politics in Social Change* (New York: New York University Press, 1936), 139. Other important publications by Merriam on the issue of planning are *What Is Democracy?* (Chicago: University of Chicago Press, 1941) and his speech from Harvard University published as *On the Agenda of Democracy* (Cambridge: Harvard University Press, 1944).

43. Merriam and Beveridge had in common their roles as academic institution builders; both even received funding from the Rockefeller Foundation at various points. Both ran unsuccessfully for public office on third-party tickets, Beveridge for the Liberal Party and Merriam for the Progressive Party. Beveridge was a noisy advocate for his ideas, but Merriam stuck to the academic lecture circuit. Incredulously, a contemporary report claims that he was barely known on Capitol Hill. See *Congressional Record,* 78th Cong., 1st sess., May 24, 1943, 4927.

44. Harris, *William Beveridge,* 90.

45. William Beveridge, *Full Employment in a Free Society* (New York: W. W. Norton, 1945), 207. Hayek's book, which was first published in 1944, was widely derided by contemporary intellectuals; see Friedrich A. von Hayek, *The Road to Serfdom* (Chicago: University of Chicago Press, 1944).

46. Merriam, *On the Agenda of Democracy,* 77.

47. Ibid., 89. My interpretation of Merriam's views on planning differs from that of James Kloppenberg, who considers Merriam to be a Deweyan social democrat and paragon of communitarianism. Merriam's personal biography and writings suggest otherwise, I think. He was an Episcopalian Republican who came to the Progressive cause as a result of his disgust with Chicago politics. Merriam cited John Dewey only in the context of social science methodology, not in support of policies he favored. Hamilton and Jefferson were Merriam's heroes. When it came to planning, Merriam did not favor local government but local planning commissions run by experts and reformers. He defended the state and the expert as the anchor for the common good. The exclusive community of experts putting their science at the disposal of the state rather than the citizenry engaged in a Habermasian social experiment in "communicative action" were to lay out the course of national policy. See James T. Kloppenberg, *The Virtues of Liberalism* (New York: Oxford University Press, 1998), 108.

48. Katznelson and Pietrykowski, "Rebuilding the American State," 314.

49. Winston S. Churchill, *The Second World War.* Vol. 6, *The Hinge of Fate* (London: Cassel, 1951), 861–62.

50. Klausen, *War and Welfare,* 131.

51. *Business Week,* March 20, 1943, 16–17.

52. *New York Times,* April 30, 1943, 8, 1.

53. *Congressional Record,* Senate, 78th Cong., 1st sess., May 27, 1943, 4924, 4929.

54. Barry Karl cites Roosevelt's letter of protest to the chairman of the House Appropriations Committee from February 14, 1943. It was important, FDR argued, to keep some civilian construction projects "on the shelf" so that the government might immediately step in should a recession arise upon demobiliza-

tion, and it was in any case cheap to keep the agency working. Piqued, he continued, "If Congress wants to . . . set up another Board with different personnel, they [*sic*] have a right to do so. . . . all they have to do is to say so quite frankly." Karl, *Charles E. Merriam,* 280.

55. Stephen K. Bailey, *Congress Makes a Law: The Story behind the Employment Act of 1946* (New York: Columbia University Press, 1950), 239.

56. V. O. Key, "The Reconversion Phase of Demobilization," *American Political Science Review* (December 1944): 1137–51. A partial list of endorsements of postwar planning by various agencies includes National Resources Planning Board, *After the War, 1918–1920. Military and Economic Demobilization of the United States. Its Effect Upon Employment and Income,* report prepared by Paul A. Samuelson and Everett E. Hagen (Washington, D.C.: GPO, June 1943); War Production Board, *War Production in 1944: Report of the Chair* (Washington, D.C.: GPO, 1945); Office of War Mobilization and Reconversion, *From War to Peace: A Challenge* (Washington, D.C.: GPO, 1945); and U.S. President, *Outline of Plans Made for the Reconversion Period: Message from the President of the United States Transmitting an Outline of the Plans Made for the Reconversion Period,* September 6 (Washington, D.C.: GPO, 1945).

57. Bailey, *Congress Makes a Law,* 10.

58. Charles E. Merriam, "The National Resources Planning Board: A Chapter in American Planning Experience," *American Political Science Review* 38 (December 1944): 1083. In collaboration with the military, the NRPB produced *Conference on Post-War Adjustment of Personnel Demobilization and Adjustment,* which was published in June 1943. Merriam also pointed to the 1945 Employment Act and the 1946 Housing Act as board achievements. Skocpol, in contrast, considers the GI Bill a disappointment, failing as it did to bestow social rights on the citizenry at large. She also denies the NRPB authorship, assigning that to the American Legion (Skocpol, "G.I. Bill," 100).

59. Henry A. Wallace, *Sixty Million Jobs* (New York: Simon and Schuster, 1945). The notion of "the nation's budget" as a planning tool was first introduced in the 1941 budget message. It was elaborated in the 1945 budget message.

60. Herbert Stein, *The Fiscal Revolution in America* (Chicago: University of Chicago Press, 1969), 173.

61. U.S. Office of War Mobilization, *Report on War and Post-War Adjustment Policies,* by Bernard M. Baruch and John M. Hancock (Washington, D.C.: GPO, 1944).

62. Bailey, *Congress Makes a Law,* 22.

63. Ibid., 140.

64. Alonzo L. Hamby, *Man of the People: A Life of Harry S. Truman* (New York: Oxford University Press, 1995), 375. Truman had met with FDR only twice since the election and appears not to have followed the congressional deliberations on planning even though he sponsored one of the various bills.

65. Truman gave the unions the green light to go ahead and seek wage adjustments, because, as he said, "there was no longer any threat of an inflationary

bidding up of wage rates by competition in a short labor market." For a discussion, see ibid., 375–81.

66. U.S. President, *Outline of Plans Made for the Reconversion Period,* 11–12.

67. Curiously, Truman claimed ten years later that the bill was a milestone and one of the most important pieces of legislation enacted while he was president. National Planning Association, *The Employment Act. Past and Future. A Tenth Anniversary Symposium,* ed. Gerhard Colm. Special Report no. 41. (Washington, D.C.: National Planning Association, 1956), x.

68. Brown, "State Capacity and Political Choice," 188–89.

69. National Planning Association, *Employment Act,* 130.

70. *Parliamentary Debates,* Commons 5th ser. (1949), col. 2499.

71. Victor G. Reuther, *The Reuther Brothers and the Story of the UAW* (Boston: Houghton Mifflin, 1976). For discussions of labor's views on postwar planning, see Christopher L. Tomlins, *The State and the Unions: Labor Relations, Law, and the Organized Labor Movement in America, 1880–1960* (New York: Cambridge University Press, 1985), and on the role of the Reuther brothers, see Nelson Lichtenstein, *The Most Dangerous Man in Detroit: Walter Reuther and the Fate of American Labor* (New York: Basic, 1995).

72. Lichtenstein, "From Corporatism to Collective Bargaining," 134.

Social Citizens of Separate Sovereignties

Governance in the New Deal Welfare State

Suzanne Mettler

Until the New Deal, most of the rights and obligations of American citizenship were defined at the state level rather than by national government. Aside from the important realm of immigration and naturalization policy, the national government had little direct effect on citizenship; rather, it occupied itself primarily in promoting commercial activity through such means as subsidies and tariffs and the development of the post office, canals, and highways. State legislatures, drawing on their "police power," fashioned electoral, criminal, moral, family, property, and commerce laws in a varied and eclectic manner that typically had more to do with preserving regional cultural norms than with extending rights to free and equal citizenship.[1] Though the Fourteenth Amendment, ratified in 1868, appeared at first to nationalize the Bill of Rights, within five years the Supreme Court had denied that interpretation.[2] The individual states thus retained the power to define most aspects of citizenship without interference from the national government.

As the twentieth century dawned, states and localities held the predominant authority for fashioning social citizenship, meaning citizens' entitlement, as an extension of their membership in the community, to the basic necessities of economic security and welfare.[3] Pensions for Civil War veterans, which had, as Theda Skocpol has shown, become a widespread and generous social policy, represented the most important exception to this pattern. Yet, such pensions still adhered to the particu-

231

laristic, patronage style of policymaking typically used by national government in that era and thus did not constitute a means of incorporating broad classes of Americans as social citizens.[4] Most new social and labor policies fashioned in the Progressive Era, such as mothers' pensions and protective labor legislation, did not involve the national government at all. They marked the elevation of responsibility for social citizenship upward from municipal governments to the states but still varied in form and extent of implementation between and within the individual states.

The New Deal heralded a transformation toward a more centralized administrative state whose reach extended into the lives of ordinary citizens. Amid the crisis of the Great Depression and the mobilization of social movements, policymakers designed national regulatory and redistributive policies. After initial resistance, by the late 1930s the Supreme Court had at last upheld such laws. Thus, a hallmark of the New Deal is the manner in which it endowed Americans with new social and economic dimensions of citizenship. The right of workers to organize and to engage in collective bargaining was institutionalized under the National Labor Relations Act of 1935; social provision for the unemployed, older adults, and single mothers with children was solidified through the Social Security Act of 1935; and minimum wages were guaranteed by the Fair Labor Standards Act of 1938. In addition to these new rights, of course, Americans acquired new obligations—namely, to pay higher taxes to the federal government and to tolerate more intervention in their personal lives.

How would the governing arrangements for New Deal policies affect the character and experience of American citizenship? Despite the current interest in welfare state development and matters of citizenship, scholars have yet to ask this question. Most policy analysts treat policy outcomes as simple reflections of the preferences of voters, politicians, or interest groups, with little heed to either the role of institutional and political dynamics or civic outcomes.[5] "New institutionalist" studies have challenged this paradigm by demonstrating, through what Skocpol calls "structured polity" analysis, how institutional arrangements, political processes, and historical precedents shape policy.[6] But while historical institutionalists have done much to explain the origins or determinants of public policies, less attention has been given to their civic and social consequences.

In this essay I explore the implications of institutionalized patterns of New Deal governance for social citizenship and American political development. I analyze social and labor policies in terms of both their policy design type—distributive, regulatory, or redistributive—and their institutional arrangements for implementation, whether primarily at the national or state level. The New Deal enhanced American social citizenship inasmuch as policymakers began to design regulatory labor policies and redistributive social policies, both of which reached citizens more broadly and made rights and obligations more standardized than had policies designed according to the distributive model, which had been the norm previously. At the same time, however, though New Dealers endowed some new policies with national administrative authority, they also retained a surprising degree of state-level authority for several others.[7]

The primary argument presented here is that through the New Deal, American social citizenship became divided into two distinct forms of governance separated by gender and race.[8] Men, particularly white men, became endowed with national citizenship as they were incorporated into policies to be administered through standardized, routinized procedures by the national government. Women and minority men were the persons most typically relegated to policies to be administered mainly by the individual states. Divided citizenship emerged, with white men incorporated within the uniform domain of national government, and women and nonwhite men left under the auspices of the states subject to highly variable forms of citizenship. These two levels of government ruled like separate sovereignties, largely because of the distinct institutional and administrative character of each realm, but also because such differences in turn permitted the application of disparate ideological norms in the definition of citizenship. National government incorporated citizens within a liberal realm of rights, where they were regarded as free and equal citizens. States made social provision conditional upon meeting obligations that pertained to hierarchical, status-bound definitions of gender norms and other social roles. The implications for American political development are striking: while the New Deal is usually understood as establishing a liberal, rights-oriented welfare state, it also perpetuated governance in a nonliberal realm that may best be described as "semifeudal."

While this interpretation of the New Deal bears some resemblance to that in other recent studies, the explanation of how such outcomes emerged diverges sharply from those analyses. Other explanations tend to assume a direct linkage between the ideas and intentions of policymakers and the consequences of policy in terms of gender, race, or political development generally. Linda Gordon and other feminist scholars, for example, explain the gender organization implicit in the New Deal welfare state as the result of gendered ideologies held by New Deal policymakers.[9] While Rogers Smith argues in a vein similar to mine that American political development has been characterized not only by liberalism but also by ascriptive, neofeudal versions of citizenship, his explanation rests almost exclusively on the role of clearly intended ideas.[10] The analysis here, in contrast to these others, suggests that such ideas played only a partial role in fashioning the fragmented welfare state of the New Deal. Far more important were choices about institutional administrative arrangements that were made with little heed to their consequences for citizenship.

Social Citizenship, Policy Design, and Institutional Arrangements

Public policies shape various dimensions of citizenship directly. First and fundamentally, naturalization and immigration policies define the *membership* of the citizenry, thus establishing the boundaries of the political community.[11] Second, policies shape *participation* among citizens, affecting the character of their involvement in public life. Whereas some policies might encourage citizens to act as rights-bearing individuals, others might render them "dependents" on the state without a sense of obligation or agency in the public realm.[12] Participatory citizenship encompasses involvement in politics and civic activities, and it is the aspect of citizenship that receives the most attention in contemporary scholarship.[13] Third, governance affects what may be called *incorporation,* the manner and extent to which people are included, consolidated, and organized as members of the political community.[14] Incorporation, a fundamental task of state building, encompasses what has been identified by Judith Shklar as "inclusion" in the political community and by T. H. Marshall as a three-step process through which civil, political, and social rights are extended.[15] A critical component of incorporation and the central concern of this essay is "social citizenship," meaning citizens' entitlement, as an extension of their membership in the political community, to the basic necessities of economic security and social well-being.[16]

Incorporation generally and social citizenship in particular have great significance for the character of citizenship in any given polity. First, the manner in which groups of citizens are incorporated into the nation imbues them with a form of status or, in Shklar's terminology, "standing" in society, as members of the political community.[17] Broad standards for social citizenship are a critical dimension of democracy, assuring citizens of not only a modicum of well-being but also a measure of dignity that is understood to befit those with the franchise.[18] As Michael Walzer explains, "Communal provision [of security and welfare] . . . teaches us the value of membership" in the community.[19] Second, the incorporation of citizens in turn shapes the *organization* of the citizenry. Broad incorporation may unite citizens in the polity, fostering the shared identity and sense of solidarity so essential, particularly in a diverse and multicultural society, to a sense of nationhood, public-spiritedness, community life, and social peace.[20] Alternatively, narrow or differentiated incorporation can stratify and divide the citizenry into groups that understand their place in public life to be distinct from that of others, promoting the pursuit of self-interest over the common good.[21] Third, incorporation establishes the ground on which *participation* in the polity occurs and affects the form it takes. Differential incorporation means that some groups have greater access to political resources and greater political leverage than others, in turn affecting the degree and form of subsequent political demands.[22]

Public policies shape outcomes for citizenship through both their policy design structure and the institutional arrangements for implementation. Policies enacted from the late nineteenth century through the Progressive Era and New Deal exhibited considerable variation in these features, as shown in Table 1. How would such design and administrative features affect citizenship?

Table 1. Social and Labor Policy Design and Institutional Arrangements

	INSTITUTIONAL ARRANGEMENTS	
POLICY DESIGN	NATIONAL	STATE OR LOCAL
Distributive	Civil War Pensions	Mothers' Pensions
Regulatory	Fair Labor Standards Act National Labor Relations Act	Protective Labor Laws
Redistributive	Old Age and Survivors' Insurance	Workmen's Compensation

Policy Design

Policy design refers to the structure of the relationship a policy establishes between government and citizens. It is important because, as Helen Ingram and Anne Schneider write, it suggests "what government is supposed to do, which citizens are deserving or undeserving, and what sort of participation is appropriate in democratic societies."[23] Features of policy design such as terms of eligibility, coverage, financing, and funding arrangements convey critical messages to citizens.[24] More important, the manner in which policies are designed has consequences for the breadth and form of citizens' inclusion in the polity.

To understand the significance of policy design for citizenship, it is useful to recall Theodore J. Lowi's classic typology, which groups public policies according to the form of political relationship that they would be expected to foster. Distributive or patronage policies, the dominant type fashioned at the national level during the nineteenth century, are highly individualistic: they are disaggregated and dispensed unit by unit, to units in isolation from each other, to reward particular behavior.[25] This policy type is exemplified by "pork barrel" legislation in the federal budget, such as research and development or highway funds earmarked for particular states or congressional districts. Civil War pensions fit the model of distributive policies: politicians retained the power to control the timing and targeting of benefits for political purposes. Implementation through the patronage party system exacerbated these tendencies.[26] Like all distributive policies, the pensions had a particularistic character that undercut their ability to promote broad and effective social citizenship. Only regulatory policies, which control the behavior of actors in the private sector through general rules and broader standards of law, and redistributive policies, which affect the entire environment of conduct, could serve to affect broad classes of American citizens. Though state governments had experimented with both from the early years of the Republic onward, the national government would only begin to use such measures in the late nineteenth and early twentieth centuries, and it waited until the New Deal years to use them for social and labor policies.[27]

Institutional Arrangements

The institutional arrangements through which policies are administered also shape the character and experience of citizenship for those covered by the policies. Of critical significance is whether policies are implemented by the state and local governments or by the national government. With the exception of veterans' pensions, social and labor policies before the New Deal were enacted and administered on the state level or, more typically, at the local level.

Several features of decentralized policies in the United States have diminished their ability to promote broad guarantees of social citizenship. The most obvious such feature is variation itself. Decentralized policies vary tremendously in scope and form, between and often within states as well. This is because the institutional arrangements of federalism permit regionally based cultural differences to thrive and to take form in public policy. In an article entitled "Federalism Means Inequality," Aaron Wildavsky pointed out that "a belief in equality, not only of opportunity but of outcome, would be hostile to noncentralization, for then there could be no substantial differences between states."[28] Accordingly, although decentralized governance may do much to preserve democratic practices in policymaking, it means that citizenship will be defined according to the political and cultural geography of federalism and that it will be different—in a word, "unequal"—from one state or region to another.

Differences in the definition of social citizenship from place to place need not necessarily detract from its quality, but two additional aspects of federalism have led, historically, to such outcomes. First, political-institutional features of the states have acted to undermine guarantees of citizenship. The U.S. Constitution left the states with command of the police power, a power defined by the mid-nineteenth-century Taney Court providing for "the public health, safety, and good order" of the community.[29] The very spirit of the police power is to promote the public good according to the local or regional norms and values. It is a governing capacity with communitarian roots that predate liberal conceptions of the rule of law.[30] The inclination of states to wield the police power in a nonliberal manner, preserving and institutionalizing social hierarchies, was possible prior to and throughout the New Deal period because the equal protection clause of the Fourteenth Amendment of the Constitution was not applied to the states until the 1950s and 1960s.

In theory, decentralized governance fosters the ideals of democracy: vibrant participation and equality. Yet, in the absence of national requirements to guarantee liberal rights, the states typically adopted paternalistic arrangements that were more in keeping with feudalism than with democratic principles. Laws such as the Married Women's Property Acts and protective labor legislation, for example, served to institutionalize women's marginal status because they rested on the notion of women's assigned role as wives and mothers rather than their role as equal citizens.[31] Similarly, states made assistance under mothers' pensions conditional on the willingness of recipients, who were often immigrant women, to adapt to restrictive cultural norms of child-rearing and housekeeping, measured through "fit mother" and "suitable home" criteria.[32] Consequently, the manner in which state-run mothers' pensions programs extended social citizenship to women failed to provide an equitable means of inclusion in public life, and it constrained beneficiaries to a role in the polity that was attached to their social role. In other words, women were incorporated into the polity on the basis of their ascribed status, based on responsibilities assigned to people of their sex, rather than as free and equal citizens.

It is worth pausing to pose the question, What was the driving force in these instances: institutional arrangements or culture? Surely cultural beliefs and values loomed large in the development of the aforementioned laws; while liberal values have long been important to Americans, so too have cultural precepts that featured social hierarchies and ascribed roles. Yet, the influence of such forces was made possible only by the political-institutional arrangements of federalism. Contrary to the assumption that decentralization fosters democratic governance, some political scientists have argued that the smaller scope of conflict at the state level has promoted domination of the political process by narrow interests, forces that seek to maintain the existing social and political hierarchy.[33] The tendency of states to enforce status-bound hierarchies was compounded by their command of the police power, which allowed them to promote cultural values through legislation. The judiciary did not require states to guarantee liberal rights but instead fiercely protected their authority to govern according to different cultural mores, often in a discriminatory fashion.[34] The importance of culture notwithstanding, it was the institutional arrangements of federalism which encouraged and permitted states to emphasize undemocratic values and which maintained them, once written into law, for so many decades.

Finally, political-economic features of American federalism have undermined states' inclinations to be generous in the realm of social and labor policy. As David B. Robertson and Dennis R. Judd observe, the Constitution created "the world's largest 'free trade' zone," because individual states have neither the power to prevent businesses from entering or leaving their borders nor, unlike the national government, the power to protect businesses within their borders.[35] The pressures of interstate economic competition make states likely to neglect standards as they engage in a "race to the bottom" to make benefits less generous in amount and more punitive in form.[36] This tendency is well illustrated by mothers' pensions: although the enactment of these policies spread "like wildfire," their implementation proved much less auspicious. Although forty-five states had enacted mothers' pensions laws by 1934, fewer than half of the local units empowered to administer the statutes actually had programs in operation.[37] National government, by contrast to the states, does not have to be as concerned about the outward flow of capital. As well, it possesses the greatest taxing power because it can tax corporations substantially and has a generally more extensive and progressive income tax system than do states and localities. Thus, whereas states have a limited capacity to incorporate their residents fully as social citizens, national government is far better positioned to do so.[38]

In sum, only regulatory and redistributive policies and only those administered on a national basis could serve to extend rights and obligations to all American citizens equally, in a manner that fostered a sense of community, solidarity, and nationhood. Though some of the early relief policies of the New Deal adhered to the patronage tradition, the enduring programs of the welfare state were designed as regulatory and redistributive programs, and thus they promised to extend social citizenship more broadly. Yet, without requirements of national standards for eligibility and administration, state-level social and labor policies are likely to institutionalize social and economic inequalities. And when some citizens are incorporated as national citizens and others as state-level citizens, fragmentation becomes inscribed in the heart of the American polity. Such were the implications of the New Deal.

The Structure of New Deal Social Citizenship

The great achievement of the New Deal was the broadening of American citizenship, through regulatory labor legislation and redistributive social legislation, to incorporate citizens more fully as members of the polity. President Franklin D. Roosevelt, in a call to further "the security of the citizen and his family," advanced the idea that citizens should be endowed with some protection against the insecurities that could emerge in a modern, industrial economy.[39] Policy officials in his administration concurred that a floor for social and labor standards, a minimum assurance of well-being, ought to be guaranteed to Americans. They fashioned policy on the premise that for persons to be meaningfully included as free, equal, and potentially active members of the citizenry, political and civil rights should be complemented by social dimensions of citizenship.

Yet, the metamorphosis of social citizenship in the 1930s had limits—boundaries imposed by prevailing ideologies pertaining to ascribed gender roles and the proper realm of governance for public policies, the political imperatives of a Democratic Party that represented diverse industrial and agricultural interests, and the institutional arrangements of federalism. In the first place, New Dealers aimed their most innovative policymaking efforts at the concerns of the "forgotten man," who had indeed been long neglected in American social and labor policy. Earlier in the century, efforts to build a "paternalist" welfare state in the United States had failed while modest "maternalist" efforts had succeeded; during the 1930s and in subsequent decades of policy implementation, policies directed primarily toward male breadwinners took center stage, and policies targeting women and children received only marginal attention from political leaders and administrators.[40] Second, and more deliberately, policymakers refashioned intergovernmental arrangements in the United States but stretched the realm of national governance only far enough to incorporate full-time, long-term wage earners under its auspices. Inadvertently, these two developments combined, as seen in Table 2, such that mostly white men became incorporated within fully national programs, while women and men of color were left to programs to be administered primarily at the state level.

Table 2. New Deal Policies by Sex of Majority of Beneficiaries and Primary Level of Administrative Authority

	PRIMARY LEVEL OF ADMINISTRATIVE AUTHORITY	
MAJORITY OF BENEFICIARIES	NATIONAL	STATE
Men	Old Age Insurance Fair Labor Standards Act National Labor Relations Act	Unemployment Insurance*
Women	Survivors' Insurance (OASI)	Aid to Dependent Children Old Age Assistance Protective Labor Laws

In time, Unemployment Insurance became a hybrid policy, typically experienced as a nationalized policy by men and as a state-level policy by women.

Social Policies

Several social policies were enacted as part of the comprehensive legislation known as the Social Security Act (SSA) of 1935. Of the four major programs in the SSA, two were tied to the employment status of recipients, whereas the other two were not. Old Age Insurance (OAI) and Unemployment Insurance (UI) made eligibility for benefits in old age and during periods of unemployment, respectively, contingent on each worker's previous employment status, the length and constancy of his or her presence in the workforce, and his or her level of earnings. Because only 25.4 percent of women in the late 1930s participated in the paid labor force at any given time, compared with 79 percent of men, and because women workers tended to have intermittent employment histories or to work part-time owing to their domestic roles, they were much less likely than men to qualify for the work-related programs.[41] While the basic framework for the legislation was created by the Committee on Economic Security within the Roosevelt administration, further occupational exclusions were written into the bill in Congress which limited its coverage even more to men, specifically white men. The omission of employees in religious and nonprofit organizations put coverage off-limits to many women who worked as teachers, nurses, and social workers in such organizations, and the exclusion of agricultural and domestic workers made coverage inaccessible to a majority of African Americans, including over 90 percent of employed African American women, as well as to high proportions of Chicanos, Mexican Americans, and Asian Americans.[42]

By contrast to the eligibility requirements for OAI and UI, those for the other two major programs in the SSA, Old Age Assistance (OAA) and Aid to Dependent Children (ADC), had nothing to do with individuals' work history, and thus women were far more likely to qualify. Old Age Assistance, a grants-in-aid program that expanded on pension programs already in place in over half the states, was included primarily to meet widespread, grassroots demands spearheaded by the Townsend organization, but also because Roosevelt administration officials knew that not all older adults would be covered in OAI, especially in the short term before the program became established. Aid to Dependent Children was fashioned by maternalist reformers in the Children's Bureau who hoped to build on the mothers' pensions model of assistance to needy children in fatherless families through a grants-in-aid program.

Unlike programs and rules established in earlier eras which distinguished clearly between citizens on the basis of sex or race, such as protective labor laws for women or Jim Crow segregation laws, the New Deal social policies were free of such language. Certainly, the fact that some programs depended on work status whereas others did not meant that a gendered division would emerge in the coverage of the programs. Nonetheless, most policymakers did not expect that difference to be of great consequence, and they certainly did not expect or intend the emergence of a higher and lower tier of social provision. In the context of the 1930s, the programs geared to white men appeared least likely to succeed: both OAI and UI lacked precedents in the United States and relied on somewhat unconventional financing arrangements, while OAA and ADC built on preexisting programs and adhered to the established grants-in-aid model. Neither is it accurate to portray OAI as a "male vision" planned by male reformers and geared toward male breadwinners:[43] the chief proponent of the program was a woman, Barbara Nachtrieb Armstrong, a law professor from the University of California at Los Angeles, and she was committed to creating a program that would reach women as well as men. Likewise, the creators of ADC cannot be interpreted as state builders who intended to relegate women to a lower tier of social citizenship; to the contrary, they were quite convinced that they were fashioning a program that would build on the best features of mothers' pensions and transcend the worst.

Nonetheless, a gendered and racialized hierarchy did emerge between the programs in the course of implementation. Its causes can be traced in part to the financing distinctions between the programs: OAI and UI were "contributory" programs, funded through automatic payroll taxes, whereas OAA and ADC depended on appropriations of funds from general government revenues. The latter approach would necessarily introduce conflict at repeated junctures in the legislative process, and it would mean that the question of whether recipients were "deserving" would be raised again and again. Overlapping with these distinctions lay another difference between the programs which would prove in time to be of tremendous consequence: national-versus state-level administrative authority.

Policy officials in the Roosevelt administration are often thought of as state builders who uniformly exhibited a clear preference for national governing authority. Many assume that the high degree of state-level authority in some New Deal programs was attributable to southern Democrats in Congress who pushed for "states' rights."[44] In fact, several leading officials in the Roosevelt administration promoted an important administrative role for the states, and they did so not just as a defensive strategy in anticipation of congressional or judicial reaction but, more important, because they were proponents of a fairly traditional understanding of American federalism. The Committee on Economic Security (CES), for instance, was divided between a small vanguard of younger policymakers who favored national authority pitted against an "old guard" of officials who had been active at the state level during the Progressive Era and who wanted to preserve programs created then. The latter group included Secretary of Labor Frances Perkins, who hailed from New York, as well as Second Assistant Secretary of Labor Arthur J. Altmeyer and CES director Edwin Witte, both of whom had prominent roles in Progressive Era reforms in Wisconsin. They preferred decentralized programs, which they thought would enable the states to function as "laboratories of democracy," and they believed that programs would function better if planned closer to those whom they would serve.[45]

Of the four programs in the SSA, OAI was the one endowed with strictly national, unified administrative authority. Just two years earlier, Armstrong had published her treatise on social insurance titled *Insuring the Essentials: Minimum Wage plus Social Insurance, a Living Wage*

Program. In it she argued that the old-age pension programs developing at the state level contained eligibility provisions that "rob [the applicant] of the dignified position of an individual."[46] She and her colleagues in the Old Age Security Subcommittee of the CES were convinced that only a fully national program could make benefits in old age a meaningful right. To defend their position, they pointed out that the mobility of the workforce would create administrative difficulties in a system resting mostly on state-level authority; a federal system would assure quicker and fuller coverage of the population, and compliance would be superior. Their position prevailed.[47] Though the program was not established easily and despite its substantial alterations through amendments in 1939 before any benefits were ever allocated, the authority of national government remained intact. In the course of implementation, the program developed into one striking for its national uniformity. Thus, the mostly male recipients enjoyed the advantages of clear, impartial, and routinized procedures administered by a single tier of government.[48] In short, benefits became, for those who qualified for them, a right of social citizenship.

The greatest battles over administrative arrangements in the CES occurred in regard to UI. The committee finally settled on a plan which offered states authority for determining eligibility but which relied on the power of the federal government to collect taxes from employers, hold such funds in a reserve, and release them to states only if they designed adequate plans for the program.[49] The politics of implementation transformed the program into one that was experienced very differently depending on one's employment status and, consequently, by sex and race. Administrators worked successfully to improve the level and duration of benefits for those at the upper end of the wage scale, mostly white men.[50] States balked, however, when the Social Security Board urged them to raise benefits for low-paid workers, meaning most women as well as most men of color.[51] In addition, although the eligibility status of white males was generally determined on the basis of the national rules alone, states developed an extra set of eligibility hurdles that applied to low-wage workers and women in particular when they sought to qualify for benefits. One variant of the state-level rules measured "attachment to the labor force" on the basis of recent work history and earnings levels and thus discriminated in a subtle manner. Another set of rules denied benefits to individuals whose unemployment was related to "domestic reasons" such as pregnancy, childbirth, or marital obligations; these overtly disqualified women on the basis of their gender roles.[52] As a result, in the experience of well-paid, mostly white male beneficiaries, UI benefits were nationalized and standardized; in the experience of low-wage workers, especially women, the benefits were administered entirely at the state level, where applicants encountered a labyrinth of eligibility rules that made their access to benefits difficult to achieve.

Both public assistance programs in the SSA were designed as grant-in-aid programs in which financing would come in part from the federal government and in part from the states in which and states would hold the primary responsibility for eligibility determination and other aspects of implementation. The inclination of officials to favor decentralized designs for OAA and ADC epitomizes incrementalism in policymaking: twenty-eight states had already established pension programs for older adults, and forty-six states had laws permitting localities to develop mothers' pension programs (though only seventeen of those offered financial support), thus it was easy to extend both programs with the assistance of national funds.[53] Yet, the existence of precedents for OAA and ADC did not by itself necessitate their decentralized design.[54] Rather than simply taking the course of least resistance, maternalist reformers in the Children's Bureau went out of their way to defend several measures of state and local authority for ADC. Grace Abbott and Katharine Lenroot did hope that the grants-in-aid approach would enable the federal government to pressure states to develop programs, make them more widespread, and raise standards, but they also believed that states must be required to shoulder a good deal of the financial and administrative responsibility.[55] While the matching grant formula for OAA was one federal dollar for each state dollar contributed, Abbott and Lenroot proposed a formula for ADC of one federal dollar for every two state dollars.[56] They also regarded the educational component of the program, through which social workers would instruct poor women in child-rearing and domestic skills, to be critical, and they thought it would be handled best by local officials.[57] Later in Congress, the Ways and Means Committee, dominated by southern Democrats, proceeded to make OAA and ADC even more reliant on state-level authority by weakening some of the few federal standards the CES had included in the bill. The committee, for example, dropped language that would have mandated that states give "assistance at least great enough to provide . . . a reasonable subsistence compatible with decency and health."[58] Instead, states were asked simply to provide assistance "as far as practicable under the conditions in each State."[59]

In the course of implementation, ADC emerged as the program least able to extend rights of social citizenship to its beneficiaries. It was the most decentralized of all the major programs in the SSA, providing states with the least incentive and assistance to develop programs and to raise standards. Though the policy design of OAA was not very different from that of ADC, the program benefited at least initially from strong grassroots support on the part of the Townsend organization and other groups struggling to improve conditions for older adults.[60] Lacking such support, ADC benefits grew little, and the administration of the program came to resemble the worst features of mothers' pensions. In determining client eligibility, for example, "suitable home" rules were used to scrutinize the lives of potential beneficiaries, evaluating their child-rearing and housekeeping abilities and the school and church attendance of their children. As well, some states and localities used "man-in-the-house" rules to withdraw aid from women suspected of or found to have "male callers." Such investigations were often conducted through "midnight raids" by local officials.[61] Thanks to its grassroots support, OAA benefits remained higher than benefits under the contributory program, which had been transformed into Old Age and Survivors' Insurance (OASI), until 1950, by which time national administrative officials had pushed successfully to enhance the latter program. Meanwhile, however, the 1939 amendments helped make procedural rules for OAA become more demanding by giving states authority to use means testing to determine program benefit levels. These features of the state-run public assistance programs combined to make coverage within them inferior to coverage under OAI and to higher wage earners' coverage under UI. As a result, the women and minority men left to such programs were governed differently as social citizens from white men, who tended to have access to nationalized social benefits.

Labor Policy

In the realm of labor as well, policies became bifurcated between national programs that reached primarily white men and state-level programs that determined the fate of women employees. The National Labor Relations Act (NLRA) of 1935 guaranteed workers the right to form and participate in labor organizations and to select their own representatives for the purposes of collective bargaining. Like the Social Security Act, the language of the law was gender-neutral and made no mention of racial or ethnic distinctions; unlike the SSA, it pertained to organizations rather than to individual citizens. The enactment of the law was followed by an upsurge in organizing and strike activity. To the extent that it gave momentum to the newly formed Committee for Industrial Organizations (CIO), which organized unskilled workers in mass production industries, regardless of sex, race, or skill, the NLRA seemed at first to promote union activity beyond the traditional realm of white, native-born, skilled male workers.[62] Yet, after the first few years, the benefits of the law for women appeared to be marginal at best as labor organizations, outside of a few industries, remained primarily a white, male enterprise. Some scholars explain the low levels of unionization of women over the next several decades as the result of job segmentation or occupational segregation;[63] others blame the design of the NLRA itself, reasoning that it fostered a hierarchical and narrow unionism, exacerbating the already male-dominated character of labor organizations.[64] In any case, women remained less than half as likely to be union members as men for the next few decades: as late as 1956, only 15.7 percent of women workers belonged to unions, compared with 32.3 percent of the male workforce.[65] Without unions to improve their collective status in the workforce, women were especially reliant on labor standards as defined by government.

Ironically, however, the Fair Labor Standards Act (FLSA) of 1938, the major piece of legislation to define labor standards for the twentieth century, carved out of coverage the low-paid women workers and men of color who most needed its benefits. Unlike the SSA, the FLSA granted authority solely to the national government. This occurred even though Secretary Perkins played as dominant a role in steering its development as she had in the SSA. She, like Roosevelt, appeared far more comfortable with national power in the regulatory arena than in the realm of redistributive policy. But like major components of the SSA, FLSA coverage rested on occupational categories, in this case on the distinction between areas of employment within the realm of "interstate commerce" and thus within the domain of congressional authority versus those which fell outside its reach in "intrastate commerce." A recent landmark decision of the Supreme Court, *National Labor Relations Board v. Jones and Laughlin Steel Corporation,* seemed to affirm a dramatically broadened interpretation of the commerce clause in which all stages of the production process were understood as interdependent and thus within Congress's power to regulate.[66] Yet, once again, New Deal officials and their associates exhibited a disinclination to encroach very far into the realm of state-level authority. Felix Frankfurter urged Perkins to craft national labor standards narrowly, leaving room for the states to experiment with their own laws for other workers.[67] The National Consumers' League and its affiliates wanted to preserve the protective labor laws for women that they had worked so hard to establish at the state level in previous decades.[68] Roosevelt himself balked at covering some categories of workers, such as those engaged in what he termed "domestic help."[69] Southern representatives, fearing that national standards would threaten the low wages that were the norm and comparative advantage of their region, resisted the inclusion of several categories of workers. The result was that labor standards were written in a manner that included mostly occupations where wages and hours already met higher standards, while excluding the categories of low-paid workers who could have benefited most. The exclusion of agricultural workers left 22.8 percent of the male work force, a group in which nonwhite men figured disproportionately, unprotected in jobs with very low wages and long hours. Nearly twice as large a proportion of the female workforce, 42.2 percent, worked in excluded occupations at wages below the minimum level, including those who were retail workers, waitresses, hotel employees, beauticians, and domestic servants and many clerical workers.[70]

In short, the New Deal had made men's working conditions the legitimate object of the new rational and efficient procedures of national regulatory policy. But because women workers were largely unaffected by the NLRA and circumvented in critical ways by the FLSA, their advocates had to return to much the same agenda as they had pursued for the three decades before the New Deal. Women's civic organizations redoubled their efforts on the state level on behalf of exploited women workers, engaging in arduous state-by-state campaigns. Yet, despite the enormous changes in national governance, states remained reluctant to engage in regulatory activism. They were willing to enact protective laws to limit women's work hours and to prevent them from working in certain occupations, but they remained resistant to enacting minimum wage laws.[71]

Implications of New Deal Policy for Citizenship

Divided between two separate sovereignties that governed through distinct institutional arrangements, Americans came to experience very different forms of social citizenship. The administrative character of each level of government allowed for the application of disparate ideological norms. The New Deal is widely assumed to have represented the culmination of American liberalism, the moment at which the national government began to extend rights beyond the basic fundamentals of naturalization to Americans.[72] Yet a careful examination of the welfare state created in the New Deal reveals the perpetuation, long afterward, of a nonliberal realm of governance.[73] It was institutionalized through the system of American federalism within the states, where most women, as well as men of color, continued to be governed long afterward.

The most innovative development of the New Deal, the aspect of political change that most dramatically qualifies it for the status of a "revolution," was surely the creation of a liberal regime of citizenship within the domain of national government. The narrow commercial republic created at the national level by the Founders could be described as ostensibly "liberal," but it did not much affect the governance of citizens, whose fates were determined primarily by the states.[74] New Deal policymakers, by contrast, reconstructed the national government into what can be called a prototypical Lockean liberal state in terms of the basis of inclusion within programs. In its new guise, national government incorporated, through OAI, UI, the NLRA, and the FLSA, those whom John Locke might have termed the "Industrious and Rational" persons.[75] To New Dealers, these persons qualified as "independent" citizens and thus as free and equal bearers of rights, on the condition that they were long-term, full-time wage earners. In classic liberal fashion, they crafted laws that were formally "gender-neutral" inasmuch as they treated individuals in an abstract manner that was blind to both biological characteristics, like sex, and to ascribed statuses, such as gender roles. As shown above, however, given the composition of the workforce, such criteria tended to include only men within their reach.

Table 3. The Incorporation of Citizens in New Deal Policies

	PRIMARY LEVEL OF ADMINISTRATIVE AUTHORITY	
IDEOLOGICAL CHARACTER	NATIONAL	STATE
Liberal	Old Age Insurance Fair Labor Standards Act	Unemployment Insurance*
Nonliberal	Old Age and Survivors' Insurance	Aid to Dependent Children Old Age Assistance Protective Labor Laws

In time, Unemployment Insurance became a hybrid policy, operating as a nationalized, liberal policy for some and as a state-run, nonliberal policy for others.

Table 3 summarizes the characteristics of the major New Deal programs. Two programs most fully combined the ethos of liberalism in their eligibility criteria with the administrative practices most common in national governance. National programs were characterized by standardized, routinized procedures and run by civil servants hired through the merit system, meaning the use of exams and fair and open competition, rather than the old-style patronage system. These programs, OAI as it was created in 1935 and the FLSA, applied, at least at the outset, primarily to men.

Feminist political theorists have pointed out that the social contract in liberal theory, through its division of the public and private realms, left the domestic sphere beyond the reach of its principles.[76] When classical liberal theorists imagined the creation of a public realm by and for free and equal citizens, they assumed the perpetuation of a nonliberal, private realm of the family, wherein a hierarchy based on ascribed roles and status could continue. Long after women have become included as citizens within the public sphere, their lives have still been defined largely within the private sphere, without the protection of rights.

Similarly, in the establishment of the "second American republic" beginning with the New Deal, most women remained beyond the purview of the new liberal realm of citizenship.[77] But the lines drawn between men and women in New Deal policies were inscribed not only on the classic liberal divide between the public and private realms but, more important, also on the distinction between national and state-level governance. Left to the states, women tended to be incorporated as social citizens on the basis of nonliberal criteria that regarded them in relational, role-oriented, or difference-based terms rather than as abstract individuals. Such criteria reflect both the "republican tradition" and the "ascriptive Americanist traditions" detailed by Rogers Smith.[78] Inclusion in OAA was rooted in ideas that predated the New Deal, through which certain citizens, in this case older adults, were considered worthy of social provision simply because of their service to society, as "good citizens," rather than because of their paid labor. Similarly, women's inclusion in ADC was based on another variant of "good citizenship": the notion that as mothers, women served the needs of the public sphere by raising future citizens.[79] Mostly left out of the FLSA provisions, women remained dependent on state-level protective labor laws to offer at least a minimal floor of labor standards; such policies had long been justified by the courts on the basis that women's innate function as actual or potential mothers provided a compelling state interest in their protection in the workplace.

In keeping with the spirit of the police power and the constraints of interstate economic competition, state governments administered these programs in a manner distinct from national government. They added layers of eligibility requirements to those stated in federal law and permitted local officials to implement rules with ample discretion. Beneficiaries became treated as dependent persons who required supervision and protection rather than as bearers of rights. Programs were characterized by invasive rules and procedures through which officials monitored and regulated recipients' moral character. While national programs evolved to be infused with the professionalism that accompanied the development of the merit system, states continued to rely on patronage procedures for selecting personnel for years to come, oftentimes using overt political influence in the allocation of benefits. Citizens left to state-level governance were endowed, furthermore, with rights and obligations that varied from state to state according to political demands, cultural norms, and economic needs of local employers. In sum, these programs perpetuated, within the states, a form of governance for women that can be described as "semifeudal." Among its hallmark features were the hierarchical and role-bound basis on which people were included within programs, the parochial administrative procedures used in their implementation, and the extent to which the programs tied citizenship to the politics of place.

Ironically, the major route through which women did gain access to the national realm of citizenship in the New Deal was through incorporation on a distinctly nonliberal basis. Through the addition of widows' and wives' benefits to OAI in 1939, women who were married to men covered by OAI became included, by virtue of being wives of "independent men," in a program that was administered according to the professionalism of national governance. Similarly, through pensions to Civil War veterans and subsequently through the GI Bill of Rights of 1944, former soldiers were included in national social provisions as a means to honor their civic virtue, an ideal that emanated from republican rather than liberal ideology.[80]

Unemployment Insurance represented a hybrid program in which inclusion was based on liberal criteria but wherein states played a significant role in administration. The program changed and developed in the course of implementation, and by midcentury most white men experienced liberal grounds for inclusion in the program and nearly national standards of administration. Women and nonwhite men, by contrast, were confronted by nonliberal eligibility rules which varied tremendously from state to state and which tended to make the program inaccessible to them. The development of UI illustrates how women can be twice ostracized under the system of American federalism. First, New Deal liberals at the national level, who viewed the beneficiary pool for UI in gender-neutral, wage-related terms, excluded most women from the policy by limiting its coverage to wage earners, and by correlating benefits to prior wages, they assured most women workers of lower benefits than men. Next, women who survived the test required by the national level faced a different set of exclusionary rules at the state level: there they were seen in a gender-particular light and frequently excluded from benefits on the basis of the notion that their husbands should provide for them. Though either system by itself would have carried substantial disadvantages, women would have been better off with either a purely liberal plan as created by the Roosevelt administration or by a nonliberal plan that ascribed people to particular roles in the democratic polity based on sex. Instead, by combining the two in a plan administered jointly by the national government and by the state, women suffered the worst of both ideologies in unemployment insurance policy.

Of course, the liberal character of the New Deal meant that its categories of citizenship were neither overtly nor rigidly defined in terms of sex. Women were entitled to the same rights and benefits as men when they fit the mold properly: as long-term, full-time participants in the paid labor force, as union members, as workers in industry. Accordingly, New Deal policies were potentially expandable, capable of including more and more women as they increased their numbers in the workforce in later decades and as they entered male-dominated occupations. But women in the late 1930s gained little from the policies because so few had sufficient records in the paid workforce and because they were likely to work in occupations excluded from coverage, to be unemployed owing to pregnancy or family responsibilities, or to be nonunionized workers.

Once established, however, divided citizenship endured in the United States for decades, with manifold implications. Most important, though men and women had unequal forms of social status in the United States before the 1930s, New Deal policies had institutionalized those disparities and inscribed them with political significance. Governed within separate sovereignties, men and women, further differentiated by class and race, gained very different and unequal forms of status as members of the political community. Those incorporated as primary beneficiaries in the national realm were viewed as worthy, independent, and free; those relegated to the states were considered dependent persons who had to be evaluated to determine whether they were deserving. What it meant to be an "American citizen" subsequently assumed a very different connotation to the retired male breadwinner, who came to expect his monthly "social security" check from the national government, from that to the poor mother, who hoped the social worker assigned to evaluate her eligibility for a meager "welfare" check would find her child-rearing and housekeeping efforts to be worthy. The first was treated with dignity and respect, as an entitled person; the latter, with suspicion and scrutiny. The bureaucracy that came to surround the administration of national programs assured beneficiaries of routine treatment, whereas citizens whose experience was defined at the state and local level could be certain only of variation, as politics shifted within the state or if they moved to a different locality.

The New Deal Legacy

Divided citizenship, as established by the New Deal, flourished throughout the mid–twentieth century owing to a combination of factors. By some indicators the national government in the early 1940s seemed to be moving toward more universal guarantees of social citizenship and greater parity between men and women. In the early part of the decade, the mobilization of women into the war effort and new national policy initiatives and rhetoric suggested that citizenship divided by gender and federalism might be on the wane. As the United States entered World War II and male workers were needed for the armed services, the War Labor Board actively encouraged women to serve on the "home front" by entering the workforce and taking high-paying, skilled jobs traditionally reserved for men. Female labor force participation climbed from 27.9 percent in 1940 to 35.8 percent in 1945.[81] At the same time, officials in the National Resources Planning Board (NRPB), who had been asked by President Roosevelt to formulate social and economic policy for after World War II, proposed building on the beginnings of social citizenship as established in the New Deal to fashion a more inclusive and comprehensive form of citizenship for all Americans. Drawing in part on plans put forward by the Social Security Board (SSB), NRPB officials suggested broadening OASI coverage, nationalizing and expanding the public assistance programs and unemployment insurance, establishing national health insurance, and providing measures for full employment.[82] Yet, most proposed reforms failed to materialize, and those which did emerged slowly.

First, when soldiers returned home from the front, government-sponsored wartime propaganda efforts were reversed: women were encouraged to leave paid work and to return to domestic responsibilities. Management and unions cooperated in efforts to reinstate traditional divisions of occupational segregation, forcing women to return to clerical and service sector jobs so that men could regain high-skilled jobs. Women lacked the seniority to compete with their male counterparts for jobs, and regardless, veterans were granted preferential treatment in hiring.[83] By 1947, female labor force participation had declined to 31.9 percent. Over the next few decades women gradually increased their numbers in the workforce through a moderated but steady growth pattern.[84] The wage gap and divisions between men's and women's jobs in terms of status and security had, however, already been reestablished. As a result, men and women were, once again, incorporated separately within the framework of New Deal social and labor policies.

Second, the hopes of the NRPB failed, for the most part, to materialize. The most generous new forms of social provision established during the period emerged in the form of the GI Bill, which was targeted narrowly to returning veterans of World War II, primarily men. Health insurance efforts floundered, and hopes for a genuine "full employment bill" dissipated with the modest Employment Act of 1946.[85]

Public assistance programs in the Social Security Act were altered only slightly, eclipsing the plans of the NRPB and the provisions of the Wagner-Murray-Dingell bills of the mid-1940s, which would have gone far to expand eligibility and to remove the aspects of financing that disadvantaged poorer states. In 1946 Congress adopted a modified version of a variable grant formula for OAA and ADC. But instead of providing for at least a minimum standard of public assistance in the poorest states, the plan changed only the matching grant ratio to depend more heavily on funds from the national government.[86] The scheme was hardly redistributive; rather, it meant that federal efforts to promote more generous benefit levels in the poorest states became contingent on higher financial obligations toward the wealthiest states. As a result, wide disparities in benefits persisted: in 1947 OAA benefits ranged from $17.32 per recipient per month in Mississippi to $53.02 in Washington state; for ADC, benefits ranged from $26.29 per family per month in Mississippi to a high of $104.63 in Washington state.[87] In 1950 a benefit for caretakers of children on ADC, a provision omitted by policymakers in 1935, was finally included in the program. Yet, despite the resulting improvement in benefit amounts, the public assistance programs continued to be run according to the same restrictive eligibility and procedural rules long utilized in the states.[88]

The full nationalization of Unemployment Insurance never materialized, and the consequences were most severe for women and nonwhite men. Both groups suffered from unemployment rates that were consistently higher than those of white men.[89] As well, they typically fared the worst at the hands of the states. Unemployment Insurance was altered slightly in 1954 to apply to employers of four or more workers instead of eight or more workers. As late as 1963, however, state laws still exempted some 15 million workers from coverage, including those in state and local government, domestic service, farm and agricultural processing, and nonprofits.[90] In 1971, moreover, twenty-three states still disqualified women from collecting UI if they left work for reasons categorized as "domestic quits," including pregnancy, childbirth, or other familial responsibilities.[91]

Most women's jobs were still concentrated in low-wage occupations excluded from coverage under the Fair Labor Standards Act. Despite repeated attempts for reform, expansion of the FLSA to include more categories of workers remained beyond the reach of women's reform organizations throughout the 1940s and 1950s. When an increase in the minimum wage was finally achieved in 1949, half a million other workers, particularly in the female-dominated clerical and service sectors, became newly excluded from the law's provisions.[92]

The primary advances in the expansion of national social citizenship in the midcentury United States involved the improvement of OASI, and even those reforms came slowly. Officials in the SSB, which became reorganized as the Social Security Administration in 1946, pressed for amendments to the program throughout the 1940s. At last in 1950, Congress expanded OASI to include about 10 million more persons, primarily the self-employed and employees in nonprofit agencies, and in 1954 the law was amended once again to include agricultural and domestic workers, thus erasing the racial cleavages that had formerly excluded most African Americans and many other nonwhites from OASI.[93]

The status of older women continued to confound reformers throughout the period, however, because many still did not qualify for either OASI or OAA. In the early 1950s the SSB research staff found that among a group of 2.6 million older Americans who had access to neither benefit type and who lacked earnings, fully 80 percent were women, and three-quarters of them were widows.[94] In 1956 Congress attempted to remedy the situation somewhat by lowering the age for OASI eligibility from sixty-five to sixty-two for women.[95] As a result of the midcentury expansions in OASI, demand for OAA slowly began to dissipate: the number of recipients dropped from 2.8 million in 1950 to 2.2 million in 1964.[96] But even then, older people who did not fit the acceptable mold for status in OASI, still mostly women, remained subject to the states and experienced citizenship in a manner that had grown distant from that of OASI beneficiaries.

Why was the reform momentum of the 1930s curbed so quickly, preventing the expansion of national social citizenship during the next two decades? First, the NRPB had to contend with the SSB and the increasingly powerful Veterans Administration, both of which had different priorities for policy development. Then, in 1943, Congress, seeking to restore congressional dominance over wartime planning, abolished the

NRPB as well as several other executive planning agencies.⁹⁷ Second, though Democrats continued to dominate Congress, conservative southern and rural Democrats became increasingly inclined to part ways with northern and urban members of their own party, and in the House their numbers made them especially powerful. Without sufficient numbers of urban Democrats to promote the social policy proposals of the NRPB and SSB, measures such as the Wagner-Murray-Dingell bill of 1943 simply died in committee. Wartime strike activity, furthermore, weakened the sympathy for labor that had existed during the 1930s, and southern Democrats began to block the efforts of their northern colleagues on labor legislation, developing what Ira Katznelson and his collaborators have called the "southern veto."⁹⁸ At the same time, Roosevelt became preoccupied with the war and ceased to push domestic policy initiatives as he had in the 1930s. After he died and Harry S. Truman became president, relations between the White House and Congress became even more strained; only modest victories were achieved in the area of social policy, and important setbacks were suffered in labor policy.⁹⁹ When Republicans took back the presidency with the election of Dwight D. Eisenhower in 1952, hopes for the expansion of the New Deal became increasingly dim, leaving the framework of divided citizenship little disturbed for yet another decade.

For those citizens whose status was still defined primarily by the states after the New Deal, the character of governance in the realm of social citizenship changed little, remaining relatively conservative well into the 1960s. For one thing, the particular features of state politics still stymied the development of governance that might have enhanced the status of those governed especially by the states. Owing to outdated apportionment, many state legislatures were dominated by rural interests, and one-party dominance and factionalism, particularly in the South, impeded possibilities for programmatic policymaking.¹⁰⁰ States had difficulty attracting administrative talent due to the continuation of the patronage tradition.¹⁰¹ Many state constitutions retained features that made innovative policies impossible, particularly if increased spending was involved. The dynamics of American federalism also continued to deter change at the state level. The threat of interstate economic competition hindered state legislators from establishing more generous programs. Southern states, anxious to protect their low-wage economies, provided particularly low public assistance benefits and had the most limited labor protections. Such tendencies, in turn, acted as a drag on the policies of other states that were concerned that higher taxes and regulations might discourage businesses from operating within their borders.[102] As well, states remained the predominant holders of the "police power," and its preliberal character still shaped the manner in which states governed. In fact, states distinguished by relatively high degrees of social spending and administrative capacity often wielded the police power in a particularly scrupulous and paternalistic fashion. Such states as Wisconsin, Massachusetts, and Washington, for example, inscribed ADC with especially moralistic "suitable home" rules and retained protective labor laws that were very restrictive of women's roles in the workforce. Such rules tied women's social provision most firmly to their ascribed gender role.[103]

From the late 1930s through the 1950s, states expanded their efforts in intergovernmental social programs only to the extent that they were effectively goaded by financing arrangements. Unemployment Insurance underwent the most substantial and widespread improvements, but the reforms did little for women. Old Age Assistance was enhanced in states where citizens' groups exerted pressure on lawmakers for more generous pensions for older adults. The majority of states continued to be sluggish, however, regarding programs for which they were left with a relatively high degree of responsibility, as in the case of ADC, or retained total autonomy, such as for labor regulations for jobs in "intrastate" commerce. The joint national-state programs in the SSA were hindered further by the multiple opportunities for state and local agendas to displace the intentions of national policymakers.[104] Consequently, the states persisted for decades in governing in a manner that set citizens within their domain apart from those incorporated within the liberal promises of national citizenship.

The Demise of Divided Citizenship

Even while divided citizenship remained entrenched, the first glimmers of change began to flicker. The *Brown v. Board of Education* decision in 1954 indicated an emerging skepticism by the Supreme Court toward classifications made by the states on the basis of race.[105] The civil rights movement started to gather momentum, pressuring states and municipalities to dismantle Jim Crow segregation.[106] Increasingly, the Court began to hold states responsible for granting "equal protection" of the law, guaranteed by the Fourteenth Amendment, to all citizens. In time, these events would lead to a second constitutional revolution that would alter how states governed.

In the 1960s and 1970s, the culmination of the civil rights movement, Democratic victories at the presidential level, and the new women's movement combined to usher in the extension of national social citizenship to groups left out in the New Deal arrangements. Many of the hopes of the most optimistic reformers of the 1930s were finally realized as New Deal laws proved to be "organic statutes" that could be built on and liberalized over time. Policymakers expanded the FLSA in 1966 to include agricultural workers and in 1974 to cover domestic service workers, retail and service workers, and most other categories of employees.[107] The Equal Employment Opportunity Act of 1972 improved women's status in UI, and the Pregnancy Discrimination Act of 1978 forbade states from denying UI to pregnant women.[108] Policymakers enacted the Equal Pay Act of 1963, followed by the Civil Rights Act of 1964, which included the prohibition of discrimination on the basis of sex as well as race.[109] In social policy lawmakers dissolved OAA in 1974 and created a new program, titled Supplemental Security Income (SSI), for older persons who are poor and person who are blind or disabled. By sharp contrast to OAA, SSI operated according to national standards, requiring uniform minimum benefits and mandatory cost-of-living increases. Gradually, given the increasing likelihood that women were covered by OASI and the elevated standards for SSI, the unequal treatment of men versus women within OASI became a more critical issue than the divergence between the contributory program and public assistance. Feminists charged that OASI discriminated on the basis of sex and pushed the courts to examine the policy. Some of the more overt gender-based distinctions regarding wives and widows were found to violate the equal protection clause of the Fourteenth Amendment. Thereafter, attention turned to less obvious issues, especially the tendency of the program to offer higher benefits to married women who never worked for pay than to women who participated in the labor force throughout their lifetime.[110]

At the same time as national social citizenship expanded, the oppressive qualities of state governance for marginalized groups became more subdued. The Civil Rights Act of 1964 restrained the states' use of the police power by striking down Jim Crow laws and by barring discrimination by states in activities that used funds from the national government. The reapportionment decisions of the Supreme Court in the early sixties forced states to reallocate membership in their legislatures in accordance with the "one person–one vote" principle and to repeat the process every ten years following each new census. As states with outmoded districting plans, especially those in the South, refigured their districts to make them equal in population, state legislatures became increasingly responsive to urban concerns.[111] The Voting Rights Act of 1965 curtailed state-level authority for voter registration and voting procedures, bringing to an end those measures which had disenfranchised southern blacks for decades. In turn, states experienced increased party competition. These changes helped awaken state legislators to broader concerns in the realm of social policymaking, and they stimulated the development of professional administrative procedures at the state level.[112]

During the 1960s, lawmakers and the courts, activated by an insurgent welfare rights movement and its lawyers, changed the ADC program in ways that made it significantly more nationalized, at least in terms of administrative procedures and eligibility rules.[113] Renamed Aid to Families with Dependent Children (AFDC) when amended in 1962, the program was transformed most dramatically through changes wrought by the judiciary through statutory review. The states lost a substantial measure of their autonomy and discretion when the Supreme Court made individual state eligibility rules invalid unless they were explicitly authorized by the federal statute or deemed to be consistent with the Court's understanding of the underlying purpose of the program.[114] These decisions abolished many of the long-standing rules that had enabled states to limit eligibility for AFDC.[115] Although financial eligibility rules and the tremendous variation in AFDC benefits from state to state persevered, some of the worst aspects of state-level administration in the areas of moral supervision were alleviated. Through such changes AFDC began to approximate an "entitlement," a benefit assured to those who fit nationally uniform, standardized eligibility criteria.

The boundaries of divided citizenship became much less distinct as policymakers expanded national programs to cover persons previously neglected and as state and local officials lost much of the discretion through which they had implemented programs previously. But just as the civil rights and women's movements prompted the Democratic Party to act on behalf of blacks and women in the 1960s and 1970s, white men—the original, primary beneficiaries of the New Deal—began to defect from party ranks. This shift continued as government deficits grew during the 1980s, leading to the revitalization of a Republican Party anxious to limit the power of national government, followed by the reposturing of the Democratic Party in the 1990s to do much the same.[116]

At the end of the century, policymakers began to reestablish some of the boundaries of divided citizenship. Most notably, the Personal Responsibility and Work Opportunity Act (PRA) of 1996 dissolved features that since the 1960s had made welfare approximate an entitlement and gave the states more authority in administering it than they had known in six decades. Granted, several features of the modern polity differ from that of the New Deal era. National policymakers today tended to be guided more by social conservatism than by liberalism; the policy result in the case of the PRA is a odd combination of states' rights conservatism and neofeudal edicts from the national level.[117] States have developed vastly improved governing capacities over the past half century and must be considerably more restrained in their exercise of the police power, though they are still affected by the forces of interstate economic competition.[118] Not all the national antipoverty policies that have emerged since the 1960s have been decimated, and the Earned Income Tax Credit was expanded under the Clinton administration. Finally, even amid the calls for overhauling Social Security and Medicare, reform plans never suggest turning authority over to the states; national government remains firmly in control of bedrock social programs whose constituencies include the middle class. Nonetheless, as critical social rights and obligations of low-income women have become defined again at the state level, the polity again appears to be acquiring some of the fractures of midcentury.

Policymakers who seek to incorporate citizens into the polity in ways that might promote the sense of social solidarity so fundamental to civic life should heed the lessons of the New Deal. First, liberal, work-oriented policies can go far, especially today, to foster social inclusivity, but they require constant attention to remedying or compensating for gender inequities in employment status. Second, policies that recognize the civic value of various forms of unpaid work, particularly the care of young children, can serve an important function in the polity. The critical caveat is that such policies must be designed to treat recipients with fairness and respect and to protect against institutionalizing social inequities. They should be extended regardless of sex, allowing responsibilities for parenting and other forms of caretaking to be shared more equitably between men and women. Third, policymakers should be mindful of the consequences of institutional administrative arrangements for public policy. While state and local officials may have some comparative advantages in the area of job creation and others, decentralized policies must include standards for social citizenship that are broad, inclusive, and national in scope if they are to endow citizens with the dignity befitting those with political membership. As those of the New Deal illustrate, policies lacking in such standards convey to citizens that they are marginal to the polity, unworthy of the provision and rights granted to national citizens. By contrast, nationally administered policies can help to knit together members of a highly diverse nation by extending a sense of social equality and community.

Notes

1. Edward S. Corwin, "The Passing of Dual Federalism," *Virginia Law Review* 36 (February 1965): 1–24; Theodore J. Lowi, *The Personal President: Power Invested, Promise Unfulfilled* (Ithaca: Cornell University Press, 1985), 24.

2. See *The Slaughterhouse Cases,* 16 Wallace 36 (1873).

3. T. H. Marshall, "Citizenship and Social Class," in *Class, Citizenship, and Social Development* (Garden City, N.Y.: Doubleday, 1964), 65–122.

4. Theda Skocpol, *Protecting Soldiers and Mothers: The Political Origins of Social Policy in the United States* (Cambridge: Harvard University Press, 1992), 82–87, 102–51. See also Theodore J. Lowi, "American Business, Public Policy, Case-Studies, and Political Theory," *World Politics* 16 (July 1964): 677–715.

5. David L. Weimer and Aidan R. Vining, *Policy Analysis: Concepts and Practice,* 2d ed. (Englewood Cliffs, N.J.: Prentice Hall, 1992).

6. For example, see Skocpol, *Protecting Soldiers and Mothers,* 1–65; Theda Skocpol and John Ikenberry, "The Political Formation of the American Welfare State in Historical and Comparative Perspective," *Comparative Social Research* 6 (1983): 87–148; Theda Skocpol and Kenneth Finegold, "State Capacity and Economic Intervention in the Early New Deal," *Political Science Quarterly* 97 (Summer 1982): 255–78; Ann Shola Orloff, "The Political Origins of America's Belated Welfare State," in *The Politics of Social Policy in the United States,* ed. Margaret Weir, Ann Shola Orloff, and Theda Skocpol (Princeton: Princeton University Press, 1988), 37–80; Ann Shola Orloff, *The Politics of Pensions* (Madison: University of Wisconsin Press, 1993); Theda Skocpol and Edwin Amenta, "Did Capitalists Shape Social Security?" *American Sociological Review* 50, 4 (August 1985): 572–75; and Margaret Weir, *Politics and Jobs: The Boundaries of*

Employment Policy in the United States (Princeton: Princeton University Press, 1992).

7. Barry D. Karl, *The Uneasy State: The United States from 1915 to 1945* (Chicago: University of Chicago Press, 1983).

8. My primary focus is on gendered divisions; for a more in-depth treatment of New Deal policies in terms of race, see Robert C. Lieberman, *Shifting the Color Line: Race and the American Welfare State* (Cambridge: Harvard University Press, 1998).

9. Linda Gordon, *Pitied but Not Entitled: Single Mothers and the History of Welfare, 1890{nd}1935* (New York: Free Press, 1994); Gwendolyn Mink, *The Wages of Motherhood: Inequality in the Welfare State, 1917–1942* (Ithaca: Cornell University Press, 1995); Alice Kessler-Harris, "Designing Women and Old Fools: The Construction of the Social Security Amendments of 1939," in *U.S. History as Women's History,* ed. Linda Kerber, Alice Kessler-Harris, and Kathryn Kish Sklar (Chapel Hill: University of North Carolina Press, 1995), pp. 87–106; Eileen Boris, *Home to Work: Motherhood and the Politics of Industrial Homework in the United States* (New York: Cambridge University Press, 1994).

10. Rogers M. Smith, *Civic Ideals: Conflicting Visions of Citizenship in U.S. History* (New Haven: Yale University Press, 1997).

11. See Smith, *Civic Ideals;* Linda K. Kerber, *No Constitutional Right to Be Ladies: Women and the Obligations of Citizenship* (New York: Hill and Wang, 1998); Virginia Sapiro, "Women, Citizenship, and Nationality: Immigration and Naturalization Policies in the United States," *Politics and Society* 13 (1984): 1–26; and Candice Lewis Bredbenner, *A Nationality of Her Own: Women, Marriage, and the Law of Citizenship* (Berkeley: University of California Press, 1998).

12. See Helen Ingram and Steven Rathgeb Smith, eds., *Public Policy for Democracy* (Washington, D.C.; Brookings Institution, 1993). See also Robert B. Reich, "Policy Making in a Democracy," in *The Power of Public Ideas,* ed. Reich (Cambridge: Harvard University Press, 1988), 123–56; Michael J. Sandel, *Democracy's Discontent: America in Search of a Public Philosophy* (Cambridge: Harvard University Press, Belknap Press, 1996); and Lawrence Mead, *Beyond Entitlement: The Social Obligations of Citizenship* (New York: Free Press, 1986).

13. The focus on participatory citizenship is evident in contemporary scholarship. Some lament the decline of social trust and civic engagement or urge its revival; for example, see Robert D. Putnam, "Tuning In, Tuning Out: The Strange Disappearance of Social Capital in America," *PS: Political Science and Politics* 28 (December 1995): 664–83, and Benjamin Barber, *A Place for Us: How to Make Society Civil and Democracy Strong* (New York: Hill and Wang, 1998). For a classic study that assesses contemporary civic engagement in a more positive light, see Sidney Verba, Kay Lehman Schlozman, and Henry E. Brady, *Voice and Equality: Civic Voluntarism in American Politics* (Cambridge: Harvard University Press, 1995).

14. Francisco Ramirez and Jane Weiss, "The Political Incorporation of

Women," in *National Development and the World System,* ed. John W. Meyer and Michael T. Hannan (Chicago: University of Chicago Press, 1979), 238–39.

15. Judith N. Shklar, *American Citizenship: The Quest for Inclusion* (Cambridge: Harvard University Press, 1991); Marshall, "Citizenship and Social Class."

16. Marshall, "Citizenship and Social Class."

17. Shklar, *American Citizenship,* 2.

18. See Fred Block, "Social Policy and Accumulation: A Critique of the New Consensus," in *Stagnation and Renewal in Social Policy: The Rise and Fall of Policy Regimes,* ed. Martin Rein, Gosta Esping-Andersen, and Lee Rainwater (Armonk, N.Y.: M. E. Sharpe, 1987); Albert O. Hirschman *The Rhetoric of Reaction: Perversity, Futility, Jeopardy* (Cambridge: Harvard University Press, Belknap Press, 1991); and Theda Skocpol, "The Limits of the New Deal System and the Roots of Contemporary Welfare Dilemmas," in *Politics of Social Policy,* ed. Weir, Orloff, and Skocpol, esp. 307–11.

19. Michael Walzer, *Spheres of Justice* (New York: Basic, 1983), 64.

20. Ronald Beiner, "Why Citizenship Constitutes a Theoretical Problem in the Last Decade of the Twentieth Century," and Will Kymlicka and Wayne Norman, "Return of the Citizen: A Survey of Recent Work on Citizenship Theory," both in *Theorizing Citizenship,* ed. Ronald Beiner (Albany: State University of New York Press, 1995), 1–28 and 283–322, respectively.

21. Gosta Esping-Andersen, *The Three Worlds of Welfare Capitalism* (Princeton: Princeton University Press, 1990); Marilyn Lake, ed., "Citizenship: Intersections of Gender, Race, and Ethnicity," special issue of *Social Politics* 2 (Summer 1995); Ann Shola Orloff, "Gender and the Social Rights of Citizenship: The Comparative Analyses of Gender Relations and Welfare States," *American Sociological Review* 58 (June 1993): 303–28; Ursula Vogel, "Is Citizenship Gender-Specific?" in *The Frontiers of Citizenship,* ed. Vogel and Michael Moran (New York: St. Martin's, 1991); Diane Sainsbury, ed., *Gendering Welfare States* (London: Sage, 1994).

22. This is illustrated very well in Skocpol, *Protecting Soldiers and Mothers* 47–57. The effect of guarantees of social citizenship for participatory citizenship has yet to be examined carefully by scholars; it remains beyond the scope of the present study. Some scholars assume that social citizenship itself undermines participatory citizenship by making citizens dependent on the state and more preoccupied by their rights than by their obligations to public life. For example, Sandel assumes that the "procedural republic" embraced by New Dealers and epitomized by "entitlement" policies was necessarily antithetical to the formative mission advocated by Progressive Era policymakers who sought to fortify civic affiliation. See Sandel, *Democracy's Discontent,* 262–73, 280–89. In a similar vein, Lawrence Mead criticizes welfare policy for undermining citizens' sense of obligation and the work ethic by placing undue emphasis on their rights. See Mead, *Beyond Entitlement,* 1–17. Such claims have yet to be tested empirically, however. It is likely that the particular design and institutional arrangement for

policies have important consequences for whether they enhance or detract from participatory citizenship.

23. Helen Ingram and Anne Schneider, "Constructing Citizenship: The Subtle Messages of Policy Design," in *Public Policy for Democracy,* ed. Ingram and Smith, 68.

24. Institutional arrangements for implementation are also a feature of policy design, but they are treated separately here to distinguish the structure of the government-citizen relationship from the administrative arrangements through which such a policy is implemented.

25. Theodore J. Lowi, "Four Systems of Policy, Politics, and Choice," *Public Administration Review* (July/August 1972): 298–310; Lowi, "American Business," 677–715.

26. Skocpol, *Protecting Soldiers and Mothers,* 82–87, 120–24, 143–48.

27. Lowi, "Four Systems of Policy, Politics, and Choice," 300–302.

28. Aaron Wildavsky, "Federalism Means Inequality: Political Geometry, Political Sociology, and Political Culture," in *The Costs of Federalism,* ed. Robert T. Golembiewski and Aaron Wildavsky (New Brunswick, N.J.: Transaction, 1984), 57.

29. David B. Walker, *The Rebirth of Federalism* (Chatham, N.J.: Chatham House, 1995), 69.

30. Christopher L. Tomlins, "Law, Police, and the Pursuit of Happiness in the New American Republic," in *Studies in American Political Development* 4 (1990): 3–34; William J. Novak, "Intellectual Origins of the State Police Power: The Common Law Vision of a Well-Regulated Society," working paper, Legal History Program, ser. 3, Institute for Legal Studies, University of Wisconsin-Madison, 1989.

31. Joan Hoff, *Law, Gender, and Injustice* (New York: New York University Press, 1991), 127–31; Rogers M. Smith, "'One United People': Second-Class Female Citizenship and the American Quest for Community," *Yale Journal of Law and Humanities* 1 (1989): 249, 253; *Muller v. Oregon* 208 U.S. 412 (1908); Alice Kessler-Harris, *Out to Work* (New York: Oxford University Press, 1982), 194, 205–14.

32. Mink, *Wages of Motherhood,* chap. 2.

33. E. E. Schattschneider, *The Semisovereign People* (New York: Holt, Rinehart and Winston, 1960), 1–19; Grant McConnell, *Private Power and American Democracy* (New York: Knopf, 1967), 3–8, 91–118, 166–95. See also James Madison's classic treatment of the subject in *Federalist* 10; James Madison, Alexander Hamilton, and John Jay, *The Federalist Papers,* ed. Isaac Kramnick (London: Penguin, 1987), 122–28.

34. See, for example, the majority opinion in *Plessy v Ferguson,* 163 U.S. 537 (1896).

35. David B. Robertson and Dennis R. Judd, *The Development of American Public Policy: The Structure of Policy Restraint* (Glenview, Ill.: Scott, Foresman and Company, 1989), 31.

36. David B. Robertson, "The Bias of American Federalism: The Limits of

Welfare-State Development in the Progressive Era," *Journal of Policy History* 1 (1989): 261–91.

37. See Eveline Burns, *Toward Social Security* (New York: McGraw-Hill, 1936), 111–12.

38. Paul E. Peterson, "Who Should Do What? Divided Responsibility in the Federal System," *Brookings Review* 13, 2 (Spring 1995): 6–11; Paul E. Peterson, *City Limits* (Chicago: University of Chicago Press, 1981).

39. Franklin D. Roosevelt, "Message to Congress Reviewing the Broad Objectives and Accomplishments of the Administration," June 8, 1934 in National Conference on Social Welfare, ed., *The Report of the Committee on Economic Security of 1935 and Other Basic Documents Relating to the Development of the Social Security Act*, 50th anniversary ed. (Washington, D.C.: National Conference on Social Welfare, 1985), 138.

40. Skocpol, *Protecting Soldiers and Mothers;* Gordon, *Pitied but Not Entitled.*

41. U.S. Bureau of the Census, *U.S. Census, 1940: The Labor Force* (Washington, D.C.: GPO, 1940), 18.

42. Department of Labor, Women's Bureau, "Old Age Security Legislation from the Viewpoint of Women," speech by Mary Anderson before the District of Columbia League of Women Voters, December 1935, microfilm 16:0133, p. 14, Labor Management Documentation Center, Catherwood Library, Cornell University, Ithaca, N.Y. (LMDC); Department of Labor, Women's Bureau, *The Negro Woman Worker,* by Jean Collier Brown, Bulletin 165 (Washington, D.C.: GPO, 1938), 2–3; Phyllis Palmer, "Outside the Law: Agricultural and Domestic Workers under the Fair Labor Standards Act," *Journal of Policy History* 7, 4 (1995): 436 n. 13.

43. Gordon, *Pitied but Not Entitled,* 146.

44. Ibid., 5. For an opposing view, see Gareth Davies and Martha Derthick, "Race and Social Welfare Policy: The Social Security Act of 1935," *Political Science Quarterly* 112 (1997): 217–35.

45. James T. Patterson, *The New Deal and the States* (Princeton: Princeton University Press, 1969), 3–4; "Reminiscences of Frances Perkins," Columbia University Oral History Collection, Columbia University, New York (hereafter OHC), vol. 2, pt. 4, 631; "Reminiscences of Arthur J. Altmeyer," OHC, 105, 187–88.

46. Barbara Nachtrieb Armstrong, *Insuring the Essentials: Minimum Wage plus Social Insurance, a Living Wage Program* (New York: Macmillan, 1932), xvii, 436.

47. "Summary of Discussion of the Old Age Security Committee of the Technical Board," September 26, 1934, CES General Records of the Executive Director and Staff, 1934–35, box 1, Record Group (RG) 47, National Archives, Washington, D.C., (NA), "Reminiscences of Thomas H. Eliot," OHC, 30; Arthur J. Altmeyer, *The Formative Years of Social Security* (Madison: University of Wisconsin Press, 1966), 25.

48. Social Security Board, "The Comparability of Public Assistance Pay-

ments and Social Insurance Benefits," by Jacob Fisher, *Social Security Bulletin* 7 (December 1944): 11.

49. See Suzanne Mettler, *Dividing Citizens: Gender and Federalism in New Deal Public Policy* (Ithaca: Cornell University Press, 1998), 121–28.

50. Edwin E. Witte, "Development of Unemployment Compensation," *Yale Law Journal* 1 (December 1945): 39–40.

51. Social Security Administration, *Social Security Yearbook, 1945* (Washington, D.C.: Social Security Administration, 1945), 116–19.

52. Mettler, *Dividing Citizens,* 150–57.

53. Committee on Economic Security, "The Report on Economic Security," in *The Report of the Committee on Economic Security of 1935 and Other Basic Documents relating to the Development of the Social Security Act,* 50th Anniversary ed., ed. National Conference on Social Welfare (Washington, D.C.: National Conference on Social Welfare, 1985), 26–28; Katharine Lenroot, "Special Measures for Children's Security," box 61, folder 3, Abbott Papers, University of Chicago Library (UC), Chicago.

54. The notion that preexisting institutional arrangements by themselves explain the arrangements for the new programs is implied in Skocpol and Amenta, "Did Capitalists Shape Social Security?" 573.

55. "Reminiscences of Katharine Lenroot," OHC, 25, 33; Katharine Lenroot, "Preliminary and Confidential Suggestions for Development of a Children's Program as Part of a Federal Security Program," 1, Abbott Papers; Lenroot to Grace Abbott, October 13, 1934, Abbott Papers.

56. CES, "Report of the Committee on Economic Security," 26–27, 36–37; "Reminiscences of Katharine Lenroot," 99.

57. "Reminiscences of Katharine Lenroot," 107–11; Lenroot, "Preliminary and Confidential Suggestions," 4, Mink, *Wages of Motherhood;* Gordon, *Pitied but Not Entitled,* 102.

58. Grace Abbott, *From Relief to Social Security* (New York: Russell and Russell, 1966), 279.

59. Public Law 271, 74th Cong., 1st sess. (August 14, 1935), *Social Security Act of 1935,* H.R. 7260, title 3, sec. 401, and title 4, sec. 401.

60. Frank A. Pinner, Paul Jacobs, and Philip Selznik, *Old Age and Political Behavior: A Case Study* (Berkeley: University of California Press, 1959), chap. 1; Abraham Holtzman, *The Townsend Movement: A Political Study* (1963; reprint, New York: Octagon, 1975); Marietta Stevenson, "Recent Trends in Public Welfare Legislation," *Social Service Review* 3 (1939): 442.

61. Winifred Bell, *Aid to Dependent Children* (New York: Columbia University Press, 1965).

62. Philip S. Foner, *Women and the American Labor Movement: From World War I to the Present* (New York: Free Press, 1980), 301–2; Robert H. Zieger, *American Workers, American Unions, 1920–1935* (Baltimore: Johns Hopkins University Press, 1986), pp. 46–55; Melvyn Dubofsky, *The State and Labor in Modern America* (Chapel Hill: University of North Carolina Press, 1994), 137.

63. Ruth Milkman, *Gender at Work* (Urbana: University of Illinois Press, 1987), 7; Richard B. Freeman and James L. Medoff, *What Do Unions Do?* (New York: Basic, 1984), 28.

64. David Montgomery, *Workers' Control in America: Studies in the History of Work, Technology, and Labor Struggles* (New York: Cambridge University Press, 1979), 165–66; Frances Fox Piven and Richard A. Cloward, *Poor People's Movements* (New York: Vintage, 1979), 155–61; Elizabeth Faue, "Paths of Unionization: Community, Bureaucracy, and Gender in the Minneapolis Labor Movement of the 1930s," in *Work Engendered: Toward a New History of American Labor,* ed. Ava Baron (Ithaca: Cornell University Press, 1991), 296–319.

65. Francine D. Blau and Marianne A. Ferber, *The Economics of Women, Men, and Work* (Englewood Cliffs, N.J.: Prentice-Hall, 1986), 273.

66. *National Labor Relations Board v Jones and Laughlin Steel Corporation,* 301 US 1 (1937); Alexander Feller and Jacob E. Hurwitz, *How to Operate under the Wage-Hour Law* (New York: Alexander, 1938), 91–99.

67. Liva Baker, *Felix Frankfurter* (New York: Coward-McCann, 1969), 114–15; Helen Shirley Thomas, *Felix Frankfurter: Scholar on the Bench* (Baltimore: Johns Hopkins University Press, 1960), 315–19, 324–25; Felix Frankfurter, *The Commerce Clause* (Chapel Hill: University of North Carolina, 1937), 21–22.

68. Minutes of the Board of Directors, National Consumers' League, March 17, 1937, p. 3, collection 5235, Labor-Management Documentation Center, Cornell University, LMDC.

69. Vivien Hart, "Minimum Wage Policy and Constitutional Inequality: The Paradox of the Fair Labor Standards Act of 1938," *Journal of Policy History* 1 (1989): 336–37.

70. Mettler, *Dividing Citizens,* 203–4.

71. Ronnie Steinberg, *Wages and Hours: Labor and Reform in Twentieth-Century America* (New Brunswick: Rutgers University Press, 1982), 99–100; Judith Baer, *The Chains of Protection* (Westport, Conn.: Greenwood, 1978), 6.

72. Sandel, *Democracy's Discontent,* 250–73; Louis Hartz, *The Liberal Tradition in America: An Interpretation of American Political Thought since the Revolution* (New York: Harcourt, Brace, 1955), 259–83.

73. For related arguments, see Rogers Smith, "Beyond Tocqueville, Myrdal, and Hartz: The Multiple Traditions in America," *American Political Science Review* 87 (September 1993): 549–66, and Karen Orren, *Belated Feudalism: Labor, Law, and Liberal Development in the United States* (New York: Cambridge University Press, 1991).

74. Isaac Kramnick, "The 'Great National Discussion': The Discourse of Politics in 1787," *William and Mary Quarterly* 45 (1988): 3–32.

75. Quote from John Locke, *Two Treatises of Government,* ed. Peter Laslett (1960; New York: Cambridge University Press, 1980), bk. 2, chap. 5, par. 34.5.

76. See especially the work of Carole Pateman, including *The Sexual Contract* (Stanford: Stanford University Press, 1988), and her edited volume, *Femi-*

nist Challenges: Social and Political Theory (Boston: Northeastern University Press, 1986), esp. Pateman's "Introduction" and Merle Thornton's "Sex Equality Is Not Enough for Feminists." See also Susan Moeller Okin, *Justice, Gender, and the Family* (New York: Basic, 1989), esp. chap. 5; Martha Ackelsburg, "Communities, Resistance, and Women's Activism: Some Implications for a Democratic Polity," in *Women and the Politics of Empowerment,* ed. Ann Bookman and Sandra Morgen (Philadelphia: Temple University Press, 1988), 297–313; and Catharine MacKinnon, *Towards a Feminist Theory of the State* (Cambridge: Harvard University Press, 1989).

77. The term "second republic" comes from Theodore J. Lowi, *The End of Liberalism,* 2d ed. (New York: W. W. Norton, 1979); see 273–74 on the transition toward it in the New Deal.

78. Smith, *Civic Ideals,* 1–13.

79. Ann Shola Orloff, "Gender in Early U.S. Social Policy," *Journal of Policy History* 3, 3 (1991): 249–81; Molly Ladd-Taylor, *Mother-Work: Women, Child Welfare, and the State, 1890–1930* (Urbana: University of Illinois Press, 1994), 147; Gordon, *Pitied but Not Entitled,* 40; Mink, *Wages of Motherhood,* 27–38.

80. Harold M. Hyman, *American Singularity: The 1787 Northwest Ordinance, the 1862 Homestead and Morrill Acts, and the 1944 GI Bill* (Athens: University of Georgia Press, 1986), 62–76; Skocpol, *Protecting Soldiers and Mothers,* 102–7.

81. Karen Anderson, *Wartime Women: Sex Roles, Family Relations, and the Status of Women during World War II* (Westport, Conn.: Greenwood, 1981); Susan M. Hartmann, *The Home Front and Beyond: American Women in the 1940s* (Boston: Twayne, 1982); Blau and Ferber, *Economics of Women, Men, and Work,* 70.

82. Edwin Amenta and Theda Skocpol, "Redefining the New Deal: World War II and the Development of Social Provisions in the United States," in Weir, Orloff, and Skocpol, *Politics of Social Policy,* 87–90.

83. Anderson, *Wartime Women;* Hartmann, *Home Front.*

84. Blau and Ferber, *Economics of Women, Men, and Work,* 70.

85. Margaret Weir, "The Federal Government and Unemployment: The Frustration of Policy Innovation from the New Deal to the Great Society," in Weir, Orloff, and Skocpol, *Politics of Social Policy,* 156.

86. Amenta and Skocpol, "Redefining the New Deal," 91; Eveline M. Burns, *The American Social Security System* (Boston: Houghton-Mifflin, 1951), 370; Jill Quadagno, *The Transformation of Old Age Security: Class and Politics in the American Welfare State* (Chicago: University of Chicago Press, 1988), 141.

87. Burns, *American Social Security System,* 306–7, 324–25.

88. Social Security Board, "Assistance Expenditures per Inhabitant, 1940–1950," by Frank J. Hanmer and Ellen J. Perkins, *Social Security Bulletin* 14 (March 1951): 12.

89. U.S. Bureau of the Census, *Statistical Abstract of the United States,* 91st ed. (Washington, D.C.: GPO, 1970), 213.

90. William Haber and Merrill G. Murray, *Unemployment Insurance in the American Economy* (Homewood, Ill.: Richard D. Irwin, 1966), 144–45.

91. Diana M. Pearce, "Toil and Trouble: Women Workers and Unemployment Compensation," *Signs* 10, 3 (1985): 452–54.

92. Phyllis Palmer, "Outside the Law," 424; Louis Weiner, *Federal Wage and Hour Law* (Philadelphia: American Law Institute, 1977), 8, 63–64, 72–74.

93. O. C. Pogge, "Old-Age and Survivors Insurance: The 1950 Amendments," *Social Casework* 32 (March 1951): 95–101; Altmeyer, *Formative Years of Social Security,* 280–83.

94. Jerry Cates, *Insuring Inequality: Administrative Leadership in Social Security, 1935–1954* (Ann Arbor: University of Michigan Press, 1983), 71–72.

95. Edwin E. Witte, "Organized Labor and the Social Security Act of 1935," in *Labor and the New Deal,* ed. Milton Derber and Edwin Young (Madison: University of Wisconsin Press, 1961), 264.

96. Gilbert Y. Steiner, *Social Insecurity: The Politics of Welfare* (Chicago, Ill.: Rand McNally, 1966), 250.

97. Amenta and Skocpol, "Redefining the New Deal," 107–8, 111, 117–18.

98. Ira Katznelson, Kim Geiger, and Daniel Kryder, "Limiting Liberalism: The Southern Veto in Congress, 1933–1950," *Political Science Quarterly* 108 (Summer 1993): 283–306.

99. Bartholemew H. Sparrow, *From the Outside In: World War II and the American State* (Princeton: Princeton University Press, 1996), 41.

100. V. O. Key, *Southern Politics in State and Nation* (New York: Alfred A. Knopf, 1949), chap. 14.

101. See Jane Perry Clark, *The Rise of a New Federalism* (New York: Columbia University Press, 1938), chaps. 8, 10; Leonard D. White, *The States and the Nation* (Baton Rouge: Louisiana State University Press, 1953), 35–64; McConnell, *Private Power and American Democracy,* chaps. 4, 6; Patterson, *New Deal and the States;* Theodore J. Lowi, "Party, Policy, and Constitution in America," in *The American Party System: Stages of Political Development,* ed. William Nisbet Chambers and Walter Dean Burnham (New York: Oxford University Press, 1967), 238–76.

102. Paul E. Peterson, *The Price of Federalism* (Washington, D.C.: Brookings Institution, 1995); Paul E. Peterson and Mark Rom, *Welfare Magnets: A New Case for a National Standards* (Washington, D.C.: Brookings Institution, 1990); Patterson, *New Deal and the States.*

103. See Bell, *Aid to Dependent Children;* Baer, *Chains of Protection;* and Russell L. Hanson, "Liberalism and the Course of American Social Welfare Policy," in *The Dynamics of American Politics: Approaches and Interpretations,* ed. Lawrence C. Dodd and Calvin Jillson (Boulder, Colo.: Westview, 1994), 132–59.

104. Russell L. Hanson, "Federal Statebuilding during the New Deal: The Transition from Mothers' Aid to Aid to Dependent Children," in *Changes in the State: Causes and Consequences* ed. Edward S. Greenberg and Thomas F. Mayer (Newbury Park: Sage, 1990), 93–114; Theodore J. Lowi et al., *Poliscide* (Lan-

ham, Md.: University Press of America, 1990), 27–28; Jeffrey L. Pressman and Aaron Wildavsky, *Implementation* (Berkeley: University of California Press, 1973).

105. 349 US 294 (1954).

106. C. Vann Woodward, *The Strange Career of Jim Crow* (New York: Oxford University Press, 1974), 150–88; Piven and Cloward, *Poor People's Movements,* 207–11.

107. Weiner, *Federal Wage and Hour Law.*

108. Pearce, "Toil and Trouble," 454.

109. Hugh Davis Graham, *Civil Rights and the Presidency* (New York: Oxford University Press, 1992), 67–86.

110. Barbara A. Mikulski and Ellyn L. Brown, "Case Studies in the Treatment of Women under Social Security Law: The Need for Reform," *Harvard Women's Law Journal* 6 (Spring 1983): 33–41.

111. *Baker v Carr,* 369 US 186 (1962), and *Reynolds v Sims,* 377 US 533 (1964).

112. Ann O'M. Bowman and Richard C. Kearney, *The Resurgence of the States* (Englewood Cliffs, N.J.: Prentice-Hall, 1986).

113. Martha F. Davis, *Brutal Need: Lawyers and the Welfare Rights Movement, 1960–1973* (New Haven: Yale University Press, 1993).

114. *King v Smith,* 392 US 309 (1968); *Shapiro v Thompson,* 394 US 618 (1969); and *Goldberg v Kelley,* 397 US 254 (1970).

115. R. Shep Melnick, *Between the Lines: Interpreting Welfare Rights* (Washington, D.C.: Brookings Institution, 1994); Steiner, *Social Insecurity;* Blanche D. Coll, *Safety Net: Welfare and Social Security, 1929–1979* (New Brunswick: Rutgers University Press, 1995).

116. Thomas Byrne Edsall and Mary D. Edsall, *Chain Reaction: The Impact of Race, Rights, and Taxes on American Politics* (New York: W. W. Norton, 1992); "Williamsburg's New Federalists," *Economist,* November 26, 1994, 32.

117. Martha Derthick, "Crossing Thresholds: Federalism in the 1960s," *Journal of Policy History* 8, 1 (1996): 78–79; Suzanne Mettler, "States' Rights, Women's Obligations: Contemporary Welfare Reform in Historical Perspective," *Women and Politics* 21, 1 (Winter 2000): 1–32.

118. On changes in state capacity, see Bowman and Kearney, *Resurgence of the States.*

The New Deal and Higher Education

Ronald Story

A Roosevelt contemporary once called the administration's contribution to higher education "inconsequential." Scholars have largely agreed.[1] Throughout the Roosevelt presidency from 1933 to the end of the war, changes occurred in postsecondary education that laid the groundwork for the entire modern academic edifice that we take for granted today, and they virtually all flowed from the policies and politics of the New Deal. Four developments in particular stand out: the impact of the New Deal on colleges and universities during the 1930s; the 1940 American Association of University Professors statement on academic freedom and tenure; the GI Bill; and federal science policy. In this essay I touch briefly on these developments and offer a few generalizations about them.

In the 1930s the federal government assisted higher education in three direct and two indirect ways. The direct ways were campus construction, work-study aid, and land-grant spending. Campus construction was mostly the handiwork of the Public Works Administration (PWA), which built several hundred libraries, dormitories, laboratories, and classrooms; the projects cost some $200 million, of which the PWA paid something more than half. Meanwhile, the Works Projects Administration undertook numerous smaller projects, supplying workers while the institutions covered materials and certain other costs. All this con-

struction occurred at public institutions because the programs were supposed to be public works projects to reduce the relief rolls and create
jobs. Money did not go to private colleges; much of higher education
was still private, but the intent of this program was not to assist higher
education per se but to put people to work, which looked easier to do,
with fewer constitutional and political constraints, at public institutions.
A few hundred buildings did not amount to much, given the enormous
institutional need. Even so—and as would happen on a far larger scale
after World War II—public institutions that were able to generate quick
proposals and find matching funds, as in Washington, Indiana, and some
other states, managed to upgrade their plants during very difficult
times.[2]

The Federal Emergency Relief Administration began the student
work program, the second direct means of assistance, for essentially the
same reason: to keep students from dropping out of school and swelling
the unemployment rolls. The National Youth Administration soon took
over the program, paying funds directly to students, who in turn paid
them to institutions as tuition somewhat in the manner of the later GI
Bill. All tax-exempt institutions were eligible, and the program clearly
worked. Over six hundred thousand students received funds, and in
1940, 1.4 million, or 15 percent of the college-age population, attended
college, up from 1 million, or 12 percent, in 1930. The median years of
schooling for seventeen-year-olds went from under eleven in 1930 to
over twelve in 1940.[3]

U.S. Department of Agriculture (USDA) money provided the big
boost to the country's land-grant colleges, which enrolled approximately 20 percent of all students in this period. Through the Bankhead-
Jones Act of 1935, funding by 1939 had risen for federal extension
work, teaching, and research support by several million dollars a year. To
be sure, the USDA under Roosevelt emphasized targeted research or off-
campus extension measures for the rural population as a whole, so that
even though the extension measures reached millions of people—over 7
million by one count—the land-grant colleges sometimes had to de-
emphasize existing programs in order to address the expectations of re-
settlement, farm credit, and other federal agencies. Fewer dollars were
available for nontargeted research, thus reducing institutional control
over the work of their science faculties. In these respects the USDA programs anticipated the patterns of federal science spending after the war.

Still, the impact was modest because the funds were modest. Moreover, Bankhead-Jones money could be spent for campus land and buildings as well as for teaching and research, and most land-grant colleges enjoyed real benefits from the program.[4]

The New Deal also had two indirect political influences of enormous long-term significance. First, the administration consulted and hired academics in unprecedented numbers. Dozens of private and public universities granted hundreds of leaves to full-time faculty, mostly in law and the social sciences, to serve in Washington. Reflecting both the influence of academy-friendly advisers such as Felix Frankfurter and Harry Hopkins and also the rush to staff up the federal bureaucracy without help from conservative businesspeople and professionals, from whose ranks top bureaucrats traditionally came, FDR's hiring of academics moved from the Brain Trust phase of 1932 to a swarm of progressive young instructors to what seemed an entire professoriat. Caricatured as bumblers, Machiavellians, or closet communists, this novel academic presence, dwarfing anything in the Progressive Era, has been as noticeable to historians as it was to contemporaries. Robert McElvaine argues, for example, that the New Deal not only fused the long-separated strands of Andrew Jackson's common-man democracy with John Quincy Adams's intellectual elite but also made intellectuals important in Washington in a way they had not been since the days of Jefferson and John Adams. David Fromkin calls the leaders of the later Roosevelt administration the first for whom college experiences and degrees were signal influences.[5]

Moreover, faculty changed politically. Already repelled by 1920s materialism and then by capitalist failure and their own straitened conditions, attracted moreover to the innovative, egalitarian strains and comparative tolerance of a welcoming New Deal, the intelligentsia, professors included, became more or less decisively liberal—or at any rate Democratic—for the first time in American history. In the words of New York critic Edmund Wilson: "To the writers and artists of my generation, who had grown up in the Big Business era and had always resented its barbarism, its crowding-out of everything they cared about, these years were not depressing but stimulating. One couldn't help being exhilarated at the sudden unexpected collapse of that stupid gigantic fraud." Boos at Groton and Harvard notwithstanding, Roosevelt attracted not only WASP economists but Jewish scientists and Catholic theologians to the Democratic cause. This was the first national administration to extend a real welcome to Catholics and Jews, a development that would not have occurred without the equally strong welcome to intellectuals and one that was not lost on hostile heartland Republicans and Dixie Democrats. The New Deal effectively married professors to liberalism for several decades, helping to create the liberal establishment that would so madden later conservatives.[6]

Given this academic presence and Democratic tilt and the cost effectiveness of the direct programs, the administration might have done more vis-à-vis higher education except for certain stubborn political facts. First, American higher education was decentralized and mixed, the preserve of jealous states and private corporations. Research science too was overwhelmingly private, indeed corporate. In 1940 twenty-three hundred industrial labs employed twenty-seven thousand research workers. The chemical industry alone spent $50 million in its own labs, more than all university research budgets combined. Except modestly with the land-grant colleges, Washington had no direct role in higher education, and FDR never demanded one.

Furthermore, most private sector administrators, from Gordon Chalmers at Kenyon College to James Conant at Harvard, were, on balance, Republican, conservative, and resistant to an expanded federal role. Even land-grant and state university officers, long accustomed to public support but now alarmed at the administration's rural planning and other socioeconomic schemes, were skittish and politically circumspect. So were the most prominent academic scientists. Fearing social science activism and geographic dispersal, research science, according to Roger Geiger, was Republican even after 1932, when the Democrats held power.[7]

Again, faculty, though pro–New Deal, were not politically strong—there were only 150,000 professors as late as 1940, nearly all earning less than in 1931—and when they did become politically active, they often merely attracted the hostility of the business community, the conservative press, the American Legion, and small-town and rural legislators. Pro-Roosevelt faculty thus helped energize Roosevelt's foes. Moreover, while faculty were liberal, they were not unionized and so lacked standing in the halls of organized labor, the country's main new political player. Labor leaders, preoccupied with immediate worker needs and their own organizational growth, also remembered campuses from the 1920s as irrelevant, even obnoxious playgrounds of youthful privilege, a view shared by such populist New Dealers as Harry Truman.[8]

Roosevelt himself was more or less indifferent to colleges per se, seeing them chiefly as recipients of public works and relief money rather than as important in their own right. In 1933, in a budget-cutting mode, FDR reduced federal funds to land-grant institutions by 25 percent, money that only strenuous farm-state lobbying succeeded in restoring. The administration later let a proposal to spend $75 million on scientific research, a third of it for universities, die without a fight, as it did a drive to establish a federal department of education with a higher education bureau. When Huey Long proposed sending every eligible boy to college, Roosevelt outflanked him with the National Youth Administration and the Civilian Conservation Corps, which could reach non–high school graduates as well as collegians.[9]

For that matter, New Deal cultural support always retained something of a New York cast. Roosevelt and Hopkins both thought that making high culture available to the masses would democratize American life, and Hopkins spent liberally on individual artists, musicians, dramatists, and writers. Had Hopkins and Roosevelt adhered to the "Wisconsin Idea," in which a major university took the lead in intellectual and cultural life, more of this money might have gone to colleges. But that was not the model in the East, from where Roosevelt hailed and where Hopkins grew to professional maturity. There, cultural workers were largely independent and cultural production largely commercial, and no large university played a role of the Madison variety. Had Roosevelt been La Follette, things might have developed not necessarily better, but at least differently.[10]

But New Deal influence on higher education in the 1930s, though not systematic or transforming, was not insignificant. The direct measures helped sustain troubled institutions and expand college attendance, while the indirect influences on faculty roles and politics would soon bear substantial fruit.

Academic freedom was a concern of individual faculty before the Civil War, especially in the South, which suppressed academic dissent and thereby consigned itself to the intellectual backwaters for several generations, and again later in the century during the controversies over evolution and the concentration of wealth and capital. Nothing could be done about this in the nineteenth century, when professors were few and opinionated lay trustees possessed (as a Harvard professor put it) "the keys and the money and the power." But in 1915, following several well-publicized dismissals, the American Association of University Professors (AAUP) issued a Declaration on Academic Freedom urging that faculty be primarily responsible for academic hiring and dismissals and that every instructor receive tenure after ten years of service. The top research universities were already moving gingerly toward this "guild" model, driven in part by the example of German research universities, where many academic luminaries had done graduate work. The AAUP, though formally powerless, hoped that bad publicity about unjust dismissals or the suppression of faculty freedom would induce other institutions to support the declaration. But faculty were fragmented, economically insecure, and worried about their public standing, while the AAUP, with just four thousand members (6 percent of all faculty), was unable to protect dissidents. In 1925 AAUP negotiations with the Association of American Colleges (AAC) produced, at the AAC's insistence, a weaker version providing for faculty consultation rather than faculty prerogative on dismissal. Even so, relatively few institutions adhered to it, and dismissals were common during the ideologically contentious 1930s.[11]

The AAUP Statement of 1940 moved things dramatically forward. Endorsed by the AAC, the Statement reduced the pretenure period from ten to seven years, called the pretenure years "probationary" to underscore the expectation of tenurability, and provided for formal dismissal hearings with written charges, a stenographic record, the right to counsel, and full faculty involvement in decision making. Dismissals could be for moral turpitude or financial exigency, but not (unlike 1925) for "treason." All teachers, whether tenured or probationary, would enjoy freedom in research and the classroom. In turn and at the insistence of the AAC, whose members were clearly concerned to protect themselves against charges of harboring dissenters and radicals, faculty would take care not to inject irrelevant material into lectures, make inflammatory public statements, or speak on behalf of the institution. Promulgated by the AAUP and the AAC, quickly endorsed by the American Political Science Association, the Association of American Law Schools, and other disciplinary bodies, this "criminal court/civil service" model, with its due process provisions and presumption of permanent appointment for good service, spread to all types of institutions. (The chief holdouts were among church-affiliated colleges and the universities of the Deep South.) Although insufficient to protect all faculty during the McCarthy era, the 1940 statement nevertheless afforded faculty an unprecedented measure of fair treatment and professional security, and it did so according to nationally understood standards rather than the mere vagaries of individual institutions.[12]

The sweeping success in 1940, after years of disappointment, is due in part to the growth of the AAUP, which by then had twenty thousand members, over 15 percent of all faculty, most of them political liberals and therefore more prone to union-like activism. Moreover, the key AAUP leaders were now lawyers who thought in terms of adversarial courtroom proceedings as well as guild collegiality, and this perspective shaped the Statement as it did academic practices. In addition, many campuses had established faculty governance committees in the 1930s, a practice especially common at the elite research universities, which second- and third-level institutions sought to emulate. Indeed, this academic pecking order lent real weight to the annual AAUP blacklist of colleges that violated academic freedom and tenure, because most of these were clearly inferior to the elite institutions that increasingly respected tenure and signed on to the Statement.[13]

The AAUP was also feeling two kinds of constituency pressure. First, although not unionized, its members knew that workers under union contracts now enjoyed elaborate rights to grieve complaints, and they wanted similar rights for themselves. Second, junior faculty conditions were very bad in the late 1930s owing to the overproduction of doctorates—3,300 in 1940 alone as compared, for example, with only 620 in 1920. Financially hard-pressed colleges hired new Ph.D.'s at below-faculty rank for dreadful pay, then released them in a year or two and hired replacements. More varied in religious and socioeconomic background—more blue-collar, more non–New England, more Jewish or Catholic—than established faculty, these junior faculty were also more receptive to union organizers, who demanded a tenure system because they believed that faculty decision making and the presumption of longevity would reduce immediate exploitation and make professorial status accessible to the young. This unionizing drive could hope for no more than limited success because faculty unions were illegal in most states. Nonetheless, the AAUP had to respond in some way to the drive. Agitation from below and expectations from within, both reflecting the triumphs of the Wagner Act and the CIO, thus pushed the AAUP toward its 1940 demands. By 1940, moreover, the House Un-American Activities Committee (HUAC) was investigating faculty radicalism. With faculty increasingly liberal, this "mini-Red Scare," as Ellen Schrecker has termed it, lent greater urgency to the quest for academic freedom and tenure.[14]

Finally, three other intertwined factors strengthened the 1940 statement. First, as noted, faculty had gained in public esteem and prestige as professors went to work for the government in the 1930s; wartime service would enhance that prestige and make faculty seem important and useful in a way they had not seemed before. Second, graduate programs had expanded during the 1930s. This generated too many doctorates for the market to absorb but also pointed to the triumph of the graduate model at the most prestigious universities, which were, emulated by other institutions. As advanced study became more important everywhere, so did the professoriat's claim to specialized expertise and therefore to a privileged place in hiring and firing. Third, wartime science, with its successful campus-based, investigator-initiated research programs, accelerated this trend. By the war's end, scientists were in a position to insist on both close peer review and a strong tenure system, which they desired in part for professional reasons unique to science. Despite the scientists' own conservatism their needs served to reinforce the 1940 AAUP Statement. By 1946, argues Martin Finkelstein, an ideal academic type had evolved connoting arcane research, full academic citizenship, and a visible and valued public role—plus better organization and more rights consciousness. Rapid acceptance of the 1940 statement was one consequence.[15]

Military veterans had received "entitlements" of pensions and bonuses, chiefly as cash payments or land, after most of the country's wars. Only the 1862 Morrill Act, which gave federal land to states willing to establish public colleges, envisioned higher education per se as a benefit. The Morrill Act was clearly a reward to the middling farmers and craftsmen who voted Republican, paid federal taxes, and sent their sons to the Union army. But the benefits were indirect, distant, and not limited to soldiers. World War I veterans received pensions and a future cash bonus, but no land, education, or other benefits. The desperate "Bonus Army" that Douglas MacArthur routed from Anacostia Flats in the nation's capital was asking for early payment of these bonuses for rent and food.[16]

Republicans in the 1920s, among them Secretary of the Treasury Andrew Mellon, resisted special benefits for veterans for cost reasons before finally acceding to a system of delayed bonuses. Franklin D. Roosevelt too resisted them, in part because, in his early tight-fisted presidential days, he agreed that straight bonuses were fiscally unwise. But FDR also argued that "no person, because he wore a uniform, should be placed in a special class of beneficiaries." In 1933 the president reduced veterans' benefits administratively (just as he did spending on the land-grant universities). Congress, responding to American Legion pressure, restored the reductions; Roosevelt vetoed the restoration; Congress overrode the veto. Relations between the veterans organizations and Roosevelt grew poisonous, but the president held his ground, having concluded that, besides his other objections, a veterans-only benefits policy would fail to ward off mass unemployment. He reversed himself only well into the war by supporting the GI Bill of 1944, whose passage entitled postwar veterans to home and business loans, jobless pay, and subsidies for education and training, including college.

Dwarfing previous programs, the GI Bill ultimately cost $20 billion and benefited 16 million veterans. Half of them received education and training payments under the bill. Of these, a third attended institutions of higher learning, public and private; a million went in the single year 1946. The college program alone absorbed $6 billion of all GI Bill expenditures.[17]

Why did Roosevelt, having resisted veterans' entitlements and major higher education initiatives, support such a massive program in 1944? A quick answer is that no one, including Roosevelt, expected the college component of the bill to be so important. One estimate was that only a hundred thousand people would use the higher education subsidy. In fact, over 2 million did, a very substantial proportion of whom either would not have attended college or, if they did, would not have graduated. A fuller answer, however, is that this program was not a bonus scheme. To FDR as to Andrew Mellon, bonuses were budget-busters, which, unlike Mellon, FDR feared because these costs might preclude loans or other benefits and would in any case simply put lump sums in veterans' pockets without giving them the means to support themselves, as grants of land had for earlier veterans. Again unlike Mellon, Roosevelt believed that passage of a bonus or other veterans-only entitlement program might also make it harder to develop the broad security and employment programs that would improve everyone's lot, veterans included.[18]

Early wartime planning groups, reflecting the views of the White House, sought for the most part to bind benefits for veterans to general needs such as providing full employment, strengthening education and social security, and insuring "fair pay" and "equality before the law." The president stressed these themes as late as his 1944 State of the Union Address, which called for a Second Bill of Rights to insure economic security and independence. But by then it had become clear that these ideas would not carry the day. Congressional conservatives increased their clout in the 1942 elections and systematically dismantled not only such New Deal agencies as the National Youth Administration, the Civilian Conservation Corps, and the Public Works Administration but also the whole postwar planning apparatus, which they saw, more or less correctly, much as Senator Robert Taft saw it—as a seedbed for "utopian" Rooseveltian planning.[19]

Moreover, the American Legion and its allies were demanding immediate measures for veterans alone, and the public was responding. Legion officials, eager to get their benefits first and foremost, called the administration's expansive early ideas "the crafty effort" of "crack-pots, long-haired professors, and radicals" to use the war for "the reorganization of the world." The Hearst press, allies of the legion, attacked the president for failing (at the behest of academic radicals) to support veterans. Senator Champ Clark of Missouri said the veterans organizations were "wrought up and bitter" over efforts to "pitchfork" veterans' rehabilitation into "a general scheme of social rehabilitation" and urged Roosevelt to serve veterans first and others only if anything remained. Then there was "Jew baiting, Negro hating" Representative John Rankin (D-Miss.), whose committee had jurisdiction over the veterans bill. Antilabor, pro-HUAC, close to the American Legion, Rankin at first opposed most of the provisions of the GI Bill as an inducement to sloth, especially among black workers: "If every white ex-serviceman in Mississippi . . . could read this so-called GI Bill, I don't believe there would be one in 20 who would approve it in its present form. . . . We have 50,000 negroes in the service from our State, and in my opinion, if the bill should pass in its present form, a vast majority of them would remain unemployed for at least a year, and a great many white men would do the same." Rankin pushed for a bonus system but finally was willing to shepherd a comprehensive bill through Congress provided it dragged no larger social schemes with it, did not raise southern wages, and did not mix the races.[20]

Finally, observers on all sides truly feared that a capitalist system that had failed so abysmally from 1929 to 1942 would never create enough new jobs to absorb millions of demobilized, probably angry, possibly antisocial veterans. Eleanor Roosevelt wrote that bringing veterans home to joblessness would produce "a dangerous pressure group in our midst" from which the country might well "reap the whirlwind." New York conservative Hamilton Fish and Texas liberal Maury Maverick argued that jobless veterans could breed "revolutionary conditions" leading to "disaster and chaos" and even "dictatorship." Legion officials themselves reminded the public, with some justification, that after World War I the United States and England were the only countries "where the men who wore uniforms did not overthrow the government on either side of that conflict" and warned that veterans could "restore our democracy or scrap it." Basically agreeing, FDR toyed with other proposals—a new Civilian Conservation Corps, universal national training, delayed demobilization—before throwing his weight behind the GI Bill, which his advisers warned him to push hard in order to outflank the conservatives. Though still doubtful whether the measure was sufficient to the nation's needs, Roosevelt by now was not hard to persuade. The bill, after all, contained no bonus. It provided education and training as the self-maintenance equivalents of land and tools. And though it entitled veterans alone to the benefits, the sheer number of veterans—the sheer magnitude of the war—meant that it was bound to have a major social impact. Keith Olson, the leading historian of the bill, is forceful on the main point. The economy needed federal help; the veterans served as a convenient, traditional, and popular means to provide that help. "Anxiety over economics," writes Olson, "preceded and dominated altruism toward veterans."[21]

Most contemporaries thought that relatively few veterans would go to college on the GI Bill. Numerous prominent educators, including James Conant at Harvard, Keith Chalmers at Kenyon, and Robert Hutchins at Chicago, hoped they would not, lest they flood the campuses with rowdy second-raters or distort the curriculum by flocking to vocational studies. Some urged low subsistence stipends to discourage "freeloaders." Nearly all feared the emergence of "an educational hobo jungle." These fears proved groundless. Veterans did opt for college. After all, a college education offered people, most of whom came from depression-era, blue-collar families, a one-time shot at white-collar status, and it was not lost on them that their wartime officers had been almost all collegians. Moreover, once enrolled, veterans by and large became what in 1947 *Fortune* magazine called "the best, most mature, most responsible, most self-disciplined group of college students in history." Far from freeloading, a substantial majority stretched their stipends with bank loans, family help, part-time employment, and working spouses. Far more than nonveterans and contrary to every expectation, they flocked to liberal arts rather than vocational programs, indicating a significant pent-up hunger for traditional learning, if not enlightenment.[22]

The consequences of the GI Bill were marked and enduring. Higher education swelled from an enrollment of 1.4 million in 1940 to 2.1 million in 1946, half of them veterans; it then grew to 2.4 million in 1949, a third of them still veterans. The GI Bill was restricted and time-limited, not permanent and general, and as the veteran pool completed its education, enrollments slipped to 2.1 million in 1952, even with Korean War soldiers eligible. But the veterans clearly helped to popularize going to college, so that enrollments started to climb again, to nearly 3 million by 1956, or 30 percent of college-age Americans. Private institutions, starved for tuition, expanded admissions faster than the public schools; half the GI Bill funds went to private institutions, a sharp departure from the 1930s. The public sector eventually moved decisively ahead, but both publics and privates (including the autonomy-loving members of the AAC) grew accustomed to admitting federally assisted students. Interestingly, elite institutions, public and private, unexpectedly expanded faster than teachers colleges, two-year campuses, urban branch campuses and other less prestigious institutions, a further indication, perhaps, of the veterans' longing for traditional liberal learning as well as their shrewd appraisal of the value of their degrees. After an initial crush, eased slightly by gifts of surplus military land and buildings, federal construction dollars began to follow enrollments to private as well as public institutions.

Faculties, too, eventually expanded, by 50 percent from 1940 to 1948. Enrollments, on the other hand, rose at a faster 75 percent pace, so that classes became larger, teaching loads heavier, graduate teaching assistants more common, and graduate programs more important even amid—indeed, partly because of—the undergraduate flood. Soon, however, the professor shortage would be noticed, and faculty numbers would increase too, though not at the same rate. Faculty pay also rose. All this occurred, moreover, within the framework of the 1940 AAUP Statement, so that security rose as well. Academics, for better or worse, thus became a more significant cultural and political presence, with cultural production and expression more centered in campuses, than they had ever been, a condition that would endure until the media revolution of the 1980s and 1990s.[23]

By far the most powerful impact on higher education came in the area of federally sponsored scientific research, which began on a large scale early in the war and has continued for decades. Wartime science policy had antecedents in the USDA research programs and in the tiny National Institute of Health and National Cancer Institute. These produced big results, among them the discovery of streptomycin and the crop yields that enabled the United States to feed the Allied armies. But they had not triggered a major federal commitment to research science. Industry, after all, conducted most scientific research without government aid, and Americans were already leading the world in scientific discoveries without it. Few saw science as a cure for the country's economic emergency, at least as compared with economic or social intervention, which seemed the province of executives, reformers, and social scientists rather than natural scientists, who were in any case mostly anti-Roosevelt Republicans.[24]

The war was another matter. Though suspicious of the New Deal, by 1940 scientist-administrators such as Conant at Harvard and Vannevar Bush from MIT were alarmed enough at Nazi aggression to believe that university science should undergird U.S. military capability. Roosevelt agreed and authorized the National Defense Research Committee, which in late 1940 became a government agency: the Office of Scientific Research and Development (OSRD), with Vannevar Bush as director. Created to generate militarily useful research, the OSRD at its first meeting decided, in the interests of speed and to avoid upsetting congressional isolationists, to use existing industrial and university facilities and personnel rather than developing its own, as the federal government had done during World War I. One important result was that research funds naturally flowed to research institutions capable of acting quickly and effectively—meaning, in the university sector, mainly high-status, chiefly private campuses. (The one gigantic exception to this pattern was, of course, Los Alamos, site of atomic weapons research, which borrowed university scientists to work in government-owned facilities.) In 1944 OSRD let $100 million in university contracts, compared with $28 million in total university research five years earlier. By 1945 the agency had expended a half billion dollars for contracted research. The results in new or improved war-wining technology—the proximity fuse, rocketry, high explosives, computers, jet propulsion, blood plasma, antimalarial drugs, mass-produced penicillin, radar, the atomic bomb—were dazzling.[25]

In the glow of Allied victory and Hiroshima, it was hard to argue against the OSRD contract system, although some people did, notably West Virginia congressman Harley Kilgore, a pro-labor, anti–big business proponent of land-grant colleges, applied research, and agricultural extension who disliked shoveling money to a handful of elite, conservative, mostly Eastern, largely Republican institutions, however good their scientists. In 1944 Kilgore, anticipating the postwar demise of OSRD, proposed a science agency with an advisory board and director appointed by the president that would dispense research contracts on a geographic basis, emphasize applied research, utilize government-owned labs rather than universities wherever possible, and fund social as well as natural science.[26]

Kilgore's proposal clearly drew inspiration less from wartime weapons research than from depression-era USDA initiatives and had a goal of improving the everyday lives of ordinary Americans in all regions of the country. Alarmed at such populism, Vannevar Bush responded that the way to improve postwar civilian life was to promote the best, most disinterested basic research possible. Bush's Senate supporters proposed an OSRD-type foundation with a presidentially appointed board, with the board, not the president, appointing the director. This agency would favor basic over applied research, use universities as well as government labs, disregard regional distribution in favor of investigator-initiated "best science" practices, and exclude social science. President Harry Truman's twenty-one-point reconversion program included "stimulate research," the only reference to higher education. But when Bush's initiative trumped Kilgore's in the Republican Congress of 1947, Truman vetoed it, largely over the issue of who would appoint the director. The

National Science Foundation (NSF) with a Bush cast eventually materialized anyway. Given the disagreement and delay in founding and funding the NSF, the Department of Defense and other agencies, including the Atomic Energy Commission, became the chief immediate postwar sources of research funds, most of which went to industry or to government labs, especially Los Alamos. But universities received a growing share of an increasing pool of federal dollars—70 percent of their research budgets came from the federal government by the early 1950s—and they did so almost exclusively by way of the contract system pioneered by OSRD.[27]

This system had and continues to have numerous fateful consequences for American higher education. University campuses became important scientific research centers in ways they had not been before 1940. Work in the physical sciences, even though mostly confined to the big doctoral campuses, thus came to exemplify, even to define, university excellence. University scientists consequently gained by leaps and bounds in status, pay, and leverage. The physicist Robert Wilson told a possibly apocryphal but certainly revealing story from the postwar years about

> a typical prosaic professor of physics who had lived in academic squalor in an inland state university, bullied in turn by his department chairman, by his dean, and by his president. He had been drafted into a big wartime laboratory; the story concerns his return to the university. For the first time in his academic career he attended a university meeting, but not to play the part of a cowering back bencher. Rather he came in late, walked right up to the presiding president and slapped down his demands. These were that a new laboratory in a new building be set up with him as director, that ten new faculty positions be created to staff it, that adequate funds be provided to match his already promised government monies, that his salary be quadrupled, and that his teaching be cut to zero so he could devote to the laboratory what little time would remain after his tight schedule of consulting in Washington. The president accepted all these demands on the spot—with a speech of gratitude—after which our friend turned on his heel and walked out to a rising ovation of the faculty!

In turn and equally significant, this glorification of research scientists created a halo effect for nonscience faculty. As science salaries rose after an initial post-1945 slump, so eventually did those of nonscientists. Because scientists insisted on and received tenure for themselves, the tenure system became stronger for all professors. And since only scientists could understand modern science, they also insisted on and got peer hiring and promotion, which strengthened the hiring and firing role of other faculty. In this way, federal science policy strengthened both the AAUP statement of 1940 and the overall position of professors in a way that the GI Bill alone would not have.[28]

But there were other, in some ways less positive, consequences as well. First, teaching eroded as an academic priority. Universities hired scientists to do research, not to teach, because research attracted the grants and prestige that university boards and administrators desired. The ability to teach science, except in tiny graduate courses, was of little concern; science teaching loads, already comparatively light, grew lighter still. One result was the virtual disappearance of good science education from the undergraduate curriculum and the spread of what Frederick Rudolph calls an "unprecedented scientific illiteracy" among most educated Americans. This was particularly the case because, in the pecking order of higher education, less prestigious institutions invariably sought to emulate more prestigious ones. Because science dollars were going mainly to elite institutions, aspiring lesser universities also hired research scientists to chase federal science dollars, thereby replicating the new pattern across the country. Equally important, as nonteaching research scientists became the stars of modern higher education, the research model gradually spread, in the familiar emulative manner, to nonscience areas, including the liberal arts, where the commitment to undergraduate teaching, though still much higher than in the sciences, likewise gave way to the dictates of research.[29]

Second, federal science policy meant that institutions gradually lost control of their programs. This was partly due to the familiar litany of federal impositions, from loyalty oaths to research secrecy to exclusion of foreign participation to the micromanagement of overhead reimbursement to diversity requirements. Far more important, it stemmed from the investigator-initiated grant system whereby agencies funded individual faculty research proposals. This system rewarded scientific initiative and creativity, as Bush, Conant, and others desired. But it also gave external agencies the power to shape the university's research agenda by commandeering the time and commitment of its faculty and triggering expenditures for scientific facilities, thereby subverting institutional autonomy. Foreshadowed by the USDA's funding of directed land-grant research in the postwar era research became, in Roger

Geiger's words, "an increasingly autonomous activity, shaped by the sources that supported its insatiable needs." Alice Rivlin, acknowledging the ravages of federal research spending on college instruction and institutional budgets, argues that federal support for basic research "should not even be viewed as aid to higher education." Having undermined higher education's instructional function, federal science policy thus converted it to a cash dispenser for other people's programs.[30]

Last and perhaps most important of all, the system undermined institutional budgets. Not only did institutions have to hire disproportionate numbers of high-priced scientists and build them expensive research facilities, but government grants also never covered the true costs of research. Not even the Department of Defense, the most generous research patron, covered all administrative and other indirect costs—nonproject equipment, library holdings, facilities maintenance, grants acquisition and administration, and the like—and other agencies reimbursed at far lower rates. The shortfall may have exceeded $35 million by 1952 and $100 million by 1960 and has risen to many billions since then. The only way to cover these costs was to draw down central institutional operating budgets, money raised from tuition or state appropriations or, occasionally to a modest degree, unrestricted endowment income. This had the effect, however, of slowly drying up positions, staff support, and facilities in the nonscience areas, and in particular the liberal arts areas that had boomed with the passage of the GI Bill. The defeated Kilgore plan for the NSF would have avoided this drain on campus resources by utilizing such government-owned facilities as Los Alamos, where the funding agencies would have had to cover all costs themselves rather than forcing universities to cover them. On the other hand, this would have drawn scientists away from campuses, thereby weakening the new tenure system and the halo effect that raised faculty salaries. It is one of history's many ironies that having boosted the security and pay of liberal arts professors, research science eroded the ground on which they stood.[31]

S̲tudents of this era have missed FDR's impact on higher education in part because the administration did not have a *policy* on higher education. It had, instead, a *practice*—of using colleges and universities for other purposes: to reduce unemployment, reward veterans, produce weapons. Higher education programs were incidental and instrumental to other concerns and thus are harder to comprehend. Moreover, on one issue—faculty security—the impact was indirect and political rather than direct and programmatic.

The significance of these developments is also obscured by the mixed nature of higher education, where chief responsibility rested with the states and private institutions. FDR never challenged this system because to do so would have entailed, among other things, having an actual higher education policy, which never materialized. This lack of a higher education policy is notable too for what it suggests about the American commitment to education as opposed to problem solving—that there was very little in the way of commitment, at least as manifested at the federal level. Only when demand or alarm—as with returning veterans— drove it did the federal government make a significant effort to support the educational function of the colleges, and even then begrudgingly.

Nonetheless, some developments were both important and mutually reinforcing. Depression-era construction and student aid sustained campuses and provided guidance in formulating the GI Bill; USDA spending anticipated aspects of wartime research. Faculty public service and liberal politics strengthened the push for a strong AAUP statement, which was strengthened further by the ascendance of science. The AAUP statement strengthened the hand of research scientists seeking security and disciplinary control. Research science elevated the status, security, and pay of the liberal arts faculty who taught the veterans.

Some developments, on the other hand, were contradictory, at least to a degree. Research science in particular tended to undermine not only higher education's own commitment to teaching but the integrity of university budgets, both of which affected undergraduates and therefore subverted in a curious way the pledge implicit in the GI Bill. Research science and the tenure system worked to release intellectual creativity and make university campuses the main source of national cultural vitality. But they also incorporated fixed costs and inflexibility into campus operations that would at times make it difficult to respond to shifting needs and demands.

The overall impact of the Roosevelt era on higher education was thus profound if unintentional. One may argue that this impact constitutes one of the administration's enduring contributions, ranking just behind support for Social Security and big labor in lasting historical significance.

As a final note, it is perhaps worth entering the realm of *mentalité* to consider whether FDR's great expansion of higher education contributed over the long run to the undermining of the New Deal coalition. Union activity, after all, produced modest individual worker gains within a narrow band through collective action. Social Security was a socialized insurance system born of mass politics that provided modest benefits within a narrow band for virtually everyone. These are quintessential New Deal attributes—collective action for equitable and generalized benefits. Higher education, by contrast, worked to expand individual consciousness and enable individual achievement. Professors told students to be individuals and think for themselves, and the students themselves capitalized on their opportunities to get ahead. Social Security and labor unions enmeshed the individual in collective bonds and provided equitable and general benefits. The means as well as the ends were to some extent collective. College education did the opposite. It liberated from prior family and community constraints, it individualized the struggle for success rather than collectivizing it as the unions and mass parties had done, and it created opportunity for widely disparate and highly personalized achievements and rewards rather than generalized and equitable ones. Students, like their professors, might have been Democratic over the past half century. College graduates, with their heightened self-awareness and greater earning power, have not been. Without insisting on the point, I would suggest that in this way one of the three great legacies of the Roosevelt years served ultimately to help break apart the collectivist politics and policies that created and sustained those legacies.

Notes

1. Hugh Hawkins, *Banding Together: The Rise of National Associations in American Higher Education, 1887–1950* (Baltimore: Johns Hopkins University Press, 1992), 130, 220; Alice Rivlin, *The Role of the Federal Government in Financing Higher Education* (Washington, D.C.: Government Printing Office, 1961), 118. The critic was George Zook, president of the American Council on Education, whose politics were unusual in higher education administrative circles for being Democratic and pro-Roosevelt.

2. Rivlin, *Role*, 98–100, 118–19; William E. Leuchtenburg, *Franklin D. Roosevelt and the New Deal, 1932–1940* (New York: Harper and Row, 1963), 121–22, 137; Clark Kerr, *The Great Transformation in Higher Education, 1960–1980* (Albany: State University of New York Press, 1991), 38.

3. Rivlin, *Role*, 3–7, 63; Hawkins, *Banding Together*, 155, 171; Ellen

Schrecker, *No Ivory Tower: McCarthyism and the Universities* (New York: Oxford University Press, 1986), 29; Christopher Jenks and David Riesman, *The Academic Revolution* (New York: Doubleday, 1968), 80–81; Martin J. Finkelstein, *The American Academic Profession: A Synthesis of Social Scientific Inquiry since World War II* (Columbus: Ohio State University Press, 1984), 7.

4. Hawkins, *Banding Together,* 126–27; Edward Danforth Eddy Jr., *Colleges for Our Land and Time: The Land-Grant Idea in American Education* (New York: Harper, 1957), 152, 169, 186–88, 235–43; Rivlin, *Role,* 25–30. Since one of the key bases of New Deal support in the 1930s was the Solid South, it is no surprise that Bankhead-Jones failed to do for the predominantly black land-grants what it did for the white land-grants. The program may even have exacerbated the inequalities between the two types of institution. So did virtually every program that lifted whites disproportionately over blacks, as was invariably the case in the segregated South. Yet the black institutions did benefit. Eight (of seventeen) initiated four-year programs or graduate programs or received regional accreditation for the first time. This was in part to keep black students from suing successfully to gain access to programs then available only at white institutions. Fred Humphries, "Land-Grant Institutions: Their Struggle for Survival and Equality," in *A Century of Service: Land-Grant Colleges and Universities, 1890–1990,* ed. Ralph D. Christy and Lionel Williamson (New Brunswick: Transaction Publishers, 1992), 5–6, 32.

5. William E. Leuchtenburg, *The FDR Years: On Roosevelt and His Legacy* (New York: Columbia University Press, 1995), 25, 244; Leuchtenburg, *Roosevelt,* 75–76, 253; Arthur M. Schlesinger Jr., *The Politics of Upheaval* (Boston: Houghton Mifflin, 1960), 32, 88, 94; George McJimsey, *Harry Hopkins: Ally of the Poor and Defender of Democracy* (Cambridge: Harvard University Press, 1987), 15, 43, 57–58, 74; Robert S. McElvaine, *The Great Depression: America, 1929–1941* (New York: Times Books, 1993), 124, 326–27; Finkelstein, *American Academic Profession,* 26–27; David Fromkin, *In the Time of the Americans* (New York: Random House, 1995), 62.

6. McElvaine, *Great Depression,* 139–45, 326–27; Finkelstein, *American Academic Profession,* 27; Leuchtenburg, *Roosevelt,* 26, 64; Leuchtenburg, *FDR Years,* 128; Schrecker, *No Ivory Tower,* 29–30. On the other hand, Roosevelt could tire of his academic advisers. He told Henry Morgenthau in mid-1939 that he was "sick and tired of having a lot of long-haired people around here who want a billion dollars for schools, a billion dollars for public health." Cited in McElvaine, *Great Depression,* 311. The Edmund Wilson quotation is also from McElvaine, *Great Depression,* 139.

7. Roger L. Geiger, *To Advance Knowledge: The Growth of American Research Universities, 1900–1940* (New York: Oxford University Press, 1986), 256–59; Hawkins, *Banding Together,* 37–40, 61–66, 128–31, 189–90; Rivlin, *Role,* 7; Eddy, *Colleges,* 172; Kerr, *Transformation,* 38. Conant may have been a Republican, but he apparently voted for Franklin Roosevelt at least twice and perhaps more, and during the war years, if not the 1930s, he was a fairly ardent supporter. For Conant's politics, see Roger L. Geiger, *Research and Relevant*

Knowledge: American Research Universities since World War II (New York: Oxford University Press, 1993), 4–5.

8. Finkelstein, *American Academic Profession,* 7; Geiger, *Research and Relevant Knowledge,* 249–50; Rivlin, *Role,* 4, 98; Schrecker, *No Ivory Tower,* 68–70; McElvaine, *Great Depression,* 251; Leuchtenburg, *Roosevelt,* 253; David McCullough, *Truman* (New York: Simon and Schuster, 1992), 219, 232. For the invisibility of higher education as a labor issue (and an exercise in negative evidence), see for example, Archie Robinson, *George Meany and His Times* (New York: Simon and Schuster, 1981); Melvin Dubofsky and Warren Van Tine, *John L. Lewis: A Biography* (New York: Quadrangle, 1977); Kevin Boyle, *The UAW and the Heyday of American Liberalism, 1945–1968* (Ithaca: Cornell University Press, 1995);

The CIO, 1935–1955 (Chapel Hill: University of North Carolina Press, 1995); George Martin, *Madam Secretary: Frances Perkins* (Boston: Houghton Mifflin, 1976); Steven Fraser, *Labor Will Rule: Sidney Hillman and the Rise of American Labor* (New York: Free Press, 1991); and Nelson Lichtenstein, *The Most Dangerous Man in Detroit: Walter Reuther and the Fate of American Labor* (New York: Basic, 1995). Faculty did not unionize in part, of course, because faculty unions were illegal. Robert K. Carr and Daniel K. Van Eyck, *Collective Bargaining Comes to the Campus* (Washington, D.C.: American Council on Education, 1973).

9. Rivlin, *Role,* 30; Hawkins, *Banding Together,* 126, 133–38; McElvaine, *Great Depression,* 311; David Fromkin, *In the Time of the Americans* (New York: Random House, 1995), 62; Leuchtenburg, *Roosevelt,* 95–98.

10. McElvaine, *Great Depression,* 267–70; McJimsey, *Harry Hopkins,* 50–59; Leuchtenburg, *Roosevelt,* 129.

11. Clement Eaton, *The Freedom-of-Thought Struggle in the Old South* (New York: Harper and Row, 1940); Ronald Story, *The Forging of an Aristocracy: Harvard and the Boston Upper Class, 1800–1870* (Middletown: Wesleyan University Press, 1980); Walter Metzger, "Academic Tenure in America: A Historical Essay," in *The American Concept of Academic Freedom in Formation: A Collection of Essays and Reports,* ed. Metzger (New York: Arno Press, 1977), 136–43, 151–52; "General Report of the Committee on Academic Freedom and Academic Tenure," *Bulletin of the American Association of University Professors* (1915), 40–41; Sheila Slaughter, "Academic Freedom in the Modern American University," in *Higher Education in American Society,* rev. ed., ed. Philip G. Altbach and Robert O. Berdahl (Buffalo: Prometheus, 1981), 80–81; Schrecker, *No Ivory Tower,* 19; Walter Metzger, "Academic Freedom in Delocalized Academic Institutions," in Altbach and Berdahl, *Higher Education,* 59; Finkelstein, *American Academic Profession,* 25; Arthur O. Lovejoy, "Academic Freedom," in *Encyclopedia of the Social Sciences* (New York, 1930), 1:387. The quotation is from a Harvard professor in the 1850s, as cited in Story, *Forging of an Aristocracy,* 73.

12. "Academic Freedom and Tenure, 1940 Statement of Principles and Interpretive Comments," in *American Association of University Professors Policy Documents and Reports* (Washington, 1973), 1–3; Walter Metzger, "Academic

Tenure," in *Faculty Tenure: A Report and Recommendations by the Commission on Academic Tenure in Higher Education* (San Francisco, 1973), 148–55; Finkelstein, *American Academic Profession*, 28–29. Metzger discusses the criminal court and civil service models in "Academic Tenure."

13. Metzger, "Academic Tenure," in *Faculty Tenure*, 155; Finkelstein, *American Academic Profession*, 29; Schrecker, *No Ivory Tower*, 22–23; Slaughter, "Academic Freedom," 81; Geiger, *To Advance Knowledge*, 250.

14. Geiger, *To Advance Knowledge*, 250; Finkelstein, *American Academic Profession*, 25–29; Schrecker, *No Ivory Tower*, 29, 52, 74–75; Hawkins, *Banding Together*, 165; Metzger, "Academic Tenure," in *Faculty Tenure*, 154–55.

15. Finkelstein, *American Academic Profession*, 25–29; Geiger, *To Advance Knowledge*, 250; Geiger, *Research and Relevant Knowledge*, 19; Hawkins, *Banding Together*, 37, 163, 206, 241; Ralph F. Fuchs, "Academic Freedom—Its Basic Philosophy, Function, and History," *Law and Contemporary Problems* (1963): 442–44.

The Association of American Colleges, whose endorsement helped legitimize the 1940 Statement, deserves discussion here. Hardly the most conservative higher education organization in all respects, the AAC was the only association to include black institutions as full members and worked constructively with the AAUP on upgrading postwar standards for faculty retirements and pensions. Moreover, the AAC kept negotiating on tenure and due process when the National Association of State Universities (NASU), for example, refused to do so. NASU actually declined to act, even when several state university presidents (in Mississippi, Wyoming, and Texas) were fired over politics, claiming that the AAUP was better able to "censure" violations of academic standards. Surely one reason postwar presidents accepted strong tenure practices was that they themselves, having obtained tenure as faculty members, would enjoy a measure of protection, a consideration hardly lost on AAC members.

But the AAC was extremely conservative on the issue of freedom from government interference at any level and eagerly sought modes of self-governance that would preclude intervention on professors' behalf by the courts, Congress, or the New Deal–drenched National Labor Relations Board. In this sense the 1940 statement represented what looked to be a wise preemptive strike. Ironically, though perhaps unsurprisingly, the 1940 statement started to gain enforceability in the early 1950s when Justices William O. Douglas, Hugo Black, and Felix Frankfurter, FDR appointees all, began issuing opinions that welded university vitality, academic freedom, and job security tightly together. Ultimately, of course, it was faculty unionization, which finally took off in the 1960s, that gave tenure provisions the real teeth of enforceability. The best description of the academic associations, including the AAC and NASU, is in Hawkins, *Banding Together*. The best discussion of the attitude of the courts, especially the New Deal–influenced Supreme Court of the 1950s, is in Fuchs, "Academic Freedom."

16. Laura S. Jensen, "The Early American Origins of Entitlements," *Studies*

in American Political Development (Fall 1966): 360–404; Ronald Story, "The Ordeal of the Public Sector: The University of Massachusetts," in *Five Colleges: Five Histories,* ed. Story (Deerfield, 1992), 52–53; Roger Daniels, *The Bonus March* (Westport, 1971); Rivlin, *Role,* 65–66.

17. Keith W. Olson, *The G.I. Bill, the Veterans, and the Colleges* (Lexington: University Press of Kentucky, 1974), 19, 43, 59; Davis R. B. Ross, *Preparing for Ulysses* (New York: Columbia University Press, 1969), 13–14, 24–28, 124, 288; Rivlin, *Role,* 65–66; Doris Kearns Goodwin, *No Ordinary Time: Franklin and Eleanor Roosevelt: The Home Front in World War II* (New York, 1994), 512–13.

18. Olson, *G.I. Bill,* 5, 13, 27–31, 118–21; Rivlin, *Role,* 65–68; Ross, *Ulysses,* 63–65, 223–24, 277; Goodwin, *No Ordinary Time,* 484.

19. Ross, *Ulysses,* 52–53, 63–65, 90–91, 277; Olson, *G.I. Bill,* 1–7; Goodwin, *No Ordinary Time,* 484–85.

20. Ross, *Ulysses,* 22–23, 41–50, 73–74, 80–81; Olson, *G.I. Bill,* 65. The characterization of Rankin as "Jew baiting" and "Negro hating" is from Democratic senator James Guffey of Pennsylvania, a contemporary of Rankin's. According to Guffey, Rankin was "against popular education and says so and he is against the Negro and boasts of it." The Rankin quote is from a letter to a constituent, as cited in Ross, *Ulysses,* 108–10. The flavor of Rankin's views is evident in this letter from a fellow southerner who wrote to Rankin in late 1943: "On my recent trip through Miss., I heard many well deserved complimentary references to your record on the race issue, Poll taxes, Marshall Field III, and the arch south hater, 'nigger' lover, chameleonic candidate for the presidency, who deadbeat his way on a world trip and now pretends such great love for 'My fellow Americans'" (quoted in Ross, *Ulysses,* 23).

21. Olson, *G.I. Bill,* 1–10, 20–24, 29; Ross, *Ulysses,* 64–65, 87; Goodwin, *No Ordinary Time,* 469, 512–13; Patrick D. Reagan, "Fighting the Good War at Home," *Reviews in American History* (September 1997): 485. Olson further argues that while there was genuine concern about angry and maladjusted veterans, there was much greater concern about joblessness, which could lead to radical economic and political changes: "The fear of unemployed veterans, not the fear of maladjusted veterans, motivated the persons who enacted the G.I. Bill" (*G.I. Bill,* 24). The quote about altruism is also from Olson, *G.I. Bill,* 24. Interestingly, the bill's sponsors modeled it partly on the Wisconsin Educational Bonus Law of 1919, one instance where the "Wisconsin Idea" bore New Deal fruit.

22. Frederick Rudolph, *Curriculum: A History of the American Undergraduate Course of Study since 1636* (San Francisco, 1977), 282–83; Olson, *G.I. Bill,* 23, 50, 78, 97–99, 111; Rivlin, *Role,* 65–69; Hawkins, *Banding Together,* 166–73; Goodwin, *No Ordinary Time,* 513. Harvard's Conant had argued that the bill would result in "the least capable . . . flooding the facilities." Robert Hutchins said it would "demoralize education and defraud the vet," who would be receiving an inferior product that would do him little good. Donald Stauffer of Princeton believed that the "old-style liberal education will be under constant bombardment." Francis Brown, president of the American Council on Educa-

tion, assumed that "the great majority of vets will desire vocational, technical, and professional training." See Olson, *G.I. Bill,* 32–33. This may have been true in the very long run at public institutions, particularly if one counts the community college sector of higher education, which eventually flourished, but it did not occur during the heyday of the veterans. After the war, business courses in particular took a nosedive, as did the agricultural sciences. Engineering, however, went up fairly sharply.

23. Olson, *G.I. Bill,* 44–45, 70–74, 86, 102; Hawkins, *Banding Together,* 165–66, 181; Hugh Davis Graham and Nancy Diamond, *The Rise of American Research Universities: Elites and Challengers in the Postwar Era* (Baltimore: Johns Hopkins University Press, 1997), 21–22; Rudolph, *Curriculum,* 258–61. With regard to its macroeconomic impact, the postwar economy unexpectedly boomed, so that the unemployment rate would have remained low in any event, but having an additional million or so young men in college assuredly helped. As for faculty remuneration, it might be noted that while salaries rose in the 1950s, in real terms professors made less in 1960 than they had in 1904.

24. Eddy, *Colleges,* 231; Graham and Diamond, *Research Universities,* 25, 31; Rivlin, *Role,* 28; Kerr, *Great Transformation,* 102.

25. Geiger, *Research and Relevant Knowledge,* 5–10; Rivlin, *Role,* 31–34; Larry Owens, "The Counterproductive Management of Science in the Second World War: Vannevar Bush and the Office of Scientific Research and Development," *Business History Review* (Winter 1994), 517–22; Graham and Diamond, *Research Universities,* 28.

26. Owens, "Science," 536, 544; Geiger, *Research and Relevant Knowledge,* 14–17; Graham and Diamond, *Research Universities,* 28–29; Hawkins, *Banding Together,* 177.

27. Geiger, *Research and Relevant Knowledge,* 14–18; Graham and Diamond, *Research Universities,* 29–32, 91; Hawkins, *Banding Together,* 177–78; Ross, *Ulysses,* 138; Rivlin, *Role,* 38–39.

28. Geiger, *Research and Relevant Knowledge,* 19, 43–45. The quotation is from R. R. Wilson, "U.S. Particle Accelerators at Age 50," *Physics Today,* November 1981, 91. I am indebted to Professor Larry Owens for bringing this anecdote to my attention. It is probably apocryphal.

29. Rudolph, *Curriculum,* 253–56; Finkelstein, *American Academic Profession,* 95; Rivlin, *Role,* 47, 59; Metzger, "Academic Freedom," 70; Geiger, *Research and Relevant Knowledge,* 296, 320. Harvard president James B. Conant was a bitter critic of his predecessor at Harvard, A. Lawrence Lowell, for favoring faculty who would "charm and stimulate the undergraduate," an attitude that to Conant amounted to almost "criminal neglect." Quoted in Geiger, *To Advance Knowledge,* 195. A. Whitney Griswold, president of Yale, was a holdout among top university leaders; he argued that educating good undergraduates would be Yale's strongest contribution to postwar America and that research at Yale should be basic, not applied, and should reinforce the undergraduate curriculum. Yale succumbed to the pressures of federal research policy and the com-

plaints of its own science faculty only in the early 1960s. Geiger, *Research and Relevant Knowledge*, 88–90.

30. Hawkins, *Banding Together,* 146, 180; Harry Gideonse, "Changing Issues in Academic Freedom in the United States," *Proceedings of the American Philosophical Society* (April 1950), 102–4; Geiger, Research and Relevant Knowledge, 40, 60–61; Metzger, "Academic Freedom," 70; Rivlin, *Role,* 121, 155. In 1950 Harry Gideonse, president of Brooklyn College, identified federal subsidies to physical and technical research as one of the three major threats to modern academic freedom, along with the Communist Party and Department of Defense research restrictions. Gideonse saw massive imbalances arising on the campuses and urged additional funds to study the social and economic by-products of the new scientific developments.

31. Lawrence E. Gladieux and Gwendolyn L. Lewis, "The Federal Government and Higher Education," in Altbach and Berdahl, *Higher Education,* 169–71; Rivlin, *Role,* 35–38, 57–58; Graham and Diamond, *Research Universities,* 91–97, 210; Geiger, *Research and Relevant Knowledge,* 41–44, 58, 106, 244; W. Lee Hansen and Jacob O. Stampen, "The Economics and Financing of Higher Education," in Altbach and Berdahl, *Higher Education,* 120–21. Faculty at Princeton and Harvard saw that nuclear physics was the key scientific field, that their universities should build strength in this field, but they warned that far from providing a financial bonanza, such an initiative would entail "large institutional investments" (Geiger, *Research and Relevant Knowledge,* 31). Alice Rivlin, writing in 1961, concluded that federal research dollars pushed institutional costs higher than if such money had been spent outside the academy "or not at all" (*Role,* 59).

Idealism, Realpolitik, or Domestic Politics

A Clinton-Era Retrospective on FDR's Foreign Policies

Seyom Brown

For present-oriented policy analysts such as myself, Franklin D. Roosevelt's statecraft is like a giant Rorschach test. What we look for and find has more to do with our current policy preoccupations than with a determination to enrich knowledge of the past for its own sake. In this essay, accordingly, I do not purport to contribute *new* information about Franklin Roosevelt's foreign policies; rather, I attempt to extract from what historians of the New Deal era have already largely elucidated and project into the scene at the close of the Clinton era those considerations that are of use to contemporary policy makers and analysts.

From the perspective of the new millennium, it is striking to realize the extent to which the foreign policies of FDR, the last pre–cold war president, prefigured the foreign policies of Bill Clinton, the first post–cold war president.[1] Like FDR's diplomacy, Clinton's diplomacy lends itself to facile caricature: as being either the product of naïve idealism, cynical realpolitik (including commercial imperialism), or domestic political preoccupations. There is some truth in these various, often contradictory, caricatures of FDR, but the larger truth lies in FDR's creative blending of idealism, realpolitik, and domestic considerations in his international statecraft. I also suggest that a contemporary U.S. statecraft somewhat modeled on FDR's could well serve the country's interests at the start of the new millennium.

In at least one of its basic characteristics, Clinton's orientation toward world affairs was in the FDR mold. Statecraft for both presidents has been what some political scientists have called "intermestic": a realm in which the country's international and domestic interests are intertwined.[2] International relations are always partly intermestic, in this sense, but for FDR, prior to World War II, and more recently Clinton, the melding of international and domestic considerations often seemed the very essence of foreign policy. Just as such intermesticity was especially prominent in early New Deal policies designed to counter the economic depression, so it was the hallmark of Clinton's post–cold war policies on trade, investment, monetary affairs, and environment and toward various foreign situations, such as the Israeli-Palestinian conflict, Haiti, and Northern Ireland. Some of Clinton's later foreign policy moves, particularly in the Balkan crises and toward Saddam Hussein, were clearly impelled by international rather than domestic circumstances, even though they were constrained by domestic political and economic considerations.

A high admixture of domestic and international considerations in the foreign policies of FDR and Clinton is clear. What is not so clear—and more interesting—is which of these two realms was the "first love" of the president and which was secondary, which was his favorite preoccupation and which is a diversion. In Clinton's case, at the start of his presidency, there could be little doubt of his preference for the domestic over the foreign arena. Even with respect to the global economy, Clinton came into office arguing that revitalization of productivity in the United States was the route toward being more competitive in international trade, not, as he later came to believe, the other way around. But Clinton soon realized that he was expected in his press conferences and daily contacts with his foreign counterparts to be no less knowledgeable about international developments impinging on the nation than about domestic political and economic events. FDR's movement during his first term and the first half of his second term was in the opposite direction, from a strong inclination to make an impact on the world stage to a determination not to let the internationally destabilizing events taking place abroad interfere with the imperatives of domestic economic recovery and, not incidental, his popularity with the American electorate. When the shock of Pearl Harbor finally allowed Roosevelt to obtain a mandate from the people to be the country's chief warrior-diplomat, which, in admiration of cousin Theodore, he always craved, all indications are that, despite his "I hate war" rhetoric, he thrived in and thoroughly enjoyed his new imperious role.

Clinton too, perhaps to his own surprise, ultimately came to enjoy being in the foreign policy limelight. He seems to have discovered early in his second term that involvement in international dimensions of policy can be more than a necessary chore, that it can be at least as intellectually stimulating as direction of the administration's domestic policy, and, moreover, that he was quite good at the nuts and bolts of foreign policy formulation and diplomatic bargaining. This realization came at just the right time for him: when serious questioning by both his political friends and enemies of his moral fitness to lead the nation provided a special need to turn the spotlight on his activities in the international arena to deflect media attention from the embarrassments of the Monica Lewinsky affair.

If Clinton and his successors did use FDR as a role model for playing the intermestic game effectively, which face of the master emerged as the most authentic and exemplary for the present era: Wilsonian idealist? Realpolitik statesman? Or democracy's quintessential diplomat?

Foreign Policy as Idealism

FDR's public embrace of the world order views of Woodrow Wilson— that world peace required a league of sovereign states collectively committed to secure them against invasion or aggression and that it was the highest calling of the United States to promote world peace through world law—was stimulated by the adulatory popular response Wilson received upon returning from the Paris Peace Conference in 1919. Those who hold that the real FDR was a Wilsonian can find support in the speeches he made in favor of the United States joining the League of Nations and in his insistent campaigning for broadened international cooperation as the Democratic candidate for vice president in 1920.

Skeptics can juxtapose the new, post–Peace of Versailles FDR with his earlier pro-military stances as assistant secretary of the navy and his admiration for the aggressive nationalism of Theodore Roosevelt.[3] But perhaps, as some biographers have suggested by citing President Wilson's emotional talks with him on the boat back from the peace conference, his was a genuine conversion.[4]

The picture of FDR as a committed Wilsonian is consistent with his persistent support for a strengthened World Court, his presidential sponsorship of world disarmament conferences during the 1930s, and his promulgation of the Atlantic Charter war aims with Churchill in 1941. Finally, Wilson's ghost could have drafted Roosevelt's address to Congress in 1945 explaining that the accords with Stalin and Churchill at Yalta were premised on "the end of the system of unilateral action, the exclusive alliances, the spheres of influence, the balances of power, and all the other expedients that have been tried for centuries—and have always failed. We propose to substitute for all these, a universal organization to which all peace-loving nations will finally have a chance to join."[5]

It is this post-Yalta statement in particular, however, that calls into question the credibility of FDR's idealism. Was the man a self-deluded utopian? Or was he a cynic of the most arrogant stripe, blatantly pandering to the uninformed hopes of his constituents for a new world order while knowing full well he had been assuring the perpetuation of the old world order? Such skepticism became common among historians and international relations specialists after the records of the Yalta conference were declassified, for they showed FDR agreeing with Winston Churchill and Joseph Stalin to allocate postwar spheres of influence among their three countries and to establish a United Nations organization wherein they would exercise predominant control in all important matters.

There were, however, two streams in Roosevelt's foreign policy—the Good Neighbor Policy toward Latin America and anticolonialism—in which the idea of what was morally right did seem to be a strong motivating force and to exercise a persisting determinative influence throughout his presidency. A third stream, support for free trade, treated as a sacrosanct moral good by its principal shepherd, Secretary of State Cordell Hull, was also a strong preference of FDR's, but his handling of this realm of policy indicated the extent to which tariffs, international monetary policy, and global economic issues were instruments of other international and domestic interests of the New Deal more than determinants of basic U.S. foreign policy.

The Good Neighbor Policy was a repudiation of Theodore Roosevelt's hegemonic Corollary to the Monroe Doctrine and even some of Wilson's interventions that FDR himself had supported while secretary of the navy.[6] By the time he was elected president, FDR had become a convert to the idea that the inter-American system, which could well be a model for the world as a whole, should be one in which countries big and small treat each other with full respect, in accord with the traditional international law of the sovereign equality of states and noninterference in one another's domestic affairs. How nations organized themselves internally, how governments treated the people within their jurisdictions, was at this stage in FDR's still-evolving worldview largely their own business. He was proud to tell the world that, by signing the Pan-American Convention on the Rights and Duties of States at Montevideo in December 1933, the United States was finally dispensing with the conceit that "the maintenance of constitutional government in other nations" in the hemisphere is the "sacred obligation" of this country. From now on, he averred, "the definite policy of the United States . . . is opposed to armed intervention."[7]

Roosevelt's anti-imperialist stance during World War II blended both authentic idealism and an "enlightened realism" premised on the recognition that the United States could advance its economic and security interests more effectively in a pluralistic and open international system than in a world dominated by rival hegemons. We can see this synthesis in the Atlantic Charter he issued with Prime Minister Churchill in August 1941, particularly in their promises to "see no territorial changes that do not accord with the freely expressed wishes of the peoples concerned; . . . respect the right of all peoples to choose the form of government under which they will live; and . . . see sovereign rights and self-government restored to those who have been forcibly deprived of them [and] . . . further . . . access on equal terms, to the trade, and to the raw materials of the world which are needed for their economic prosperity."[8] These commitments were, no doubt, partly the result of political calculation: As with Wilson's Fourteen Points, a statement of principles was important for generating public enthusiasm for U.S. participation in the war against Germany, which the president had already decided was in the nation's interest. Such commitments were also important for inducing peoples in the colonized world to side with the Western democracies against the Germans and the Japanese, who were then assiduously courting their participation in an "anti-imperialist" front. FDR's insistence that an Anglo-American declaration of principles with an anti-imperialist thrust was crucial in the struggle against the Axis powers persuaded Winston Churchill to endorse the charter, even though the language might ultimately be turned against the British Empire.[9]

Churchill's unease was warranted, for the Atlantic Charter did turn out to be more than an instrument for mobilizing domestic and international support against the Axis powers. The Lockean/Jeffersonian/Wilsonian "progressive" liberalism which FDR had made a part of his political rhetoric on the way to the presidency and which was now being projected onto the world stage had apparently become very much a part of his own Weltanschauung. As he put it to the squirming British prime minister at the Atlantic Charter conference, "I can't believe that we can fight a war against fascist slavery, and at the same time not work to free people all over the world from backward colonial policy."[10] As victory in the war neared, much to the chagrin of Churchill and Charles De Gaulle, FDR reaffirmed that he had been dead serious in putting the anticolonial commitments into the Atlantic Charter.

The Soviets were relieved that Roosevelt did not explicitly brand as colonialism their determination to maintain a dominant presence in eastern Europe at the end of the war. But Roosevelt, supported by Churchill, was able to persuade Stalin to accept in the Declaration on Liberated Europe FDR's favorite self-determination and consent-of-the-governed concepts as part of the final package negotiated at Yalta. The text of the declaration, signed by the Big Three on February 11, 1945, jointly committed them to "processes which will enable the liberated peoples . . . to create democratic institutions of their own choice. This is a principle of the Atlantic Charter—the right of all peoples to choose the form of government under which they will live—the restoration of sovereign rights and self-government to those peoples who have been forcibly deprived of them by the aggressor nations."[11] Where the exercise of these rights required a period of transition to establish law and order and provide the populace with necessary goods and services, the victorious powers further promised to "jointly assist the people in any European liberated state . . . to form interim governmental authorities broadly representative of all democratic elements in the population and pledged to the earliest possible establishment through free elections of governments responsive to the will of the people."[12]

FDR's interjection of Wilsonian concepts of national self-determination into what was otherwise consummate realpolitik bargaining over the fate of postwar Europe was, of course, strongly prompted by his need to reassure the Democratic Party's ethnic constituents in the Midwest that he was not selling out their east European brothers and sisters.

Churchill had a similar constituency problem and had committed his government to secure an influential role in liberated Poland for the Polish exiles residing in Britain. The British prime minister was not all that pleased, however, at the American delegation's determination that references to the universalistic Atlantic Charter be included in the declaration, fearful that the Yalta accords could then be turned against British and French efforts to reconsolidate their imperial spheres in Africa, the Middle East, and Asia. FDR, alert to the sensitivities of both his counterparts, was not beyond tweaking Churchill's anxieties about American anticolonialism in front of Stalin in order to gain the latter's confidence.

Yet the ideals of the Atlantic Charter had become more than mere instruments of the president's other interests. Even if the initial reasons for his public embrace of the Wilsonian concepts had been narrowly political, FDR's encounter during the war with the passion of people for national self-determination, together with how this affected their willingness to side with either the Allies or the Axis powers, made him even more aware that the global influence of the United States after the war would depend substantially on the credibility of commitment to such ideals. FDR's appreciation of the extent to which the furtherance of the Atlantic Charter values could advance the enlightened self-interest of the country had become inseparable from the belief that the United States of America had been "chosen" by destiny to be the noble embodiment of these ideals.

Foreign Policy as Realpolitik

What Roosevelt told the general public he was trying to accomplish internationally did often depart considerably from the bargains he struck with other world leaders. Were these bargains simply a pragmatic accommodation of American idealism to a world of nation-states still highly resistant to any infringement of their sovereignty? Or was the basic thrust of FDR's foreign policy the product of an even more fundamental "realist" or "realpolitik" worldview—that a basic restructuring of the anarchic international system is inconsistent with the natural need of humans to seek protection and well-being in a particular national community and that such national communities will always feel it imperative to secure their territory, material assets, and way of life against envious or aggressive outsiders? Did Roosevelt accordingly—underneath the Wilsonian rhetoric—actually believe that the national leader's highest priority was to maintain the nation's coercive power intact and, if possible, superior to that of one's potential adversaries?

Perhaps the authentic FDR was (at least in his psyche, if not necessarily in a fully worked-out Weltanschauung) the dashing assistant secretary of the navy, consumer of Admiral Mahan's geopolitical treatises, aspiring soldier-statesman in the heroic mold of cousin Theodore, who would serve his country and the world best by helping his fellow public servants to avoid the illusions of Wilsonian liberalism. His big-navy and global-interventionist views were well known to the Wilsonians ("Our national defense must extend all over the western hemisphere, must go out a thousand miles into the sea, must embrace the Philippines and over the seas wherever our commerce may be").[13] Indeed, they put him at odds with many of his superiors in the Wilson administration, including Secretary of the Navy Josephus Daniels.[14]

It is thus quite plausible that his soon-to-be-displayed international liberalism was a carefully tailored political cloak designed to appeal to the constituencies whose support he calculated was necessary for the attainment of his destiny—to be the nation's president—and then to sustain himself in office. Such a personal political strategy would be consistent with various of the flip-flops historians have recorded in his public stances on the way to the White House and as the country's chief executive: appearing at times as global free trader, at times almost a populist protectionist; sometimes taking a position in favor of substantial disarmament, at other times an unapologetic champion of national preparedness; insisting on a number of occasions that Britain did not need the United States to fight alongside her to stop Hitler, even when Germany attacked Poland on September 1, 1939, and assuring his fellow Americans that he would do everything possible to keep the United States out of the European war, while predicting that victory for Hitler would jeopardize the institutions of democracy throughout the Western world.

A consummate manipulator of public opinion, FDR should not be expected to have revealed his actual philosophy of statecraft forthrightly if he truly was a practitioner of realpolitik in Wilsonian clothing. What then can we learn about the authentic Franklin Roosevelt from his behind-the-scenes policymaking and secret diplomacy? The picture that emerges is still mixed but quite coherent in its larger outlines.

By the time Roosevelt had formulated the Lend-Lease stratagem in mid-1940 that let the British and other enemies of Germany "borrow" military equipment from the United States in return for giving the United States permission to use ("lease") some of their strategically located bases and other facilities, he had determined that U.S. participation in the war was practically inevitable and imperative for preventing an irreversible shift in the global balance of power. Hitler was on the brink of accomplishing what Mahan and other prominent geopolitical thinkers warned against: an expanding "heartland" power was about to achieve control over the "rimland" as well, which in combination would give it the power to rule the world.

But Prime Minister Churchill and war hawks within the U.S. government, such as Henry Stimson, were concerned that FDR's public denials of the need to become an active belligerent—denials the president felt were required to induce Congress to approve even lend-lease assistance—were making it increasingly unlikely that he could ever get a declaration of war from Congress. They pleaded with FDR to reveal his private thoughts and go before the American people in the spring of 1941 to preempt an isolationist backlash. But the president, not wanting to revive the coalition that just a few years ago had tried to clip his national security powers with a constitutional amendment,[15] refused to be pushed to do premature battle in the domestic political arena. Assuring his hawkish critics that they would not have to wait too much longer, he predicted that sooner or later there would be a major "incident" (presumably a dramatic destruction of U.S. seaborne commerce by German submarines) that would galvanize public opinion and force Congress to declare war on Germany. As it turned out, it was not a German attack on U.S. ships or facilities but Hitler's declaration of war against the United States in response to the U.S. declaration of war against Japan for the attack on Pearl Harbor that brought the United States into the war against Germany.

In Asia FDR showed himself to be fully aware of the geopolitical threat that an expanding Japan posed for the regional and global balances of military and economic power, yet quite coolheaded about how to put the onus on Japan for starting any war that might embroil the United States—a requirement for generating sufficient public support for such a war. His strategy of severely tightening the economic screws on Tokyo (freezing their financial assets so as to deny them oil) in response to Japan's move into Indochina in 1941, while deploying naval forces to Hawaii to enhance deterrence, did force Japan to make its stark choice for war sooner rather than later and in that sense can be regarded as a miscalculation by the U.S. strategists.

The most controversial of FDR's foreign policies with geopolitical implications—the Yalta negotiations and accords—continue to be analyzed by historians and political scientists for what they reveal about this extraordinary statesman's philosophy of international relations. There is still considerable disagreement over whether Roosevelt was taken advantage of by Stalin at Yalta or whether his behavior reflected a realistic appreciation of the connection between the disposition of the forces of the victors at the war's end and their bargaining power vis-à-vis one another. Many of the old questions persist: Did Roosevelt pay too high a price in conceding a Soviet sphere of influence as far west as the Elbe and in giving Stalin virtually everything he demanded in Asia in order to secure his entry into the war against Japan? Did he really believe that Stalin would permit reasonably free elections in Poland and other countries under Soviet occupation? Did he assume that the wartime cooperation with the Soviets would be sustained sufficiently into the postwar world to permit the United Nations to function as a weighty collective security institution?

My revisiting of the accumulated evidence about the period and of the records of the discussions at Yalta leads me conclude that FDR was quite aware of what he was doing. Retrospective judgments of his having been too soft in conceding to Stalin's demands tend to ignore the military backdrop to the Big Three encounter in early February 1945. Robert Dalleck reminds us that on the western front, the Allied forces were just regaining their balance after one of the most costly firefights of the war, the terrible Battle of the Bulge to regain control of the Belgium city of Bastogne and the Ardennes. The Americans and the British were only now beginning to resume the offensive that would take them deep into Germany. As the Yalta Conference commenced most of their forces were still at the German borders with France and Belgium. But on the eastern front, the Soviets were already well into their culminating victory drive and were only forty miles from Berlin as Stalin offered an outstretched hand to Roosevelt at the Black Sea resort.[16] Moreover, the president's military advisers were anxious for him to get a firm commitment from Stalin to enter the war in Asia as soon as possible following the defeat of Germany, and he had no reason as yet to count on the atomic bomb being ready to use against Japan.[17]

Whether from the vantage point of more than a half century after Yalta FDR's assessments of the military and political realities of 1945 look wise or unduly optimistic or pessimistic, one feature is clear: Roosevelt, hardly the naïve idealist of his caricatures, was focusing intently on the geopolitical situation and bargaining primarily in a realpolitik mode with Churchill and Stalin.

Foreign Policy as Domestic Politics

Idealist or realist in his views on the desirable and feasible world order, FDR's actual foreign policies were highly constrained by his keen perception of what the domestic political traffic would bear. Consistent with the political style assumed early in his career, Roosevelt would lead the charge on policies that were good domestic politics (good for his popularity, that is) and retreat on policies that were politically costly for him.

To maintain the tactical flexibility this required at high policymaking levels, he made sure that ardent internationalists in his administration were kept in check by officials with more nationalist views, and vice versa. Thus Roosevelt's appointments to key subcabinet posts in the State Department included a number of hawkish nationalists who would counter and undercut Secretary of State Hull's passionate commitments to free trade (which FDR was basically for but felt needed to be subordinated to the exigencies of domestic economic recovery) and disarmament (which FDR felt should be handled as a negotiating tool for sustaining military balances favorable to the United States). In his administration staffing policies and in his notorious penchant for playing off assertive aides against one another, FDR was an artist—particularly in the foreign policy field—in preserving maneuvering space for himself to pursue the national interest as he saw fit.

Brilliant political tactician that he was, he nevertheless sometimes faltered embarrassingly, as in his 1935 advocacy of U.S. participation in a strengthened World Court—a development that FDR did strongly favor. Starting out with an estimated two-thirds of the Senate in favor, the president beat a hasty retreat in the face of angry opposition from the Hearst press, the Hiram Johnson progressives, and the American Liberty League. When Republican senator Arthur Vandenberg offered an amendment restating America's presumed commitment to the principle that countries should not interfere in the internal affairs of other states, Roosevelt, hoping to undercut the extreme nationalists, gave the amendment his blessing. And to stave off the growing congressional support for additional restrictive legislation, he reluctantly signed a bill requiring Senate approval of any effort by the executive to take an issue to the World Court. Instead of retrieving his lost support, these concessions only created a bandwagon for the isolationists, with the result that FDR's initiative was ultimately defeated.[18]

As wartime leader too, Roosevelt the geostrategist never stopped being the domestic politician. There is no other explanation for his unconscionable decision of February 1942 to intern 110,000 Japanese Americans in concentration camps on the West Coast. The pressures for this move, although it had tepid support from the War Department as a means of precluding Japanese Americans from engaging in acts of subversion and sabotage, were almost entirely from politicians catering to racist constituencies. Historian James MacGregor Burns describes the situation impinging on the Oval Office:

> More and more, Washington felt the heat. California officials—notably Governor Culbert L. Olson and Attorney General Earl Warren, working in close touch with sheriffs and district attorneys—threw their weight behind the campaign for evacuation. In Washington the West Coast congressional delegations put unrelenting pressure on the Justice and War Departments and on their regional officials. Congressmen denounced as "jackasses" those who had failed to deal with sabotage and espionage at Pearl Harbor.[19]

Burns attributes this, "one of the sorriest episodes in American history," not only to populist racism but also to a "great negative factor—the opposition never showed up. . . . Doubting administration officials did not carry their protests to the Chief Executive."[20] While this blatant contradiction of the values for which the United States claimed to be fighting had little effect on the conduct of the war or U.S. foreign policy, it did exhibit how FDR's domestic political instincts could overwhelm his statesmanship—sometimes with momentous consequences for basic U.S. national interests and the fate of the world.

Such was the case with the war aim of "unconditional surrender" by Germany and Japan. Although designed in part to discourage members of the anti-Axis coalition from attempting to negotiate a separate peace, it was expected to help sustain a popular will to bear the costs of war over the long haul. The enemies were portrayed as absolutely venal and not deserving to be brought back into the international system after their defeat.

The need to be faithful to FDR's unconditional surrender promise was one of the clinching arguments used by Secretary of State Jimmy Byrnes to convince President Harry Truman to explode the atomic bombs on Hiroshima and Nagasaki and not to take up the Japanese bid to keep their emperor as a part of the surrender arrangements. Ironically, after the bombs were dropped, with Byrnes continuing to argue against the deal, Truman did finally allow the Japanese to keep their emperor, albeit subordinated to the American occupation regime. The other persuasive reasons for using the bomb, to avoid the need to sacrifice hundreds of thousand of U.S. soldiers in an invasion of the Japanese home islands and the geopolitical value of preventing the Soviets, who were about to enter the war, from sharing in the spoils of victory, might have been satisfied by the alternative of an earlier conditional surrender that included some deal on the emperor. Historians who have mined Japanese archival materials continue to debate whether the Japanese would indeed have surrendered, even after the Soviets entered the war, before the shocks of Hiroshima and Nagasaki. As it turned out, however, the modified post-Nagasaki "conditional" surrender terms that the Japanese did finally accept were approved by Truman only after he himself was shocked at the reports of the instant nuclear incineration of women and babies.

FDR in the Eye of the Beholder

Internationalism/nationalism, realpolitik/idealism, elitism/populism— no one of the Rooseveltian Janus faces, no particular angle of vision on them, adequately captures the often elusive character of his international (or "intermestic") statecraft. Perhaps this is the kind of foreign policy leadership the country needed during those tumultuous twelve years, in that a less enigmatic and skillful politician probably could not have fended off the isolationists during an era when the depression seemed to demand inward-looking public policies, and a less internationally oriented and geopolitically sophisticated president of this democratic republic might not have tried.

The current generation of policymakers could do worse in selecting as their role model the last pre–cold war president. To be sure, the Great Depression presented a more stark and identifiable array of threats to American society than the United States has yet had to face in the post–cold war era, nor has an impending dangerous change in the global balance of power, such as the world faced in the early 1940s, necessitated a systematic and ruthless prioritization of the country's interests. Yet when Roosevelt began to plan for the postwar world, he contemplated an evolving global polity and economy in some ways more like the world contemporary policymakers must deal with than the materially polarized and ideologically divided world of the cold war that U.S. presidents had to operate in for over four decades.

If there is a dominant axis of alignment and antagonism in today's world, it is, as during the 1930s, not one that pits the United States and its allies against some definable set of enemy nations (certainly not "the West" against "the rest," as fantasized in Samuel Huntington's *Clash of Civilizations*).[21] Rather it is one in which the allies and antagonists characteristically traverse national and continental lines—the conflict in every country and region of the world between those who welcome the expansion of contacts and competition and those who oppose it. Simplified by the code word "globalization," the increasing mobility of goods, persons, and information is being embraced by those who perceive they will be the winners in larger and more open markets and political systems. The same phenomena are feared and opposed by those who perceive they will lose—relatively, if not absolutely—in material well-being, political power, and social status if such globalization continues apace.

Cultural affinities and antagonisms are often interlinked with the cosmopolitan versus parochial lineup on economic issues. The technological revolutions in transportation and communication both challenge and reinforce ethnocentric attitudes, leading in many places to renewed efforts to thicken barriers at least to the mobility of people. Thus opposition to expanding the depth and scope of regional and global economic markets tends to go hand in hand with the revival of restrictive immigration policies in many countries.

This was Mr. Clinton's world and will be the world of at least the next president, George W. Bush: a world that has returned to the complex evolutionary, yet fitful development of a global economy and world polity that was interrupted by the cold war. Historians of Rooseveltian foreign policy issues, looking back from the first decade of the new millennium, should have a sense of déjà vu. In the eye of this beholder, much is there to mine.

Notes

1. President George H. W. Bush is sometimes accorded the role of first post–cold war president, but inappropriately. To be sure, Bush presided over the end of the cold war. Yet many of his foreign policies, while directed toward the dismantling of inherited cold war arrangements, were still largely influenced by cold war attitudes toward the new leadership in Moscow. Even Bush's Gulf War statecraft, much of it focused on influencing Mikhail Gorbachev, cannot be separated from this legacy. See George Bush and Brent Scowcroft, *A World Transformed* (New York: Knopf, 1998).

2. The term was coined by Bayless Manning, the former dean of Stanford University Law School and president of the Council on Foreign Relations, in his article "The Congress, the Executive, and Intermestic Affairs," *Foreign Affairs* 55, no. 2 (1977): 306–24, in which he defined "intermestic" affairs as those which are "simultaneously, profoundly and inseparably both domestic and international" (309).

3. Frank Freidel, *Franklin D. Roosevelt: The Apprenticeship* (Boston: Little, Brown, 1952), calls this essentially a politically "opportunistic" switch.

4. See Robert Dalleck, *Franklin Roosevelt and American Foreign Policy, 1932–1945* (New York: Oxford University Press, 1979), 11.

5. U.S. Department of State, *Foreign Relations of the United States, Diplomatic Papers: The Conferences at Malta and Yalta, 1945* (Washington, D.C.: GPO, 1955), 975.

6. The so-called Roosevelt Corollary to the Monroe Doctrine was a series of statements by President Theodore Roosevelt, in response to domestic turmoil and financial instability in various Latin American countries, that the United States, while opposing imperialistic interventions against the sovereign independence of its sister republics in this hemisphere, could not itself sit idly by in the face of the developing chaos. TR's clearest articulation of this interventionist policy came in his annual message of 1904, putting the world on notice that "chronic wrongdoing, or an impotence which results in a general loosening of the ties of civilized society, may in America, as elsewhere, ultimately require intervention by some civilized nation, and in the Western Hemisphere the adherence of the United States to the Monroe Doctrine may force the United States, however reluctantly, in flagrant cases of such wrongdoing or impotence, to the exercise of an international police power." *A Compilation of the Messages and Papers of the Presidents* (Washington, D.C.: Bureau of National Literature, 1911), 9:7053–54.

7. Speech before the Woodrow Wilson Foundation, quoted by Tony Smith, *America's Mission: The United States and the Worldwide Struggle for Democracy in*

the Twentieth Century (Princeton: Princeton University Press, 1995), 121. According to article 8 of the 1933 Inter-American Convention on the Rights and Duties of States, "No state has the right to intervene in the internal or external affairs of another." See *Convention on the Rights and Duties of States.* Done at Montevideo, December 26, 1933. Entered into force for the United States on December 26, 1934, 49 Stat. 3097, T.S. no. 881, 3 Bevans 145, 165 L.N.T.S, 19.

8. The Atlantic Charter of August 14, 1941, *The Public Papers of Franklin D. Roosevelt,* 10:314.

9. Lloyd Gardner, "The Atlantic Charter: Idea and Reality, 1942–1945," in *The Atlantic Charter,* ed. Douglas Brinkley and David R. Facey-Crowther (New York: St. Martin's, 1994), 45–81.

10. FDR quoted by Elliot Roosevelt, *As He Saw It* (New York: Duell, Sloan and Pearce, 1946), 37.

11. U.S. Department of State, *Foreign Relations of the United States, Diplomatic Papers,* 972.

12. Ibid.

13. FDR quoted by Robert Dalleck, *Franklin Roosevelt and American Foreign Policy,* 9.

14. Gaddis Smith quotes a revealing comment from FDR's private correspondence concerning the outbreak of World War I in Europe, in which FDR seems to delight in how his boss was "feeling chiefly very sad that his faith in human nature and civilization and similar idealistic nonsense was receiving such a rude shock." Gaddis Smith, "Roosevelt, the Sea, and International Security," in Brinkley and Facey-Crowther, *Atlantic Charter,* 36.

15. Proposed by Representative Louis Ludlow of Indiana and brought to the floor in the House in December 1937 following the sinking of the U.S. gunboat *Pinay* in the Yangtze River by the Japanese, this constitutional amendment would have required a national referendum before the United States could become involved in a war. See Frank Freidel, *Franklin D. Roosevelt: A Rendezvous with Destiny* (Boston: Little, Brown, 1990), 289–91.

16. Dalleck, *Franklin Roosevelt and American Foreign Policy,* 508–9.

17. The Soviets probably would have entered the war against Japan anyway (without British and American inducements) in order to be in on the division of the spoils and to establish a foothold for their territorial claims. But given Stalin's record of double dealing with Hitler prior to the war and his coyness about becoming a belligerent against Japan, FDR could not rule out some new Kremlin stratagems—such as connivance with Tokyo to let the Soviets walk into northeastern China and Korea unopposed so as to allow Japan to redeploy its forces from these areas to the home islands for the final stand against the American invasion.

18. Dalleck, *Franklin Roosevelt and American Foreign Policy,* 96–97.

19. James MacGregor Burns, *Roosevelt: The Soldier of Freedom, 1940–1945* (New York: Harcourt Brace Jovanovich, 1970), 213–17; quotation from 215.

20. Ibid., 216.

21. Samuel P. Huntington, *The Clash of Civilizations and the Remaking of World Order* (New York: Simon and Schuster, 1996).

The New Deal and Progressivism

A Fresh Look

Morton Keller

For most of its sixty years, the historiography of the New Deal has been dominated by two major perspectives: pro- and anti-. These have been as much normative as descriptive approaches: they seek to explain not only how the New Deal happened and of what it consisted but also why it was a Good Thing or a Bad Thing.

The major conceptual basis of this literature is its distinction between a recovery-minded First New Deal rooted in the past, and a reform-minded Second New Deal that under the political, intellectual, and demographic pressures of change unfolded into something broader and more original. Its major expositors—Basil Rauch, William Leuchtenburg, Arthur Schlesinger Jr., Frank Freidel, Richard Hofstadter—had in common a more or less strong political and ideological identification with their subject. They sought to strengthen the New Deal's historical bona fides by dwelling not only on its broad popular appeal in the 1930s but as well on its deep roots in a tradition of American reform. Hofstadter made it part (though in some respects a discordant part) of an Age of Reform stretching back to the end of the nineteenth century. Schlesinger reached even further back into the American past, finding affinities between the Age of Jackson and the Age of Roosevelt, thereby positing a reform tradition almost as old as America itself.[1]

The odd men out from this Whiggish view of the New Deal were no less motivated by political and ideological leanings. Conservatives Raymond Moley and Edgar Robinson and men of the Left Barton Bernstein and Paul Conkin came at their subject from opposite ends of the ideological spectrum. As so often is the case, there was a symmetry to these antipodal dissents: a shared distaste for FDR as an agent of (in the one case) capitalism or (in the other) socialism; a shared derogation of the New Deal as a movement dedicated either to subverting or propping up the existing system.[2]

Over time, a more analytic and nuanced approach has taken hold. A suggestive more recent work is *The New Dealers,* in which author Jordan Schwarz interprets the New Deal as an exercise in state capitalism. From this perspective the usual key figures—Raymond Moley, Harold Ickes, Harry Hopkins, Rexford Tugwell—yield pride of place to such seemingly un-New Dealish characters as Reconstruction Finance Corporation chairman Jesse Jones and western entrepreneur Henry J. Kaiser and to so un-New Dealish a policy as expanding credit to make possible industrial development in the South and the West. Theda Skocpol and Kenneth Finegold's *State and Party in America's New Deal,* in which they examine the Agricultural Adjustment and National Recovery Acts as instances, respectively, of successful and failed state building, is of the same fresh genre. And while Alan Brinkley's *The End of Reform: New Deal Liberalism in Recession and War* is more old-fashioned and judgmental, it strikes a new note in relating the New Deal not only to its antecedents but also to the political environment that followed.[3]

Where do we go from here? Because historians are even worse at predicting the future than at explaining the past, it would be rash to point firmly to the future direction of New Deal historiography. But the essays in this volume provide some clues. Here are fresh and adventurous treatments of traditional themes such as FDR's impact on the presidency and the party system, the New Deal's labor and economic regulatory policies, Social Security and welfare. Other chapters open up previously unexplored areas of inquiry such as the New Deal and higher education and the New Deal's post–World War II planning seen in comparative perspective. At the twentieth-first century's beginning, as this book makes clear, the lengthened perspective provided by the passage of time makes it possible to see the New Deal more clearly in its complex, nuanced whole. And the bottom line is that it was an even more important event in the history of American politics and government than previously thought.

I should like to reinforce this view of the New Deal's historical legacy by comparing it with its closest predecessor, the Progressive movement of the early twentieth century. How did the two differ? And, more important, why was it that the New Deal, and not Progressivism, came to be the true watershed dividing the American political and governmental past from the regime under which we live today?

Aside from Arthur Schlesinger's bold attempt to turn Andrew Jackson into a proto-FDR and his Kitchen Cabinet into a preview of the Brains Trust—an effort rightfully consigned to the historiographical dustbin—it is the Progressive Era that most often attracts the attention of those who seek to set the New Deal in the larger context of American history. Just think of the points of similarity: the centrality of executive leadership (TR and Wilson; FDR); the fact that FDR and many of his associates cut their political and ideological teeth during the Progressive period; the degree to which experts and expertise framed social and economic legislation; the experimental mindset so conspicuous in the two periods' policymaking; even the chronology of a rising tide of reform cut short by war. All this reinforces the conventional view that Progressivism and the New Deal were parts of a larger historical process, an American reform tradition.

But our greater distance from both Progressivism and the New Deal lends itself to a different perspective. For all their structural, stylistic, and policy similarities, the two movements had very different characteristics and consequences. In the case of Progressivism, it should by now be evident that the First World War did not so much mark the end of reform as it reinforced purposes and attitudes that from the first were an integral part of the Progressive movement. True, new elements in American life—professional expertise, immigrants, minority advocates, socialist-minded social reformers—had a place in the public life of the Progressive Era far more important than ever before. But at its core the Progressive movement appealed to native, white, Protestant, middle-class Americans, galvanized to political action by the changes that industrialization, immigration, and the growth of cities wrought in American life. The First World War diverted that political energy from domestic to international matters. At the same time it unleashed—or, more accurate, fueled—xenophobic, preservationist attitudes present before the war but overshadowed by broader social reformist goals.[4]

Prohibition and immigration restriction emerged around the turn of the century as issues with significant social reform dimensions. Prohibition offered the promise of a healthier population, fewer abused wives and children, less socially dysfunctional working-class families, and better race relations in the South. Immigration restriction held out the hope of less poverty and social pathology in the cities and a higher standard of living for American workers. But during and after the First World War, the darker implications of those causes came to the fore. Prohibition came to be identified more closely with fundamentalist Protestantism, anti-Catholicism, and small-town native American hostility to foreigner-filled cities. The case for immigration restriction relied increasingly on anti-Semitism, antiradicalism, and xenophobia.

Much the same may be said of woman's suffrage, the third great policy achievement of the time. Its original justifications were gender-free civil rights and the cleansing of a corrupt political system. But by the time the Nineteenth Amendment was adopted in 1920, there was increasing stress on its potential to strengthen the political power of the white, native-born middle class.

It can be argued that the First World War and its aftermath marked not the end of Progressivism but the triumph of its deepest underlying intent: to restore an idealized American past. That Herbert Hoover, who came to be the embodiment of what the New Deal sought to change in American public life, had been little more than a decade before a major representative of the Progressive impulse is a measure of the gulf in sensibility separating the two movements.

The New Deal's trajectory was very different from that of Progressivism. Its origins lay in the Great Depression and the felt need to change a dysfunctional economic order, not from a desire to preserve an older America in the face of new social, political, and economic conditions. True, like Progressivism it adopted a more forceful and challenging agenda as it matured. In this sense the First New Deal and early TR/La Follette Progressivism had much in common, as the New Nationalism/New Freedom programs of TR and Wilson would have echoes in the later New Deal. But the Second World War made clear how different a country the United States of the 1940s was from a quarter of a century before, and how different the New Deal's legacy would be from that of Progressivism.

From the hindsight of more than half a century, we can see that what emerged from the New Deal and World War II was not renewed xenophobia (Japanese American internment and segregated armed forces to the contrary notwithstanding) or traditional laissez-faire conservatism (the union-limiting Taft-Hartley Act notwithstanding). Rather, the basic New Deal themes of a broad, inclusive, democratic cultural nationalism and a readiness to use federal programs and deficit financing when necessary to secure prosperity and meet large domestic or international needs turned out to be the primary characteristics of American public life during the second half of the twentieth century.

The loyalty-security/McCarthyism excesses of the 1950s were transient, subject to rapid reversal after the end of the Korean War. No one would propose, from today's vantage point, that civil liberties and academic freedom are more constrained than they were in 1930. Similarly, American xenophobia and racism slowly gave way to a new ecumenicism that over the decades eroded anti-Catholicism, anti-Semitism, and even, gradually, the segregation of blacks in American life. The Great Society legislation of the 1960s was the fulfillment of much that was implicit in the New Deal: it was an extension of its predecessor rather than a distinctively different political movement. The recurrent, totemic identification of Democrats with FDR and the New Deal suggests that its central impulses—active government, an inclusive rather than exclusionist cultural nationalism—are alive and well. The New Frontier, the Great Society, and even Bill Clinton's Hope (more accurately put, Hot) Springs Eternal evocations contrast starkly with the vague, barely visible legacies of Theodore Roosevelt's New Nationalism or Woodrow Wilson's New Freedom.[5]

Nor has this been a one-party inheritance. A more than superficial relationship links the Tennessee Valley Authority, Dwight D. Eisenhower's Interstate Highway System, the space program of John F. Kennedy and Lyndon Johnson, and the arms buildup under Ronald Reagan. These are descendants of the New Deal's readiness to take on large-scale public works dedicated to ambitious domestic or foreign policy goals: an inclination that (aside from the brief World War I interlude) was conspicuously absent in the Progressive period.

Looking back from the beginning of the twenty-first century, it appears that the Progressive movement was the last gasp of a polity seeking to preserve what it could of a (rapidly receding) American past. In this sense, the antitrust movement, conservation, prohibition, immigration restriction, and even woman's suffrage were the products of a powerful preservationist impulse more than of a forward-looking quest for social and economic change. The New Deal and what came after evolved very differently: as a continuing effort to adapt to and shape the American present and future, rather than to restore or preserve the American past.

This was not foreordained. The early New Deal relied heavily on the government's experience in the First World War for its legal authority and its justification for emergency action. Nor did the New Dealers, true to the Progressive tradition, show much concern for the situation of blacks in American life. But the ideological evolution of the New Deal, fed by the new political and cultural conditions, began to change that. One measure: the 1938 Federal Housing Administration Act required that Federal Housing Administration–insured home mortgages have racially restrictive covenants. Only two years later the Fair Employment Practices Commission (FEPC) was established by executive order. No one would claim that this marked a sea change in New Deal racial attitudes: the wartime segregation of the armed forces is testimony to the persistence of traditional racial views. Nevertheless, the FEPC, for all its inadequacies, was the first instrument of the federal government since Reconstruction specifically aimed at alleviating racial discrimination.[6]

American politics and government in the second half of the twentieth century was dominated not by a rejection of the New Deal's legacy but, in its spirit, by a continuing adaptation to the demands of a changing American society. The New Deal's two most characteristic features—a readiness to turn to the federal government to deal with domestic and foreign problems and an inclusive popular nationalism—have been the hallmarks of American public life during the past fifty years. Evidence abounds: constitutional amendments (the Twenty-third, enfranchising voters in the District of Columbia; the Twenty-fourth, the anti–poll tax amendment; the Twenty-sixth, giving eighteen-year-olds the vote); major legislation on civil rights, voting rights, immigration liberalization, and the environment; Harry Truman's Fair Deal, John F. Kennedy's New Frontier, Lyndon Johnson's Great Society.

The continuing salience of the New Deal has not been unchallenged or uninterrupted. Hostility to the civil rights and cultural revolutions of the 1960s and suspicion of the active state continue to have a prominent place in American political conservatism. And a Left unable to come to terms with the failures of socialism finds little ideological sustenance in the New Deal tradition. But surely any long view of American public life over the past half century suggests that we have lived—and live today— in a polity best defined as the lengthened shadow of the New Deal.

So from our present perspective the New Deal seems more than ever a watershed, rather than an ephemeral event that separates politics past from politics present and future. If that is indeed its deepest historical meaning, then a second large question surfaces: How and why was this the case?

It is not difficult to pose a counterfactual: an American politics that responded to decades of Depression, war hot and cold, and rapid social and cultural change by emphasizing the more atavistic, separatist strands of the American political tradition, rather than building on the implications and precedents of the New Deal. (Indeed, the Left would say that that, in fact, is what has happened.)

There were alternatives: the nationalist and/or totalitarian politics of the Right as in Germany, Italy, Japan, China; totalitarian Socialism as in the former Soviet Union. Set against this world backdrop, the New Deal, and indeed the American polity since then, is as distinctive, as American- exceptionalist, in its character as, say, was the early Republic. So we have to ask: Why the roads not taken? Why the road taken?

One answer, surely, is demography: the coming of age of the new im- migrants. Over 90 percent of new voters in 1936—disproportionately the children of the more fecund newcomers—voted for FDR. These, along with blacks, organized labor, and a growing share of the chatter- ing classes (in the universities, the media, the professions), constituted a core New Deal constituency with far greater diversity, depth, and stay- ing power than those who identified themselves as Progressives in the early twentieth century.

True, the Roosevelt coalition of the 1930s was soon eroded by new conditions. The Spanish Civil War and the World War II alliance with the Soviet Union weakened Irish, Italian, and East European Catholic sup- port. The mass movement of blacks northward and the civil rights revo- lution all but destroyed the FDR/New Deal core of northern ethnics and southern whites. But when political and social conditions warranted it—in 1948, in 1960, in 1964—much of the old coalition coalesced and prevailed. The major demographic changes of the past half century—the flow of blacks northward and westward and into the political mainstream; the arrival of Hispanics and Asians in ever greater numbers—have put pressure on both parties to avoid drawing racial and ethnic lines as blatantly as they did in the old days. In this sense the political coming-of-age of the new immigrants in the 1930s was not an isolated event but one of a continuing series in which emerging groups—blacks, women, Hispanics, Asians, gays—each with its own distinctive political consciousness, have played and replayed a political drama that drew on and echoed the rise of the Roosevelt coalition of the 1930s.

No less important in shaping the modern American political landscape is the intellectual and cultural transformation of the past half century. Again, the consequence has been an ongoing reinforcement of the proactive, pluralist approach that characterized the New Deal. The most notable instance of this was the intellectual and then the popular abandonment of the belief that race or ethnicity is a prime determinant of social attributes and ultimately of inclusion within the larger polity. It was in the New Deal that the first substantial absorption of Catholics and Jews into the political mainstream took place. It saw also the first chinks in the armor of racial segregation and discrimination. Politics and public policy since then have (with fits and starts) expanded on and enriched those assumptions. Nothing more profoundly makes the point that the political regime starting in 1933 is the regime in which we still live. It is incontestable that there has been an evolution of ethnic and then racial politics from the New Deal to the present that in its totality is the mirror image of the persistent, indeed deepening racism of the pre-1930 polity.

The prevailing political culture of our own time—weakened parties, an unstable electorate, influential mass media, agenda setting by varied interest groups—is another inheritance of the 1930s and 1940s rather than of the century-long regime of parties, machines, and bosses that preceded it. True, party machines and partisan politics flourished during the New Deal. But no president before FDR had so tumultuous a relationship with large segments (the South, conservative northern Democrats) of his own party. And it was during the 1930s that massive swings in the political loyalty of social groups and American regions began to be a hallmark of American politics. During the sweep of time from the Civil War to the New Deal, the Solid South and the generally Republican North were the controlling facts of American public life. During the comparable sweep of time since then, more like the opposite has been the case. A similar contrast can be drawn between the voting preferences of Irish Catholics and (when these could be exercised) of blacks.

A comparable sea change has occurred in American government. The Great Depression–World War II experience locked in lessons about the active state that still have great political vitality. What happened (or, more to the point, what did not happen) to the federal government during the Eisenhower, Nixon, and Reagan presidencies is in its way as much a measure of the depth of the New Deal revolution as what happened during the Truman, Kennedy/Johnson, and Clinton years. Like American politics, American government during the almost seventy years since the onset of the New Deal has had a coherence that sharply distinguishes it from what went before.

This is what the New Deal means—or should mean—to us today. It should be remembered not as an episode in some imagined long march of American reform but as a defining time, like the Revolution and the establishment of the new nation, that set the stage for and defined the terms of American politics and government for generations to come.

Notes

1. Basil Rauch, *The History of the New Deal* (New York: Creative Age Press, 1944); William E. Leuchtenburg, *Franklin D. Roosevelt and the New Deal 1932–1940* (New York: Harper and Row, 1963); Arthur M. Schlesinger Jr., *The Age of Roosevelt*, 3 vols. (Boston: Houghton Mifflin, 1956–60); Frank Freidel, *Franklin D. Roosevelt*, 4 vols. (Boston: Little, Brown, 1952–1973); Richard Hofstadter, *The Age of Reform: From Bryan to FDR* (New York: Knopf, 1955); Arthur M. Schlesinger Jr., *The Age of Jackson* (Boston: Little, Brown, 1953).

2. Raymond Moley, *After Seven Years* (New York: Harper and Row, 1939); Edgar E. Robinson, *The Roosevelt Leadership, 1933–1945* (Philadelphia: Lippincott, 1955); Barton J. Bernstein, "The New Deal: The Conservative Achievements of Liberal Reform," in *Towards a New Past: Dissenting Essays in American History,* ed. Bernstein (New York: Pantheon, 1967), 263–68; Paul Conkin, *The New Deal* (London: Routledge and Kegan Paul, 1968).

3. Jordan A. Schwarz, *The New Dealers: Power Politics in the Age of Roosevelt* (New York: Knopf, 1993); Theda Skocpol and Kenneth Finegold, *State and Party in America's New Deal* (Madison: University of Wisconsin Press, 1995); Alan Brinkley, *The End of Reform: New Deal Liberalism in Recession and War* (New York: Knopf, 1995).

4. The foregoing analysis is based on Morton Keller, *Regulating a New Society: Public Policy and Social Change in America, 1900–1933* (Cambridge: Harvard University Press, 1994), chaps. 4, 7, 9.

5. William E. Leuchtenburg, *In the Shadow of FDR: From Harry Truman to Ronald Reagan* (Ithaca: Cornell University Press, 1989).

6. William E. Leuchtenburg, "The New Deal and the Analogue of War," in *Change and Continuity in Twentieth-Century America,* ed. John Braeman et al. (Columbus: Ohio State University Press, 1964), 81–143; Harvard Sitkoff, *A New Deal for Blacks: The Emergence of Civil Rights as a National Issue* (New York: Oxford University Press, 1978), 321–23; Kenneth T. Jackson, *Crabgrass Frontier: The Suburbanization of the United States* (New York: Oxford University Press, 1985), 208. See also David Kryder, *Divided Arsenal: Race and the American State during World War II* (Cambridge: Cambridge University Press, 2000).

Contributors

Donald R. Brand is associate professor of political science at the College of the Holy Cross. He is author of *Corporatism and the Rule of Law: A Study of the National Recovery Administration* as well as numerous articles in edited volumes and leading political science journals.

Seyom Brown is professor of politics at Brandeis University. He is author of *The Causes and Prevention of War; New Forces, Old Forces, and the Future of World Politics;* and *The Faces of Power: Constancy and Change in United States Foreign Policy from Truman to Reagan.*

Morton Keller is professor of history at Brandeis University. He is author of *Affairs of State: Public Life in Late Nineteenth-Century America; Regulating a New Economy: Public Policy and Economic Change in America, 1900–1933; Regulating a New Society: Public Policy and Social Change in America, 1900–1933;* and coeditor of *The Encyclopedia of the United States Congress.*

Jytte Klausen is associate professor of politics at Brandeis University. She is author of *War and Welfare: Europe and the United States, 1945 to the Present* and editor of *European Integration in a Social and Historical Perspective: From 1850 to the Present.*

Marc Landy is professor of political science at Boston College. He is coauthor of *The Politics of Environmental Reform* and *Presidential Greatness* and coeditor of *The New Politics of Public Policy* and *The Nature of Politics: Selected Essays by Bertrand de Jouvenel*.

William E. Leuchtenberg is professor of history at the University of North Carolina. He is author of *The Perils of Prosperity, 1914–1932; Franklin D. Roosevelt and the New Deal, 1932–1940; In the Shadow of FDR: From Harry Truman to Bill Clinton; The Supreme Court Reborn;* and *The FDR Years*.

Nelson Lichtenstein is professor of history at the University of California, Santa Barbara. He is author of *The Most Dangerous Man in Detroit: Walter Reuther and the Fate of American Labor; Who Built America? Working People and the Nation's Economy;* and *Politics, Culture, and Society*.

Suzanne Mettler is associate professor of political science at Syracuse University and author of *Dividing Citizens: Gender and Federalism in New Deal Public Policy*.

Jerome M. Mileur is professor of political science at the University of Massachusetts Amherst. He is editor of *Liberalism in Crisis: American Politics in the Sixties,* coeditor of *Challenges to Party Government* and *America's Choice: The Election of 1996,* and serves as coeditor of the University of Massachusetts Press series Political Development of the American Nation.

Sidney M. Milkis is the James Hart Professor of Politics and senior scholar at the Miller Center of Public Affairs, University of Virginia. He is the author of *The President and the Parties: The Transformation of the American Party System since the New Deal* and *Political Parties and Constitutional Government: Remaking American Democracy;* coauthor of *The Politics of Regulatory Change, The American Presidency: Origins and Development, 1776–1998,* and *Presidential Greatness;* and coeditor of *Remaking American Politics* and *Progressivism and the New Democracy*. He also serves as coeditor of the University of Massachusetts Press series Political Development of the American Nation.

Ronald Story is professor of history at the University of Massachusetts Amherst. He is author of *The Forging of an Aristocracy: Harvard and the Boston Upper Class,* coauthor of *Generations of Americans: A History of the United States,* and editor of *Five Colleges: Five Histories.*

Index